DATE DUE

DEMCO 38-296

HISPANIC BALLADRY TODAY

THE ALBERT BATES LORD STUDIES
IN ORAL TRADITION
(VOL. 3)

GARLAND REFERENCE LIBRARY
OF THE HUMANITIES
(VOL. 765)

THE ALBERT BATES LORD STUDIES IN ORAL TRADITION
John Miles Foley
General Editor

Center for Studies in Oral Tradition
English Department
University of Missouri
Columbia, Missouri 65211

HISPANIC BALLADRY TODAY

Ruth H. Webber

GARLAND PUBLISHING, INC. • NEW YORK & LONDON
1989

Library of Congress Cataloging-in-Publication Data

Hispanic balladry today / Ruth H. Webber.
    p. cm. — (The Albert Bates Lord studies in oral tradition ;
vol. 3) (Garland reference library of the humanities ; vol. 765)
    Bibliography: p.
    Contents: The artisan poetry of the romancero / Diego Catalán—
Survival of the traditional romancero / Ana Valenciano—Migratory
shepherds and ballad diffusion / Antonio Sánchez Romeralo—In
defense of romancero geography / Suzanne Petersen—Hunting for
rare romances in the Canary Islands / Maximiano Trapero—
Collecting Portuguese ballads / Manuel da Costa Fontes—The living
ballad in Brazil / Judith Seeger—The traditional romancero in
Mexico / Mercedes Díaz Roig—The Judeo-Spanish ballad tradition /
Samuel G. Armistead, Joseph H. Silverman—The structure and
changing functions of ballad traditions / Beatriz Mariscal de Rhett.
    ISBN 0–8240–4035–X (alk. paper)
    1. Ballads, Spanish. 2. Ballads, Spanish—History and criticism.
3. Ballads, Portuguese. 4. Ballads, Portuguese—History and
criticism. I. Webber, Ruth H. II. Series. III. Series: Garland
reference library of the humanities ; vol. 765.
PQ6196.H5 1989
861'.04409—dc20   89–7669
                                    CIP

Printed on acid-free, 250-year-life paper
Manufactured in the United States of America

Contents

Introduction

The ballad or *romance*, as it is commonly called, has played a vital role over the centuries in Hispanic culture as an orally transmitted narrative song. It is characteristically the product of people who have had to look to themselves for entertainment. From the end of the fifteenth to the early seventeenth century, the *romancero* (balladry) enjoyed a great vogue among learned poets and their audiences, especially in the Spanish and Portuguese courts. There are poets and writers in almost every subsequent generation who drew inspiration from the *romancero*, from Cervantes to Antonio Machado and García Lorca in our own century, to cite several notable examples. But whether visible or not at the level of "artistic" poetry, the *romancero* has continued to live among the Hispanic peoples as part of their cultural heritage and has gone with them wherever they chanced to go, whether throughout the Spanish empire to other parts of Europe, to the Atlantic islands and on to the New World, or, with the Sephardic Jews, expelled from Spain during the Diaspora at the end of the fifteenth century, to areas around the Mediterranean and many places in eastern Europe. Now with the advent of radio and television in even the most remote areas, the tradition of ballad singing, unfortunately, is vanishing.

Our intent here is to survey and to assess the state of the *romancero* today, not only in Spain and Portugal, but also in peripheral areas where it has migrated and taken root. In the following essays you will find accounts of the efforts that have been and are continuing to be made to capture on tape the *romances* that are still being sung before they are lost forever, together with an evaluation of the material that is being collected and examples of various ways in which the *romancero* is being studied. Above all we hope to convey, despite the fact that they are now probably doomed to oblivion, the tremendous appeal of the *romances*, many of which are true poetic gems, as well as an understanding of why these little songs have delighted and maintained a hold in the minds and memories of so many people for such a long time.

The center of worldwide *romancero* studies is located in Madrid in the Seminario Menéndez Pidal, a university research institute. Diego Catalán and his staff coordinate and direct ballad-collecting activities, sponsor international meetings of ballad scholars, publish several series of *romancero* collections and studies, and are hard at work on the huge task of assembling, analyzing, and cataloguing all Hispanic ballad texts old and new to make this material accessible for scholars. Three volumes of this catalogue (the *CGR*), written in both Spanish and English, have already come out. In the initial essay Diego Catalán describes the unique character of *romances* and the problems involved in their study. He also surveys the results of recent ballad-collecting projects and analyzes in some detail, according to the system developed by the Seminario, the poetic language and narrative structure of several *romances*.

Between the years 1977 and 1985 the Seminario Menéndez Pidal organized ten large-scale ballad-collecting expeditions in various parts of Spain as well as several smaller ones. Ana Valenciano, the coordinator of field expeditions for the Seminario, reviews in her essay the history of ballad collecting and the outcome of several of these recent expeditions. She presents the problems experienced by the ballad collector who goes out into the field, gives advice as to how to proceed, recounts from her own experience exactly what ballad collecting can be like, and emphasizes that the greatest chances for success these days are to be found in small, out-of-the-way villages.

There have been many additional ballad-collecting expeditions carried out through individual initiative. The Seminario Menéndez Pidal has always been willing to be consulted and to encourage such undertakings and has sometimes cooperated in the publication of the results. Antonio Sánchez Romeralo, who has collaborated in a number of the Seminario's projects, undertook to identify and survey the age-old routes followed by Spanish shepherds in their seasonal migration with their livestock from north to south and back again. The full account of this investigation was published in his *Romancero rústico* (1978). In his study here he has assembled all known versions of a popular shepherd's ballad, *La loba parda* (The Brindled She-Wolf) in order to demonstrate how these ballad versions tend to cluster along the principal migratory routes.

The mechanics of ballad transmission, clear enough in the case of the migratory shepherds, in reality represent a complex set of phenomena. Pioneer work on ballad geography done in 1920 by Menéndez Pidal, who plotted on maps the locations of certain ballads and their variants, was taken up and continued thirty years later by Diego Catalán and Alvaro Galmés. These two studies revealed the independent life in the transmission process of each and every ballad motif rather than that of the whole version. When Suzanne Petersen became interested in the problem of measuring ballad variation, she developed by means of the computer a series of ingenious techniques to plot both variation and modification in certain ballad narratives throughout Spain and to detect thereby regional tendencies, all of which is set forth in her essay.

Whereas ballad hunting in the Iberian Peninsula itself has become less fruitful except in remote areas still relatively unaffected by the inroads of modern life, explorations undertaken on the island possessions of both Spain and Portugal have proved to be remarkably successful. The Canary Island are a case in point. Maximiano Trapero, who has been systematically searching for ballads there, reviews the present-day state of the *romance* tradition in the Canaries. He describes how he has been able to make some extraordinary new finds along with superior versions of the more familiar *romances* and presents several unique ballad texts.

Manuel da Costa Fontes, who himself was born in the Azores and attributes his interest in balladry to his upbringing, has had great success collecting ballads in Portugal, in the Azores, and among Portuguese immigrants (mostly from the islands) now living in Canada, New England, and California. Each one of these expeditions has resulted in a rich volume of ballad texts. He recounts his varied experiences when, accompanied by his wife, he traversed Trás-os-Montes, a mountainous province of northeastern Portugal, recording ballads.

Realizing the necessity of collecting as many ballads as possible before it was too late, Manuel da Costa Fontes succeeded in covering a great deal of territory in a short time. Judith Seeger took a different tack. Settling down in a small coastal town in Brazil, she immersed herself in the local rural environment, hoping to be able in time to record *romances* in a natural setting. Although progress was slow and her harvest lean, she managed to record two exceptional versions of a well-known ballad. Here she tells how it came about and analyzes both the words and the music of her texts.

As the *romance* moved westward first with the explorers, then with early settlers, and finally with more recent immigrants to the New World, its traditional life continued, albeit diminished and contaminated with locally developed lyric and narrative song forms. Although it generally has been believed that in Mexico the *romance* was supplanted by the *corrido*, Mercedes Díaz Roig presents a convincing case to the contrary. She not only examines the role of the *romance* in Mexican culture but also the specific ballads that have kept reappearing, commenting upon the particular characteristics of these versions in comparison with their other Spanish-American counterparts.

The Sephardic Jews with their conservatism and adherence to long-established customs have kept alive over the years a vast store of *romances*, some even dating back to the time of the Diaspora. Sephardic ballad tradition is customarily divided into two sectors, the Eastern (eastern Mediterranean), which suffered a greater variety of outside influences, and the Moroccan (North Africa), in which closer contacts were maintained with Spain. Samuel Armistead and Joseph Silverman, who have long been the authorities on the Judeo-Spanish ballad tradition, survey the Sephardic ballad repertory, its regional characteristics, ballad collecting, and principal collections of this important branch of the *romancero*.

The *romance* always tells a story, and therein lies much of its appeal. Since this story is often fragmented and incomplete, the analysis and classification of ballads have provided a challenge for the ballad scholar. Beatriz Mariscal de Rhett accepted this challenge in a long study that forms part of her edition of *La muerte ocultada*. By way of conclusion to this series of essays, she discusses and illustrates how the functions and the narrative structures of the *romances* that have survived over the centuries have been modified in response to the ever-changing social environment.

The *romance* line is usually eight syllables long with a stress on the seventh, although six-syllable forms are not uncommon, nor are occasional irregularities characteristic of sung verse. Normally there is assonance (vowel rhyme) in alternating verses unless they are written in long lines divided into two hemistichs, as sometimes happens, in which case every line is assonating. The same assonance is generally maintained throughout although exceptions are to be found. Inasmuch as the *romance* is a narrative song, words and music are inseparable. The importance of the melody must not be underestimated despite the focus here on the poetic and narrative aspects. In the present-day state of the *romancero*, however, recitation sometimes alternates with singing, or the *romance* may simply be recited.

Since the *romance* is transmitted orally, it bears no title; nor is there any standardized system for naming *romances*. Therefore, the same ballad may be referred to in more than one way. For this reason there is included a list of titles of all the ballads cited, whether in Spanish, Portuguese, or English. All *romance* texts are accompanied by English translations, which have been kept as literal as possible. Because ballad language is apt to be both figurative and elliptical, a translation rarely is able to convey the poetic quality of the original.

Grateful acknowledgment is made to Dean Stuart M. Tave for the contribution of The Division of the Humanities of the University of Chicago to the original publication of this book as an issue of *Oral Tradition*, to John M. Foley for permission to reprint *Hispanic Balladry Today* and to include it in his Albert B. Lord Studies in Oral Tradition, to Charles E. Gribble of Slavica Publishers for his generous offer of the use of their typography, and to Samuel G. Armistead for his expert help.

R.H.W.

Hispanic Balladry Today

The Artisan Poetry of the *Romancero*[1]

Diego Catalán

The Spaniard who does not know of the existence of the *romancero* is rare. Some have come to know of it by learned means, through school books and literature classes in high school or even in the university; others because they have listened to folk singers, and still others because they have witnessed its oral transmission as part of local popular culture. But, despite this familiarity, ideas about the *romancero* continue to prevail today that have little correspondence with its essence. And precisely the most "cultured" people—according to official standards—are the ones who are most confused in their evaluation of the *romancero*. It is the specialists in Spanish literature who are propagating the most inexact ideas about ballads. Accustomed to examining texts that are both fixed and datable, which printed literature has accustomed us to since Gutenberg's time, erudite men of letters find it difficult to comprehend the special problems of poems elaborated by traditional "literary artisanship."

For the majority of students of Spanish literature, the word *romancero* evokes the Middle Ages (in its final period). Others, more conscious of bibliographical facts, remember that the classic corpus of ballads came to us from the printers of broadsides and of pocket-sized songbooks during the first half of the sixteenth century, and they classify the *romancero* as an old-fashioned genre during the Renaissance. But both groups, by trying to confine the *romancero* to a time frame and placing it within the sequential chain of literary products with which the history of literature concerns itself, do not take into account the essential quality of the artistic object being studied: its traditionality. And even if they do not overlook that aspect, they do not understand it.

During the eighties of this century, the richest archive of the *romancero* is not in any private or public library, but in the

1

collective memory of singers of *romances* throughout the Spanish-speaking world.   Neither the advances achieved by bibliographical research in the second half of this century, nor the accelerated expansion of both a school and a consumer culture at the expense of traditional forms of culture has been able to modify that reality which historians of literature forget about.   From the Middle Ages up to today, *romances* continue to be poems that are stored in the memory of custodians of traditional culture and are transmitted by word of mouth (most of the time with musical support) from one generation to another without any need to resort to writing.

The recognition of this fact forces us to redefine the *romancero*.   Ballads, as the object of investigation of literary criticism, cannot be enclosed within the chronological limits imposed upon them by histories of literature. Their existence and their value as artistic creations do not depend upon the fact that in the time of Alphonse V, Henry IV, or the Catholic Monarchs they were sung by ladies and gentlemen and served as a pretext for guitarists and court poets to show off their creative abilities; or upon the fact that printers and booksellers of the first two-thirds of the sixteenth century used them for a lucrative editorial business since there existed a broad consumer market for printed matter that was both cheap and easily comprehensible. There is no doubt that these "successes" of the genre have made it possible for us to reconstruct the *romancero* diachronically, since, if they had not come about, we would know nothing about the ballads that were sung such a long time ago (consider the scarcity of evidence in existence today about gypsy songs from only the day before yesterday).   Obviously these "successes" have to be the object of study in any historical vision of Spanish history or culture.   But its importance does not justify the error of confusing sociological or cultural matters, like the penetration of the *romancero* into certain markets or consumer groups, with the longer-lasting and more essential phenomenon of the creation, transmission, retention, and re-creation of an artistically organized "discourse" by a very great number of "speakers" capable of using the poetic language we call *romancero*.   Not to be aware of "literary artisanship" at the end of the twentieth century is as absurd as throwing out of art history architecture without architects or artisan gold and silver work, imagery, and ceramics.

It is necessary, therefore, to rescue the *romancero* from the hands of critics who close their eyes to the poem/song and who only consider as poets those pedants of former times whose poetry may have taken on interest but not, of course, quality, with the passing of the centuries.   The poem/song must not be confused with the sort of document that shows it turned into a written poem, fixed by writing or print and bound by a circumstantial poetics dependent upon a literary fashion belonging to a certain epoch.

Traditional models, whether poetic creations or popular creations in ceramics, in gold work, in architecture, in cuisine, are characterized by being trans-temporal (which does not mean ahistoric), and by having survived throughout the ages.   That has been possible thanks to the open character of their structures and thanks to their capacity to adapt themselves to the surroundings in which they are reproduced and re-created. Openness must not be confused with freedom in the creative process, since every artisan, even while innovating, claims above all that he is a faithful transmitter of the cultural inheritance of which he feels himself to be the repository.

Each ballad is not a closed fragment of discourse like the poems or stories of non-traditional literature, but a virtual model which is realized successively (and simultaneously in different places) in the form of poetic objects or individual versions that are always different.   But the singers, who keep on altering the structure little by little, do not freely create "their" versions (as the oralist critics believe) on the basis of a narrative skeleton; rather they reproduce, albeit with originality, the model they have received with all of its traditional details. The various realizations of a ballad differ among themselves in the same way that changing realizations of the ceramic model *botijo*, or the culinary model *gazpacho*, or the model for the rural dwelling *masía* differ.   It is the temporal and spatial difference between the manifestations of the model that makes possible an ever-increasing variety of results. In this way, by means of small innovative acts, either confirmed or corrected by successive singers, the narration keeps on adapting itself, both aesthetically and ethically, to the changing systems of values of the social groups that make use of *romances* to express their most deep-seated, local, and intimate culture.   Thanks to the inherent variability of the *romancero* transmitted orally, ballads preserve an eternal immediacy for their singers.

This openness, which we can observe today if we are able to

listen to the *romancero* being sung, is not an exclusively modern phenomenon. It comes from far-off times in which popular culture still had not been submitted to the process of the written word, which, until a little while ago, seemed to us, as people of bookish culture, to be the only way to preserve knowledge, but which, as we are beginning to understand today, only represented one important stage in the storage of mankind's knowledge. Up until the last several decades, we found ourselves so immersed in a "textualized" world, so accustomed to the consumption of discourse closured by the fixative power of the printed word, that it was difficult for us to recognize the characteristics of open traditional discourse, adaptable, in each memory in which it is stored, to the modifying pressure of personal or group experience. However, the storage and transmission of organized, but not fixed, knowledge throughout the living, human archives constituted by the memories of individuals pertaining to a cultural community are a reality which existed before writing and continued to do so after the fixing of discourse by means of writing. Recently the electronic revolution has come to strip the trans-linguistic (that is, organized in semic units superior to the sentence), structured discourse of its traditional textual closure. Computer terminal screens and print-outs coincide with the voice of the transmitters of oral literature in offering us only transitory or, at most, provisional realizations of memorized discourse. The information stored in electronic memories has lost the textual rigidity characteristic of the written document, making it resemble traditional discourse transmitted from one human memory to another without recourse to writing. Thanks to modern technology, humanistic sciences, traditionally hostile to all knowledge not dignified by *littera*, are becoming more receptive to the special problems offered by art stored and re-created in human memory. Recently, traditional discourse is attracting the interest of researchers for precisely what it has that is foreign to "literary" (in the most restricted sense of the word) discourse: its variability and its dynamism.

The study of the *romancero*, like that of other creations of popular culture, demands of us who have been brought up in an official, urban civilization, a great and humble effort of adaptation if we truly want to understand the language that those creations use and not merely collect strange artifacts. On taking upon ourselves, as collectors and readers of *romances*, the role of receivers or legatees of the messages that those *romances* express (without really being so since we are outside the chain of transmission made up of successive bearers of traditional knowledge), our objective should be to try to reproduce, to simulate the recognitory, decodifying activity of the consumer/ producers of the *romancero*. But we must do it fully aware that we are learning a foreign language which, in turn, its speakers use both actively and passively (by speaking it and listening to it) as part of naturally acquired knowledge.

The artisans of oral narrative songs are not depersonalized producers of poetic objects, unaware of the model they are reproducing. When they actualize, by singing or reciting, the virtual structures received from tradition, they do not desemanticize them. The transmission of ballad messages presupposes a knowledge, although not necessarily complete, of the language in which these messages are codified. Even the most impassioned devotees of traditional poetry often fall into the contradiction of considering the bearers of *romances* to be incapable of fully understanding the meaning of the marvelous creations they are transmitting, as if those creations were waiting for a literary critic in order to acquire all of their meaning. It is true that the experience of collecting ballads reveals at times that an individual singer of a *romance* does not understand the poem he is transmitting; but should his faulty comprehension not be corrected immediately by the interpretative capacity of other singers, his "error" would generate a variant of the poem that would lead to the elimination of the incomprehensible part. If in a dynamic structure, an open poem, there survive images, symbols, and messages which the literate reader considers to be outside of the knowledge of the habitual transmitters of the poem, it is because those images, symbols, and messages are understood by a large part of those in whom the tradition reposes; that is, they form an effective part of the poetic vocabulary of the singing community.

In contrast to the natural speakers of the *romancero* language, we see ourselves obliged to try to learn that language without speaking it, without participating in acts of re-creative transmission, by going to the study of its "grammar," discovered by means of analyzing written or recorded samples of ballad discourse. Therefore, the importance of the variant in order to achieve a complete reading of the *romances*. Thanks to the confrontation of the many and varied manifestations that a structure can offer us, we students of the *romancero* language can

DIEGO CATALÁN

6 DIEGO CATALÁN

recognize the semantic invariants that lie behind particular motifs and expressions. It is the variation found in the individual versions that enables us to discover the units that are manipulated by the unique poetics of the traditional *romancero*.

These considerations are at the base of recent systematic efforts to recover the *romancero* for the cultural history of the Hispanic peoples.

Collection and Creation of Audio Archives

The first and most urgent task that the *romancero* presents to us today is the creation of an audio-visual archive of the Pan-Hispanic ballad, by means of an international effort, which will preserve for tomorrow in organized form the largest number and the most varied manifestions possible of the ballads that are still being sung in the Spanish, Portuguese, Catalan, and Judeo-Spanish world. The audio archive should be enriched year after year by means of systematic collecting campaigns (like those organized since 1977 by the Seminario Menéndez Pidal in Spain,[2] and since 1969 by various professors, both local and from afar, in Portugal[3]), as well as by the efforts of individual researchers or groups of scholars dedicated to intensive exploration of a specific branch of the Pan-Hispanic tradition or of ballad lore of a particular district.[4] Although every contribution to knowledge about the *romancero* is welcome, it would behoove specialists to instruct collectors in the "art" of field research if the proliferation of amateur folklorists is not to become a threat to oral tradition. It is necessary to save the *romancero* from the hands of collectors of literary artisanship, who in their indiscriminate evaluation of what is popular or antique, place in the same sack whatever piece turns up, acting not very differently from the way exploitative antiquarians of rural culture act, who are always ready to put up for sale any shapeless pot or rusty nail. The collector must acquire as complete a knowledge as possible of the regional tradition he is attempting to investigate by the preparation of a collector's manual in which *romances* are duly classified according to their greater or lesser rarity and greater or lesser interest for the reconstruction of the "ballad map" of the Hispanic world. Collectors must compete in knowledge with the native repositories of tradition in order to gain their respect and collaboration and discover the deepest strata of the local corpus of ballads.[5]

It is also necessary for ballad collectors to have a clear idea of the difference between the orally transmitted *romancero viejo* and *romancero vulgar* (the distinction does not matter here) and the *romances de ciego* or *de pliego de cordel* (chapbook) distributed in Spain up until a few decades ago by blind singers who sold them with the help of a guide (and in other countries by different kinds of professional singers).   The coexistence in the memory of men and women in the small towns in Spain and other Hispanic countries of poems coming from these chapbooks with the open poems of the *romancero* does not mean that those blind men's ballads can be considered oral poetry. The editors of *romances de ciego* who supplied the popular market were not interested in the existence of the oral *romancero* except in rare cases; nor were they concerned about adjusting their product to the aesthetics or the ethics of the traditional culture expressed by the oral *romancero*. The rural consumers of chapbooks capable of memorizing the long stories of the blind men have been reproducing them in general without making them their own, respecting the "artificial" language of their verses, keeping the strictly narrative modality (contrary to the dramatic conception of traditional ballads) in which the events are told, and repeating their simplistic moralizations, which are also far removed from the ideological complexity of the oral *romancero*. Since these *romances* remain invariable except for the omission of verses and the introduction of lexical and syntactical errors, only the sociological fact of their acceptance, and not their texts, needs to be recorded.   Only in those cases in which a chapbook ballad has acquired textual variability and has been enriched and transformed in accord with the re-creative mechanism of poetry that is truly oral will we be able to consider it part of the oral *romancero* and of traditional culture.

Ballad collecting still holds, even from a thematic point of view, unexpected and extraordinary surprises in store for researchers.   In the seventies and eighties *romances* which nobody had expected to find in the modern oral tradition were discovered in Spain and Portugal.[6]   And along with these extraordinary specimens of Hispanic balladry, wonderful new versions of most of the rare *romances*, the existence of which in modern oral tradition had been attested to since the beginning of exploration in 1825.

The interest in having recourse to the living archive of popular memories does not reduce itself to the always fortuitous possibility that an undocumented or almost undocumented theme might emerge.   Because of the open nature of ballad narratives, tradition will always hold inexhaustible treasures of poetry which have never been fixed in writing or recorded in any one of the regions or places where *romances* are sung. Alongside of the widely distributed "vulgate" versions of scant variability, there still live and continue to be created regional, district, and village versions with extraordinary personality. It is precisely the variability of these versions that enables us to understand the mechanisms of collective creation, the poetic art of tradition.

Editing the Texts

The study of the *romancero* poetics requires that we have at our disposal ahead of time complete bodies of versions that have been conveniently transcribed and organized. For audio archives to be useful and manageable, it is necessary that the versions stored in them be edited, whether in conventional printed form or transcribed in an electronic archive that can be reorganized and consulted whenever necessary. During the seventies and eighties we can attest to renewed efforts for making accessible the *romancero* stored in manuscripts and field tapes.

Since 1957 the Seminario Menéndez Pidal has been publishing in the *Romancero tradicional de las lenguas hispánicas* all known data related to each *romance* being studied, including every version, old or modern, available at the moment of publication.[7] But the complexity and slowness of the task has brought about the simultaneous adoption on the part of the Seminario itself of other models for the publication of *romances*, like the *Fuentes para el estudio del romancero* (Sources for the Study of the *Romancero*) in its several series: *Sefardí,*[8] *Luso-brasileira,*[9] *Ultramarina,*[10] etc., and the application of computers, creating an *Archivo Internacional Electrónico del Romancero* (AIER), with its corresponding series of publications.[11]

Outside of the domain of the Seminario Menéndez Pidal, the publication of ballad collections, fruit of systematic field expeditions, either individual or collective, has also taken on in recent years a very hopeful rhythm.[12]

Description of the Poetics of the *Romancero*

The third activity that poems transmitted from memory to memory demand from students of balladry is the description of their poetic language, of the characteristics of their art. This task, no less fundamental than collecting and publishing oral manifestations, requires a thorough understanding of the significative complexity of ballad stories. Not an easy task, as I have proven by personal experience. Although from childhood I had been a reader of *romances*, it was only on trying to analyze systematically and exhaustively corpus after corpus of *romances* for the *Catálogo general descriptivo del romancero* (*CGR*), in company with a group of collaborators (especially J. A. Cid, B. Mariscal, F. Salazar, A. Valenciano, and S. Robertson),[13] I became aware of how simplistic are our readings as men of letters of traditional *romances* and the richness and significative depth of most traditional structures. The existence in the multiple manifestations of a *romance* of expressive variants at each level of semantic articulation makes it possible to recognize the invariables that hide behind them, and thus assures that our analyses are not misguided. Variation enables us to discover in the dramatized poetic narratives of the *romancero* a plurality of structured semantic levels that occupy the ground between the purely linguistic signs, whose highest level of integration is the sentence, and the primary semantic structures manifested through them, structures emulating the social, economic, and ideological systems of the referent (and, in that respect, the possible object of extra-semiological disciplines).

Figurative Language

The first level of poetic articulation is made up of a discourse which actualizes content or plot. Within the corpus of a *romance*, the same plot segment can and usually does manifest itself in different versions with discourse that varies as much in mode as in the figurative units of which it is composed.

For example, the monorhymed octosyllabic version (unique today) of *El caballo robado* from Lumbrales (Salamanca) and the Catalan and Sephardic strophic and hexasyllabic versions all contain the same story:

En los palacios del rey	In the king's palaces
faltara el mejor caballo.	the best horse was missing.
El rey le pregunta al conde:	The king asks the count:
—¿Eres tú el que lo ha robado?	"Are you the one who stole him?"
(Salamanca)	
Al palau del rey	In the king's palace
hi falta un caballo.	a horse is missing.

El rey dice al comte
si l'havia hurtado.
     (Catalonia)

The king asks the count
if he had stolen him.

En casa del rey
se le fue un caballo,
decían que el conde
lo había robado.
     (Morocco)

In the king's house
a horse disappeared,
they said that the count
had stolen him.

— — — — —

El rey lo mandó prender,
tres cadenas va arrastrando,
una le traba las piernas
y las otras dos las manos.
     (Salamanca)

The king ordered him detained,
he is dragging three chains,
one fetters his legs
and the other two his hands.

N'agafan al comte
i l'encarcelaron,
con grillons als peus,
manillas a las manos.
     (Catalonia)

They seize the count
and they put him in prison,
with fetters on his feet,
handcuffs on his hands.

Ataron al conde
al pie de una torre,
cadena al pescuezo,
su cuerpo en prisiones.
     (Morocco)

They tied the count
at the foot of a tower,
a chain around his neck,
his body in shackles.

Arrimóse el conde
al pie de una torre,
sus pies en cadenas,
su cuerpo en prisiones.
     (Eastern Sephardic)

The count rested against
the foot of a tower,
his feet in chains,
his body in shackles.

— — — — —

—Carpintero, carpintero,
di por qué repicas tanto.
—Estoy haciendo la horca
para un conde ajusticiado.
—Hazla bien alta y derecha,
que yo soy el sentenciado,
y no quiero que los perros
me coman por los zancajos.
     (Salamanca)

"Carpenter, carpenter,
say why you are pounding so."
"I am making a gallows
for a condemned count."
"Make it tall and straight,
for I am the sentenced one,
and I don't want the dogs
to nibble on my heels."

—Carpintero noble,
¿per qui son les forcas?
—Per vos son, el comte,
per vostra persona.
—Feu que sean altas,
altas y espayosas,
no coman los perros
de mis carnes dolças.
     (Catalonia)

"Noble carpenter,
for whom are the gallows?"
"They are for you, count,
for your person."
"Make them tall,
tall and roomy,
so the dogs don't eat
my sweet flesh."

Vido al carpintero	He saw the carpenter
la horca que haze.	who is making a gallows.
—Maestro, maestro,	"Master, master,
así Dios te guarde,	may God keep you,
hazedla muy alta	make it very tall
y angosto el collare,	and the collar narrow,
no me coman perros	so the dogs don't eat
mi hermosa faze.	my handsome face."
(Morocco)	
Vido al carcelero	He saw the jailer
haziendo la horca.	making the gallows.
—Así logréis, carcelero,	"May you succeed, jailer,
que me la hagas honda	in making it deep
que mis pies son blancos,	for my feet are white,
no me los coma el perro.	may the dog not eat them."
(Eastern Sephardic)	

and so on for the rest of the *romance*.

In the ballad of *La condesita* the sequence "the countess disguises herself as a pilgrim in order to go in search of her husband" is expressed by stating the action:

Se ha vestido de romera	She has dressed as a pilgrim
y le ha salido a buscar.	and set out to look for him.

or by visualizing it with some concrete detail:

Se vistió de rica seda	She dressed in rich silk
y encima un tosco sayal,	and on top coarse sackcloth,
con la cayada en la mano	with her staff in her hand
ha empezado a caminar.	she has begun to walk.

or by describing in detail how the countess changes from noble robes into beggar's clothing:

Se ha encerrado en un cuarto,	She has shut herself in a room,
se principia a desnudar,	she begins to undress,
se quita basquiña 'e seda,	she removes her silken petticoat,
se la pone de percal,	she puts on one of percale,
se quita medias bordadas,	she removes embroidered hose,
se las pone sin bordar,	she puts on plain ones,
se quita zapato de ante,	she removes soft leather shoes,
se le pone 'e cordobán,	she puts on some of cordovan,
ha cogido un baculillo	she has taken a small staff
para poder caminar.	in order to be able to walk.

or by making use of direct discourse, in a scene in which the abandoned wife seeks her father's help before departing:

—Cómpreme, padre, un vestido,	"Buy me, father, a dress,
que le quiero ir a buscar;	for I want to go to seek him;
no se lo pido de seda,	I don't ask that it be of silk,
ni de oro, que cuesta más,	nor of gold, which costs more,

que se lo pido de lana,	I ask that it be of wool,
de eso que llaman sayal.	of the kind called sackcloth."

or in which she receives instructions from her father:

—Ponte unos ricos galones	"Put on rich adornments
y encima un sobresayal,	and on top sackcloth,
ves en villita en villita,	go from town to town,
ves en ciudad en ciudad.	go from city to city."

This variability clarifies the purely expressive function which those forms of discourse have with respect to the invariable semantic content of the plot.

The openness of the discourse of a *romance* is unlimited in principle, but in practice it is subject to the pressures, both selective and restrictive, of the genre. The speakers of the *romancero* language make use of a traditional discourse, based on a lexicon and a grammar (at the figurative level), in other words, a poetics.

The plainness of expression, the "naturalness," considered since the Golden Age as the salient quality of the "old" *romances*, does not mean that the oral *romancero*, ancient or modern, rejects figurative language. This so-called lack of artifice is simply the absence of the stock phrases which characterize the literary forms of each period (at the end of the Middle Ages, in the Renaissance, the Baroque . . ., in the literature of today). The *romancero* has its own artifice, its own different and little understood poetics. There is no other unlearned song save that of the birds. At the level at which the discourse reveals a plot, that is, a narrative content already aesthetically organized, the artisans of the ballad construct and reconstruct their models employing a poetic language acquired through oral tradition, which they revert to as naturally as any individual speaking a language in which he or she is fluent.

The figurative language of the *romancero* uses the formula as its basic unit. Formulas are tropes; they mean something different from the phrases of which they are made up. Although the literal information that a formulaic expression offers cannot be rejected as not being pertinent, since it generally represents a realistic visualization of the plot, what matters for the development of that plot is the "lexicalized" meaning of that expression. The formula is synecdochic in that it designates by means of a restricted, concrete representation something of a broader or more abstract reality.

For example, in the ballad of *Belardo y Valdovinos*, Belardo comes upon his cousin lying on the ground in the middle of a field and discovers that he is badly wounded.   In several versions the sick man explains:

Estoy mirando al caballo
para el agua que bebía,
y también para la sangre
que de mis venas corría.
(Lugo)

I am looking at the horse
at the water he is drinking,
and also at the blood
that is running from my veins.

Estoy mirando al caballo
cómo las hierbas pacía;
también miro mis heridas
cómo la sangre vertían.
(León)

I am looking at the horse
how it grazes on the grass;
I also look at my wounds
how they spill out blood.

This formula can be substituted by another one related to it:

Estoy mirando el agua clara
que de esta fuente salía;
también estoy mirando el cuervo
que de mi sangre bebía.
(Oviedo)

I am looking at the clear water
coming out of this fountain;
I am also looking at the crow
who is drinking my blood.

or by others that are very different:

Con un concho de naranja
curando mortal herida.
(Santander and similar phrases in Trás-os-Montes)

With an orange skin
dressing a mortal wound.

Con tres heridas mortales,
con tres mortales heridas,
por una le entraba el viento,
por otra el aire salía,
por la más chiquita de ellas
un gavilán volaría.
(Zamora, Orense)

With three wounds that are mortal
with three mortal wounds,
through one the wind entered,
through another the air came out,
through the smallest of them
a hawk would fly.

Siete heridas tiene el cuerpo,
la menor era mortal,
la más chiquita de ellas
entra y sale un gavilán,
con las alas bien abiertas
y sin la carne tocar.
(Zamora, León)

Seven wounds the body has,
the smallest was mortal,
[through] the tiniest of them
a hawk goes in and out
with its wings wide open
and without touching the flesh.

All of these expressions, translated into simple, non-poetic language, say the same thing: "I have (he has) mortal wounds."

The purpose of the *romancero* discourse formulas is to dramatize the narration through concrete, vicarious acts which help to visualize the essential events of the plot. In the example cited, the horse that drinks or feeds freely, the crow that drinks the blood, the orange skin, the three or seven mortal wounds, and the hawk that flies in and out of them with his wings open have no existence other than at a dramatic level appropriate to the discourse, but not at the narrative level of the plot, where the only thing that matters is the meaning of the trope: "I have (he has) mortal wounds."

The simplicity of the meaning of the formulas makes it possible for each one of them to appear in various *fabulae*. For example, "I have (he has) mortal wounds" is a plot element that we also find in the ballad of the *Pérdida de don Beltrán*:

Três feridas tem no peito,	I have three wounds in my breast,
todas três eram mortal,	all three are mortal,
por uma entrava o sol,	through one the sun enters,
pela outra entra o luar,	through another the moon,
pela mais pequena delas	through the smallest of them
um gavião (aguia, pomba) a voar	a hawk (eagle, dove) flies
com suas aças bem abertas	with its wings wide open
sem as ensanguentar.	without bloodying them.
(Trás-os-Montes)	

and in the *Sueño de doña Alda*:

Siete puñaladas tiene	He has seven dagger wounds
al derredor del collare,	around his throat,
por la una le entra el frío,	through one the cold enters,
por la otra le entra el aire,	through another the air enters,
por la más chiquita de ellas	through the smallest of them
entra y sale un gavilane,	a hawk goes in and out,
con las sus alas abiertas	with its wings open
no le toca en la su face.	it doesn't touch him on the face.
(Morocco)	

and in the *Partida del esposo* combined with the *Vuelta del hijo maldecido*:

Tres cuchilladas tenía	He had three slashes
que eran dadas de duxmán,	that were given by an enemy
por la una entra el sol,	through one the sun enters,
por la otra entra el lunar,	through another the moon enters,
por la más chica de ellas	through the smallest of them
entra y sale un gavilán.	a hawk goes in and out.
(Eastern Sephardic, Morocco)	

The fact that expressions of discourse of one *romance* reappear in others is not what permits us to identify them as formulas. We recognize them at once, from the first encounter, by their unitary semantic value and by the basically figurative nature of their literal information. But, although in order to recognize them as such, it does not matter whether or not they are present in a number of ballad corpora, the meaning they have at the plot level makes them easily transferable from one context to another.

The Plot

An analysis of the corpus also makes it obvious that the plot, the artistically organized narrative, is at the same time the particularized expression adopted by the *fabula* (or causal series of cardinal events which follow upon one another in a chain supported by the natural passing of time). Suffice it to observe how in the totality of the versions of one *romance*, there can alternate in a given syntagmatic context several plot segments that are narratively equivalent, how some versions complicate the telling of an event with specific details that others ignore, or how the facts that permit the listener to reconstruct the logical/temporal sequences of the *fabula* are sometimes incorporated into scenes visualized in the narration and other times merely by means of references to past facts and offside stage directions, or by vague suggestions (*indicia*) incorporated in other sequences. The exposition of a *fabula*, that is, the plot, can upon occasion complicate the story with secondary incidents, and, in contrast to what has usually been affirmed, can easily break up the *ordo naturalis* of the narrative. The receivers, the hearers of a *romance*, are accustomed, just as are the readers of "literary" works, to reconstruct synthetically in their minds the logical/temporal succession of events which in the narration are presented reorganized according to an *ordo artificialis*.

Let us take as an example the ballad of *Bernal Francés*. The story as it is narrated is made up of the following logical/temporal sequences:

1. Departure of the husband (X leaves home and the village where he resides leaving Y alone).
2. Adultery (Y substitutes Z for X).
3. Return of the husband (X returns to his village and home).
4. Deception (X presents himself to Y pretending to be Z).
5. Proof of the crime (Y receives pseudo-Z in her home and bed).
6. Revelation of identity (Pseudo-Z identifies himself to Y as X).
7. Punishment or vengeance (X kills Y).

Among the individual versions we have, this *fabula*, so ordinary in itself, appears artistically elaborated by means of a violent dystaxia. The narration begins in the fourth sequence (Deception) without explaining to us the identity of the characters, or the situation in which they find themselves:

—¿Quién es ese caballero que en mi puerta dice: "Abrir"? —Don Francisco soy, señora, que vengo para servir, 5 de noche para la cama, de día para el jardín. —Aguarda, mi don Francisco, para encender el candil. —No lo encienda, señora, 10 no lo encienda para mí, que he dejao tres hombres muertos y otros tres para morir, toda la justicia viene en seguimiento de mí; 15 si ven la luz encendida, dirán que yo estoy aquí— Le he agarrado de la mano y en la cama le subí, en una cama de flores 20 donde el rey puede dormir. (Molinos del Razón, Soria)	"Who is that knight who at my doorway says: 'Open'?" "I am Don Francisco, my lady, I am coming to serve you, at night in bed, by day in the garden. "Wait, my Don Francisco, until I light the lamp." "Don't light it, my lady, don't light it for me, for I have left three men dead and three more dying, all the police are coming in my pursuit; if they see the light burning, they will say I am here." I grasped him by the hand and I put him on the bed, on a bed of flowers where a king could sleep.
—Franciscana, Franciscana, la del cuerpo muy gentil, abre puertas y ventanas a quien las sueles abrir!— 5 Se levanta la güitada, desvelada en el dormir, se lava los pies y manos con agua de torongil. Y a la vuelta del capote 10 él le apagaba el candil. (Granadilla, Tenerife)	"Franciscana, Franciscana, of the very lovely body, open doors and windows for me as you are wont to do!" The unfortunate one gets up, not having slept, she washes her feet and hands with balm water. And with the fold of his cloak he put out the lamp.

It is only thanks to the suprasegmental allusions or *indicia*, and not by means of the distributional or sequential units, that the receiver of the message gradually becomes aware that the amorous encounter contains within itself elements leading to a tragedy. The two characters who are speaking are defined by means of expressions such as "of the very lovely *body*", "*my* Don Francisco", "as *you are wont* to do", "at night in bed, by day in the garden", which, without clarifying for us the adulterous situation, indicate the clearly illicit existence of a continuous and voluptuous sexual relationship. But the listener who is sensitive to the signs can go one step further and begin to suspect that the situation and the identities that have been established involve a

trap.   In the version of Granadilla, the wakefulness of the woman
is an *indicium* that already puts us on guard, and the epithet *la
cuitada* attributed to the lady when it is simply relating how she is
preparing herself sensually and ritualistically to offer her lovely
body to the one who is accustomed to enjoying it, turns out to be
truly alarming.   In the other version, from Molinos del Razón, the
romance opens with a question: "¿Quién es ese . . .?," prefiguring
what is going to be the cause of the whole tragedy: the doubtful
identity of the person who says "Abrid."   Alerted by these signs,
the receiver of the ballad message is prepared to interpret the
darkness brought about by the knight at the time he crosses the
threshold (motif of the lamp) as a potential threat to the beauty.
Nevertheless, if we limit ourselves to holding in mind the chain of
events, the *fabula* will only begin to unveil itself during the course
of the dialogue provoked by the sexual indifference of Z:

Y a eso de la media noche	And by around midnight
no se había vuelto a mí.	he had not turned to me.

or:

—¿Qué traes tú, don Alonso,	"What is the matter, Don Alonso,
que no te viras pa mí?	that you don't turn to me?"

Only by means of the lady's words do we discover that she is a
married woman and her husband is away:

No temas a mi marido	Don't be afraid of my husband
que está muy lejos de aquí;	for he is very far from here.
(Molinos del Razón)	

. . . o temes a mi marido.	. . . or you're afraid of my husband.
Bien lejos está de aquí.	He is very far from here.
(Granadilla)	

and we have to wait until the adulterous wife observes the trap
into which she has fallen to recognize the true identity of the
knight who knocked at the beauty's door:

—Si eso hiciera usted, señora,	"If you did that, lady,
pagao sería de mí:	I would pay you
le daré saya de grana	by giving you a skirt of red cloth
y jugón de escarlatín,	and a bodice of scarlet,
gargantiña colorada,	a red necklace,
la que a ninguna le di.—	such as I have given to no one."
A las últimas palabras,	At his final words,
yo, triste, le conocí.	I, alas, knew who he was.
(Molinos del Razón)	

—Tu marido, Franciscana,	"Your husband, Franciscana,
está aquí al lado de ti.	is here beside you.

Media noche está pasada	Half of the night has passed
y otra media por venir,	and the other half is coming,
y en viniendo la otra media	and when the other half comes
te cortaré de vestir:	I will cut clothes for you:
te cortaré manto y nagua	I will cut you a cloak and skirt
y mantón de carmesí,	and a bright red shawl,
gargantilla colorada	a red necklace
que te pertenece a ti.	which you deserve."
(Granadilla)	

And observe that the solution to the enigma can even be postponed until the appearance of the final sequence of the *fabula*, the punishment or vengeance, a sequence that does not have to be expressed in the form of action that we witness or about which we are informed.

But whichever narrative units were resorted to or whatever their organization may be, the plot always constitutes a concretion of the story structure, a particularized representation, among the many that are possible, of what is signified by the *fabula*. For that reason the *fabulae* of the *romancero* can and in fact do manifest themselves in the individual versions of oral tradition by means of various plots. The study of the artistic structuralization of the *fabulae* of the *romancero*, with a web of variable interrelationships of the characters, constitutes another inevitable area whenever one tries to describe the *romances*.

Fabula and Functional Model

The *fabula* itself, at the deepest interpretative level (or the highest, if one prefers to use another metalanguage), also appears to us, in turn, like a particular expression of the functional structures within which the roles of the *dramatis personae* and what the characters do become integrated so as to offer the receiver unified messages. At this level of organization of the narrative, the *fabulae*, so closely linked to the referent through the simulation of human behavior, are only "historical," circumstantial manifestations of more general and more abstract structures (actantial or functional models) which syntagmatically organize atemporal, "mythical" contents. Within those more abstract structures, the characters shed their semantic traits in order to remain identified merely with the principal roles of the narrative's "grammar."

In order to exemplify the relationship between the *fabula* of a *romance* and the actantial structure revealed in it, the *romance* of the *Infante parricida* will serve as an example:

Preñada estaba la reina	The queen was pregnant
de tres meses que no mase,	three months no more,
hablóle la criatura	the child spoke to her
por la gracia de Dios padre:	by the grace of God the Father:
5 —Si Dios me deja vivir,	"If God lets me live,
salir de angosto lugare,	and leave this confined place,
mataría yo al rey,	I will kill the king,
también la reina mi madre;	also the queen my mother;
porque durmieron a una	because they slept together
10 la noche de las verdades,	the night of truths,
me quitaron mis virtudes	they took away my virtues
cuantas Dios me diera y mase,	all that God gave me and more,
que si unas me quitaron,	for if they took some away
otras más me volvió a dare. —	still others he gave me."
15 Oídolo había el buen reye	The good king heard it
desde su sala reale:	from his royal hall:
—La [reina], si pares niña,	"Queen, if you bear a girl,
cien damas la han de criare;	a hundred ladies will rear her;
la [reina], si pares niño,	Queen, if you bear a boy,
20 a la leona le he de echare. —	I'll throw him to the lioness."
Van días y vienen días,	Days come and go,
la [reina] parió un infante.	the queen bore a prince.
Toda la gente se alegra;	All the people rejoice;
el buen rey que se atristare.	the good king is saddened.
25 Envolvióle en seda y grana,	He wrapped him in red silk cloth,
a la leona le fue a echare.	he threw him to the lioness.
La leona vido ese hijo	The lioness saw that child
que era de sangre reale,	was of royal blood,
quitó leche de sus hijos	she took milk from her offspring
30 y al infante fuera a dalle.	and gave it to the prince.
No es el niño de cinco años,	He was not yet five years old,
parecía un barragane;	he seemed like a young man;
no es el niño de diez años,	he was not yet ten years old,
las armas supo tomare;	he knew how to handle arms;
35 no es el niño de quince años,	he was not yet fifteen years old,
a cortes del rey fue a entrare.	he entered the king's court.
Hubo de matar al rey,	He killed the king,
también la reina su madre.	also the queen his mother.
40 Otro día en la mañana,	The next morning
ya reinara en su lugare.	he was reigning in their place.
(Sephardic tradition of Morocco)	

Actantially, two characters compete for the role of subject: R^1 (the king A) and R^2 (the prince or king B). The story makes us witness two parallel processes with a contrary sign: the fall of R^1 and the accession of R^2. The process of the fall is initiated with the *breaking of the pact (sustainer of the monarchy)* on the part of R^1, and the process of accession with the *establishment of a new pact (sustainer of the monarchy)* on the part of R^2. The two complementary cardinal functions are expressed in the first sequence: *conception of an heir by transgressing a sacred prohibition* (they engender him on Christmas or an analogous night). As a consequence of this first cardinal action, the circumstantial attributes of the characters and the terms of their interdependence are modified, according to what we consider necessary for the existence of a sequence: R^1 (and R-) deprive R^2 of his natural virtue; D (God), as an automatic response, transfers his alliance from R^1 to R^2 (see verses 6 and 7: "they took away my virtues, / all that God gave me and more, // for if they took some away, / still others he gave me.").

The second function consists of a *divine sign (of the transference of the alliance).* In terms of the *fabula,* the withdrawal of God's protection from R^1 and the election of R^2 are shown in the second sequence: *revelation of the destiny of the crown prince.* Observe that another type of sign could easily have been substituted: manifestation of divine anger in the form of a plague, for example.

These first two sequences of the *fabula* acquire visibility in the plot by means of one single scene: the threat or challenge of the fetus to his parents with which the action of the *romance* opens.

In the process of accession, the next functional act is the *birth (of the chosen one),* conceived as the overcoming of the danger of abortion ("to leave this confined place") and of the proof represented by the alternative male/female (". . . if you give birth to a girl . . .//. . . if you give birth to a boy . . .//. . . she gave birth to a prince"). Its parallel, in the process of the fall, is the *persecution (of the chosen one)* by R^1. In the *fabula* these functions are represented in two plot sequences, 3 and 4, *birth of a male heir* and the *king's renunciation of his heir,* which, at the level of the plot, are interchanged, converting the decision of the king into a warning directed to the queen before the birth (verses 9-10).

The next functional act in the process of R^1's fall is the *sacrifice (of the chosen one),* which brings as a counterpart the resurrection or *rebirth (of the chosen one)* in a new nature. In the *fabula* the sequence of the *sacrifice of the crown prince* perhaps requires some commentary: R^1, on trying to deprive his son of life and, thereby, his right to be king, does not take away from him his royal insignias ("he wrapped him in red silk cloth"); it is a question, therefore, of an expiatory sacrifice, of the immolation of the fruit of sin, for the purpose of placating the divinity, and not a mere act of self-protection by R^1. The change of the nature of R^2 is made explicit by means of the two following sequences: the sixth, *adoption of the child by a lioness*, carried out by RA- (the lioness), who recognizes him, that is, she identifies herself with him as having in common a royal nature and nurses him; and the seventh, *upbringing of the hero*, in which the son of the lioness assumes the role of subject and reveals his new nature, both royal and animal, as he proves himself both as a man and as a warrior without need of the teachings of a tutor and at an exceptional age.

The last functional act in both processes consists of the *substitution of the king under divine disfavor for the new king blessed by God.* Sequentially, the three actions of the plot, the penetration into the royal abode, the killing of the parents, and the accession of the prince to the throne constitute a single cardinal action: *the prince kills his parents and installs himself as king.*

Paradigmatic Reading

The reading of the ballad seems so obvious that we could be asked why we have chosen this story as an example. But the clarity of the text is deceptive. To put an end to our optimism, all we have to do is ask one basic question: what is the nuclear message of the *romance*? Evidently the story has to do with the monarchy; it comments upon the divine origin of royal authority, but what does it say?

The victory of the hero confirms the inevitability of divine designs: the child heir, destined by the finger of God to be king, passes over not only the obstacle of parental opposition (based, more than on egotistical reasons, on a misinterpretation of the function of the king as a pastor of the people), but rather that of the sin which is at the base of his existence. When the "restorer" mounts the throne, it is evident that a new order is taking over in the kingdom (or in the *civitas*). Once the tyrant is dead (and also his wife), the stain that contaminates the people has been washed away and the pact with the divinity, basis of the monarchy, has been renewed and the authority has recovered its legitimacy. But there is something disturbing in this restoration: the hero, the chosen one, in order to begin his reign has had to commit a new crime, the double parricide, the licitness of which is more than doubtful.

Can we consider the narration to be closed, as sufficient unto itself? Is not the *romance* a macrosequence of an untold story, of a story that never will be told but whose parameters are well defined?

Like every hero, the child-slayer of his parents is born "marked." The sin, the transgression that accompanies his engendering, turns him into the chosen one. But at the same time, he is tragically conditioned by the fact that his exaltation at being king can only be realized after a new sin. The kingdom, the city, which has been freed from a curse by sacrificing its own king like an expiatory goat, finds itself, at the end of the tale, with the paradox that the savior on carrying out the liberating act, the death of the tyrants, is again bringing divine anger upon his people.

The insufficiency of analyses, of descriptions limited to the syntagmatic projection of the web of paradigmatic relationships that ballad narrations show seems to me to be an obvious fact. If we want to understand the message of the *romance* of the *Infante parricida*, one must incorporate into the semiotic study of the text a "vertical" reading of those relationships. It is necessary to recover the underlying ideology, which is mythic and at the same time historic, although on doing so it seems more obvious than ever to us that the essential property of traditional creations is their openness.

Instituto Universitario "Seminario Menéndez Pidal"
Universidad Autónoma de Madrid
University of California, San Diego

Notes

[1]Translated from the Spanish by the editor and the author.

[2]In 1977 the Seminario Menéndez Pidal and the Universidad Complutense de Madrid initiated a plan to recover as quickly as possible the store of *romances* still hoarded in the living archives of tradition. The method used has a double purpose: to cover a broad territory quickly and, at the same time, to penetrate into the most hidden recesses of traditional knowledge. Therefore, (a) the need to have recourse to large teams for the field expeditions (from twenty to thirty-five people each time), made up of investigators of very different origin but previously trained and directed afterwards in the field by a group of expert monitors, and (b) the careful preparation of special manuals for field work for each region under investigation. Since 1977 the following large-scale field expeditions have been

carried out: Northern Field Trip - 1977: in Santander, northern Palencia, northern León, Sanabria (Zamora), and Ancares (Lugo); Southern Field Trip - 1978: in the mountains of Cazorla and Segura and contiguous areas in Albacete, Murcia, Jaén, and Granada; Northern Field Trip - 1979: in Fornela and the upper valley of the Sil; Northern Field Trip - 1980: in the north and west of León and the west of Asturias with brief incursions into Orense, Zamora, and Segovia; Zamora Field Trip - 1981: in the northwest of Zamora and in the northeast and southwest of León; Segovia Field Trip - 1982: Segovia; Galician Field Trip - 1982: in the east of Orense and the south of Lugo; Galician Field Trip - 1983: in the north of Lugo and the north of La Coruña; Castilian Field Trip - 1984: in Burgos, in the east of Palencia and the west of Soria; León Field Trip - 1985: León. In addition, the Seminario Menéndez Pidal has carried out several other field expeditions of lesser duration with smaller teams: in the northwest of Salamanca and the southwest of Zamora - 1981; in Ciudad Real and contiguous areas in the south of Toledo, the east of Badajoz and the north of Córdoba - 1982; in the center and south of León - 1984; and in La Gomera - 1985.

[3]Intensive collecting with modern recording equipment was begun in both insular and continental Portugal in 1969 by Joanne B. Purcell, who had previously familiarized herself with the Portuguese tradition of insular origin among emigrants residing in California. Following in her footsteps, Manuel da Costa Fontes and Maria-João Câmara Fontes, after extensive collecting among the emigrants from the Portuguese islands living in California, New England, and Canada, carried out numerous field expeditions in São Jorge (Azores) as well as in Bragança (Trás-os-Montes) in 1977 and 1980. During the eighties several researchers living in Portugal who had previously taken part in field expeditions of the Seminario Menéndez Pidal in Spain, Pere Ferré, Vanda Anastácio, José Joaquim Dias Marques, and Ana Maria Martins, have been carrying out splendid exploratory work in various insular and peninsular districts.

[4]The most studied branch of the Pan-Hispanic tradition is, beyond a doubt, the Judeo-Spanish, in which for several decades S. G. Armistead and J. H. Silverman have been the active leaders with the collaboration of I. J. Katz as musicologist. They were the ones who established models for the collection of Sephardic ballads with modern technical aids and who have served both as guides and as a stimulus for young investigators who are working in this field in various American universities. The Catalan branch, which was so rich in the last century and during the first third of this one, seems to have lost more of its traditional store than any other from the time of the Civil War on. At least this is the impression derived from recent explorations by Salvador Rebés and Isabel Ruiz in territories that formerly were very rich in ballads. The Canaries branch, on the other hand, continues to furnish notable surprises concerning the preservation of themes not previously known in the area, as is shown by the collections of Maximiano Trapero and of Benigno León Felipe among others. Another branch of the *romancero* up to a short while ago not identified in old samplings is the gypsy branch from western Andalusia, the last examples of which have been saved by Luis Suárez. In Castilian territory there are very strong contrasts: the field work of S. G. Armistead and of Luis Díaz Viana in Soria gives evidence of an impoverished tradition, an impression also formed by the field expeditions of the Seminario Menéndez Pidal in the same area, while areas not very distant from Palencia and Burgos preserve a much richer *romancero*.

[5]Although every "document" of a traditional version is a useful datum for the investigator of the *romancero* and although a few texts of great rarity come from fortuitous finds carried out by first-time or chance investigators, as a whole, knowledge about the traditional *romancero*, today as yesterday, owes more to a select group of specialized collectors than to the many amateur folklorists or to the musicologists interested in the popular song in general. Therefore, the Seminario Menéndez Pidal considered it important to organize four intensive theoretical/practical courses about research in the oral *romancero* in 1980, 1981, 1982, and 1985 (which thirty to thirty-five students attended each time) with the aim of instructing new investigators about the oral traditional *romancero*.

[6]They include themes as rare as: *Lanzarote y el ciervo del pie blanco* (Jaén, Tenerife, La Gomera), *Gaiferos rescata a Melisendra* (León, Orense), *Mocedades de Gaiferos* (Segovia, Santander), *Durandarte envía su corazón a Belerma* (Asturias, Cádiz), *Valdovinos sorprendido en la caza* (Asturias), *La muerte de don Beltrán* (León), *La caza de Celinos* (Lugo, León, Burgos), *Las quejas de doña Urraca* (Zamora, Madeira), *Destierro del Cid* (Madeira), *El Cid pide parias al moro* + *El tornadizo y la Virgen* (La Gomera), *El moro que reta a Valencia y al Cid* (Asturias, León), *Rodriguillo venga a su padre* (Madeira, Asturias, La Palma), *Afuera, afuera, Rodrigo* (Madeira), *Nacimiento de Bernardo del Carpio* (Madrid), *Bernardo reclama la libertad de su padre* (Cádiz), *Bañando está las prisiones* (Cádiz), *Río Verde* (La Gomera), *Muerte del maestre de Santiago* (Segovia), *El hijo póstumo* (Lugo), *Don Manuel y el moro Muza* (Asturias, León), *Merienda del moro Zaide* (Palencia, Santander, Lugo), *Isabel de Liar* (Lugo, La Coruña), *Marquillos* (León), *Espinelo* (Zamora, Burgos), *El tornadizo y la Virgen* (La Gomera), *Virgilios* (El Hierro), *Paris y Elena* (La Gomera), *El alabancioso* (León), *El sacrificio de Isaac* (Palencia, León, Orense), *El esclavo que llora por su mujer* (Gran Canaria), *La mujer de Arnaldos* (León), *Canta, moro* (León), *El bonetero de la Trapería* (León, Asturias), etc.

[7]The *Romancero tradicional de las lenguas hispánicas* is now up to volume 12, which has just been published: *La muerte ocultada* (1984-85), edited by B. Mariscal de Rhett.

[8]Seven volumes in the Sephardic series have been published up to the present. They include works by S. G. Armistead and J. H. Silverman, I. J. Katz, R. Benmayor, and O. A. Librowicz.

[9]Three volumes by M. da Costa Fontes have come out in this series, and a fourth, which begins the publication of the collection of J. B. Purcell, has been edited by I. Rodríguez and J. das P. Saramago.

[10]Aside from the two volumes of *La flor de la marañuela* edited by D. Catalán and his collaborators in 1969, which are being reissued with additions, two volumes have been published by M. Trapero, *Romancero de la Isla de Hierro* (1985) and *Romancero de la Isla de La Gomera* (1987).

[11]An example of the results of an intensive effort of collective field work is the Northern Field Trip - 1977 of the Seminario Menéndez Pidal, prepared by J. A. Cid, F. Salazar, and A. Valenciano with the collaboration of B. Fernández and C. Vega (see note 2, above) and edited by S. H. Petersen, which bears the title *Voces nuevas del romancero castellano-leonés* (1982), AIER 1 and 2. Since then the stock of ballads of the AIER has been increased by means of ongoing processing of versions from Segovia, León, and

Galicia gathered during different field expeditions of the Seminario Menéndez Pidal, together with unedited texts from those same districts that are in the Menéndez Pidal archives, which were begun in 1900.
[12]Of special importance is the fact that S. G. Armistead, J. H. Silverman, and I. J. Katz have begun the systematic publication of the store of Sephardic ballads in a series entitled *Folk Literature of the Sephardic Jews*, the second volume of which is now in print: *Judeo-Spanish Ballads from Oral Tradition: I. Epic Ballads.* Other splendid private collections include P. Ferré, V. Anastácio, J. J. Dias Marques, and A. M. Martins, *Subsídios para o Folclore da Região Autónoma da Madeira. Romances tradicionais* (1982) and M. da Costa Fontes, *Romanceiro Português do Canadá* (1979), *Romanceiro Português dos Estados Unidos: 1. Nova Inglaterra* (1980), *2. California* (1983), *Romanceiro da Ilha de S. Jorge* (1985).
[13]Volumes 2 and 3 of the *CGR* have already been published: *El romancero pan-hispánico. Catálogo general descriptivo / The Pan-Hispanic Ballad. General Descriptive Catalogue* (1982 and 1983), preceded by an introductory volume: *Teoría general y metodología del romancero pan-hispánico. Catálogo general descriptivo* (1984), the English version published in 1988. In the *CGR* there are descriptions of all accessible versions, edited and unedited, of every *romance* in existence in the oral tradition of any one of the branches of the Pan-Hispanic tradition: Castilian, Galician-Portuguese, Catalan, and Sephardic.

Survival of the Traditional
Romancero: Field Expeditions[1]

Ana Valenciano

Research work in the humanities and the social sciences at times demands two kinds of parallel and complementary activities: first, obtaining material directly from the context in which it is produced and, second, processing the data later outside of its context. The ways in which the fieldwork should be organized as well as where and how it is to be carried out depend upon the objective that is being pursued.

Oral literary genres differ in the ways they are transmitted, but we can find them together in the same cultural environment. Narrations in prose, like stories or legends, live together in the collective memory along with proverbs, riddles and sayings, and poetic forms, among which are included *canciones* (songs), *coplas* (couplets), and *romances* (ballads).

Our primary objective in going out on collecting expeditions is to obtain examples of the traditional *romancero*. It is not a question of storing literary fossils for the mere desire of increasing the number of texts in existence in present-day collections, but rather of trying to gather, in so far as it is possible, new data which will help to illustrate and clarify the various questions that have arisen in this literary field.

Some of the conditions that in principle are required in order to undertake the task of collecting *romances* do not differ substantially from those that are necessary for obtaining other categories of oral texts: a certain amount of previous knowledge in order to keep the data from turning into a mosaic of confused information, a permanent way to store and assemble interesting information when the opportunity arises, and an adequate knowledge of the language of the interlocutors (Lacoste 1981:141), which means in our case, the poetic discourse in which traditional ballads are expressed.

Direct contact with the reality in which the *romancero* survives today is not going to tell us anything about the exact moment in which a version became fixed in the memory of each one of its "authors" nor, consequently, about the evolutionary process of each one of its most significant variants, since the most important transformations seem to be produced during an apprenticeship period, and we will never be able to witness that process. Despite the fact that as students of the *romancero* we are outside of the chain of traditional transmission, we have an advantage over the reciters in being able to observe simultaneously a greater number of ballad *fabulas* (themes) in their multiple divergent realizations (versions), and that possibility is what will permit us to interpret the meanings that the poems offer at different levels. Therefore, the more abundant and the more varied are the examples that we have at our disposal on carrying out an intertextual comparison, the better command we will have of the poetic language in which *romances* are expressed and the closer we will come to an understanding of their mechanisms of transmission.

The *Romancero*

The *romancero*, the most important living oral literary tradition in the western world, has been stored up to the present in the collective memory of the Hispanic peoples and has come to occupy potentially the same area as that of the languages in which it can be expressed: Spanish, Galician-Portuguese, Catalan, and Judeo-Spanish.

We can come close to a knowledge of the *romancero* of the past thanks to fifteenth- and sixteenth-century printers who published in chapbooks and songbooks not only poems composed by authors who were more or less learned, but also *romances*, which were circulating orally at that time in a society interested in transmitting them. Certain kinds of information printed in works of a very different sort offer invaluable material for the reconstruction of the history of the genre. The Golden Age theater frequently makes use of fragments of *romances* which must have had wide circulation among the people who habitually attended the performances. Ballad stories themselves have inspired various re-elaborations of a theme transmitted to us by printed literature.

The survival today of many themes present in medieval tradition, of which there are early printed examples, does not at all suppose that we can consider the thematic panorama of the *romancero* to be limited to the sixteenth century, since from that time on poems with a very different origin have become popular, alongside of older stories, to the extent that they have considerably enlarged repertories with new types or subtypes of traditional *romances*.

When we attempt to reconstruct the history of the *romancero*, the eighteenth century appears to be a silent parenthesis. We know, nevertheless, that those poetic narrations which delighted ladies and gentlemen and even Queen Isabel in the fifteenth century gradually disappeared from courtly circles and ended up taking refuge in rural environments. Except for the Sephardic *romancero*, which went far afield with the expulsion of the Jews from Spain in the fifteenth century and generally reappeared in urban areas, the inhabitants of the towns and villages of Portugal and Spain have become the outstanding repositories of this valuable cultural inheritance.

The diachronic study of this type of poetry helps us to understand its evolution and consequently its process of adaptation. By knowing the history of the genre, we can try to calculate the approximate age of the traditional texts that we find and locate their sources: whether they are related to the epic, whether they have a historical base, whether they enter into the large group we customarily call folkloric, whether they began to circulate from chapbooks sung by blind men, or whether their origins are nearer at hand. Nevertheless, none of the foregoing seems to be of concern to the traditional transmitter, who belongs to a cultural environment in which the poems are inherited from his immediate forebears without any importance being given to the age or the original text of the stories that are memorized. On being integrated into the chain of traditional transmission, the folkloric subject learns naturally the poetic discourse in which *romances* are expressed, and he makes use of them to set forth and to comment upon problems that interest or affect in some way the society in which he happened to be born. What has definitely kept the *romancero* alive up to the present is its intrinsic capacity to accommodate itself to the successive societies that have kept re-creating it.

History of Ballad Collecting

Collecting the modern *romancero* has its own history. At the end of the first quarter of the nineteenth century, almost simultaneously in Portugal and in Spain, Almeida Garrett and Bartolomé José Gallardo collected the first versions, which mark the initial moment of the reappearance of the traditional *romancero*. From that date up to the middle of the twentieth century, when collecting methods change, we can distinguish four great stages in the exploration of the *romancero*: (1) the era of the pioneers of the nineteenth century when collecting was centered particularly in Portugal and Catalonia; (2) the first period of Menéndez Pidal and María Goyri, when we began to be aware of the continued presence of the *romancero* in Castile (1900-10); (3) the most fruitful period (1911-20); and (4) the middle years (1921-51) (see Catalán 1979:217-56; Armistead 1979c:53-60).

Since the first texts were collected, the contributions of hundreds of fieldworkers have put at our disposal thousands of versions, published or unpublished, which have offered abundant data for study (see Sánchez Romeralo 1979a:2:15-51 and *Bibliografía* 1980). But until a few years ago, in the majority of the cases we could only count upon the testimony of the poems themselves, and we knew little or nothing about the experiences or the collecting methods that our predecessors used. Aside from the commentaries of Menéndez Pidal in some of his works dedicated to the *romancero* (1953:2:291-439; 1973:403-45), certain allusions in prologues of printed collections and some correspondence between collectors of unpublished versions (part of which is preserved in the Menéndez Pidal archives) constitute the only "bibliography," which is far from complete, of the topic in question. It was María Goyri, pioneer of ballad collecting, who, after rediscovering the Castilian *romancero* in the company of her husband Ramón Menéndez Pidal, published the first field manual. This little book, in which she makes explicit allusions to methodology, has served as a guide to succeeding generations (1906:10:374-86, 1907:11:24-36; Torner 1929).[2]

It is also necessary to recognize that this type of fieldwork has generally not been systematic and has depended on chance. The great collection of Menéndez Pidal could be assembled thanks to the collaboration of family and friends, students, and correspondents, the quantity and the origin of the contributions depending upon the personal circumstances of the collectors.

Outside of the Menéndez Pidal archives, the totality of regional or local printed collections does not reflect either greater or less vitality of the traditional *romancero* in different communities of the Peninsula because collecting and, especially, editing ballad texts have always depended upon interests of the moment.

This situation was beginning to change at the time of the Primer Coloquio Internacional sobre el Romancero held in Madrid in 1970.[3] The harvest of traditional *romances* and the methodological aspect this task involves seem to have awakened great interest among researchers in the field, and this revitalization of the collecting activity, together with the new possibilities offered by technological advances (tape recorders, etc.) have produced a spectacular enrichment of ballad archives in recent years.[4]

Point of Departure: My Collecting Experience

My first field trip in search of *romances* goes back to July, 1977, the beginning of the series of large field expeditions organized by the Seminario Menéndez Pidal.[5] In the village of Tresabuela del Valle de Polaciones, Santander, I found myself for the first time face to face with one of the authentic recreators of the traditional *romancero*. She was Adela Gómez, a sixty-year-old resident of Salceda, who happened to be in Tresabuela that day. Although she did not have much time, she was kind enough to recite and sing for us a splendid version of a Carolingian ballad.

Adela was the first person we came upon when we entered the town. We asked her directly if she knew any *romances*, and we were lucky in that one of the ballads that she knew, *Belardo y Valdovinos*, includes in one of its formulaic verses a reference to the singing of a *romance*. Therefore, she began at once to recite to us:

Tan alta iba la luna	The moon was as high
como el sol al medio día	as the noonday sun
cuando el buen conde Belarde	when good Count Belarde
de sus batallas venía.	came from his battles.
Cien caballos trae de rienda,	He has a hundred horses on rein,
todos los ganó en un día,	he won them all in one day,
y los echaba a beber	and he let them drink
en la reguera de Hungría.	in the canal of Hungary.
Mientras los caballos beben	While the horses are drinking
este romance decía: . . .	he recited this ballad: . . .

At the same time, another one of our ballad-collecting teams was working in Salceda and, as a result of information from other villagers, they waited for Adela's return in order to question her. Adela repeated for them afterwards the same version of *Belardo y Valdovinos* without introducing a single important variant.[6] Our next expedition, in the summer of 1978, was in the south of the Peninsula, where our activities were centered in the province of Jaén and the southern part of Granada, but we also covered the northwest of Murcia and the south of Albacete. The contrast between the two areas was evident from the very beginning. Given the large size of the towns in comparison with the scantily populated villages of the north, it was impossible to try to interview a significant number of inhabitants in one day. For that reason it became necessary to keep returning to the same locality, since the most infrequent *romances* might survive in one spot without our coming upon them in several trips.

Although in the expedition of 1978 no texts of extraordinary rarity appeared, in general the *romancero* came to us in very complete versions with themes like *Conde Claros en hábito de fraile*, *La bastarda y el segador*, *La mala suegra*, etc., which showed a tradition in a better state of preservation than we had found in 1977.

The ballad reciters of the south are apt to be relatively younger than those of the north. Certain farm tasks, like harvesting grapes or olives, which still bring two or even three generations into contact, have undoubtedly contributed to the fact that oral tradition is still alive among young people and even among Andalusian children, who still sing *romances* as an accompaniment to their games. Andalusia is also the home of the versions called *vulgatas* which, with melody and text practically fixed, cover long distances and in some areas come to take the place of regional types.[7] In contrast to these *vulgatas*, which spread very easily, there also exists in Andalusia a small group of *romances* of very limited circulation which have been incorporated into Andalusian gypsy song and which in most cases "belong" to certain gypsy families who originally came from Puerto de Santa María, Cádiz.[8] These are very special versions of the epic or historical cycles, some of which derive from post-sixteenth century printed re-elaborations.

Subsequently rural areas of the northern half of Spain have been preferred for our exploratory activity in the thirteen additional expeditions sponsored and organized by the Seminario Menéndez Pidal in the last seven years (1979-1985).[9] As an example of the situation concerning the *romancero* found in these northern zones and the urgent need to carry out both extensive and intensive field work in various districts, I am going to comment in some detail about our experience in an isolated corner of the northwest part of León, the district of La Fornela, made up of seven villages in close communication with one another: Cariseda, Chano, Faro, Fresnedelo, Guímara, Peranzanes and Trascastro.[10]

In the final period of the northern field expedition of 1977, a team made up of permanent members of the Seminario Menéndez Pidal, Diego Catalán, Jesús Antonio Cid, Flor Salazar, and Ana Valenciano, went on the nineteenth of July to La Fornela. After a stop in Cariseda,[11] we proceeded to the village of Trascastro, where, according to the inhabitants themselves, scarcely thirty-five families were living in a somewhat unsatisfactory situation.[12] The elementary school had been closed by the government for lack of children of school age and, as a result, the smallest children were transported daily to various centers, while those who were fourteen or older and wanted to continue their studies had to reside as boarding students in the private high schools of Ponferrada and only returned home during vacations.

That day in Trascastro two subteams, the composition of which changed during the day, worked independently until well after nightfall, managing in this way to contact almost all of the villagers.[13] Among the men who remembered *romances* and who on that occasion far surpassed our feminine informants was David Ramón, age 69, a true representative of the great ballad singers, who died the following year. Among the women, Gloria Álvarez, age 67, gave us fifteen magnificent versions one after another. Out of a total of eleven informants, we succeeded in collecting forty texts which corresponded to twenty-eight different ballad stories, many of them belonging to the most hidden depths of ballad tradition.[14]

The excellent results obtained in Trascastro showed us the category of the ballad store that the remaining villages of La Fornela could offer us. For that reason we believed it to be important to return to such a promising district and to devote to it a good part of the northern field expedition of 1979. Six collectors participated in this work during the first two days (September 20-21) dedicated to exploring the area around the upper valley of the Sil. The group was reduced to four during the remaining days (September 22-25) centered in La Fornela. We systematically divided up into two teams and when circumstances required, one or another of the investigators would go off to do individual interviews.   During this expedition we were lodged in Villafranca del Bierzo.

During those four days in September of 1979 the number of informants who sang or recited ballads for us came to more than forty.   Although a few men, like Felipe Cerecedo García , age 56, from Chano, showed that they had exceptional knowledge of traditional poems, the women we interviewed surpassed the men, in contrast to what had happened two years before in Trascastro. Among the women who stood out for their familiarity with *romances* were Joaquina García, age 81 (mother of Felipe Cerecedo) and Eva Robledo, age 72, of Chano, and Valenta Fernández, age 79 and Adelaida Álvarez, age 83, of Peranzanes.[15]

All but one of the *romances* collected in Trascastro reappeared in La Fornela two years later, but, in addition, alongside of these ballad themes, magnificent versions of many others enlarged the repertory of 1977.   Only an enumeration of these oral poems can show the enormous variety and wealth of the *romance* versions that were stored in the memories of the inhabitants of La Fornela in 1979.[16]   These magnificent results obtained in the exploration of La Fornela in 1979 instilled in us a certain amount of optimism concerning the possibility of survival of the *romancero* in regions with more conservative traditions. Unfortunately that optimism has not been maintained as we have continued our collecting activities in the decade of the eighties.

During the northern field trip in 1980, devoted to the exploration of the *romance* tradition of western León and Asturias from its base in Villablino (León), one of our teams went as far as Peranzanes and Guímara, where *romances* were collected from four informants, three of whom had been interviewed in 1979.[17]   Again during the León field trip in 1985 another team went off from the capital of the province on July 18 to the village of Chano, where eleven versions were collected, including the reappearance of several interesting themes like *Belardo y Valdovinos, La caza de Celinos, El conde Grifos Lombardo, Flores y Blancaflor (Hermanas reina y cautiva).*

The situation that was found in this last field trip is quite discouraging for the future of the *romancero* in the district.   Two great reciters interviewed in 1979, Joaquina García and Eva Robledo, had died, together with another of our informants, Arturo

Fernández; others had moved away, and among our former informants who remained in the village, one of them did not even remember having been interviewed by us six years before. The disappearance of these witnesses of the continued existence of the *romancero* has not been compensated for by the discovery of younger informants of analogous character. This rapid deterioration of the ballad tradition in one of the areas that had been most fruitful in the search for *romances* is related to a sociological change which seems to be irreversible: the progressive extinction of the small villages as a result of the rapid reduction of their population.

If we go back to the last century, we know that a few years before 1849 the district of La Fornela had a total of 1337 inhabitants distributed among 295 families (an average of 4.53 members per family). This population increased during the course of the century, reaching 1709 in 1888. In this century, after the civil war (1936-1939) the number of inhabitants in La Fornela stayed about the same, 1758, but in 1970, as a result of the emigration of people from the country to the cities during the sixties, the total of the inhabitants remaining in their villages was reduced to 1253, distributed among 325 families (an average of 3.85 per family). After that date the reduction in population accelerated enormously, since, according to the most recent census of 1981, the number of inhabitants, after eight more years of emigration, has been reduced to 446 for the whole district, distributed among 175 families (an average of 2.45 per family), that is to say, a third of those who were still living in La Fornela in 1970.

In the winter of 1981, thanks to a generous invitation from Professor Aaron V. Cicourel of the University of California, San Diego, I had the opportunity of collaborating with his teams set up for a sociological project. One of the phases of the project consisted of carrying out interviews in towns in various regions of Spain with people who had been selected in advance by means of a questionnaire. During the period of my collaboration we visited several villages of Las Hurdes Altas (Cáceres) and the town of Cortes de la Frontera (Málaga). Encouraged by Professor Cicourel, I took advantage of the opportunity and devoted my free time to searching for ballad texts. The results were again encouraging since, in a very limited period of time, I managed to gather a sizable number of versions in Las Hurdes as well as in Cortes de la

Frontera.[18]

That experience was different from the field trips of the Seminario Menéndez Pidal and therefore rewarding. It made me realize that, although the aims were not the same, in practical terms and in technique they had much in common. The length of a field expedition, the time of year in which it takes place, the number of investigators, whether it is more desirable to have a fixed base which facilitates a continual exchange of experiences or to be free to move on to more promising areas—all have to be taken into consideration in organizing a field expedition for sociological purposes, for collecting *romances*, or for any comparable research project.

Aims Pursued.   Data Pertinent to the Classification of Materials

The principal objective in our field expeditions is to collect texts that are as complete as possible and to record the melodies to which they are sung. If it is not possible to collect a sung version, it is necessary to ascertain whether the reciter memorized it with or without the music. The *romances* we have found in our explorations in recent years have not always been offered to us in sung form. Although sometimes the reciters acknowledge that they learned them with music, advanced age, mourning, or insecurity prevent them from giving us versions accompanied by their *son* or *tonada*, as they call it. We have also been able to determine that many poems have been transmitted by recitation only, although possibly they began by being sung. Thanks to the tape recorder, it now possible to record the melodies that accompany traditional poetry. Thus these new audio archives will be able to provide valuable data for scholars interested in the study of traditional music.

In order to collect a text, aside from the actual recording, it turns out to be useful, while the recitation or singing is going on, to take notes that will facilitate the transcription and the processing of the information afterwards. It is also interesting to obtain information about the various designations that are used to identify the ballad themes they know and even to ascertain the personal interpretation of each reciter of certain passages in their stories. In practice, however, this type of question can produce serious interference at the moment of performance and spoil the results. The delivery of traditional ballads demands a certain rhythm on the part of the reciters to which they adapt themselves as they gain self-confidence. They re-create their versions recalling them verse by verse, for which reason forgetting a single verse in the middle destroys the fluidity of the recitation. Their memory becomes recharged after the delivery of each *romance*, and in this way the informant remembers more easily the rest of the themes that make up his repertory. For all of these reasons the ballad collector must try to stimulate the recitation, taking care not to spoil with inappropriate questions the effort that the informants are making to recall poems that they memorized in the past.

Nevertheless, there are data that are indispensable for this kind of research, and they are readily accessible. The place of origin of a version or of a repertory does not always coincide with the locality where it is collected. It is advisable, therefore, to find out where the informant came from and to ask him (or her) directly where and when he remembers having memorized his poems, even though, in the case of widespread themes, the definitive location will be able to be made later by means of a comparison of the texts obtained with others typologically similar. The testimony of the reciters themselves often turns out to be confused because natural forms of interference have been produced (which they are not even aware of) between imported versions and ballad types and repertories from the place where they live. As for the circumstances that surrounded their apprenticeship and the origin of the versions (the person or the printed source from which they learned them), these are data that go far back in time and not even the reciters can recall them clearly. This information generally emerges in a spontaneous fashion during the interview, and if it is of interest, it should be noted down.

Other data that should be recorded are the age and sex of the informants, their first name and family name (and their nickname if they have one), provided that obtaining this information does not disturb ballad collection, because, after all, the reciters who generously offer us their poems have the right to remain anonymous if they so desire. The date of the field trip and the names of the team members are facts that should be recorded in the field workbooks at the beginning of each day. The classification of the poetic genres transmitted orally is somewhat outside the cultural world that produces them, since it is the students of balladry, foreign to this world, who have "baptized" the different genres in order to compartmentalize their field of research.

Perhaps the first problem faced by the investigator who sets out to collect traditional *romances* is to make himself understood when he tries to identify the genre he is looking for, because, except in unusual cases, *romances, canciones,* and *coplas* are mixed together in the memory of their transmitters. Aside from the always useful allusion to the names of the most popular ballad protagonists (Gerineldo, Sildana, Delgadina, etc.) or reciting to them fragments of ballads supposedly widespread in the area, it is helpful to find out the designations applied to the different categories of poems in the zone under investigation. It is normal for nearby towns or those in close communication to use a common term for the *romancero: coplas, canciones antiguas, cantarías, cántigas,* etc., but rarely *romances.*

Context in which Traditional Poems Are Delivered

The social or folkloric circumstances in which ballads are propagated in principle does not modify the ballad that is collected, but community tasks like harvesting, grape-picking, or gathering olives can serve as a reference point for categorizing certain repertories that are considered appropriate for singing while these activities are being carried out (even though now they are almost never actualized in these contexts). *La bastarda y el segador,* for example, is usually included among harvest songs (*canciones de segada*), and *La dama y el pastor, La loba parda,* along with other *romances* with a similar theme, belong primarily to shepherds' repertories, although any one of the themes alluded to may have been memorized by any villager interested in these narrations at a given moment.

Any reference to artisan work realized as a common endeavor or to any kind of gathering in the past in which the villagers, male and female, had a good opportunity to sing poems, goes back to bearers of folklore in distant times in which the re-creation of *romances* was more integrated into the daily life of the community. As for the officially sponsored *fiestas,* many of which are artificially revitalized, they do not seem to have been, as a whole, particularly favorable moments for the singing of traditional *romances.* This kind of poetry does not need especially qualified interpreters for its actualization, which are the kind that usually perform in public upon such occasions.

Ritualization

When a *romance* becomes ritualized, for example, in songs for children's games or in prayers, the content of the narration tends to lose its function and, as a consequence, the poem loses its open quality and becomes fossilized or greatly deformed. Although, except for these cases, ritualization is not very frequent in peninsular tradition, there are some very interesting exceptions. Refunctionalization has been the reason for the survival of two old historical themes, *La merienda del moro Zaide* and *La muerte del maestre de Santiago*, which, if they had not developed a petitionary function, would undoubtedly have ceased being transmitted, as has happened with the majority of ballads on contemporary events (*romances noticieros*).[19]

In the ballad that tells of the death of the Maestre don Fadrique, the printed version of the sixteenth century would seem to suggest indirectly that Doña María, the mistress of King Don Pedro, had asked the king for the head of Don Fadrique, since the king, on receiving his brother in the palace, says to him:

—Vuestra cabeza, maestre,	Your head, master,
mandada está en aguinaldo.	has been claimed as a gift.

    (*Cancionero de Amberes sin año*)

The second hemistich was without doubt the point of departure for the incorporation into the *romance* of the introductory formula referring to Christmas gift requests with which it is sung today:

Hoy es día de los Reyes,	Today is Twelfth Night,
día muy aseñalado	a very important day,
cuando damas y doncellas	when ladies and maidens
al rey piden aguinaldo.	ask the king for a present.
Unas le pedían seda,	Some asked him for silk,
otras sedilla y brocado	others satin and brocade,
a no ser doña María	except for Doña María,
que se lo pidió doblado,	who asked that it be doubled,
que le pidió la cabeza	for she asked for the head
del maestre de Santiago.	of the master of Santiago.

Something similar must have occurred with *La merienda del moro Zaide* (Catalán 1969b:83-99). The two cases cited suggest that the possible existence of petitionary songs should be investigated while ballad collecting. The opening formulas are used not only in these two historical ballads but also in other Nativity ballads and in many different kinds of songs.

Strata of the Traditional *Romancero*

In the totality of orally transmitted genres, our collecting experience seems to indicate that the *romancero* is found in the memory of the subjects who are the repositories of folklore in a deep substratum from which it can only be actualized spontaneously with difficulty. Within the *romancero* itself we can distinguish, in turn, several levels of diffusion among the community of reciters.

In the most superficial level or stratum are found the *romances* often classified as *infantiles*, which were memorized to serve as an accompaniment to children's games. In them interest in the story that is being told has been lost, for which reason they generally show up in very degraded versions that are resistant to variation. Included in these repertories there are not only poems like *Don Gato, Mambrú,* or *Hilo de oro,* which are at the outer limits of the genre, but also another series of versions which, although coming from stories with traditional roots, on being incorporated into this superficial level lose their capacity for openness, thereby checking their natural evolution. Among the latter are to be found *La doncella guerrera* with the opening "En Sevilla [a] un sevillano / siete hijas le dió Dios" (In Seville to a Sevillan / God gave seven daughters); *Ricofranco,* "En Madrid hay una niña / que la llaman la Isabel" (In Madrid there is a girl / whom they call Isabel); *La vuelta del marido,* "Estaba una señorita / a la sombra de un laurel" (There was a young lady / in the shade of a laurel tree); *El quintado,* "Mes de mayo, mes de mayo, / mes de mayo, primavera" (Month of May, month of May / month of May, spring); or *Albaniña,* "Estando la Catalina / sentadita en su balcón" (While Catalina is / seated on her balcony). With these and other similar openings these ballads appear in practically every region of Spain alongside of "vulgate" versions of *La hermana cautiva,* "El día de los torneos / pasé por la morería" (The day of the tourneys / I passed through the Moorish district); *Las tres cautivas,* "A la verde, verde, / a la verde oliva" (At the green, green, / at the green olive tree); or *Santa Iria,* "Estando tres niñas / bordando corbatas" (While three girls were / embroidering neckties).

In a second stratum are located the *romances* which belong to what we may call the *romancero común.* These are quite widespread themes known to us in a great variety of regional and local types, forming the most extensive block of ballad stories.

Finally, the third category of *romances* is formed by those themes that have only been preserved by exceptional ballad-singers, who are usually not young. For present-day collectors these singers constitute the great "finds" during their days of fieldwork. There survive in the memory of these "specialists" versions of *romances* of medieval origin which have been almost lost today, along with many others of limited circulation unknown to the majority of their fellow villagers.

At the same time, within the corpus of a *romance* belonging to what we have called the *romancero común*, it is possible to distinguish different groups of versions: independent versions, few in number, which are barely related to other versions in the vicinity; regional versions, which coincide in most of their motifs and in their basic structure with many nearby versions; and what we have called "vulgate" versions, which go beyond the traditional folkloric frontiers and take the place of the specific ballad types of a given district.

There is one additional category of versions, initially developed outside of the traditional culture, which with their influence can wipe out natural frontiers of folklore geography. Sometimes these are factitious versions made up by scholars from verses that are mostly traditional in origin, like those of the *Flor nueva de romances viejos* of Menéndez Pidal (1928); other times they are versions chosen by chance by professional singers or folklore groups. The latter are circulating today with a melody that has been artifically adapted to their new commercial function.

Although these texts make use of a language that is recognizable as their own by authentic speakers of the *romancero* language, they can re-enter traditional culture through scholarly books or other published means and through commercial tapes and radio broadcasts. Once they have been memorized by traditional singers or reciters, they live today alongside the versions and the melodies characteristic of each region; they can maintain themselves just as they are or, with the passing of time, they can incorporate words, formulas, and motifs from the specific version of the area (cf. *Romancero tradicional* 1971-72:5:227-55). Although in some cases it is difficult to identify them, it is necessary to detect this kind of version at the moment of processing the results of a field expedition in order to avoid erroneous conclusions.

Contamination

What has been called "contamination" is in reality one of the most frequent aesthetic devices used in traditional transmission. Speakers of this poetic language manipulate in a natural way a great abundance of lexicalized words and verses which they transfer from one *romance* to another, either keeping the same meaning or adapting it to the new context into which it is inserted. But the informants themselves are totally unaware of this phenomenon, since they recount to us in their poetic language stories that have a beginning, a development, and an ending that form a unit.

Contamination is detected after the fact by students of the *romancero* when they submit the samples they have obtained to comparative analysis. Since these samples of oral tradition are not always presented to us in a good state of preservation, when two or more *romances* are crossed, it is necessary to determine whether it is contamination with a traditional base, or whether, on the contrary, it is no more than the result of an artificial attempt at reconstruction caused by the uncertain memory of the informant at the moment of re-actualization.

The Fieldwork Manual

The fieldwork manual, together with the tape recorder and the field workbook, is a basic tool for the task of ballad collecting. Its function is to anticipate in so far as possible what *romances* will appear and to remind the collector of them by means of a version as close as possible to those they expect to find. It should include a complete inventory of themes known in the area that is being investigated, as well as in nearby areas, with alternate openings and the most representative segments of discourse, as well as complete versions of the *romances* that offer the most interest because they still are poorly documented. Whenever possible it should include names of reciters and collectors of the past, a list of the localities already searched, and demographic data that will help to select the localities they are going to visit. As for the internal organization of the manual, it is a good idea for each *romance* to occupy a loose, independent sheet to facilitate later reordering in accord with the preferences that we know are characteristic of the tradition of each subarea under investigation. The manual must not be considered a closed book; the new data collected during the course of the expedition must be entered in the manual to serve as future reference.

Variation, a characteristic of traditional poetry, has not imposed itself sufficiently upon modern oral tradition to break up to any substantial degree the repertories and models of each theme implanted from past times in a given area. The use of the manual during field explorations has shown that the majority of *romances* and *romance* types that had been sung in a region reappear in the present. Although it will be necessary to wait for the complete processing of all the data obtained in the field expeditions of recent years, we can state that the ballad tradition has not remained static and that phenomena of poetic re-creation are still being produced similar to those which occurred in past times. Alongside a large number of versions that have a tendency to summarize stories, there also appear others that are amplified in a discursive way or that have transformations that affect the plot and even the structure of the *fabula*. Certain themes like *Gerineldo* or *El conde Niño* are in a state of regression in zones where they had attained great popularity, while others, generally in "vulgate" versions like *Tamar* or *La doncella guerrera*, are expanding with great rapidity. The type of *La serrana de la Vera* that begins "Allá en Garganta la Olla, / siete leguas de Plasencia" (There in Garganta la Olla / seven leagues from Plasencia), which up to 1977 was only known in Extremadura and thereabouts, has traveled as far as the province of Lugo, where it was documented in recent field trips in Galicia. Also the appearance of new hybrid versions of previously well differentiated types of *La muerte del príncipe don Juan* serve as an example of the transformations that a traditional theme can still suffer by means of contact between repertories of contiguous communities.

Teams and Functions of their Members

Any individual investigator can, of course, devote himself to ballad collecting. This is what has habitually been done in the past, and it is continuing to be done with great success in many cases. But there are many advantages to undertaking this task as a team, in addition to sharing experiences with colleagues or collaborators of different origin.

It does not seem to us to be a bad idea to have in a well organized collective field expedition a large number of participants, some of them lacking experience, since didactic aims can be integrated into the practical experience of field trips without disturbing the progress of ballad collecting. But it is necessary, in the cases of "massive" participation, to distribute the collaborators in teams of no more than four people, to be sure that they are always directed by monitors who are experts in ballad collecting, and to assign ahead of time a task to each person so that there will not be any sort of interference that could affect the investigation. Taking notes by hand about unusual versions, recording information about informants and, above all, taking down systematically the incipit of each sample that is collected together with the identification, whenever feasible, of corresponding themes, can enormously facilitate the processing of the data at the end of each expedition.

Choosing the Area of the Field Trip

Choosing a small or very limited area seems indispensable for certain kinds of fieldwork carried out by sociologists, ethnographers, or anthropologists who include personal interviews in their methodology, since in this way they have the possibility of selecting their informants according to their different interests.

In the case of the traditional *romancero*, the selection in advance of a concrete locality or an excessively small area always carries with it the risk of finding wasteland and the conviction, albeit with reservations, that the *romancero* does not survive at that moment in that place. The seeker of *romances* will never cause by his presence, however prolonged it may be, a text to be produced that did not exist before his arrival. *Romances*, as we have said, can be in the memory of any speaker of the Ibero-Romance languages: men, women, young or old, even children. But at the same time whole communities, even though they speak those languages, have lived on the margin of *romancero* transmission or, what is more frequent today, they have forgotten it because of the absence or the death of the last repositories of this tradition. For these reasons it is wise to select a zone that is large enough to permit movement in several directions depending upon the state of the ballad tradition.

Insistence upon Areas with the Greatest Continuity in their Ballad Stores

Naturally, continued residence in one place or returning to a town already visited offers more opportunites for coming upon informants and situations that are more favorable for carrying out interviews than a rapid visit in the course of one day.

On the other hand, we have been able to confirm repeatedly how the presence in the villages of skilled fieldworkers brings a resurgence of interest in the poems with which people entertained themselves in the past. Listening to fragments of ballads which they recognize as something familiar or hearing the recitations of one of their neighbors revives the memory of those who had lost their remembrance of ballads and stimulates them to contribute to the process of recuperating the traditional store. Therefore, when a district or a locality is identified as a zone of special interest because of the characteristics of its traditional repertory, it is indicated that we should return to the same place as many times as is necessary.

Access to Rural Media

The best way to gain access to community repositories of oral tradition is conditioned by the personality of each fieldworker, and it differs according to the circumstances, including climatic factors, at the moment of beginning a day of ballad collecting.

In urban areas it seems necessary for the one who is trying to investigate the living reality of the *romancero* (and we have abundant examples of this in fieldwork on the Sephardic ballad) to belong to the community or be introduced into it by some relative or common friend of the subject one wants to interview. In this kind of fieldwork, establishing a relationship with potential informants by means of people with a certain amount of prestige seems to offer good opportunites for the investigator.

On the contrary, in rural areas of the Peninsula, using as intermediaries people who are socially outstanding does not usually give good results. It is difficult for the school teacher or the priest of the town, often as much of an outsider as the interviewer, to be well informed about the identity of the authentic ballad singers. On the other hand, if they are present at the interviews, by representing authority they can provoke auto-censorship in the informants.

At present, for obvious reasons, there is greater comprehension than there was in the past among individuals who belong to urban cultures and among people who still adhere to rural culture. But the arrival in a town of a group of investigators continues to excite natural curiosity in the inhabitants to find out the reason for the presence of strangers in the community. Presenting ourselves as we really are, field investigators of oral poetry, and showing at once our knowledge of the genre that we are looking for seems to us to be the most honorable and effective way to explain our presence in a cultural world that is foreign to us. Peasants who have had some contact with the ballad tradition and who have been witnesses to how, with the passing of time, these poems have ceased to be sung, understand immediately our interest in saving from oblivion the *romances* that some members of the community can still recall.

It can happen that the first people whom the investigator encounters know nothing about the *romancero* and are not even capable of identifying it. In those cases they will direct us toward the most erudite or the most knowledgeable person in the town, or, in some cases, toward the one who is known for his (or her) ability to sing any kind of song but who is not necessarily a good repository of tradition. But with a little practice, in most instances it is possible to avoid these false paths without losing too much time and to obtain trustworthy information about those who may be well informed about the *romancero*.

Although it is preferable to try to contact the oldest people, any one of the town's inhabitants can be, in principle, an active speaker of the traditional poetic language or at least a passive speaker who has listened to it and can recognize it on hearing it again. For this reason, it is essential to try to establish relations with the greatest number of individuals possible until we come upon the person who can offer us the information that we are seeking.

Once we have succeeded in identifying the *romancero* as the object of our interest for our informants, even though we may have hardly collected a fragmentary sample, names of people suggested by them who may be acquainted with the *romancero* usually lead us to discover individuals who knew *romances* at least at one time.

The Interview: Collector, Informant, Manual

Approaching people in their homes, generally elderly people who are not at all prepared for the presence of an investigator, in order to ask them to tell us what they know about traditional texts doubtless supposes an action that is not without an appearance of aggressiveness, since the collector, who knows very well why and for what purpose he is in a given place, is the one who is breaking into the peasants' daily life. But in my long collecting experience, I have proven, day after day, that the "traditional" hospitality of rural folk shown to the stranger who knocks at his door continues to function as the norm in all rural communities. Provided the investigator from outside knows how to wait for a favorable opportunity and not interfere with sometimes pressing obligations in which the peasants are occupied, he will find the means to establish an excellent relationship. The collector and the informant do not know each other, but they have in common their knowledge of the *romancero*. This shared culture is, in my opinion, what contributes most to the opening up of communication between them. The two interlocutors have made a discovery: the investigator foresees the possibility of listening to some admirable, hitherto unknown texts, and the one who is being interviewed discovers that "his" *romancero* is recognized and appreciated by someone who is not an integral part of his traditional culture.

Good results are obtained when interviews are carried out in the presence of relatives or neighbors of the informants so that everybody can collaborate, but this situation, which often presents itself, creates difficulties that the collector has to overcome so that the texts being collected are comprehensible despite the interferences that are naturally produced on such occasions. In these collective interviews it is also important to understand the various levels of authority that are in effect in each case. The acceptance of certain hierarchies (between husband and wife, parents and children, good and bad singers, etc.) can cause even the most talented singer to remain silent since, despite his knowledge, he respects the role of protagonist assumed by another one of the group. Just as there are many styles among those who devote themselves to collecting oral texts, the bearers of traditional knowledge offer us varied personalities that make us adapt collecting techniques to each particular situation.

The various levels of the *romancero* that different types of reciters can offer oblige us to choose our questions during the interview in such a way as not to discourage our interlocutors by insisting upon *romances* that almost surely they are not going to recognize. Therefore, it is wise to use the manual and alternate popular themes with those that appear less frequently. Whenever possible the initiative should be left to the informants themselves so that they will offer us their whole repertory, but this does not always turn out to be possible, owing to the fact that the transmitters, because of the crossing of genres in their minds, easily turn to singing or reciting *coplas, canciones,* or even songs from *zarzuelas,* or tangos learned in their youth.

Not having been re-actualized in years, the ballad texts that we find in our current field trips almost always remain in a state of lethargy from which they must be brought out. It is surprising, nonetheless, how the first actualization with omissions and verses that are incoherent or out of place, with our help, turn into a magnificent version delivered all in one piece once the reciter gains self-confidence. Therefore, the collector can and must, with or without the help of the manual, make suggestions in order to bring a recitation to a good conclusion, although in no case should he propose perfect verses or hemistichs that are then integrated into the version after being respectfully accepted by the informant. The first rule of collecting is not to alter or deform a ballad text at any time on the basis of our own knowledge.

The collector must be patient and devote all the time that is necessary to every interview in order to overcome the natural resistance of the transmitter to give us fragmentary texts. The most important key to awakening the memory of the reciters is to hit upon an incipit that makes them recall the opening of one of their own versions, because if the beginning does not come out right, it is not likely that they will go on to sing (or recite) the rest of the *romance.*

If the poem was learned with its melody, we must ask the informant to repeat it by singing, and if this is not possible, to intone at least four to six verses, since the melody that accompanies ballad texts keeps repeating itself with scarcely any variation. Aside from the musical interest of the melody, singing can facilitate the collecting of a more perfect text. Between two consecutive actualizations of a well-remembered version, we are not going to find significant differences, but when a ballad is not remembered with precision, the melody memorized with that version usually helps the singer produce one verse after another more easily. Nevertheless, it must be emphasized that, even though the melody or the assonance helps the informant recall verses that he did not manage to actualize correctly or had omitted, he always has the option while reciting of stopping to think or to correct his words, or add or remove verses or hemistichs afterwards. However, the desire not to disturb the continuity of the performance while singing will oblige him to

accept verses whose traditional form he does not remember well or
else to omit them completely.

All the informants we have been referring to up to now are
those we have encountered most frequently during the course of
our ballad collecting, but this does not mean that there do not still
exist exceptional ballad singers, men or women who continue to
practice singing or reciting themes that are very scarce in modern
oral tradition and who have the ability to produce dozens of
versions without the least hesitation.   There is no definable
prototype of this kind of individual and, although, unfortunately,
they are usually elderly people who have kept their memory intact,
we can also find middle-aged "specialists," often the children or
grandchildren of expert reciters who know they are repositories of
an important family heritage.

The knowledge of a ballad collector and even the data
accumulated in the field manual can turn out to be insufficient
when we find ourselves face to face with these balladeers.   The
investigator must accept the fact that his interlocutor is the one
who is truly knowledgeable about the traditional language. At the
same time he must profit by every opportunity to plumb the
depths of the store of *romances* hoarded in that privileged memory.
This traditional transmitter usually accepts our questioning with
good grace, pleased to be able to offer us the information that we
are seeking, but it is not easy for him (or her) to give us
fragmentary texts, however important we consider them to be;
rather, if he is unable to recall the complete story, he will refuse
to give it out.

The periods of time shared with informants with an
exceptional traditional memory are the best reward that the fieldworker who devotes himself to ballad collecting can receive, but
these rare encounters warp for a while our evaluation of the true
state of health of the ballad tradition by making us believe in the
survival of the *romancero*.

Unfortunately, taking the tradition as a whole, there is no
reason for optimism concerning the possibility of the *romancero*'s
continuing to be re-created in the future.   The singers and reciters
whom we have met during our field trips in recent years are much
older on the average than the informants interviewed by ballad
collectors up to the middle of this century.[20]   In the time that
passed between the northern field trip of 1977 and the expedition
of 1985 in León, we have been able to confirm the rapid

disappearance of traditional culture as a result of the depopulation of the small rural communities in which the *romancero* was being kept alive.

This pessimistic assessment, in which can be foreseen the end of authentic singing of traditional *romances*, is only partially compensated for by the fact that, even today, the research worker interested in searching for *romances* still has before him a great deal of terrain in which he can discover for himself the enormous quantity of devices that traditional creativity utilizes, as demonstrated by transmitters of the *romancero* when encountered at the right time and place and under propitious conditions.

Instituto Universitario "Seminario Menéndez Pidal"
Universidad Complutense, Madrid

Notes

[1]Translated from the Spanish by the editor.

[2]Upon their return to Madrid from their honeymoon, María Goyri wrote a note (which is in the Menéndez Pidal archives) in which she explains in detail the circumstances that surrounded their discovery.   Doña María tells how, when she was lodged in an inn in Burgo de Osma (Soria), while she was helping a woman (who was from La Sequera, Burgos) with domestic tasks, it occurred to her to sing the *romance* of *La condesita*.   On hearing it, the woman began in turn to sing *romances* among which was found the first Castilian version of the *Muerte del príncipe don Juan*. This manuscript note of María Goyri has been reproduced in an interesting work which has to do with various aspects of ballad collecting written by one of the most enthusiastic and successful collectors of the Portuguese *romancero*, my good friend, who died recently, Joanne B. Purcell (1979:61–73).

[3]The papers presented in the Primer Coloquio bring out the interest on the part of the students of the *romancero* in questions related to the collection of traditional texts in very different geographical areas.   Between 1971 and 1979, date of the publication of *El romancero hoy: nuevas fronteras*, the acts of the Segundo Coloquio Internacional sobre el Romancero, there was a great increase in the amount of ballad collecting being done.   In the Tercer Coloquio Internacional sobre el Romancero y otras Formas Poéticas Tradicionales, organized by the Colegio de México and the Universidad Autónoma of Madrid in 1982, a considerable number of papers were read about the successes obtained by an ever larger group of fieldworkers dedicated to collecting oral texts.   The acts of the Tercer Coloquio are in press at the present time.

[4]In the field expeditions organized by the Seminario Menéndez Pidal (1977-1985) in all 845 tapes were recorded, which are to be found in the ASOR (Archivo Sonoro del Romancero).

[5]I am referring to the Northern Field Trip of 1977. The 687 oral versions collected during that search were published in *Voces nuevas del romancero castellano-leonés* (1982). For the methodology used in that expedition, see F. Salazar and A. Valenciano (1979:361-421).

[6]The full text of the ballad with variants is found in *Voces nuevas del romancero castellano-leonés* (1982:1:23-24).

[7]An example of the expansion of these *vulgatas* can be seen in the ballad of *La muerte ocultada*. Out of a total of 300 versions, almost two-thirds correspond to the *vulgata* type. See B. Mariscal de Rhett (1984-85).

[8]We can find references to this very special tradition in two articles published by Diego Catalán (1972:88-89; 1979:232-236). On the other hand, a few months ago Luis Suárez, an expert in Flamenco singing and very knowledgeable about folklore themes related to his native Andalusia, made contact with the Seminario Menéndez Pidal and informed us that for several years he had been investigating the genealogy of the gypsy families who were repositories of this kind of ballad and had collected several versions from the mouths of the few transmitters who were still alive. At the present moment Luis Suárez is preparing a book that has the suggestive title *Rosas y mosquetas de romances viejos*, which will include these rare Andalusian *romances*.

[9]For a list of these expeditions, see note 2 of the preceding article by Diego Catalán. Most of the fieldwork of the Seminario Menéndez Pidal has been carried out during the summer months with a sizable number of participants (from 15 to 45). Among them there have been experienced research workers, students, and dedicated amateurs who were novices in collecting oral texts.

[10]The transmission of oral poems is more favorable in small rural communities in which the peasants have the possibility of establishing contact with other nearby localities, since inhabitants of very small and excessively isolated villages have fewer opportunites for collective re-creation of traditional *romances*.

[11]There most of the villagers were working in the fields. We only interviewed Catalina Carro, age 94, originally from Fresnedelo, who sang for us *Gerineldo* followed by *La condesita* and a quite fragmentary version of *La serrana de la Vera*, all learned in her native village.

[12]According to the census of 1970 Trascastro had 291 inhabitants distributed among 81 families. By the census of 1981 the number of inhabitants was reduced by more than half, 148 inhabitants and 48 families, a larger number than the villagers themselves had given us two years earlier.

[13]At the beginning of the day the teams were Flor Salazar/Antonio Cid and Diego Catalán/Ana Valenciano, but when Antonio and Diego were summoned by the men in the tavern, Flor and I continued our interviewing along the village streets. That was one of the occasions in which the advantages of organizing teams with researchers of both sexes were made clear to us.

[14]Versions of the following *romances* were collected in Trascastro and subsequently published in *Voces nuevas del romancero castellano-leonés* (1982): *El moro que reta a Valencia, Belardo y Valdovinos, El conde Grifos Lombardo,*

Hermanas, reina y cautiva (*Flores y Blancaflor*), *Gaiferos libera a Melisendra,
La doncella guerrera, El conde Niño, Las mala suegra, La muerte ocultada, Las
señas del esposo* (*La vuelta del marido*), *El quintado* + *La aparición de la
enamorada, Albaniña, Tamar, Delgadina, La hermana cautiva, Los soldados
forzadores, Una fatal ocasión, Conde Claros en hábito de fraile, Gerineldo,
Gerineldo* + *La Condesita, La dama y el pastor, La bastarda y el segador, La
serrana de la Vera, La Gallarda, La loba parda, La difunta pleiteada* and a
romance from a late broadside that showed incipient traditionalization.

[15]I interviewed this exceptional reciter on the twenty–fifth of September.
The father-in-law of the owner of the inn where we ate every day had
spoken to us about Adelaida on several occasions, but since she had been ill
in bed, it was not possible for us to see her until the last day of our visit.
During the interview, her enthusiasm for the *romancero* made her forget her
state of health, and it was I who had to stop and make her rest after singing
each poem.   According to what she told me, she had been interviewed several
months before by a journalist from the province, but the lack of knowledge of
the *romancero* on the part of the interviewer had confused Adelaida, who was
only able to give her a version of *Gerineldo*.   For me she sang, among other
romances: *Belardo y Valdovinos, Gaiferos libera a Melisendra, El moro que
reta a Valencia, El conde Grifos Lombardo, Sacrificio de Isaac,* and *El robo del
Sacramento* + *La penitencia del rey don Rodrigo.*   Given her situation, I did
not want to prolong the interview excessively, for which reason the following
year I recommended her name to one of the teams of the Seminario Menéndez
Pidal, which made a detour to Peranzanes.   See note 17.

[16]These texts include: *El moro que reta a Valencia, Don Manuel y el
moro Muza, Pérdida de don Beltrán* (found only once before in Spain) with
several verses taken from *El marqués de Mantua* and *Belardo y Valdovinos,
Gaiferos libera a Melisendra, El conde Grifos Lombardo, La caza de Celinos*
(not found here before 1979), *Sacrificio de Isaac, Muerte del príncipe don Juan,
Conde Claros en hábito de fraile, El robo del Sacramento* (which almost always
ends with the *Penitencia del rey don Rodrigo*), *El veneno de Moriana* (not
found here before 1979), *Una fatal ocasión, El ciego raptor* (which usually goes
on with *La noble porquera* and *La casada de lejas tierras*), *Flores y Blancaflor*
or *Hermanas reina y cautiva,   Gerineldo* + *La condesita, La condesita, La
muerte ocultada, La infanta preñada* (*La mala hierba*) + *La infanta parida,* a
fragment of *El conde Alarcos, El conde Niño, Blancaflor y Filomena, La
serrana de la Vera, La gallarda, La dama y el pastor, La bastarda y el segador,
La loba parda, Los primos romeros, Los mozos de Monleón, El mozo arriero y
los siete ladrones, La Virgen romera, La devota de la Virgen en el yermo, La
difunta pleiteada, Cristo testigo* + *El difunto penitente, La infanticida, El galán
y la calavera, El quintado* (which usually goes on with *La aparición de la
enamorada*), *La mala suegra, La casada de lejas tierras, Albaniña, La doncella
guerrera* (which may go on with *El ciego raptor* and *La casada de lejas
tierras*), *La vuelta del marido, Las tres cautivas, Santa Iria, Ricofranco, La
hermana cautiva, ¿Dónde vas, Alfonso XII?, Don Gato, Atentado anarquista
contra Alfonso XII* and *La muerte de García y Galán.*   Among traditional
religious themes are: *La Virgen y el ciego, ¿Cómo no cantáis, bella?* (a lo
divino) and *La confesión de la Virgen.*   In addition, there are several old
Christmas songs with verses that belong to *La muerte del maestre de Santiago,*
a few blind men's ballads with partial traditionalization, several *canciones* and
coplas, prayers, prose stories, and a few poetic compositions about political
events that took place recently.

[17]On June 29, one of our best informants from 1979, Adelaida Álvarez, repeated for the 1980 team some of the *romances* collected from her before, but she added to her previous repertory *El conde Niño*, *La serrana de la Vera*, *La loba parda*, *La doncella guerrera*, *La Virgen y el ciego*, and a *copla*. They again encountered Valenta Fernández, who did not offer anything new this time, and Narciso Álvarez, who added to what he had recited in 1979 the ballad of *La muerte ocultada*. They interviewed Primitiva Fernández Román for the first time, who recited a version of *Gerineldo* and another of *La loba parda*.

[18]The *romances* that I collected in Las Hurdes (January 25–29) and in Cortes de la Frontera (February 6–10) correspond to themes that have been well documented in both geographical zones. In Las Hurdes: *Conde Claros en hábito de fraile*, *Gerineldo*, *La condesita*, *La muerte ocultada*, *La infantina* + *El caballero burlado*, *El conde Niño*, *La serrana de la Vera*, *Tamar*, *Blancaflor y Filomena*, *La vuelta del marido*, *La doncella guerrera*, *El quintado* + *La aparición de la enamorada*, *Los mozos de Monleón*, *La casada de lejas tierras*, *La bastarda y el segador*, and *La loba parda*. In Cortes de la Frontera: *Silvana*, *Delgadina*, *Gerineldo*, *El conde Niño*, *La mala suegra*, *La casada de lejas tierras*, *La bastarda y el segador*, *El quintado*, *La vuelta del marido*, etc.

[19]These two *romances* have been used in Christmas festivities as a petitionary song to solicit money or food. In the province of Segovia the theme of the *maestre* is also sung at Christmas time in a festival called "El Reinado" (the selection of a boy and girl as king and queen who collect money from the townspeople). On this occasion the ballad ends by saying: "Aquí se acaba la historia, / aquí se acaba el reinado, / aquí se acaba la historia, / señores, de hoy en un año" (Here the story ends, here the reign ends, here the story ends, gentlemen, for a year). During the field expedition in Segovia in 1982, I collected in the towns of Siguero and Sigueruelo two good versions of *La muerte del maestre de Santiago* which were very similar to those that Diego Catalán had collected in the same villages in the fifties, but neither of the two reciters, who were about seventy, remembered having taken part in the festival of "El Reinado."

[20]The advanced age of our informants is a fact that has been observed daily during our recent field trips. Taking as a base the *romance* of *Gerineldo* in the province of León, from the beginning of modern ballad collecting up to approximately 1950, the average age of the informants familiar with this theme was slightly over 43. In the Northern Field Trip of 1977, the reciters in the province of León who knew this same theme had an average age of almost 70. The difference in age between the two groups of reciters coincides with the number of years that passed between the two periods of fieldwork.

Migratory Shepherds and Ballad Diffusion[1]

Antonio Sánchez Romeralo

In 1928, in his now famous anthology of Spanish ballads, *Flor nueva de romances viejos*, Ramón Menéndez Pidal included the following comment concerning a *romance* that is very well known throughout the central regions of the Iberian Peninsula, particularly among shepherds:

> This attractive, authentically pastoral ballad, of purely rustic origin, had its origin, I believe, among the shepherds of Extremadura, where it is widely sung today, accompanied by the rebec, especially on Christmas Eve. Nomadic shepherds disseminated it throughout Old and New Castile and León; I heard it sung even in the mountains of Riaño, bordering on Asturias, at the very point where the Leonese *cañada* [nomadic shepherds' path] comes to an end. But it is completely unknown in Asturias, as well as in Aragon, Catalonia, and Andalusia. This means that areas which did not get their sheep from Extremadura did not come to know this pastoral composition. (Menéndez Pidal 1928:291).

Years later, in 1953, Menéndez Pidal was to modify his commentary on the ballad's geographic diffusion, extending it to "all provinces crossed by the great paths of migration, those of León and Segovia, which go from the valleys of Alcudia, south of the Guadiana, to the Cantabrian mountains and El Bierzo," and would now make no definite statement concerning the composition's exact origin (Menéndez Pidal 1953:2:410). The ballad to which these comments refer is *La loba parda* (The Brindled She-Wolf). The present article will discuss two of Menéndez Pidal's assertions regarding this *romance*: a) its supposedly rustic, pastoral character ("de pura cepa rústica . . . auténticamente pastoril") and b) its

53

diffusion, coincident with the regions traversed by the nomadic routes ("las dos grandes cañadas de la trashumancia, la leonesa y la segoviana") and contiguous areas. We will use this ballad to illustrate an interesting feature of the *romancero*, which possibly is little known to readers not familiar with Hispanic balladry: the role of shepherds and their migration routes (*cañadas*) in the diffusion of Spanish ballads.

The Ballad of *La loba parda*

The following version of this *romance* was collected by Ramón Menéndez Pidal in 1905, in the village of Bercimuel (judicial district of Sepúlveda, Segovia Province). This text was edited, along with many other versions of the *romance* (a total of some 192) in the *Romancero rústico* by Sánchez Romeralo (1978:130-31; abbreviated henceforth *Rr*). The volume brings together all known versions of four rustic ballads, concerned particularly with shepherds: *La loba parda* (The Brindled She-Wolf); *La mujer del pastor* (The Shepherd's Wife); *El reguñir, yo regañar* (He Grumbles and I Scold); and *La malcasada del pastor* (The Shepherd's Mismated Wife). Here is our version of *La loba parda* (*Rr*: I.111):

Las cabrillas ya van altas
la luna va revelada;
2 las ovejas de un cornudo
no paran en la majada.
Se pone el pastor en vela
vio venir la loba parda.
4 —Llega, llega, loba parda,
no tendrás mala llegada,
con mis siete cachorrillos
y mi perra Truquillana,
6 y mi perro el de los hierros
que para ti solo basta.
—Ni tus siete cachorritos,
ni tu perra Truquillana,
8 ni tu perro el de los hierros
para mí no valen nada.—
Le ha llevado una borrega
que era hija de una blanca,
10 pariente de una cornuda
y nieta de una picalba,
que la tenían los amos
para la mañana 'e Pascua.
12 —Aquí, siete cachorritos,
aquí, perra Truquillana,
aquí, perro de los hierros,

The Pleiades are at their height,
the moon is well in sight;
The accursed sheep of a cuckold
are restless in the fold.
The shepherd begins his watch;
he saw the brindled wolf:
"Come, come, brindled wolf,
a fine welcome you'll surely have,
with my seven little dogs,
and my Truquillana bitch,
and my dog of the iron collar
that alone is enough for you."
"Your seven little dogs,
your Truquillana bitch,
your dog of the iron collar
don't mean a thing to me."
She has taken a lamb of his,
that was daughter of a white one,
a relative of a horned one,
granddaughter of a white-nosed one,
that the owners had kept
specially for Easter morning.
"Come here, seven little dogs,
come here, Truquillana bitch,
come here, dog of the iron collar,

a correr la loba parda!—
14 La corrieron siete leguas
   por unas fuertes montañas,
   la arrastraron otras tantas
   por una tierras aradas,
16 y al subir un cotarrito
   y al bajar una cotarra,
   sale el pastor al encuentro
   con el cuchillo a matarla.
18 —No me mates, pastorcito,
   por la Virgen soberana,
   yo te daré tu borrega
   sin faltarla una tajada.
20 —Yo no quiero mi borrega
   de tu boca embaboseada,
   que yo quiero tu pelleja
   para hacer una zamarra;
22 siete pellejitas tengo
   para hacer una zamarra,
   con la tuya serán ocho
   para acabar de aforrarla;
24 las orejas pa pendientes,
   las patas para polainas,
   el rabo para agujetas
   para atacarme las bragas,
26 para poder correr bien
   la mañanita de Pascua.

give chase to the brindled wolf!"
They chased her for seven leagues
over the rugged mountains;
they urged her on as many more
over the plowed fields,
and going up a gully
and coming down a ravine,
out comes the shepherd to meet her
with the knife to kill her there:
"Don't kill me, little shepherd,
in the sovereign Virgin's name.
I'll give you your lamb
without even a morsel less."
"I don't want my lamb,
all frothy from your mouth,
what I want is your hide
to make a shepherd's coat;
seven little hides have I
to make a shepherd's coat;
with yours there will be eight
to finish lining it;
the ears for earrings
and the legs for leggings,
the tail for laces
to tie my breeches with,
so I can run well
on the morning of Easter.

The Ballad's Rustic and Pastoral Character

Just as there are women's *romances* (associated in some way with the work or household tasks of women, and therefore conserved particularly by women), there are also, for the same reason, *romances* that are specifically attributable to men. The ballad of *La loba parda* is such a man's *romance* or, more concretely, a shepherd *romance*, remembered and known by shepherds, or by men, women, or children connected with them.[2] In his *Flor nueva de romances viejos*, Menéndez Pidal stated that, at that time (1928), the ballad was widely sung by shepherds "accompanied by the rebec, especially on Christmas Eve" ("al son del rabel, sobre todo en Nochebuena" (Menéndez Pidal 1928:291). The *rabel* (*rebec* in English and French) is a very crude, stringed instrument, characteristically played by shepherds.[3] Federico Olmeda (1903:43, 56, 57) published the music of three versions of the ballad, from Burgos, along with the complete text of one of them, and presented them as songs typical of the shearing season (*esquileo*), which was considered as a "great event," when shepherds "began the day singing, sang while shearing the flocks, resumed after eating, and continued after the day's work was done" (1903:54).

La loba parda is also a rustic ballad in its theme and in its expressive elements. The theme can be seen as rustic, if we recall that *rústico* comes from the Latin *rusticus*, which in turn derives from *rus* "campo" (field), as Alonso de Palencia observed, in his *Universal vocabulario* (1490): "ca *rus* es donde tiene miel y leche y ganado, donde se llaman rústicos los que entienden en estas cosas" (for *rus* is where they have honey and milk and cattle, where those who are knowledgeable about these things are called rustics). The ballad is rustic in expression, according to the two definitions of rusticity (*rusticidad*) given in the dictionary of the Royal Spanish Academy of 1726 (known as the *Diccionario de autoridades*): "la sencillez, naturalidad y poco artificio que tienen las cosas rústicas . . . [y] la tosquedad, aspereza y rudeza de las cosas rústicas" (The simplicity, naturalness, and lack of artifice of rural things . . . [and] their coarseness, harshness, and rudeness).[4]

The Ballad's History

There are no early printed versions of this ballad. The earliest texts we possess belong to the first decade of the present century. However, we know that the ballad was already old and popular (in the sense of belonging to and being transmitted in popular oral tradition) by the end of the sixteenth century. We can be certain of this because the ballad's opening lines (as they also appear in some modern versions) were known to the late sixteenth- and early seventeenth-century scholar, *Maestro* Gonzalo Correas. Correas was a professor of Greek and Hebrew at the University of Salamanca. When he died in 1631, at the age of 60, he left an unpublished *Vokabulario de refranes i frases proverbiales* (Glossary of Proverbs and Proverbial Expressions), which is one of the richest and most interesting collections of Spanish folk-speech ever assembled. The proverb collected by Correas (1967:211) reads as follows:

> Las kabrillas se ponían,
> la kaiada ia enpinava
> las ovexas de una puta
> no kieren tomar maxada.

In a slightly bowdlerized version, this text could be translated:

> The Pleiades were setting,
> the Big Dipper was on the rise;
> these damned sheep
> won't go into the fold!

This is obviously the beginning of a text of *La loba parda*. Correas' citation is very similar to the opening lines of some versions that are still sung today.   Compare, for example, the following texts (as well as the Bercimuel version transcribed above):

Las estrellas ya van bajas   y la luna revelada;
las ovejas de un cornudo   solas duermen en majada.[5]

Rr I.83

Ay qué alta va la luna   y el aire que la meneaba,
las ovejas de un cornudo   se salen de la majada.[6]

Rr I.117

Flock Migration in Spain: The *Mesta*
and the *Cañadas Reales*, Past and Present

In 1910, in an important article on flock migration in Spain, André Fribourg stated:

> For almost a thousand years, flock migration has been carried out in Spain to an extent and under conditions unparalleled in any other part of Europe.   From north to south, from east to west, immense flocks were moved, until only yesterday, from the Pyrenees to the Ebro, from Galicia and the Cantabrian mountains to La Mancha and Extremadura, from the Iberian mountains to New Castile, from Andalusia to Valencia; like an ebb and flow of wool in a rhythmic oscillation of flocks.   In groups of 10,000, following special routes, the sheep went, devouring the grass, trampling and beating down the earth.   Each group was divided into smaller flocks, of from 1000 to 1200 head each.   At the front of each group was an overseer (*mayoral*); the head shepherds (*rabadanes*), with the help of the other shepherds, urged the animals along.   Armed with slings and carrying long crooks, the shepherds traversed the Peninsula, twice a year, with their mules, their cooking pots, and their

dogs (1910:231-44).[7]

When this passage was written, in 1910, the situation was already changing, but the migrations continued and, even today, are still carried out, although under different conditions.

To explain the migrations' historical and, although lessened, present importance, one must remember that, due to its climate and topography, Spain is a land of violent contrasts; and that, although its latitudinal variation is only eight degrees, it includes some of the rainiest and some of the most arid regions of continental Europe. Such circumstances mean that, in any season of the year, shepherds can find sufficient pasturage for their flocks by merely moving to wherever the grazing is good. Moreover, the continual state of war throughout the Middle Ages, during the centuries of the Reconquest, encouraged the development of livestock raising. Stock was an easily transportable commodity, preferable to the products of agriculture, which were subject to periodic devastation.

The origin of the migration seems, however, to predate the Arab invasion. It already existed in Visigothic Spain, and possibly in Roman and even in pre-Roman times. It is said that the Carthaginians in Spain were aided in their war against Rome by seemingly nomadic shepherds. The *Fuero Juzgo*, an important seventh-century Visigothic legal code, reserves established passageways for the transit of migratory stock.[8] These routes are mentioned, already as fixed and established, in diverse documents from the beginning of the Middle Ages, covering the period from the reign of Sancho the Elder (970-1035) until the founding of the *Mesta* (the sheep raisers' union) in 1273. By the end of the twelfth century, the migratory routes were already known as *cañadas*. The Royal *Fuero* of 1254 grants to the Crown ownership rights to all these routes, whatever their characteristics may be. A royal charter of 1284 specifies their full legal width as "seys sogas de marco de cada quarenta y cinco palmos la soga", (six *sogas*, at 45 spans per *soga*), equivalent to 90 Castilian *varas*, or 75.22 meters. If the Reconquest, during the entire Middle Ages, contributed to the development of an economy based on livestock rather than on agriculture, the introduction into Andalusia of merino sheep from North Africa (around 1300) helped to further its development. This produced a strong demand for Spanish wool, which in turn led to new forms of government protectionism.

In 1273, the Crown brought all the various associations of

sheep owners into a single organization, which later became known as the *Mesta*. In return for financial contributions, the Crown granted the *Mesta* important privileges, often in conflict with the interests of farmers, without regard for the complaints and resolutions of the courts that attempted to restrain the abuses perpetrated by the stockmen. The *Mesta* had its own tribunal and was entrusted with the supervision and regulation of the migratory movements of sheep. We find the term *reales* (royal) applied to the *cañadas* for the first time in a charter of 1462. The royal *cañadas* became especially important in the sixteenth century, when the wool of the migratory merino sheep became the principal economic resource of the country. The wool's high quality was largely due to continuity and homogeneity of pasturage, which was achieved by means of migration. The routes were wide enough to allow passage of over three million head of sheep, at the height of the season. Gradually, the *Mesta* ceased to be an owners' association and became, instead, a tool of the Crown. In 1500, an advisor to the king, Pérez de Monreal, became its president. In 1511, the Council of the *Mesta* entrusted to a jurist, Palacios Rubios (also advisor to the king and queen and second president of the *Mesta*, 1510-1522) the task of gathering all dispersed charters and ordinances that proved the legality of the organization's privileges and submitting the resultant compilation for ratification by the king.[9] Thanks to this compilation, we know today the workings of the Honorable Council of the *Mesta* and the privileges it enjoyed for many years, making it a formidable enemy of the farmers.[10]

There were four basic privileges: 1) the right of the *Mesta* flocks to graze and drink water on all Castilian lands except for those that were referred to as the five forbidden things (*cosas vedadas*): orchards, sown lands, vineyards, mowed fields, and those devoted to the pasturage of oxen; 2) exclusive rights to the use of paths, tracks, trails, and resting places (*cañadas, cordeles, veredas, descansaderos*);[11] 3) exemption from many taxes; and 4) the right to cut smaller trees as fodder during the winter, or when pasturage was scarce, which effectively left the forests at the mercy of the flocks. These privileges were especially protected by the *Mesta*'s court of first appeal, which had its own judges, as well as its own administration and budget.[12] As the economic importance of wool waned, there was a corresponding reduction in royal protection of the *cañadas*. During the reign of Carlos III (1759-88), the relationship between farming and stock ranching underwent a radical change. The construction of roads, canals, and bridges over the length and breadth of Spain made it possible to market wheat, and agriculture began to escape from the suffocation that had inhibited it for centuries. The relationship between city and countryside also began to change. Madrid was being transformed into the economic center of Castile, La Mancha, Extremadura, and part of Andalusia. A livestock-based economy was giving way to a system based on grain. Campomanes conducted a series of inquiries on the *Mesta*, followed by measures aimed at reducing its privileges.[13]   Years later, Jovellanos would defend the right of agriculture to develop, free from the obstacles imposed by the *Mesta* (*Informe sobre la ley agraria*, 1795). The courts of Cadiz and the constitution of 1812 reinforced this policy. In 1815, the right to enclose town commons was legally recognized and, in 1835-36, the *Mesta* and its special tribunal were discontinued. Its interests were taken over by the *Asociación General de Ganaderos del Reino* (Royal Association of Sheep Owners and Breeders). The *Asociación* acquired the *Mesta*'s files and added to them the reports of their special *visitadores* (inspectors). These archives continue to be the main source of information on the *cañadas*.[14]

Migration did not disappear along with the *Mesta*. The number of nomadic sheep decreased to half a million by the middle of the last century, but increased again toward the end of the 1800s. In 1910, the *Dirección General de Agricultura* (General Agriculture Administration) estimated the number at 1,355,630 (migratory) head, approximately one tenth of the total Spanish flock (figured then at 13,359,473 head of sheep).[15] What did decrease and deteriorate notably was the network of pastoral roadways. The less travelled ones were encroached upon by farmers in many places along the way and some disappeared altogether.

At the beginning of the present century, a new blow was struck against the conservation and use of the *cañadas*: the railroads. In 1899, the Madrid-Zaragoza-Alicante railroad company established a special service for transporting migratory sheep and goats and, in 1901, the Madrid-Cáceres-Portugal line followed suit. This service was to change radically the character of the migration along the great *cañadas* and their use would be notably reduced. Since that time, and still today, the great majority of flocks make the journey from the northern pastures to the winter grazing land, in lower Extremadura or in the southern part of La Mancha, in railroad cars prepared especially for them. Thus the railroads came to resolve the serious problem that had confronted stockmen and farmers for centuries, making it possible to utilize the winter pastures on the plains and in the valleys of the south and the summer pastures in the mountains, without impeding the agricultural development of the lands in between.

Toward the middle of the last century, the *Asociación General de Ganaderos* published a series of bulletins containing detailed descriptions of the main *cañadas* and many pastoral trails. There are eight pamphlets in all, with the following titles:

> *Cañada de La Vizana y parte del cordel de Babia de Abajo. Empieza en el puerto de Bahabrán, límite de Asturias y León, y termina en el puente de La Lavandera (provincia de Cáceres).* n.p., n.d. (Map; circa 1866) (The *cañada* of La Vizana, with part of the track of Babia de Abajo: It starts at the pass of Bahabrán, on the border between Asturias and León, and ends at the bridge of La Lavandera in Cáceres Province).

> *Descripción de la cañada leonesa, desde Valdeburón a Montemolín.* Madrid: Imprenta de Manuel Minuesa, 1856 (Description of the Leonese *cañada*, from Valdeburón to Montemolín).

> *Cañada leonesa desde El Espinar a Valdeburón.* n.p., n.d. (Map; circa 1860) (The Leonese *cañada*, from El Espinar to Valdeburón).

> *Cañada occidental de la provincia de Soria.* Madrid: Imprenta de Manuel Minuesa, 1856 (The western *cañada* of Soria province).

> *Descripción de la cañada segoviana, desde Carabias al valle de la Alcudia.* Madrid: Imprenta de Manuel Minuesa, 1856 (Description of the *cañada* of Segovia, from Carabias to the valley of Alcudia).

> *Descripción de la cañada soriana, desde Yanguas al valle de la Alcudia.* Madrid: Imprenta de Manuel

Minuesa, 1857 (Description of the *cañada* of Soria, from Yanguas to the valley of Alcudia).

Descripción de los ramales de la cañada soriana desde Villacañas y Quero al valle de la Alcudia [with an appendix: "Descripción de la cañada real de la provincia de Córdoba"]. Madrid: Imprenta de Manuel Minuesa, 1858 (Description of the branch routes of the *cañada* of Soria, from Villacañas and Quero to the valley of Alcudia, with an appendix: "Description of the Royal *Cañada* of Córdoba Province").

Descripción de las cañadas de Cuenca, desde Tragacete y Peralejos, al valle de la Alcudia, al campo de Calatrava y a Linares. Madrid: Imprenta de Manuel Minuesa, 1860 (Description of the *cañadas* of Cuenca, from Tragacete and Peralejos to the valley of Alcudia, the Calatrava region, and Linares).[16]

The descriptions contained in these pamphlets are, in general, quite complete, as far as the principal routes described in them are concerned, but there are *cañadas* and *ramales* whose descriptions were never published. Detailed information concerning many of them has been preserved, still in unedited form and in various stages of completion, in the holdings of the Archivo Histórico Nacional, waiting for some scholar to undertake the difficult task of putting in order and studying these documents. In any event, the pamphlets published in the nineteenth century are, as of now, the most important source of information available for mapping the network of migratory livestock trails across the Iberian Peninsula.

On the map that accompanies these pages, our layout of the *cañadas* was made by following the descriptions in the pamphlets of the *Asociación General de Ganaderos del Reino*. First of all, I marked the municipal districts through which the various routes passed, according to the descriptions, on an official highway map (*Mapa oficial de carreteras*, Ministerio de Obras Públicas, scale 1/400,000; 8th ed., 1969). Then, as faithfully as possible, I transferred this drawing to another blank map, on a smaller scale. On our present map, the reader can follow the routes of the six main *cañadas*, with the branches corresponding to the Leonese *cañada* and the *cañada* of Cuenca. They are as follows: 1) the track of Babia de Abajo, the *cañada* of La Vizana, and branches to

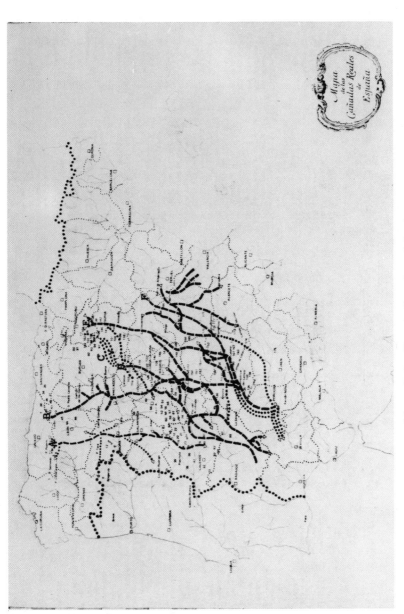

Map of the Royal *Cañadas* of Spain

MAP OF THE ROYAL CAÑADAS OF SPAIN

Place of origin of the versions of La loba parda, indicated on the map by the numbers 1-182

A. Cordel of Babía de Abajo, cañada of La Vizana and its ramales to the west.

1. San Martín de Suarna
2. Abedes
3. Villablino
4. Quintanilla de Babia
5. Zureda
6. Villamanín
7. Vinhais
8. Uva
9. Villarino de Manzanas
10. Nuez
11. Sejas de Aliste
12. Ferreruela (de Tábara)
13. Zamora
14. Fornillos de Fermoselle
15. Candelario
16. Candelario
17. Garganta de Béjar
18. Garganta de Béjar
19. El Cabrero
20. [Gargenta la Olla]
21. Gargenta la Olla
22. Villanueva de la Vera
23. Malpartida de Plasencia
24. Malpartida de Plasencia
25. Malpartida de Plasencia
26. Serradilla
27. Cañaveral
28. Portaje
29. El Pero
30. Villa del Campo
31. Santiago de Cerbajo
32. Arroyo de la Luz
33. Aliseda

B. Royal Leonese cuñada.

34. Tudance
35. Belmonte
36. Lurieza
37. Dobres
38. Cosgaya
39. Oceño
40. Riboia
41. Osela de Salambre
42. Osela de Salambre
43. Osela de Sajambre
44. Besande
45. Crémenes
46. Villalquite
47. Montaña de León
48. Horcalo de las Torres
49. Maello
50. Guijasalbas
51. Peguerinos
52. Burgohondo
53. Hoyocasero
54. Hoyocasero
55. San Martín del Pimpollar
56. Hoyos del Espino
57. Hoyos del Espino
58. Hoyos del Espino
59. Hoyos del Espino
60. Hoyos del Espino
61. Navacepeda de Tormes
62. Navacepeda de Tormes
63. Bohoyo
64. Bohoyo
65. Navamediana
66. Provincia de Avila
67. Almorox
68. Almorox
69. Almorox
70. Almorox
71. El Real de San Vicente
72. Navalcán
73. Navalcán
74. Torralba de Oropesa
75. Torralba de Oropesa
76. Valdverdeja
77. Valdverdeja
78. Valdverdeja

79. Trujillo
80. Trujillo
81. Huertas de la Magdalena
82. Montánchez
83. Alcuéscar
84. Alcuéscar
85. Helechosa
86. Castilblanco
87. Orellana de la Sierra
88. Campanario

C. Royal cañada of Soria (western route).

89. Baltanás de Cerrato
90. Cerezo de Riotirón
91. Cerezo de Riotirón
92. Pineda de la Sierra
93. Barbadillo de Herreros
94. Huerta de Arriba
95. Berbadillo del Mercado
96. Alcubilla de Avellaneda
97. Quintanar de la Sierra
98. Viniegra de Arriba
99. Viniegra de Arriba
100. Viniegra de Arriba
101. Ventrosa
102. Anguiano
103. Villaverde de Rioja
104. Torre en Cameros
105. Almarza de Cameros
106. El Royo
107. Calatañazor
108. Calatañazor
109. Calatañazor
110. Torreblacos

D. Royal Segovian cañada.

111. Berchimuel
112. Fresno de la Fuente
113. Riaza
114. Riaza
115. Sepúlveda
116. Aguilafuente
117. Sigueruelo
118. Somosierre
119. Arcones
120. Aylión, Arcones, Vega de Santa María (versión factica)
121. Robregordo
122. Serrada de la Fuente
123. Serrada de la Fuente
124. Rascafría
125. Rascafría
126. Rascafría
127. S. Agustín de Guadalix
128. S. Agustín de Guadalix
129. Navas de Estena
130. Arroba de los Montes
131. Corral de Calatrava
132. Veredas
133. Hinojosas de Calatrava
134. Hinojosas de Calatrava
135. Fuencaliente
136. Fuente el Canto
137. Córdoba

E. Royal cañada of Soria (eastern route).

138. San Pedro Manrique
139. Castillfrío de la Sierra
140. San Andrés de Soria
141. San Andrés de Soria
142. Renieblas
143. Villaciervitos
144. Las Fraguas
145. Valdetorres del Jarama
146. Valdevero
147. Los Santos de la Humosa
148. Extremera

149. Villarejo de Salvanés
150. Los Yébenes
151. Los Yébenes
152. Los Yébenes
153. Alcázar de San Juan
154. Malagón
155. Malagón
156. Ciudad Real
157. Manzanares
158. Manzanares
159. Almagro
160. Almagro
161. Valdepeñas
162. Valdepeñas
163. Valdepeñas

F. Cañadas of Cuenca and ramales in the extreme east of this province.

164. Cañamares
165. Vega del Codorno
166. Tragacete
167. Pineda de Gigüela
168. Acebrón
169. Torrubia del Campo
170. Hontanaya
171. Honrubia
172. Villanueva de los Infantes
173. Villanueva de la Fuente
174. Torre de Juan Abad
175. Jódar
176. Villarrobledo
177. Villarrobledo
178. Villarrobledo
179. Villarrobledo
180. El Bonillo
181. El Bonillo
182. Alcaraz

the west of it; 2) the royal Leonese *cañada*; 3) the royal *cañada* of Soria (western sector); 4) the royal *cañada* of Segovia; 5) the royal *cañada* of Soria (eastern sector); 6) the *cañadas* of Cuenca and branches at the extreme east of this province, which are, from west to east, as follows: a) *cañada* of Beteta; b) *cañada* of Rodrigo Ardaz; c) *cañada* of Cuenca (or Tragacete); d) *cañada* of Jábaga; and e) *cañada* of Hoyo and Sisante.[17] Neither the *Mesta* nor the *Asociación General de Ganaderos* ever managed to draw a map of the *cañadas*, although in the nineteenth century the *Asociación* planned to do so.   Mapped trails are included in the works of Julius Klein, Robert Aitken, André Fribourg, and Juan Dantín Cereceda.   In an article about the *romancero rústico* in Albacete, Francisco Mendoza Díaz-Maroto (1980) includes a map showing the approximate itineraries of pastoral roads and trails and the locations of versions of *La loba parda*, *El reguñir, yo regañar*, and *La dama y el pastor*, collected in Albacete.[18]   Finally, the volume published in 1984 (see n. 16) also includes a schematic map of the *cañadas*.

Location and Geographic Diffusion of the Ballad

When I studied the 192 known versions of *La loba parda* in preparing the *Romancero rústico* and classified them according to their geographic origin, I was able to demonstrate that the ballad's area of diffusion coincided with the regions traversed by the various migratory shepherds' routes.   On the map elaborated in that volume, the ballads' versions correlate, very precisely, to the various migratory *cañadas*, or to areas very near to them, as the reader of the present article can verify by consulting the reproduction of that map and the "List of geographic origins of the versions" indicated on that map by the numbers 1 to 182.[19]   This fact was indicative of the relationship between migratory shepherds and the ballad's diffusion and could, possibly, help to explain some of its characteristics: 1) the existence of some few distinctive features in each group of versions as defined in relationship to a given *cañada*; 2) and, in spite of this, a greater homogeneity in the case of this ballad—in comparison with others—which could, in turn, be explained by communication between shepherds from different areas, thanks to the existence of secondary transverse paths connecting the various *cañadas* with one another and, even more, to interchanges during the months of common winter pasturage at the *cañadas'* various southern terminals (Valley of Alcudia, Campo de Calatrava, Campo de Montiel, La Serena).[20]

The copious material collected since the publication of *Rr*—thanks principally to a series of field expeditions carried out by the Seminario Menéndez Pidal between 1978 and 1984 and a few other versions made available in various publications—have served to corroborate our observations in *Rr*. The 171 new versions of *La loba parda* which are catalogued below can also be geographically categorized in relation to some of the *cañadas*, *ramales*, and *veredas* which make up the network of migratory livestock trails. These versions also confirm the observation offered in *Rr* regarding the ballad's relative homogeneity in the various areas where it is current, together, even so, with some distinctive features characteristic of each geographic subgroup. A good example of this latter fact is a motif—already taken into account in *Rr*—which is exclusively characteristic of versions collected along the Segovian *cañada*. In these versions, the wolf, after being chased by the dogs, comes face to face with the shepherd, who has come out to meet her "with a knife to kill her" or "a knife without a scabbard" ("con un cuchillo a matarla"; "con un cuchillo sin vaina") (*Rr* I.110a, 110b, 111, 112, 117, 120a, 127, 128, 130); in other versions from the Segovian *cañada* the *cuchillo* does not appear, but the shepherd's role as the one to whom the wolf begs for mercy is maintained (*Rr* I.113, 114, 116, 119, 124, 129, 137), instead of the dogs being begged as in versions from the other *cañadas*. Some apparent exceptions to this rule (Segovian versions without the shepherd motif or versions from other *cañadas* that include it) can be satisfactorily explained in terms of the proximity of or communication between the *cañadas* in question (*Rr*:21-22). The very abundant new material (70 versions) corresponding to the Segovian *cañada* conclusively confirms our observations in *Rr*.

The New Versions: Their Geographic Distributions Relative to the Six Major Migratory *Cañadas*

From 1977 to 1982, the Seminario Menéndez Pidal (*SMP*) carried out a series of field expeditions in various areas of Spain. The following eight field trips are of interest to us here, inasmuch as they involve versions of *La loba parda*: "Sur 78" (Jaén); "Norte 80" (NW and W of León and W of Asturias, with side trips to the SW of León, NE of Orense, and NW of Zamora);

"Salamanca-Zamora 81" (NW of Salamanca and SE of Zamora); "Norte 81" (W of Zamora, SW of León, and SE of Orense); "Ciudad Real 82" (W of Ciudad Real, side trips to N of Córdoba and E of Badajoz); "Segovia 82" (Segovia); "Noroeste 82" (N of Orense, S of Lugo, side trips to SW of León and W of Pontevedra); "Castilla 84" (Burgos, E of Palencia, W of Soria, and W of Logroño).[21] To these collections must be added the *Voces nuevas del romancero castellano-leonés* edited by Suzanne H. Petersen (1982) (abbreviated here *VN*), which also includes versions of *La loba parda* documented in the present article. Finally, a series of publications and still unedited collections of diverse origin have provided various additional versions of the ballad, which will be indicated (together with their sources) at the appropriate juncture.

On the following pages, I offer a catalogue of the new versions of *La loba parda*, classified, according to their proximity to the various *cañadas*, in six different groups, following the procedures used in *Rr*. The corresponding versions are designated by their place of origin (the name of the town) and arranged by provinces. These editorial criteria are followed in this catalogue: 1. Together with the name of the town, the pertinent administrative area (p.j. = *partido judicial*) is indicated in italics and parentheses. But when a series of towns belongs to the same administrative area, the latter is indicated only at the end of the series. The transition from one administrative area to another is indicated by a semicolon (;). When more than one version originates in the same town, the number of versions is indicated in parentheses following the name of the town. For example: Belmonte, Salceda (2), Caloca, Enterrías (p.j. *San Vicente de la Barquera*); 2. The source (*SMP* field trip, publication, etc.) is indicated following a version or at the end of a series of versions when all originate in the same source. The designation of the source will be enclosed in brackets. For example: Santa Cruz de los Cuérragos, Carbajalines (p.j. *Alcañices*); El Cubo de Tierra del Vino (p.j. *Fuentesauco*) [*SMP* "Salamanca-Zamora 81"].

A condensed description of the various *cañadas* can be found in *Rr*: pp. 28, 56-60, 108, 128, 162, 182-184.

A. THE *CORDEL* OF BABIA DE ABAJO, *CAÑADA* OF LA VIZANA AND ITS *RAMALES* TO THE WEST

[Description in Rr:281]

ASTURIAS

Riera de Somiedo, Arbeyales, Coto de Buena Madre (p.j. *Belmonte*); Taladrid, Brañas de Arriba (p.j. *Cangas de Narcea*) [*SMP* "Norte 80"].

LEÓN

Genestosa (2), Torrebarrio (2), Villargusán, La Majua, San Emiliano (2), Aralla-Cubillas de Arbas, Casares (3), Abelgas (2), Bonella, Torrecillo, Salientes (2), Matalavilla (2), Valseco (4), Murias de Paredes, Senra (2), Posada de Omaña, Fasgar, Rioscuro (p.j. *Murias de Paredes*); Peranzanes (p.j. *Villafranca del Bierzo*); Fresnedelo (2), San Martín de Moreda (p.j. *Ponferrada*); Truchillas (p.j. *Astorga*); Marzá San Martín de la Tercia (p.j. *León*) *SMP* "Norte 80"].

ORENSE

Rubiana (p.j. *El Barco de Valdeorras*) [*SMP* "Noroeste 82"]; Berrande (2) (p.j. *Verín*) [*SMP* "Norte 81"].

ZAMORA

Villárdiga (p.j. *Villalpando*); Moraleja del Vino (p.j. *Zamora*) [*SMP* "Norte 81"]; Toro (p.j. *Toro*) [Díaz 1982:13-15]; Santa Cruz de los Cuérragos, Carbajalinos (p.j. *Alcañices*); El Cubo de Tierra del Vino (p.j. *Fuentesauco*) [*SMP* "Salamanca-Zamora 81"].

TRÁS-OS-MONTES (PORTUGAL)

Freixiosa de Vila Chã (c. *Miranda do Douro*) [Armistead 1982:80]; Duas Igrejas, Aldeia Nova (c. *Miranda do Douro*) [Fontes 1979:164-65].

SALAMANCA

Torresmenudas, Valverdón (p.j. *Salamanca*); Mieza (p.j. *Vitigudino*) [*SMP* "Salamanca-Zamora 81"].

CÁCERES

La Fragosa (p.j. *Hervás*) [Encuesta Valenciano-Cicourel].

B. ROYAL LEONESE *CAÑADA*
[Description in *Rr*:58-60]

SANTANDER

Belmonte, Salceda (2), Caloca, Enterrías (p.j. *San Vicente de la Barquera*) [*VN*].

PALENCIA

Herreruela de Castillería (3), Celada de Robleceda, San Juan de Redondo, Santa María de Redondo (p.j. *Cervera de Pisuerga*) [*VN*].

LEÓN

Siero de la Reina, Casasuertes (2), Prioro (4), Soto de Valderrueda (p.j. *Cistierna*) [*VN*].

BURGOS

Revilla-Vallegera (p.j. *Castrojeriz*) [*SMP* "Castilla 84"].

VALLADOLID

Villabrágima (p.j. *Medina de Rioseco*); Mojados (p.j. *Olmedo*) [Díaz et al. 1978:152]; Bocigas (p.j. *Medina del Campo*) [*SMP* "Norte 80"].

SEGOVIA

Chaña (p.j. *Cuéllar*); Miguel Ibáñez, Pinilla Ambroz, Tabladillo, Marugán, Muñopedro, Monterrubio (2) (p.j. *Santa María la Real de Nieva*) [*SMP* "Segovia 82"].

CÁCERES

Valdecasa del Tajo (p.j. *Navalmoral de la Mata*) [Coll. A. Sánchez Romeralo and Soledad Martínez de Pinillos].

C. ROYAL *CAÑADA* OF SORIA (WESTERN ROUTE)
[Description *Rr*:108]

LOGROÑO

Trevijano de Cameros, Torrecilla de Cameros (p.j. *Logroño*) [Gomarín Guirado 1981].

BURGOS

Huerta de Arriba (p.j. *Salas de los Infantes*) [F.

Gomarín Guirado 1981].

D. ROYAL SEGOVIAN CAÑADA
[Description in Rr:128]

SEGOVIA

Rebollo (p.j. Sepúlveda); Cuellar (p.j. Segovia) [SMP returning from "Norte 80" field trip]; Santibáñez de Ayllón, Maderuelo, Aldealuenga de Santa María, Alconada de Maderuelo, Ribota, Cedillo de la Torre, Fresno de Cantespino, Pajares de Fresno (p.j. Riaza) [SMP "Segovia 82"]; Montejo de la Vega (p.j. Riaza) [Castro Rey et al. 1981:203-7]; Laguna de Contreras, Pecharromán, Tejares, San Miguel de Bernuy (2), Olombrada, Sanchonuño (2) (p.j. Cuéllar); Bercimuel (2), Navares de Enmedio, Urueñas, Santa Marta del Cerro, Valle de Tabladillo, Castrillo de Sepúlveda (3), Consuegra de Murera, Duratón (4), Aldealcorvo, Navalilla, Sabulcor, Cantalejo, San Pedro de Gaillos, Ventosilla y Tejadilla (3), Sigueruelo, Cosla (3), La Velilla (4), Cañicosa (4), Gallegos (2), Aldealuenga de Pedraza (2) (p.j. Sepúlveda); Abades, Hontoria, Hotero de Herrero, Sauquillo de Cabezas, Vegas de Matute, Zarzuela del Monte, Casas Altas (p.j. Segovia) [SMP "Segovia 82"].

CIUDAD REAL

Horcajo de los Montes, Anchuras (p.j. Piedrabuena); Viso del Marqués (p.j. Valdepeñas); El Hoyo, Solana del Pino (p.j. Almodóvar del Campo); Fuencaliente (p.j. Almadén) [SMP "Ciudad Real 82"].

E. ROYAL CAÑADA OF SORIA (EASTERN ROUTE)
[Description Rr:162]

SORIA

Arguijo, Sotillo del Rincón (p.j. Soria) [Díaz Viana 1982]; Villaciervitos (p.j. Soria) [Díaz Viana 1983:45-46].

F. CAÑADAS OF CUENCA AND RAMALES
TO THE EXTREME EAST OF THIS PROVINCE
[Description in Rr:182-84]

ALBACETE

Chinchilla de Monte Aragón (p.j. *Albacete*); Casas de Lázaro, Salobre (p.j. *Alcaraz*) [Mendoza Díaz-Maroto 1980].

JAÉN

Beas de Segura (p.j. *Villacarrillo*) [*SMP* "Sur 78"]; Jamilena (p.j. *Martos*) [Checa Beltrán 1981].

University of California, Davis

Notes

[1]Translated from the Spanish by Samuel G. Armistead and Karen L. Olson.

[2]Version I.133 in *Rr*, collected in Valle de Alcudia in 1975, was sung by a woman during a shearing at the Grazurango farm, but she herself explained that she had learned the *romance* from her father, a shepherd, who used to sing it, accompanying himself on the rebec, to her and her brother when they were children in order to put them to sleep. She also recalled that the music was so sad that it made them cry.

[3]Corominas and Pascual (1980-83:4:743) document the name as early as 1135, giving the etymology as Arabic *rabéb* 'a kind of violin'. The same origin is adduced by Sebastián de Covarrubias, in his *Tesoro de la lengua castellana* (1611), where he defines it as an "Instrumento músico de cuerdas y arquillo; es pequeño y todo de una pieça, de tres cuerdas y de vozes muy subidas. Usan dél los pastores, con que se entretienen, como David hazía con su instrumento" (A musical instrument with strings and a small bow; it is small and all of one piece, with three strings and very high-pitched. It is played by shepherds, who entertain themselves with it as David did with his instrument).

[4]Similar meanings occur in English: "*rustic*: 1. Of or pertaining to the country, rural . . . ; 2. Awkward, rough, unpolished . . . ; 4. Simple; artless; unadorned; unaffected . . ." (Webster 1949: s.v.).

[5]Version from Baltanás de Cerrato (Palencia); collected by Manuel Manrique de Lara in 1918.

[6]Version from Sigueruelo (Segovia); collected by Diego Catalán in 1947. See also *Rr*.I.47, 102, 104, 110*b*, 113*a*, 116, 119, 120, 120*a*, 128, 130, 147. However, most of the modern versions have lost this rather strange introductory couplet, and begin with the story itself.

[7]Other works referred to in summarizing the past and present states of migration are: Julius Klein's fundamental study (1920), and the article by Robert Aitken (1945). For the *cañada* of Vizana, Juan Dantín Cereceda's article is crucial (1942).

72 ANTONIO SÁNCHEZ ROMERALO

[8]Lib. 8, tít. 3, ley 9; tít. 4, leyes 26–27; and tít. 5, ley 5 (*Fuero Juzgo* 1815:139, 146, 149).

[9]This compilation of 1511 supplemented earlier ones, especially that of 1492, carried out by Malpartida, legal counsel to Fernando and Isabel.

[10]See *Libro de los Privilegios y Leyes del Ilustre y muy Honrado Concejo general de la Mesta y Cabaña real destos reynos de Castilla, León y Granada* (Madrid: Pedro Madrigal, 1586); and the more complete *Libro de las Leyes, Privilegios, y Provisiones reales del Honrado Concejo general de la Mesta* (Madrid, 1595), compilation later revised, in 1609, 1639, and 1681. The most complete code of the *Mesta*'s laws and ordinances is the one published by Andrés Díez Navarro, *Quaderno de Leyes y Privilegios del Honrado Concejo de la Mesta* (Madrid, 1731). There is a description of this latter work in Pérez Pastor (1891–1907:vol. 1).

[11]In theory, the width of the *cañadas, cordeles*, and *veredas* was fixed at 90, 45, and 25 *varas*, respectively (i.e. 75, 37.50 and 20.80 meters). The width of the *descansaderos* was indeterminate. In fact, however, the limits were not respected.

[12]The hostility of municipalities toward the abusive privileges of the *Mesta* was expressed in a proverbial phrase in the seventeenth century: "Entre tres *Santos* y un *Honrado* está el reino agobiado" (Between three Saints and one Honorable [association], the kingdom is oppressed). The saints were the Holy Brotherhood (*Santa Hermandad* or rural police), the Holy Crusade, and the Holy Office of the Inquisition, and the *Honrado* was the Honorable Council of the *Mesta*.

[13]*Memorial ajustado del Expediente de Concordia que trata el Honrado Concejo de la Mesta con la Diputación General de Extremadura ante el Conde de Campomanes*, 2 vols. (Madrid, 1783).

[14]When the *Asociación General de Ganaderos del Reino* (General Association of Stock Owners of the Kingdom) was founded in 1836 as a confederation of guilds to protect the economic interests of stock owners, but now without the former privileges and power of the *Mesta*, one of its first concerns was that of reestablishing the exact boundaries of the early *cañadas, cordeles*, and *descansaderos*, abandoned and blurred, due to the grave disruptions of the war against Napoleon's armies. To this purpose a royal commission was created which, at the same time, named a series of royal superintendents (*comisarios*) charged with establishing the exact limits of royal *cañadas* in all disputed areas. For years, these patient superintendents (Celestino del Río, Juan Manuel Escanciano, Aquilino Téllez, Eladio de Matesau, and several others) traversed the entire area of Spain occupied by the traditional *cañadas*. Always requiring that they be accompanied by two local shepherds, they overcame innumerable difficulties, as well as the hostility of the peasantry and village mayors—sometimes having recourse to provincial governors so they could be protected by soldiers. Without resources and with little help, they forwarded, during a number of years, their exact, meticulous reports to the *Asociación General de Ganaderos*. The dossiers of these worthy functionaries—preserved today in the Archivo Histórico Nacional (Madrid)—were the basis of a series of pamphlets describing the *cañadas, cordeles*, and *veredas*, printed in Madrid, between 1852 and 1860, concerning which we will have more to say later.

[15]Fribourg (1910:235). The number of migratory sheep in 1910 was,

then, less than half the number in 1482.

[16]These pamphlets, except the first one, were published in one volume with the title: *Descripción de las cañadas reales de León, Segovia, Soria y ramales de la de Cuenca y del valle de Alcudia* (Madrid: Ediciones El Museo Universal, 1984).

[17]Besides the great *cañadas* of the central system, André Fribourg mentions three groups of less important paths: one that goes from Gibraltar, through the south of Andalusia, to Valencia; another to the north of the Júcar River, of short branch roads (*ramales*) that descend from the plains to the coast; and, finally, the *ramales* and *veredas* of Aragón, which were used by flocks coming down from the Pyrenees.

[18]Francisco Mendoza Díaz-Maroto's map (indicating the *cañadas* in the province of Albacete) is based on the one included in Panadero Moya (1976: 108).

[19]The ten versions not included on the map were assigned the following numbers: 4a, 8a [in an appendix], 30a, 38a, 42a, 110a, 110b, 113a, 120a and 126a (according to their position on the map).

[20]See my observations in this regard, referring to the valley of Alcudia (Sánchez Romeralo 1979).

[21]For more information on these *SMP* expeditions, see Diego Catalán's article in the present volume (n. 2).

In Defense of *Romancero* Geography

Suzanne Petersen

> Folklore materials derive their
> defining characteristics from their
> behavior within the space-time
> coordinates as they are subjected
> to certain forces and influences
> through environment and the
> very mechanisms of transmission
> (Foster 1968:247).

Ramón Menéndez Pidal's pioneering essay "Sobre geografía folklórica. Ensayo de un método" (1920) constituted the first full-scale implementation of geographic methods in *romancero* studies.[1] At a time when the very concept of traditionalism was hotly debated and the centrality of the transmission process to a definition of traditional poetry was largely ignored, this study provided Menéndez Pidal with several valuable insights into the mechanisms of variation governing orally transmitted Hispanic ballads. By meticulously plotting the geographic dispersion of key motifs present in two widely disseminated modern *romances*, each represented by some 160 traditional versions, he found that each independently conceived motif, each element that appears in a traditional *romance*, attains its own continuous and compact, but ever-evolving area of diffusion and has a history distinct from that of every other motif or element in the text.[2] In addition to documenting the important role played by the independent propagation of individual motifs in the continuous transformation of oral *romances*, his geographic study of these two sizeable bodies of evidence also revealed the existence of clearly discernible "local types" or groups of versions in geographic proximity which manifest considerable thematic uniformity and a high proportion of common

74

variants. In the face of the "prodigiously multiform" variation to which his two corpora attested, this evidence further supported his recently formulated theory of collective re-creation, exemplifying the way and extent to which individual creative freedom is restricted and partially neutralized, by the pressure of communal sensibilities and attitudes (artistic, moral, and ideological).

When some thirty years later Diego Catalán and Álvaro Galmés again studied the same two ballads (1954), then represented by more than a thousand traditional versions, the addition of a temporal factor to Menéndez Pidal's geographic method allowed them to reconstruct with far greater precision the paths of dissemination and the complex history of the two ballads.[3]   With heightened awareness of the diachrony implicit in folklore geography and less preoccupied than their predecessor with hypothetical prototypes, Catalán and Galmés were able to identify three successive, but overlapping stages in the evolutionary development of these two ballads: an initial and most truly "traditional" stage characterized by the independent propagation of isolated motifs, resulting in numerous highly diversified local forms; a subsequent phase in which a particular version or versions, having gained exceptional prestige, were for a time propagated *en bloc*, leading to the implantation throughout entire regions of highly uniform "types" that competed with and modified pre-existing local forms; and, in more modern times, a third stage brought on by the recent invasion of modern civilization and the rapid erosion of traditional rural society, and characterized by the tendency toward peninsular uniformity in conjunction with the ever more accentuated expansive force of Andalusian ballad types.

While the particular history of each ballad is, of course, unique and the specific details of the Catalán-Galmés study with regard to the propagation of isolated motifs, the formation of compact as opposed to diffuse geographic areas, the creation of fixed "types," the southern invasion of the north and its reaction, as well as the chronology and rhythms of change are valid only for the two ballads studied, subsequent research has shown that the major evolutionary tendencies and patterns identified in this historical-geographical study are, for the most part, characteristic of the modern oral *romancero* tradition.

To be sure, the importance of geography and the utility of geographic methods have frequently been questioned in subsequent years and, on occasion, flatly denied in Hispanic ballad criticism.

In this regard *romancero* studies have not been remiss in reflecting major trends in contemporary Western ballad scholarship. Yet, contrary to prevailing opinion in many of its sister disciplines, and despite repeated attacks, geographic considerations play a very significant role in much of *romancero* criticism to this day.

To explain and justify the continued reliance on geographic data in this branch of balladry, I will first examine the explicit and implicit objections of those who have proposed alternative approaches to the study of the modern oral *romancero*. In so doing, my aim is not to deny that subsequent criticism has accurately identified certain shortcomings in one or another geographic study, or that it has legitimately taken issue with certain procedures and even with portions of the results of *romancero* geography studies undertaken to date. My objective is rather to demonstrate with supporting evidence from recent scholarship that despite the difficulties inherent in the use of both space and time factors, these two variables are nonetheless essential to any theory which purports to define the processes of transformation and reproductive mechanisms of the *romancero* and similar bodies of traditional folk literature in which the processes of creation and transmission are inseparable. It is my contention that rather than seek to discredit or supplant folklore geography, what we require are more appropriate tools for incorporating it in our analyses. To this end I will conclude my review and defense of historical-geographical methods with sample analyses which illustrate how time and space as well as numerous interdependent, internal variables were integrated in a pilot program of computer-aided literary analysis specifically designed to facilitate exploration of the processes of variation in traditional ballad narratives.

As I hope to make clear in the following pages, the modern oral Hispanic ballad tradition differs significantly in a number of ways from many of the models of oral poetic discourse with which contemporary ballad research concerns itself. One very distinctive feature whose importance should not be overlooked or underestimated in seeking to justify the prevalence of geographic and historical-geographic studies in *romancero* scholarship is the unparalleled spatial and temporal span of the Hispanic *romancero* tradition.[4] Documentary evidence of this tradition not only encompasses six centuries of uninterrupted traditional poetic activity, but exists, often in abundance, for nearly every region inhabited by speakers of one of the four Hispanic languages.[5]

As we would expect, the earliest and most unconditional denials of the value of geographic considerations issue from those *romancero* scholars most closely allied with the individualist position. Thus the French critic Jules Horrent, in affirming the essential similarity of the creative processes in learned and traditional poetry, voices strenuous objection to the aforementioned studies by Menéndez Pidal and Catalán-Galmés primarily on the grounds that their focus on development and transformation tends to obscure the fact that "the innumerable variants that give the ballad its continual and unique movement, they too are individual in essence" (1957:392).

From a similar position Daniel Devoto launches a scathing attack on the same two studies in folklore geography, insisting that "the accent of the investigation ought to be put, above all, on the individual folkloric act, the conduct of *that* individual, of the *individual* alone, capable of varying the ballad each time he brings it to life" (1955:253).[6]   When Devoto asserts that geographic methods are invalidated by the very fact that variations inevitably arise in successive repetitions of a ballad by the same subject (253), he, like Horrent, attributes to the individual singer a degree of freedom and independence from the tradition far in excess of that which documentary evidence bears out.   No one would deny that each and every variation that arises in the course of a ballad's oral life originates with an individual (or specific individual situation), but, as the evidence of folklore geography has demonstrated time and again, once the variant has been accepted by the tradition, and in fact becomes the tradition, that element conditions subsequent individual folklore behavior to a far greater degree than Devoto is willing to acknowledge.[7]

At the root of Devoto's dissatisfaction with these geographic studies is his conviction that such methods are virtually useless for the study of what really matters, namely, the underlying reasons for the behavior of folklore materials (1955:250).   His contention that the study of this behavior leads to the discovery of the "sentido profundo" of the recurrent, invariant motifs of the tradition has considerable merit, but in rejecting the traditionalist conception of collective re-creation and with it the relevance of geographic data, Devoto takes his argument too far, insisting that this invariant latent symbolic content informs all versions of a ballad, old and modern alike.   When he counsels that our attention

should be directed to the question of how the words can vary
while the essential content remains unchanged, he not only
overlooks the significance of the ways in which, at the lexical and
morphological level, local geographic traditions determine and
explain individual behaviors, but more importantly, he fails to
perceive how, at the semantic level, these essential contents (the
meanings of myth) can and frequently do undergo profound
alteration.   In seeking to identify and explain that which is
constant, Devoto largely ignores the equally important, opposing
(but complementary) forces responsible for innovation. As a result,
he underestimates and unduly trivializes the creativity of the
modern *romancero*, whose narratives have retained their relevance
and thus survived only by adapting to the diverse and
ever-evolving social and historical contexts in which they are
reproduced.   To perceive how the latent content of inherited
narrative structures is subject to profound and often radical revision
as it is reinterpreted in ways consistent with the prevailing
attitudes and values of culturally bound collectivities, we need only
compare the dominant regional types within a well-documented
corpus of versions of a single modern ballad—one that adequately
represents the geographic and cultural diversity of the Hispanic
world.

      Exemplary in this sense are the very disparate reactions
manifested in the different areas of the modern tradition to the
problem of sibling incest posed in *Amnon y Tamar*. Within Spain
alone the tradition proffers a wide variety of potential "solutions"
to the family crisis created when the father/king unwittingly hands
over his daughter to be brutally ravaged by her brother. In the
various northern traditions these solutions range from the victim's
conventual reclusion, her suicide, or the vengeful murder of the
rapist, to conjectured papal sanction of the marriage of brother and
sister—all but the last in keeping with traditional morality, but
denounced as insensitive, useless, or unjust and regarded as equally
unsatisfactory.   By contrast, in the vulgate versions originating in
the southern half of the Peninsula, rather than explore ways to
deny, cover up, atone for, or legitimize sinful behavior, the reaction
to the incestuous act is one of open consent and even defiant
maternal defense of the singularly beautiful offspring proudly
baptized "son of brother and sister."[8]

      As numerous recent studies devoted to the analysis of
variation have demonstrated, this ongoing process of reactualization

is possible by virtue of the essential, unique property of oral narrative structures: their openness to unlimited and potentially irreversible transformation at all levels of articulation.[9]   However, it is the *romancero*'s re-creative process, its particular brand of orality, that determines the *modus operandi* of this characteristic feature of all oral discourse.

Like the individualists (and Devoto) who emphasize the importance of the individual creative act in the folkloric performance, the oralists who attempt to apply to the modern *romancero* the principles of oral-formulaic composition established by Parry and Lord fail to make the necessary distinction between an oral tradition carried on by a small core of trained semi-professionals and one that has survived for centuries as a communal activity in which any and all can participate.   In the oral epic tradition of the Balkans an individual singer selects elements from the body of stock epithets, phrases, and forms the tradition offers, to create a text at the moment of each performance.   By contrast, in the *romancero* those traditional elements form part of a text, an organic whole, endowed with its own structure, which the individual subject has memorized.   In the "performance" what the singer actualizes is the text she has learned.[10]   While motifs, formulas, and verses can and often do travel from one text to another, their normal existence is as part of a larger unit, which is the text, the *romance*.[11]   Precisely because Hispanic ballads are not individual creations that come into being on the occasion of a public performance, but re-creations of a text previously committed to memory, they are characterized by a high degree of fidelity to local tradition in both of the complementary aspects of traditionality: the retention of inherited narrative structures and their renovation in response to communal attitudes, values, and aesthetic sensibilities.

A verse by verse comparison of two versions of *Muerte del príncipe don Juan* collected in the same town (Uña de Quintana, Zamora, Spain), one in 1912 and the other in 1981, illustrates the "permanence" of a text in a given geographic location.

Muy malo estaba don Juan,   muy malo estaba en la cama.
Muy malo estaba don Juan,   muy malo estaba en la cama,
(Don Juan was gravely ill, gravely ill in his bed;)

siete doctores lo curan   de los mejores de España;
siete doctores lo curan   de los mejores de España;
(seven doctors attend him, among the best in Spain.)

aún faltaba por venir　　　　aquel dotor de la Parra,
y aún faltaba por venir　　　aquel dotor de la Parra,
(There was yet to arrive that doctor La Parra,)

que dicen que es gran dotore,　　gran dotor que adivinaba,
que dicen que es gran dotor,　　　gran dotor que adivinaba.
(a wise doctor they say he is, a wise doctor who reads signs.)

Trae solimán en el dedo　　　y en la lengua se lo echara.
Trae el veneno en el dedo　　y en la lengua se lo echara.
(He brings poison on his finger and places it on his tongue.)

—Tres horas tienes de vida,　　la media ya va pasada:
—Tres horas tienes de vida,　　la una ya va pasada:
("Three hours of life you have, a half has already gone by:)

una para confesarte　　　y otra pa enmendar tu alma
una para confesarte,　　　otra para enmendar tu alma
(one to make your confession, another to attend to your soul)

y otra para despedirte　　de la tu esposa doña Ana.—
y otra para despedirte　　de la tu esposa doña Ana.—
(and another to bid farewell to your wife doña Ana.")

Estando en estas razones　　entró doña Ana en la sala.
Y estando en estas razones　　entró doña Ana por la sala.
(At this very moment doña Ana entered the room.)

—¿Tú qué tienes, el don Juan,　　tú qué tiés en esa cama?
　　　　　—　　　　　　　　　　　　　—
("What is ailing you, don Juan, what ailment keeps you abed?")

—Tengo mal de calentura,　　que otro mal no se me hallaba.
　　　　　—　　　　　　　　　　　　　—
("I have a very high fever, no other ill has been found.)

¿Dónde vienes, la mi esposa,　　dónde vienes, doña Ana?
—¿Dónde vienes, la mi esposa,　　dónde vienes, doña Ana?
("Where have you been, my wife, where have you been, doña Ana?")

—Vengo del templo de Dios,　　del convento 'e Santa Clara;
—Vengo de rezar por ti　　　del convento 'e Santa Clara;
("I come from the temple of God, from the Convent of Saint Clare;)

vengo de rezar por ti　　　te levantes de esa cama.
vengo de rezar por ti　　　te levantes de esa cama.
(I have been praying for you, that you get up from that bed.")

—Yo sí me levantaré,　　antes de por la mañana,
—Yo sí me levantaré,　　antes de por la mañana,
("Yes, I will surely get up before a new day comes,)

para unas andas de pino,　　para una igresia sagrada;
　　　　　—　　　　　　　　　　　　—
([headed] for a pine bier, for a holy church;)

verásme cerrar los ojos,   los dientes hechos en tabla;
verásme cerrar los ojos,   los dientes hechos en tabla;
(you will see me with my eyes closed, my teeth clamped tight;)

verás el cura a la puerta,   los confrades con las hachas;
verás el cura a la puerta,   los confrades con las hachas;
(you will see a priest at the door, the brothers with their torches;)

verás el Cristo en el medio,   diciendo que salga, salga;
verás el Cristo en el medio,   diciendo que vaya, vaya;
(you will see Christ in the middle, saying 'Begone, begone;')

verásme coger al hombro,   verásme sacar de casa,
        —   —
(you will see me on their shoulders, taken from the house,)

verásme ir pa la iglesia   onde el cristiano arremata;
        —   —
(you will see me going to the church where all good Christians end up.)

verásme meter n'el hoyo   y tú te irás para casa,
tú te vendrás para adentro   y te quedarás en casa,
(you will see me put in a grave and you will go back home,)

verás las paredes negras,   las puertas todas trancadas,
verás las puertas...
(you will see the walls in black, all the doors boarded up,)

la hacienda pa la justicia,   para mis hijos no hay nada.
        —   —
(My estate for the judges, for my children there will be nothing.")

Estando en estas razones,   doña Ana se desmayara;
Estando en estas razones,   ella quedó desmayada;
(At this very moment, doña Ana faints away;)

ni con agua ni con vino   no l'hacen que recordara.
        —   —
(neither with water nor wine are they able to revive her.)

Luego le sacan un niño,   parece un rollo de plata;
Luego sacaron un niño,   parece un rollo de plata;
(Then they deliver her of a child, as beautiful as silver;)

se lo llevan a su padre   que la bendición le echara.
lo llevaron a don Juan   que la bendición le echara.
(they take it to its father to receive his blessing.)

—Si eres, mi hijo, varón,   rey has de ser en España;
—Si eres, mi hijo, varón,   has de ser rey en España;
("If, my child, you are a male, you will be king of Spain;)

y si eres, mi hija, hembra,   serás monja 'e Santa Clara.
si eres, mi hijo, hembra,   serás monja en Santa Clara.
(if, my child, you are a girl, you will be a nun in Saint Clare.")

The extreme similarity between these two "individual" re-creations of the ballad—identical save for minimal verbal variation and minor gaps in the later version—clearly points to two acts of memorization of a common model.[12]

Proponents of ethnographic and anthropological approaches who contend that in order to understand the behavior of this body of folklore material the primary focus of critical attention must be the specific social context of each individual performance similarly overlook the larger implications of the distinctive character of *romancero* orality. It being the case that the process of transmission routinely begins with an act of memorization, we must bear in mind that this activity is, at one and the same time, a creative, interpretive act. What is learned is not what was emitted, but what the receiver heard and/or was able (wanted) to understand. Consequently, the most significant adaptation or change with respect to the model occurs in the acquisition phase, rather than in subsequent executions of the "text" that has been committed to memory. Thus, as a rule, it is not primarily the immediate, external circumstances surrounding a given performance, but the broader sociocultural context and the ballad's coexistence and contact with other traditional texts that together condition change.

Moreover, for the vast majority of traditional *romances*, execution is not normally tied to specific social events as is frequently the case in neighboring European oral traditions. As long as traditional Hispanic cultures survive, open-structured *romancero* narratives can and do maintain their cultural relevance by adapting to changes in the referent, but the possibility for profound change is lost when the narrative itself ceases to function as a reflection on life. This is just what has occurred with the relatively small number of ballads that owe their continued existence largely to their having become ritualized (e.g., ballads sung in chorus as part of children's games or those sung only on certain holidays or as part of specific social events). As J. Antonio Cid (1979:329) so aptly points out, in these exceptions to the norm the context has come to prevail over the text with the result that "variation approaches zero."[13] For this reason the study of the contexts in which these particular ballads are reproduced, however interesting, can shed little light on the mechanisms governing variation in truly traditional re-creative activity.

Finally, although in the past the *romancero* enjoyed an active life in rural areas, forming part of everyday traditional communal activities, today it only rarely surfaces spontaneously even among those who participated most actively in former times. Many of the best of today's informants admit to not having sung the ballads in twenty or thirty years (and particularly not in public). Thus today very few opportunities arise to witness the spontaneous reproduction of ballad themes in their natural, immediate contexts. In the face of this reality, folklorists and ballad specialists anxious to document what most have assumed to be the final stages of a dying plurisecular tradition have been forced in recent decades to seek out prospective informants and induce them to reactivate their fund of traditional knowledge. The intense collecting activity of the past ten years has extracted in this manner an unprecedented wealth of ephemeral documentary evidence from the "archive" of popular memory.[14] In these circumstances, however, considerable temporal distance often separates the elicited execution and the primary interpretive activity which configured the text committed to memory. Consequently, much of the variation that arises in this process is the result of vacillation as the singer struggles to retrieve her "text" from the depths of her memory. Simple memory lapses, together with the interference of variants recalled from competing local versions and the intertextual contamination of motifs and sequences (or even entire *fabulae*) among several ballads in the singer's repertoire are increasingly characteristic of today's recitations. These phenomena are by no means anti-traditional in nature, but given the dormant state of the tradition, the transformation they occasion is less likely a reflection of current social values and collectively (or individually) held opinions on present-day life than was the case in former times when traditional re-creative activity was vastly more intense and flourished naturally.[15]

Although Menéndez Pidal's concept of traditionalism had gained general acceptance by the sixties, the methods of folklore geography continued to be viewed with skepticism by several of the neo-traditionalists most actively involved in the nascent critical re-evaluation of the *romancero*. In seeking to counter early traditionalism's overriding concern with the retentive aspects of the *romancero* while avoiding Menéndez Pidal's occasionally excessive reliance on the fragmented evidence of independent variants, both Paul Bénichou (1968a) and Guiseppe Di Stefano (among others) wisely advocated the straightforward synchronic comparison of texts or groups of texts as a more appropriate method of evaluating the creative aspects of orally transmitted poetic structures.

Bénichou, the most outspoken critic of the earlier geographic studies, echoes Devoto in arguing that in view of the genealogical and chronological uncertainty with regard to the derivation of the texts, the history of a ballad is an inaccessible goal with or without geography (1968b:328). While he concedes its occasional utility as a tool with which to investigate the processes of traditional re-elaboration, he maintains that the labor-intensive methods of folklore geography generally provide no better nor more conclusive evidence than can be obtained through simple comparison of the texts. Despite the implicit skepticism of such remarks as ". . . but this does not keep us from asking ourselves just what end this method serves and what difference knowing the geographic origin of each text makes when considering a group of versions of a ballad" (327), much of Bénichou's own extremely insightful work makes readily apparent the relevance of geography.

When Bénichou sets out to evaluate the creative activity and poetic value of the modern tradition in *Creación poética en el romancero tradicional* (1968a), he focuses primarily on the "variety of content and structure of the modern versions, *in their different families*" (95, italics mine) to demonstrate how this activity in modern times is neither substantially different from, nor inferior in its results to that which produced the venerated *romances tradicionales* of the sixteenth century.

In each of his three comparative studies of modern ballad texts Bénichou establishes these different families or groups of versions on the basis of common motifs and similar thematic structure—the two criteria used by proponents of *romancero* geography to identify the various local traditions of a given ballad.[16] Not suprisingly, in all three studies his families of versions coincide with recognized traditional geographic areas and even highly localized traditions. To cite but one example, in this same essay on *Muerte del príncipe don Juan* the author observes "this group [*La Montaña*], geographically very near the first, has a totally distinct physiognomy" (1968a:103). In his study of forty-one modern versions of this ballad, Bénichou dramatically demonstrates how in four distinct areas of the modern tradition the ballad's transmitters have variously developed the latent poetic content of the primitive historical *romance*, transforming it in both form and spirit. After meticulously examining the narrative function of the motifs that characterize each group of versions,

Bénichou affirms:

> . . . we find innovations that change the spirit and the
> construction of the ballad: in the Castilian versions of
> the first group, the anticipated description the sick man
> makes of his funeral and of the helplessness of the
> young widow; in some versions from *La Montaña*, the
> final scene of tenderness between husband and wife and
> their death; in the Portuguese versions, the scruples of
> the dying protagonist and his parents regarding the
> dishonored mistress; in the Jewish versions, the family
> lament (118).

In his eloquent defense of the modern tradition Bénichou's
case for the freedom with which modern transmitters of the ballad
have exercised their poetic creativity is well made, but the
limitations within which that freedom is seen to operate clearly
indicate the relevance of geography to the processes of traditional
re-elaboration.   He concludes his study of the ballad with the
astute observation that the real difference between the old and the
modern traditions is that they reflect different worlds (123).
Bénichou's analysis admirably demonstrates traditional poetry's
ability to adapt to the changing environments in which it is
reproduced, but these "different worlds" are not merely those of
the sixteenth and twentieth centuries, as his introductory comments
make abundantly clear:

> The ballad has been transforming itself in environments
> so distinct and distant from one another as Old Castile,
> Portugal, Morocco, and the Eastern Sephardic
> communities and *therefore*, in the main, has experienced
> a very high degree of differentiation (97, italics mine).

By respecting the integrity of the poetic structure and shifting
the focus of attention to the creative reinterpretation and
restructuring of poetic content, Bénichou as well as Di Stefano,
Catalán, and others avoid some of the undeniable limitations
inherent in the earlier geographic and historical-geographic studies.
Nevertheless, their findings invariably confirm the significant role of
geography in the transformation of collectively re-created poetic
narratives.[17] Despite methodological improvements, the more recent
investigations that stress synchronic comparison of ballad texts also
impose severe restrictions on the analysis of transformation
processes.   If the early studies in *romancero* geography could

analyze an exhaustive corpus only by virtually limiting analysis to a single variable (thereby ignoring numerous other interdependent factors), more comprehensive analysis based on the "simple comparison of texts" has proven feasible only by limiting the textual evidence to a relatively small, but manageable sample. This restriction inevitably tends to undermine the possibility of identifying and comparing genetically related structures and thus jeopardizes our ability to determine exactly how orally transmitted poems are reproduced. The Hispanic *romancero* constitutes an ideal corpus for exploring the mechanisms of transmission in a dynamic open-structured model precisely because it offers bodies of evidence of unprecedented numerical, spatial, and temporal amplitude.

With the advent of modern electronic data processing, rigorous, systematic analysis of large, highly complex corpora such as that constituted by the oral *romancero* became a real possibility for the first time. Computers capable of storing, sorting, tabulating, and cross-correlating vast quantities of data can perform exhaustive synchronic and diachronic comparisons of hundreds (or thousands) of traditional poetic texts. By exploiting this potential in conjunction with appropriate samples of the *romancero*, we can explore the processes of variation at all levels of organization of the narrative(s) and, in the case of multiple manifestations of a single theme, examine and measure the dynamic interaction among these levels.

The first attempt to devise a computer-based system of literary analysis designed to facilitate a comprehensive description of the reproductive patterns and system of poetic communication of the *romancero* was undertaken in the early seventies. The data base for this pilot project consisted of 612 versions of *La condesita*, a modern ballad first documented in 1820 and widely diffused in all areas of Spain.[18] To maximize the potential for subsequent comparative operations, this entire corpus was first segmented into various smaller units of analysis. These included the three most obvious breaks in the chain of discourse—the version, the hemistich (the basic unit of composition), and the word—as well as three other units of analysis related to the narrative structure and its dramatic presentation: the dramatic scene, the thematic segment, and the element of narrative information. In order to generate these and other paradigmatic groupings related to the poetic structure or to the spatial and temporal classification of the material, eleven different sets of codes were manually or mechanically assigned to each of the 34,233 hemistichs of the corpus.

Each version was defined with a code identifying 1) its place of origin (province and region), 2) its date of collection (year and period), 3) the nature of its testimony (distinguishing between fragmentary and more or less complete versions) and 4) its ballad type (distinguishing among oral versions of the autonomous ballad *La condesita*, oral versions of the double ballad *Gerineldo + La condesita*, non-traditional versions propagated by virtue of the popularity of certain published texts, and versions derived from Menéndez Pidal's influential composite text published in *Flor nueva de romances viejos*).

The text of each hemistich was defined with a code to:

a) insert it into its immediate syntagmatic context;

b) identify it as a 1st (non-rhyming) or 2nd (rhyming) hemistich;

c) attribute it to a particular narrative sequence, specifying the dramatic scene and thematic segment in which it appears;

d) classify it by its mode of narrative discourse, identifying 1st or 3rd person narration or direct discourse;

e) identify the speaker, if part of a direct discourse;

f) identify the type of narration, if part of a narrated sequence, distinguishing among inter- and intra-scenic narration, narration denoting a time/space transition, narration announcing the entrance or exit of a character in the drama, or narrative introduction to direct discourse;

g) specify the element of narrative content it carries, identifying it with one of 250 minimal elements of narrative information;

h) specify the invariant or "archetypal" hemistich of which it is but one manifestation, identifying it with one of 1,937 archetypal hemistichs;[19]

Finally, each of the 170,978 words in the corpus was assigned a code to 1) identify its position in the hemistich, 2) identify its grammatical function and part of speech, and 3) define its function in the metric scheme by identifying the words that carried the assonance.

Although much of the above information is logically associated with a particular level or unit of analysis, by uniformly encoding each and every hemistich with all the information it was all retained and available at all levels of analysis or subdivisions

thereof.   The capacity to correlate any number or any combination of variables allows taking into account simultaneously all
the simple and complex variable factors that must be weighed in
order to determine which are responsible for a given phenomenon,
a particular aspect of variation.

    In testing the applicability of a system with almost unlimited
potential for generating and tabulating information on significant
subsets of the data base, we focused primarily on problems that
had consistently defied analysis with more traditional methodologies,
that is, those that required either a multilevel analysis or the
interpretation of large batches of sorted and tabulated data.
Geographic and temporal variables figured prominently in a number
of   our   computer-aided   analyses   of   lexical   variation   and
lexical-syntactic, semantic, and structural transformation.   In view
of the fact that a serious limitation of the earlier geographic studies
was their inability to adequately assess structural transformation in
the versions whose variants they studied, the examples selected all
utilize   geographic   and/or   temporal   variables   to   analyze   an
important aspect of this process.

    As illustration of even the simplest of the analyses requires
some familiarity with the ballad studied, the following description
of the narrative content of *La condesita* will serve to introduce
both the ballad and two of the units of analysis that figure in the
subsequent examples.

ACT #   SEGMENT #

1 Separation of the spouses   10 Semi-autonomous introduction
                               11 The husband is called to war
                               12 Grief of the spouses in the face of
                                  forced separation
                               13 Estimated duration of the separation
                               14 The husband's departure

2 The wife decides to go in   21 The estimated time limit on the
   search of her husband   separation elapses and the husband
                                  has not returned
                               22 The wife's family pressures her to
                                  remarry
                               23 The wife discusses going in search of
                                  her husband with a member of her
                                  family
                               24 The wife, disguised in a pilgrim's
                                  garb, leaves in search of her
                                  husband

3 Encounter with an informant 31 After long travels the "pilgrim"

(wife) encounters an informant
32 First news of the husband
33 The "pilgrim" is appraised of how
and where to gain an audience with
her husband

4 Recognition
41 The "pilgrim" manages to obtain an
interview with her newly affianced
husband
42 Dialogue culminating in the
revelation of the "pilgrim's" true
identity
43 The husband's reaction
44 The rival fiancée's reaction on
learning what has transpired
45 The husband decides which of the
women he wishes to claim as his
wife
50 Final comment, marginal to the
story line

The first example, in which geographic considerations are
brought into play only in a second stage of the analysis, illustrates
how the coding system enables us to analyze the transformation of
individual invariant hemistichs—the underlying base structures or
"archetypes" that generate the 34,233 hemistichs (19,403 variant
hemistichs) of the *La condesita* corpus.

Segment 44, in which the count's new fiancée [N] or a
member of her household [T] comes upon her betrothed [C] lying
in a dead faint before a pilgrim whom he has just discovered to be
his long-abandoned wife [R], frequently begins with one of two
hemistichs that carry the information coded as element 505 (Curses
cast on the pilgrim): *Damn the pilgrim* [44505111] and *You,
Pilgrim (~ Madame), are the Devil* [44505511]. A sample listing of
17 of the 87 variant hemistichs that manifest archetype 44 505 511
reveals how, in the course of its reproduction, this archetype has
acquired new semantic values and taken on different functions in
the final scene of the ballad.

Hemistich	Speaker	Segment	Element	Archetype
12939A Vaya al diablo la romera	N	44	505	44 505
23330A Eres el diablo romera	N	44	506	44 505
19929A Eres mujer o demonio	N	44	506	44 505
22522A Mujer es usted el demonio	N	44	506	44 505
21627A Que mujer o que demonio	T	44	506	44 505
28733A Que demonio de princesa	N	44	506	44 505
51117A Que diablo de romera	C	42	462	44 505
56219A Eres er diablo niña	C	42	462	44 505

52718A	Romera eres el demonio	C	42	462	44 505
61949A	Tu eres el mismo demonio	C	42	462	44 505
25116A	Vete romera del diablo	C	42	438	44 505
19540A	Mujer eres el demonio	N	45	472	44 505
20428A	Hombre tu eres el demonio	N	45	471	44 505
50367A	Que romera ni demonios	N	42	410	44 505
25116A	Vete romera del diablo	C	42	438	44 505
54053A	Vete demonio e romera	C	41	433	44 505
65954A	Sera mujer o demonio	N	41	433	44 505

The allusion to the devil that appears frequently in conjunction with archetype 44505111, *Damn the pilgrim, / (who in) the devil brought her here,* is here formulated as an insinuation that the pilgrim might herself be the devil: *You, Pilgrim (~ Madame), are the devil / who has come to tempt him* (element 506).   Once the association surfaces as an insinuation or expression of doubt, it can readily be transferred from the irate fiancée [N] to the count himself [C], whereby the same archetype comes to express his last moment of vacillation between committing himself to his present life or accepting the superior claims of his first love [C 42 462]: *You, Pilgrim, are the devil / who has come to tempt me.*

As revealed by other discrepancies between the archetype code and the codes identifying the segment in which the hemistich actually appears and the information it actually carries, this archetype occasionally takes on other meanings as well.   It travels intact to segment 45 where, as an accusation lodged either against the count (element 471) or the countess (element 472), it functions to express the rival's protestations in the face of her defeat: *You, Madame (~ Sir), are the devil / who came to insult me (~ for you have deceived me).*   With only minor lexical variation ("Qué mujer o qué demonio" ~ "Qué romera ni demonios"), the same base structure can introduce the pilgrim's revelation of her true identity (element 410): *What pilgrim or devil?, / I'm your lawful wife!.*   With similar ease the curse is transformed into an expression of disgust at the pilgrim's haughty refusal of alms (element 438) and finally, reformulated yet again in segment 41, it functions as an order for the alms-seeking pilgrim to withdraw from the palace door, thus replacing the more usual expression *Get you back, Madame,* issued either by the fiancée or the count himself.

By providing data that allows us to analyze each archetype's capacity for acquiring new semantic values and functioning in different contexts, the codes allow us to detect all instances of syntagmatic reorganization of the narrative, including those with repercussions on the paradigmatic plane. The relative importance of the syntagmatic reorganization occasioned by the mobility of archetypes can be measured for parts or all of the narrative simply by tabulating occurrences of discordance between the two sets of codes. Not surprisingly, these statistics reveal that structural transformation in *La condesita* is most radical in the final scene, where discordance between the ideal and the actual position of the hemistichs averages 43% (as compared to 30% for the corpus as a whole). In other words, only 57% of hemistichs that reproduce an invariant ideally belonging to a particular segment in the fourth act actually appear in that segment.   Mobility is most extreme precisely in segment 44, where 54% of the hemistichs we expect to find there have travelled to another segment (this, compared to the minimal variation attested to in segment 13 of act 1, for example, where discordance drops to 10%).[20]

Table I

Region	number of versions	% of versions with 44505511	occurrences 44505511 by BT	breakdown by function	breakdown of function by BT
1 (Northwest)	84	4.7%	75% BT I		
2 (Leonese area)	79	3.8%	100% BT II		
3 (Old Castile)	83	4.8%	75% BT I		
4 (Extremadura)	78	16.7%	62% BT I	N44 = 54% C42 = 46%	BT I: N44 88% C42 12% BT II: C42 100%

5 (New Castile)	72	40.3%	62% BT I	N44 = 72%
				C42 = 17%
				N45 = 7%
				N41 = 3%
					BT I: N44 83%
					       C42 5%
					       N45 11%
					BT II: N44 54%
					       C42 36%
					       N45 9%

6 (Andalusia)	86	23.3%	92% BT II		
7 (Levant)	66	16.7%	82% BT I		

(BT = Ballad type)

Regional Classification of Provinces

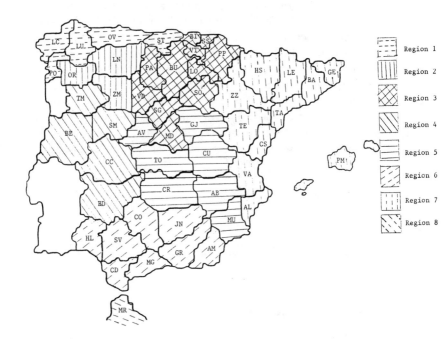

Key to Regions and Provinces

Regions	Provinces
1 Northwest	LC = La Coruña PO = Pontevedra LU = Lugo OV = Oviedo ST = Santander
2 Leonese Area	LN = León ZM = Zamora OR = Orense Z = Unspecified within region
3 Old Castile	BU = Burgos PA = Palencia VD = Valladolid SG = Segovia MD = Madrid SO = Soria LO = Logroño VT = Álava BI = Bilbao [Vizcaya] SS = San Sebastián [Guipúzcoa] PP = Pamplona
4 Extremadura	SM = Salamanca TM = Trás-os-Montes BE = Beira AV = Ávila CC = Cáceres BD = Badajoz
5 New Castile	TO = Toledo CR = Ciudad Real AB = Albacete MU = Murcia CU = Cuenca GJ = Guadalajara
6 Andalusia	CO = Córdoba SV = Sevilla HL = Huelva CD = Cádiz MG = Málaga GR = Granada JN = Jaén AM = Almería A = Unspecified within region HS = Huesca ZZ = Zaragoza TE = Teruel GE = Gerona

7
Levant
BA = Barcelona
LE = Lérida
TA = Tarragona
CS = Castellón
VA = Valencia
AL = Alicante
PM = Palma de Mallorca
[Baleares]

8   M = Morocco

In order to perceive any significant pattern in the reproduction of any of the 1,937 invariant hemistichs of the corpus across time and space, we need only sort the data already obtained on the reformulations of archetypes by the appropriate temporal and/or geographic variables.[21] Internal sorting of the 87 variant hemistichs of archetype 44505511, for example, reveals very definite trends in its implantation in the tradition. The preceding Table I summarizing the output of several cross-tabulations on this archetype allows us to identify these trends as well as the relationship between external factors (time and space) and structural characteristics of the ballad.[22]

It is immediately apparent (col. 3) that while archetype 44505511 appears in all regions of the Peninsula, it can only be said to characterize a significant number of versions in four of the seven regions (4-7), with notable prevalence in region 5 (where a full 35% of all the manifestations of this invariant hemistich occur). The next column clearly suggests that the archetype, where used, is found primarily in versions of the autonomous ballad (type I), the descendants of the older structure. (In the Leonese area, where the archetype is unknown to type I versions, its three occurrences in the more modern double ballad are statistically irrelevant and in Andalusia, where the double ballad constitutes 95% of all known versions, the archetype nevertheless occurs in 50% of the four documented type I versions.) The most significant patterns in the reproduction of this archetype emerge in the last two columns, which register, within each region, the proportionate use of each of the reformulations of the archetype (col. 5) and within that context, their proportionate use in the type I and type II versions (col. 6). In Extremadura, although the archetype functions with approximately the same overall frequency, now as a curse on the pilgrim uttered by the irate fiancée [N44], now as an expression of the count's vacillation [C42], the latter reinterpretation corresponds exclusively to versions of the more modern ballad type, while 88% of the versions in which the invariant functions as an expression of the rival's outrage correspond to the older autonomous ballad (type I). Manifestations of the archetype in Andalusia fully corroborate the correlation between type II versions and the archetype's reformulation in segment 42. In region 5, where re-creative activity has produced maximum diversification in the reinterpretation of this archetype, its function in the context of the rival's reaction clearly dominates

(72%) over all other reformulations. So tenacious is this interpretation in New Castile that it has seriously compromised the normal syntagmatic organization of type II versions, prevailing in 54% of the area's double ballad texts that retain the archetype.[23]

Syntagmatic reorganization of a higher order can be analyzed in a similar fashion simply by substituting or incorporating additional variables in the cross-tabulation program and changing the internal sorting priority. This procedure allows us to explore three key processes of transformation intimately related to the poetic restructuring of the narrative for dramatic effect: the distortion of the natural order of the narrative (Petersen 1976a:190-92; Catalán 1976:72-74); modifications in the absolute and relative length of the ballad and of its dramatic scenes and segments; and variation in the proportionate use and distribution of direct discourse and narration.

A brief look at some statistics on the average length and proportionate use of direct discourse in the second act of the ballad will serve to illustrate how electronic processing of secondary data can identify important evolutionary trends in the structural transformation of the ballad across time and space.

Table II lists the average length of act 2 of all non-fragmentary versions in each of the seven peninsular regions (and in parentheses, the percentage of the overall narrative those figures represent), followed by a breakdown of the same information by ballad type.

Table II. Length (in hemistichs) and Relative Weight of Act 2

Region	avg. length	%	BT I avg. length	%	BT II avg. length	%
1	9	(13%)	11	(14%)	6	(11%)
2	9	(14%)	11	(15%)	5	(10%)
3	13	(18%)	14	(20%)	9	(14%)
4	11	(17%)	13	(18%)	7	(17%)
5	14	(23%)	14	(23%)	12	(24%)
6	6	(14%)	7	(14%)	6	(14%)
7	13	(22%)	13	(22%)	12	(23%)
8	8	(18%)	15	(25%)	5	(13%)

The average length of the second act is seen to vary considerably from region to region, from maximum elaboration in New Castile (14 hem.) to minimum elaboration in Andalusia (6 hem.). In all areas, however, the average length of the act is

greater in the autonomous ballad (type I) than in its more modern
counterpart, and in several regions the contrast is extreme.   In
regions 1, 2, and 4 the second act is approximately twice as long
in type I versions.   The two radically different conceptions of the
narrative suggested by the dramatic contrast in Morocco (region 8)
between versions descended from the older ballad structure and
those which reproduce the more modern double ballad theme is
entirely consistent with the well-documented duality of the
Moroccan tradition wherein, even today, the poetic legacy of the
Sephardic communities coexists with recent importations from the
Peninsula.   Equally significant are the figures for regions 5, 6, and
7, where we find no appreciable differences between type I and
type II versions in the average length of the second act.   This
similarity suggests an approximation between the two ballad types
in these areas, particularly in regions 5 and 7 where the
importance accorded to act 2 is maintained even in type II
versions (24% and 23%).

    As the next table reveals, the proportionate use of direct
discourse in the ballad's second act also varies radically from region
to region.

Table III.   Proportionate Use of Direct Discourse in Act 2

Region	% dir. disc.	BT I % dir. disc.	BTII % dir. disc.
1	59.6%	73.9%	30.8%
2	49.4%	59.3%	16.7%
3	62.2%	64.3%	47.0%
4	48.9%	53.7%	19.8%
5	62.3%	68.0%	67.0%
6	25.0%	36.4%	24.7%
7	59.9%	60.9%	52.7%
8	42.8%	56.8%	25.6%

The breakdown of direct discourse percentages by ballad type
confirms and reinforces the structural tendencies seen in the
previous table.   Just as the average length of the ballad is greater
in all type I versions, so too is the proportionate use of dialogue
always higher in these versions than in the double ballad.
Moreover, the greatest contrasts between the two ballad types
occur in the same regions that manifested the greatest contrast in
average length (regions 1, 2, 4, 8), as do the regions where the
contrast is minimal (regions 5, 6, 7).

    Setting aside other important regional differences that point to a need for further investigation, the numerous parallels we have identified between length and proportionate use of dialogue are also born out in a global comparison of the autonomous and double ballad structures, both for the second act alone and for the entire narrative.   The following table summarizes these statistics for the non-fragmentary oral versions of *La condesita*.

Table IV

	Act 2		Acts 1-4	
	BT I	*BT II*	*BT I*	*BT II*
avg. length	13	7	69	47
% dir. disc.	63%	35%	67%	63%

The most interesting statistic here is the percentage of direct discourse for all type II versions of the ballad taken as a whole (63%).   The dramatic contrast seen between the two ballad types in act 2 largely disappears, indicating that the use of direct discourse for dramatic effect has not been replaced by narration in the double ballad, but rather that it has been used, very extensively, at other points in the narrative.   The redistribution of discursive modes signalling important shifts in the focus of interest is a clear indication of profound reinterpretive activity.

The sample analyses discussed thus far have demonstrated that certain structural characteristics of the ballad are manifested, not in isolated versions, but in whole groups of versions, and that the poem adjusts itself to a number of very different poetic molds, with certain structural characteristics tending to dominate in certain regions and at certain stages in the ballad's oral life.   The evidence clearly suggests that the study of any structural aspect of a traditional ballad requires an analysis of its transformation across time and space.   While the study of the effects of these two factors on individual, simple variables provides valuable insights into the ballad's evolution, the most interesting comparative operations are those that allow correlating the data on all relevant variable factors so as to determine the effect of each one and the relationship or degree of interdependence among them.   The final example illustrates how a first-generation computer cartography system was used to display the results of global comparative operations in such a way as to make the effects of time and space visually discernible.[24]

Whereas the earlier manual geographic studies could only aspire to cartographically illustrate affinity among certain versions

of a ballad based on a number of subjectively selected hemistichs
(i.e., one variable), computer cartography and geographic
information systems allow us to take into account the geographic
distribution of all the hemistichs and consider concurrently any
number of variable factors (length of the poem, length of its scenes
and segments, sequences of narrative events, discursive modes
employed throughout, etc.).   In this particular application, the
geographic processing package was used to determine the degree of
narrative affinity among all strictly oral, non-fragmentary versions
of *La condesita* and to measure the extent to which that affinity is
conditioned by the time and space factors, while the mapping
program (primitive by today's standards) provided visual display of
those relationships.

The first step in determining narrative affinity among versions
was to create a base structure to which individual versions or
groups of versions could be compared.   To do this we chose to
generate not one but several model or archetypal versions, each
representative of the poem's dominant narrative structure in one of
the temporally and spatially restricted subsets of the total corpus.
Using the *ballad type* and *region* variables for the temporal and
geographic subclassification of the texts, a representative version
was mechanically generated for each of the two traditional ballad
types (I and II) in each of the seven peninsular regions.

To assure that the fourteen archetypal versions faithfully
reproduced the narrative structure of the ballad characteristic of
the group of versions used to generate it, the computer first
tabulated for each group of versions the total number of versions in
the subset, the average length (in hemistichs) of the versions, the
number of versions in which each of the poem's thematic segments
appears, and the average length of each segment.   With these
statistics it created a "skeleton" defining, in outline form, both the
narrative content and the syntagmatic structure of the narrative in
each group of versions.

To give concrete form or "texture" to the narrative skeleton
of each model version, a second program, run once for each subset,
listed and tabulated occurrences of all archetypal hemistichs present
in each of the poem's thematic segments.   Based on their number
of occurrences in these lists, the most representative archetypal
hemistichs (that is, those of maximum incidence in each segment)
were then selected to fill in the corresponding, predetermined
"slots" in each narrative skeleton.

Map 1   Archetypal Version of *Region 1, BT I*
against all *BT I* versions

Map 2   Archetypal Version of *Region 5, BT I*
against all *BT I* versions

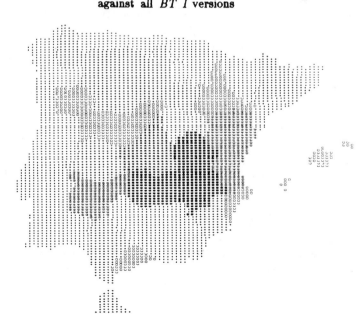

To evaluate affinitive relationships among the versions of the corpus, we elected to determine the precise degree of narrative affinity between each of the archetypal poems and all the real versions of each *ballad type* in each *province*, using as a measurement the average proportion of a model version's archetypal hemistichs preserved in the real versions of each temporally and geographically defined subset. Once the computer had determined, for a given archetypal version, the average proportion of affinity of all versions of a given *ballad type* in each *province*, it merely converted those proportions into a number on a graduated scale of ten values and then printed those values, translated into one of ten corresponding graduated over-print symbols.

The first map produced in this way constitutes a province by province comparison of the model versions of *ballad type I - region 1* with all 288 non-fragmentary versions of the autonomous (type I) ballad. As Map 1 reveals, this archetypal version represents a highly regionalized ballad "type" with its center in the Asturian provinces of Oviedo and Santillana (today, Santander). Lugo, the third of the three provinces in region 1 whose versions served to generate the model, is shown to be no more closely related to the nuclear group than the neighboring province of León (region 2). A considerable part of Old Castile, excluding the eastern portion (Logroño, Soria), maintains an attenuated second and third degree relationship of affinity with the model. The difference between the provinces of Palencia and Valladolid (degree 4), more akin to the model, and Burgos, Segovia, and Ávila (degree 3), bears out the progressive debilitation in relative affinity as one moves from west to east within the Castilian area. Aside from this zone adjacent to the nuclear area, the affinity between the archetypal version of *region 1 - type I* and the remaining type I versions is minimal. In reconfirming the existence of a regional Cantabrian "type" previously identified by Catalán and Galmés (1954) on the basis of nine invariants, this computer map confirms the validity of both this and the earlier geographic studies. In addition, the computer generated map visually displays not only the implantation of this regional "type" and the greater or lesser conformity of the versions included in the Cantabrian region to the details of the "type," but also the degree of affinity between it and the contiguous versions not belonging to the regional type.

To further test the validity of this regional archetypal version, the computer generated another map of narrative affinity using as the basis of comparison the oldest real type I version from the northwest, rather than a composite, artificial model. As expected, the numerous inevitable singularities of a real version resulted in a general debilitation of the degrees of affinity, but in all other respects this comparison reproduced the same image as Map 1.

Map 2 compares the archetypal version generated from the thirty-four ballad type I versions of region 5 (New Castile and Murcia, excluding the province of Madrid) with all 288 type I versions. This map, like the first one, reveals the importance of the spatial factor in the transformation of a ballad narrative. Again we find a nucleus of marked affinity (degree 9) in the Manchegan provinces of Ciudad Real, Albacete, and Cuenca in the center of the region, and a secondary zone (degree 6) that includes not only Toledo, but Madrid, therein belying our conviction (influenced by the maps in *Cómo vive un romance*) that the versions from Madrid ought to be grouped with those of Old Castile. Conversely, the affinity of the versions from Guadalajara (degree 1) and Murcia (degree 2), used to generate the model, is considerably less than that of other provinces outside the region. As in the case of the first map, here too there exists in the periphery of the region a third zone of somewhat less pronounced affinity that includes, to the west, the province of Badajoz (degree 4) and, to the east, the kingdoms of Valencia and Aragón (degrees 3-4). No less significant and logical is the higher proportion of affinity with respect to the model in the versions from the southern band of the northern plateau than in those of the northern part of this plateau.

Not all the ballad type I maps are similar to the two described thus far because not all regions have a dominant "type" with marked regional characteristics. In contrast to regions 1 and 5, regions 2, 3, and 4 (Zamora-León, Old Castile and Extremadura) generate maps in which there is no nucleus of maximum affinity clearly identifiable with the center of the region that has served to generate the model. Although geography is still seen to be relevant in that the focus of affinity shifts (from the Leonese area in region 2), now to the east (region 3), now to the southwest (region 4), in all three maps we find that the versions which contributed to their respective regional models show no greater affinity to those models than the versions from surrounding provinces that did not contribute to the model. Moreover, in all three cases the patches of attenuated affinity extend to provinces

Map 3 Archetypal Version of *Region 6, BT II* against all *BT II* versions

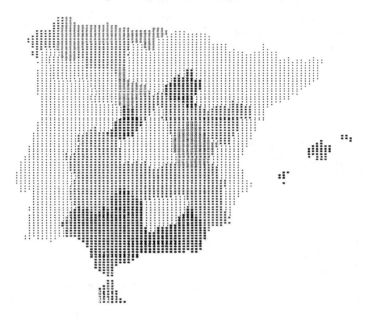

Map 4 Archetypal Version of *Region 2, BT I* against all *BT I* versions

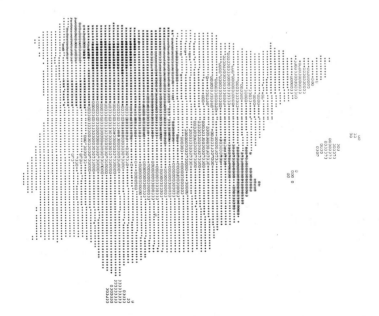

at considerable distance from the region whose model serves as the basis of comparison.   Both these characteristics demonstrate that the model versions representative of these regions contain numerous archetypal hemistichs of non-regional character, that is, hemistichs that very nearly approach a universal ballad type I model.   It is in these three areas where we find the vast majority of what Catalán and Galmés call the "independent versions" representative of the oldest surviving tradition of the ballad.

In contrast to the maps generated from versions of the autonomous ballad, Map 3 confronts the *ballad type II - region 6* model generated from the seventy-six Andalusian versions with all 208 ballad type II versions.   The most striking feature of this map is the absolute homogeneity of the Andalusian region that has served to generate the model: all seven of the provinces with type II versions reflect the maximum degree of affinity.   (Jaén, which is virtually unexplored, as well as Madrid and Toledo, have no versions of this type.) Equally evident is the fact that the fourteen Moroccan type II versions are intimately related to their Andalusian counterparts (unlike the five Moroccan type I versions). The affinity of the periphery of Andalusia with the Andalusian model encompasses Murcia as well as all of Extremadura (degree 6) and the Manchegan provinces of Albacete and Ciudad Real (degree 5).   However, the greatest novelty of this map with respect to all those that compared type I versions is that here the highest degrees of affinity (8 and 9) with the archetypal version occur no less in the Balearic Islands than in Soria, in Ávila, and, to a significant degree (6), even in La Coruña.   It must be noted that in all these provinces ballad type II is represented by no more than one or two versions—a circumstance which indicates that the double ballad *Gerineldo + La condesita* is a rarity of recent importation in these areas.   Of greater importance is the fact that in a province such as León, with as many as eighteen type II versions, the affinitive relationship is still quite pronounced (degree 5).   The fact that in areas far removed from Andalusia rather dense populations of ballad type II versions manifest a high degree of affinity with the Andalusian model seems to confirm the hypothesis that, in the last analysis, ballad type II depends on the success achieved by some individual initiative to fuse into a single *romance* the two Andalusian ballads *Gerineldo* and *La condesita.*

The remaining maps generated from ballad type II models all reflect a certain affinity with the Andalusian double ballad, but at the same time each manifests strong regional characteristics that contrast sharply with one another. This tendency is particularly in evidence in the entire northwestern part of the Peninsula (regions 1 and 2), where an exceedingly compact area of maximum degrees of affinity denounces the existence of a very pronounced and firmly established regional "type" whose unique personality renders it utterly distinct from the type II versions in the eastern half of the Peninsula.

The first series of fourteen maps treats the ballad narrative as a whole, but the coding system also allows us to explore independently the different behavior of the various parts of the overall narration. Thus, in a second series of maps, we elected to use as contrastive units the ballad's four dramatic scenes or acts. The earlier analyses suggested that the archetypal versions of *region 2 - ballad type I* and *region 6 - ballad type II* were ideally suited to this purpose, as these two geographically and temporally defined subsets illustrate extremes in the total corpus. As Map 4 demonstrates, in region 2 no pronounced regional "type" prevails; the majority of the versions that have contributed to the generation of the archetypal version are representative of local models devoid of expansive force. This model therefore constitutes a good example of the more traditional, conservative geography. In contrast, *region 6 - type II* (Map 3) generates a model of unified regional character that enjoys tremendous expansive force in modern times. (The four period maps that display the relative proportion of type I and type II versions collected in each province in each of the four *periods of collection* established for this corpus confirm the expansive power of the double ballad and its decided triumph over the autonomous *La condesita.*)

Maps 5-8 constitute an act by act comparison of the *region 2 - type I* model with all 288 type I versions (subclassified by act).

Even the most casual sequential "reading" of these four maps exposes the contrast between act 4 and the other three. In spite of their differences, Maps 5, 6, and 7 have in common an essential feature: in all three the distribution of the diverse degrees of affinity is not organized around a focus or geographic nucleus more or less identifiable with the region that has served to generate the model. None of the three reproduces the configuration depicted in Map 4, the map that displays an image of the global comparison

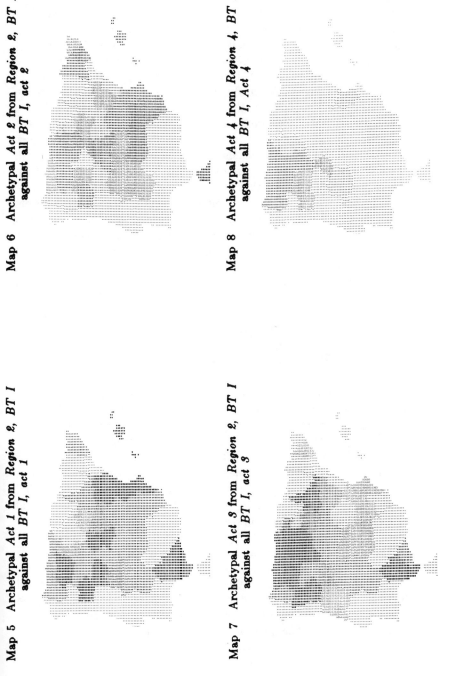

Map 5 Archetypal *Act 1* from *Region 2, BT I* against all *BT I, act 1*

Map 6 Archetypal *Act 2* from *Region 2, BT I* against all *BT I, act 2*

Map 7 Archetypal *Act 3* from *Region 2, BT I* against all *BT I, act 3*

Map 8 Archetypal *Act 4* from *Region 4, BT I* against all *BT I, Act 4*

of the *region 2 - type I* archetypal version with the 288 type I versions. It is obvious that acts 1, 2, and 3 of the model versions generated from the thirty-nine type I versions of León, Zamora, and Orense are not regionally defined. In Maps 5, 6, and 7 geography is shown to be relevant in some cases, but only in a negative sense: for example, in act 1, Catalonia, with proportions of affinity oscillating between degrees 2 and 9, maintains a certain personality in the face of the model; in act 2, Andalusia is the region to separate itself most ostensibly from the norm (as opposed to what happens in acts 1 and 3); and in act 3 regions 5 (New Castile) and 7 (Levant), *en bloc*, demonstrate the relative strength of their respective "types" in differentiating themselves more than the others from a model that is seen to be quite universal.

In sharp contrast to the first three acts of this model version, act 4 is seen to be eminently regional. Map 8 clearly depicts a focus of greater affinity, comprised of the nineteen Leonese versions, surrounded by a very limited area of moderate affinity (degrees 5 and 4) which includes, to the north, three provinces of region 1, and to the east, Palencia and Valladolid (region 3). A second band with weak proportions of affinity (Zamora, Trás-os-Montes, and Ávila) serves only to emphasize the regional character of the last act. As in all maps that manifest a well-defined geographic nucleus, we once more observe here that the nuclear region is redefined, or rather redefines itself, thereby correcting our regional classification of provinces. In this case two of the provinces within region 2, although they contribute 46% of the versions used to generate the model, have a lower degree of affinity than other adjacent provinces in regions 1 and 3. It is apparent that act 4 and only act 4 is responsible for the clearly delineated geographic focus displayed in Map 4. The possibility that a single act can account for the general outline of a map generated on the basis of an entire version (Map 4) is not so surprising if we keep in mind that in the model version under consideration the archetypal hemistichs of act 4 constitute 51% of the whole poem. What does merit emphasizing is the fact that the individual geographic study of the four acts demonstrates that the only part of the ballad to contain a high proportion of distinctive creations is the final scene.

The obvious contrast between the configuration of Map 8 and that of Maps 5, 6, and 7 must not obscure the similarity, in another important aspect, between Maps 6 and 8 as opposed to Maps 5 and 7. The first and third act maps both display large patches of elevated degrees of affinity: in the first, these are dispersed throughout the most diverse regions of the Peninsula; in the third, they are basically concentrated in two separate areas in the northwest.   Conversely, acts 2 and 3 have in common the absence of all degrees of affinity superior to 6 (except in the second act of the five Moroccan type I versions).   This indicates that these are the two acts which are subject to the greatest amount of revisionary activity, the two which most attract the creative attention of the artisans of the traditional ballad.   With respect to act 4 we already knew this to be the case, but the act by act comparison of type I versions also offers objective proof that act 2, the act in which the wife decides to assert her rights and abandon her family and native land, represents a secondary focus of creative activity.   In this second act the personality of the various type I versions undoubtedly achieves maximum definition within region 2 itself, since the three provinces whose versions have generated the model of the archetypal act offer even lower proportions of affinity to that model than provinces outside the region.

The four acts of the *region 6 - type II* model version also produce highly contrasting maps.

The two most outstanding features of Map 9 are the almost absolute uniformity of the degrees of affinity in all provinces with type II populations and the fact that the maximum degree (9) is maintained both without and within the region that has generated the model.   Clearly, the Andalusian act 1 model serves to define the first act of the double ballad *Gerineldo + La condesita* in the Spanish oral tradition such as it is known in modern times.   This uniformity is not so surprising in type II versions where the first act functions as a transition between the two fused ballads, retaining in its six hemistichs only the essential information: the proclamation of war, mobilization of the count, and estimated duration of the protagonists' forced separation.   Only in region 5 do we find a more limited affinity with the Andalusian model (Murcia, degree 8; Albacete, 6; Cuenca, 7; and Guadalajara, with only one version, degree 4).   In the preliminary statistical analyses of different aspects of the ballad's narrative structure, both the type I and type II versions from region 5 were seen to be often at variance with the general tendencies manifested by the rest of the

Map 9   Archetypal *Act 1* from *Region 6, BT II*
         against all *BT II, act 1*

Map 10   Archetypal *Act 2* from *Region 6, BT II*
         against all *BT II, act 2*

Map 11   Archetypal *Act 3* from *Region 6, BT III*
         against all *BT II, act 3*

Map 12   Archetypal *Act 4* from *Region 6, BT II*
         against all *BT II, act 4*

corpus. In the map of act 1, the versions from this region once again demonstrate their independence from the other type II versions of *La condesita*.

The map of act 3 is more significant. First, unlike the other three, it comes quite close to duplicating the map generated from the global comparison of all type II versions with the *region 6 - type II* model version (Map 3). The strong affinity between the Andalusian model of act 3 and the third act of the poem in the vast majority of provinces where the double ballad is known confirms the high degree of uniformity among ballad type II versions, for, unlike the abbreviated first act, the third act of the Andalusian archetypal poem constitutes 36% of the entire model and is proportionately far more important than in the Leonese type I model. On the other hand, the map clearly reflects a contrast between the south, where the highest degrees (7-9) prevail, and the central and northwestern portions of the Peninsula, where the affinity ranges between degrees 4 and 6.

The regional character of act 4 (Map 12) is readily apparent. The affinitive relationship between the versions from Andalusia and those from the north virtually ceases to exist. The affinity between the model version and the whole of region 5 also diminishes greatly. Far more surprising is the fact that even Extremenian versions have little similarity to the Andalusian model of act 4 despite the extraordinary similarity between the two maps that compare the Andalusian archetypal version and the Extremenian model to all type II versions. These two maps reveal that while the vast majority of hemistichs characteristic of the Extremenian type II model survive in the Andalusian model, a lower proportion of the latter's hemistichs are retained in the Extremenian versions. Map 11 proves that this attenuation is largely the result of the singularity of the final act of the ballad in Andalusia. This observation is further confirmed by the Moroccan versions, which, on the whole, are also closely akin to those of Andalusia (see Map 3) and yet maintain only slight affinity (degree 3) with the Andalusian model of the last act. Unlike the situation in the previous series of maps for region 2, the regional character of the fourth act in the Andalusian model is not sufficient to determine the map image produced from the global comparison of the Andalusian model version with all type II versions (Map 3). This is due to the fact that in this model the final resolution, although distinctive, is proportionately less important: act 4 here represents only 31% of the total narration as opposed to 51% in the *region 2 - type I* model (Map 4). The variability of the final act is, nonetheless, apparent within Andalusia itself. Whereas Cádiz (degree 9), Granada (8), Huelva, Sevilla, and Córdoba (7) offer quite high proportions of affinity, Málaga (6) and Almería (5) denounce the existence of very real divergencies in the dénouement of their versions.

Map 12 is the most surprising of the series. The second act of the seventy-six Andalusian versions that have served to generate the archetypal act of the region do not seem to be particularly homogeneous since, in general, they have less affinity with the model than the versions from region 5 (New Castile and Murcia) and its prolongation as far as Teruel. Even two provinces as densely populated with type II versions as Huelva and Almería (which together make up 41% of the Andalusian type II versions) have a very limited affinitive relationship (degree 4) with the act 2 model they have largely defined. This can undoubtedly be explained by the fact that nearly half of the Andalusian versions lack two of the three segments that survive in the archetypal second act of the region.

Considered together, these fragmented act by act maps provide objective proof that, as Menéndez Pidal argued, the ballad narrative does not undergo parallel transformation throughout. The opening up of the system is manifested above all in the last act of the ballad, whether this act is accorded maximum development and elaboration or is reduced to a bare minimum. The singers of each region, and even within each region, inevitably exercise the greatest amount of creative activity after they have received the better part of the ballad's actantial message. While this fact merely confirms an observation made on other occasions, its verification with this corpus is extremely important, for it proves that even a final resolution so readily anticipated and highly formulaic as that of our ballad provokes variable reactions in those who carry on the modern oral ballad tradition. The initial act, on the other hand, is less susceptible to regionalization, undoubtedly because its functions, in addition to being highly formulaic, must lay the groundwork for the narration. Acts 2 and 3 are more open to regionalization. Act 3 (the encounter between the wife and the informant), more episodic and formulaic in nature, tends to be expressed via more universal archetypal verses (maps 7 and 11). Nevertheless, we can perceive in it, more than in act 1, certain regional tendencies (namely, the divergent personality of New Castile and Morocco in type I versions and the differentiation between type II versions in the south and those of New Castile and the north of the Peninsula). The most outstanding characteristic of act 2 (Maps 6 and 10), which relates the wife's departure, is its very great instability, even among versions of the same region or province. This instability is an indication of the singers' very diverse reactions to the act's functions which (as was demonstrated in other analyses) are of far greater transcendence for the underlying message of this ballad than a casual reading leads us to believe.

Unquestionably, the 612 ballad texts studied in this pilot project represent a mere fraction of those elaborated at one time and place or another in the oral life of *La condesita*. Nonetheless, as the preceding examples demonstrate, with the aid of modern technology statistical evidence can be obtained from the diachronic and synchronic analysis of this sample which clearly identifies a number of important, interrelated evolutionary trends—trends that cannot be perceived by simple manual comparison of the texts. Computer-based geographic and temporal analysis of the material, while only one method and one focus among many, can substantially enhance our knowledge of a ballad's history (a history less inaccessible than many have claimed). In this undertaking we stand to gain valuable insights into the mechanisms of reproduction and transformation of orally transmitted poetic narratives.

University of Washington

Notes

[1]For his comments on the affinities and differences between his methodology and that of the early Finnish folklorists, see Menéndez Pidal (1973:304, n.2).

[2]Following the generally accepted convention in *romancero* studies, I retain Menéndez Pidal's distinction between *version* ("complete or fragmentary text of a ballad, taken as a whole") and *variant* ("each of the details of which the version is comprised, in so far as this detail differs from the analogous contents of the other versions") (1973:299). Thus I use interchangeably the terms motif, element (of content), and variant.

[3]Interest in synchronic and diachronic consideration ought not to obscure the fact that in living folklore traditions spatial projection is in no small measure a reflection of diachronic movement. Consequently, time and space factors should not be conceived as two independent dimensions of

transformation.   Transmission theories often tend to suggest just such a dichotomy.   For example, J. W. Foster states "though the spatial dimension of transmission may in certain cases be more important than the temporal, most transmissionists think of transmission as a process in time" (1968:239).

[4]See, for example, S. G. Armistead's comments on the chronological and geographic continuity of the Hispanic ballad tradition (1985:109-10).

[5]Classification on the basis of linguistic areas traditionally distinguishes (minimally) among the following branches of the oral *romancero* tradition: 1)Peninsular Castilian linguistic domain, 2)Canary Islands, 3)Spanish-speaking America (South and Central America, Mexico, and Southwestern United States), 4)Moroccan Sephardic, 5)Eastern Sephardic, 6)Galicia, 7)Portugal, 8)Portuguese islands and overseas communities, 9)Brazil, and 10) Catalan linguistic domain.   A simple list of the Judeo-Spanish communities represented in but one major ballad collection (of 2150 texts) will suffice to underscore the geographic and cultural diversity implicit in this broad classification.   *Eastern Sephardic:*   Sarajevo, Belgrade, Vienna, Istib, Sofía, Stanke Dimitrov, Tatar-Pazardjik, Plóvdiv, Ruse, Bucarest, Rósiori, Salonika, Vérroia, Kastoría, Lárissa, Edirne, Istanbul, Bursa, Tekirdağ, Çanakkale, Izmir, Rhodes, Beirut, Damascus, and Jerusalem; *Northern Africa:*   Tangier, Tetuán, Arcila, Larache, Alcazarquivir, Casablanca, Morocco, Gibraltar, and Oran.   See Armistead (1978:1:34.)   For information on ballad-collecting activity in the various branches of the modern tradition, see A. Sánchez Romeralo (1979a:15-51), S. G. Armistead (1979c:53-60), and D. Catalán (1979:217-56), all in *The Hispanic Ballad Today: New Frontiers.*   For recent, major bibliographic sources for the various branches of the tradition, see S. G. Armistead (1985:111).

[6]See D. Catalán's reply (1959b:149-82) and Devoto's counter-reply (1969:11-44).

[7]This phenomenon will be discussed and documented at several points in the ensuing pages.   For further discussion of the extent to which the individual's possibilities of selection and invention are governed by local tradition, see D. Catalán, (1970-71:18-19).   Catalán's observations are substantiated in his reply to Devoto (1959b:155ff).   Even casual perusal of the geographically, temporally, and thematically organized ballad corpora published in the *Romancero tradicional del las lenguas hispánicas* series makes apparent the pressure of local tradition.

[8]See D. Catalán's detailed analysis of the final sequences of the ballad (1986:94-97).   Catalán's study further documents the profound alteration of latent semantic content in response to social changes in the referent with partial analyses of *Una fatal Ocasión, Muerte del duque de Gandía, Fratricida por amor, El moro que reta a Valencia,* and *Muerte del príncipe don Juan.* For other studies that discuss the relationship between prevailing social structures and traditional Hispanic narratives, see D. Catalán (1978:245-70), Manuel Gutiérrez Esteve (1978:551-72), J. Antonio Cid (1979:281-359), and Beatriz Mariscal de Rhett (1984-85:19-56 and 281-333).

[9]Since the early 1970's the majority of publications by D. Catalán and members of the Instituto Seminario Menéndez Pidal which he directs have dealt with multi-level analysis of variation and include theoretical discussion of the *romancero* as a model of open-structured narratives.   The basic tenets of this conception of the *romancero* first appear in D. Catalán (1976:55-62).   My doctoral dissertation (S. H. Petersen 1976a) constitutes the most exhaustive

analysis to date of poetic, verbal, and semantic transformation of a single Hispanic ballad.

[10]I refer to individual informants as "she" in recognition of the dominant role women have played as singers of *romances* in the last two centuries.

[11]Any field researcher who has recorded *romances* sung or recited by a group of informants has witnessed the lively debates that often ensue among neighbors or family members who argue over the "correct" text ("No, mama, that's not the way it goes. Let's see if I can get it right . . ."). Equally indicative of the textual memorization process are the comments made by informants who, upon faltering in their recitation, almost invariably either lament the passing of a friend or relative whose memory was vastly superior to their own or recommend consulting other family members or friends from whom they learned the ballad or with whom they used to sing (e.g., Felisa Fernández Naranjo, age 44, from Hinojosas de Calatrava, who, having forgotten portions of *La loba parda*, suggested the collectors seek out her father who learned the ballad as a boy and used to sing it to her and her brothers when they were children to put them to sleep. As promised, Eusebio Fernández Martínez, a 72–year–old shepherd, later sang a more complete, but otherwise essentially identical text with the help of his wife. See A. Sánchez Romeralo 1977:155–57.)

[12]The texts (cited from *CGR* 1A:199–200) also illustrate one of the difficulties of using the date of collection as a basis for measuring diachronic movement. As the older version was sung by a woman of 31 and the more recent version, by an 80–year–old woman who learned the ballad in her youth, the temporal "distance" separating the two is, in fact, minimal. On the other hand, as some areas of the tradition are extremely conservative and others highly innovative, the rhythm of change varies greatly from area to area, with the result that a considerable temporal "distance" often exists between contemporary versions originating in geographically distant areas. For other examples of the enormous fidelity to local tradition as well as additional commentary on the rhythms of transformation in the *romancero*, see *CGR* 1A:195–204.

[13]See Cid's lucid exposition of the larger implications of ritualization, contamination, and other factors that restrict traditional variation (325–35).

[14]For example, in 1985 the Seminario Menéndez Pidal's three–week field trip to León yielded some 2700 ballad texts on 110 traditional themes. Approximately 545 informants from 255 Leonese towns and villages contributed to this sizeable corpus. Naturally, not all the evidence recorded during these recent campaigns is of equal value, but superb versions of rare ballads—traditional *romances* scarcely documented in this century—continue to surface with surprising frequency. A list of some of the most invaluable testimony unearthed in the last fifteen years appears in D. Catalán's article in this issue.

[15]On the other hand, recent critical interest in traditional Hispanic cultural activities, and specifically the field research on the *romancero*, has served to rekindle popular interest in traditional cultural products and has thereby contributed to affirming and prolonging the life of this body of oral poetic discourse.

[16]In his study of *Muerte del príncipe don Juan* (1968a), for example, Bénichou explains "versions PV and RC contain the dying protagonist's

declaration that the wife he leaves behind is pregnant; therefore I include them in this group" (98–99), and further on, "As for the details or poetic elements that are scarcely found outside this group . . ." (101), and again, "They [the Portuguese texts] total sixteen versions, which must be divided into two subgroups on the basis of their divergent endings, that is, first, the ending with the projected marriage, and second, the ending with the young woman's complaint" (106, n.18).

[17]Although from a different perspective, few studies provide such conclusive evidence of the importance of geography as A. Sánchez Romeralo's article in this volume on *La loba parda*, a modern shepherd's ballad propagated exclusively along the six migration routes that traverse the Peninsula from north to south. Both in the relative homogeneity of the ballad (owing to the crisscrossing and convergent patterns of the sheep tracks and the common winter pastures) and in the few distinctive characteristics of one or another of the six groups of versions, geography is seen to function with singular clarity.

[18]The test ballad was selected on purely practical grounds (its availability in published form), but our prior knowledge of it (owing to the two earlier major geographic studies) proved extremely useful in anticipating system design requirements and in providing some means of verifying the validity of computer-generated analyses. The system, designed to accommodate many different types of ballad corpora, is fully described in my dissertation (Petersen 1976a). Numerous publications that include sample analyses have appeared since the mid-seventies: Catalán et al. (1975), Catalán (1976), and Petersen (1976b, 1978, 1979).

[19]For the present discussion only the first five digits of this eleven digit code require some explanation. They define each hemistich with reference to the thematic segment to which it "ideally" belongs (2 digits) and the element of information it "ideally" carries (3 digits). Any discrepancy between these five digits and the five that identity the thematic segment in which a given hemistich actually appears (*c* above) and the element of information it actually carries (*g* above) automatically denotes some type of reorganization or modification of the narrative structure and content of the poem. Both these interrelated phenomena—the archetypes' potential for opening up and acquiring new semantic values and their mobility (or capacity to function in different contexts within the overall narrative)—constitute an important mechanism of variation and are central to the whole question of structural transformation in oral poetic discourse.

[20]The figures become more significant when cross-tabulated to indicate precisely where the hemistichs that reproduce the archetypes of a given segment have travelled to. This information is even more useful when further broken down by geographic areas, period, or any other relevant internal variable.

[21]Given certain characteristics of our data base, the particular history of this ballad, and our coding system, the classification of versions by ballad type and region was considered the most valid and useful procedure for establishing diachronic and synchronic breaks in the corpus. The two oral ballad types (BT I and II), which largely eliminate the interference of diachrony from geography, constitute a more valid means of temporally classifying the versions of *La condesita* than the time periods that can be established for this corpus (see Petersen 1979:175–76, n.11). With respect to geography, although all

versions were identified by both province and region, only the latter classification guaranteed comparison of roughly equal populations. (With a larger data base, smaller geographic units—province, or provincial districts, or even townships—would be possible and clearly preferable.)

[22]To avoid unnecessary confusion in reading the chart, I have suppressed statistically irrelevant data.

[23]In as much as only 15% of the Levantine type I versions make use of archetype 44505511, little significance can be attributed to the apparent contradiction in Levant to the trends identified above.

[24]For a more detailed description of this system and the results of its application, see Petersen (1979:176–228 and 1976a:212–82). Future applications of this sort will benefit enormously from recent technological advances in computer cartography. Graphics–oriented microcomputers (with appropriate peripherals and software) provide a sophisticated tool for geographic data processing and mapmaking and largely free the individual researcher from costly and cumbersome mainframe computing.

Hunting for Rare *Romances* in the Canary Islands[1]

Maximiano Trapero

What is a Rare *Romance*?

Diego Catalán published in 1959 an article with this same title (1959a:445-77), dedicated to the Portuguese ballad tradition, in which he brought out the importance of that tradition for the knowledge of certain *romances* which because of their rarity were overlooked or lived in fragmented form in the oral life of other Hispanic traditions. Four *romances* were studied there,[2] four very powerful examples of how an oral text, a single version, can be the key to the correct interpretation of several *romances* which tradition has not preserved very well. Here we should like to call attention to the Canarian tradition as one of the most extraordinary in its preservation of *romances* that are extremely rare in modern oral tradition.

Ballad collecting can be compared to going hunting. One must always go out well prepared. It is true that the prey—the *romance*—appears when it is least expected and, frequently, when that type of example was not foreseen in that particular zone. But the search constitutes a very pleasant adventure. Ballad collecting today, given the extreme state of decadence in which the subject lives, is now an adventure on its own account, but if in addition those that are being sought are rare, the ones that are scarce everywhere, then the search turns into a true big-game hunt. Going out into the field and collecting whatever is there is the obligation of every collector, but if something valuable comes out of it, the obligation turns into joy. And what causes one *romance* to be more valuable than another? Evaluative judgments about traditional songs are very diverse and the criteria upon which they are based, very subjective. As Diego Catalán says:

In the "permanence" of the medieval historical *romancero* we do not know what to admire most, the collective memory, capable of retaining century after century details of a song that refers to a past event, whether real or imaginary, or the re-creative capacity of oral transmission which, at the same time that it recalls a poetic text, gives it new life, omitting, adding, or modifying certain motifs that make up the story (1969b:8).

If the phenomenon *romancero* were a closed genre, that is, a fixed repertory, and that repertory were considered to be the same at a given historical moment, it would seem obvious that selective criteria would favor aesthetic values only, but if, as it happens, it is a living phenomenon which perpetually renews itself, making and remaking itself during transmission, a changing repertory in which there are *romances* that are forgotten and die in oral life and others that are born and become popular, a phenomenon that goes beyond time and adapts itself to historical moments as disparate as the Middle Ages and the present, evaluative criteria necessarily become very heterogeneous. And in any case, the criteria of the scholar are not, nor are they ever apt to be, the same as those of the public singer.[3] The traditional singer always has a limited repertory and he clings to it as if it were the best and the only one. The investigator, for his part, is trying to put together a "puzzler" of a thousand and one entries in which many are always missing, and furthermore, a "puzzler" with an unknown number of entries. No one will ever be able to say what is the total ballad repertory of an epoch, that is, the oral *romancero*, or of a district, or even of a single informant. Novelty and surprise are always possible in a genre that lives by surprises, buried in the collective memory of a marginal people, without census or nomenclature.

The traditional *romancero*, despite the more or less systematic extensive searches that have been carried out during the twentieth century—and before—through all the territories where it is still alive, continues to be a source of frequent surprises such as the appearance of a still unpublished *romance* or others only known in fragmentary or contaminated versions which are insufficient for a true knowledge of the *romance* in question. The accumulation of many versions of the same ballad theme in a genre which is by definition changing and multiform is an absolute necessity for its study. From this point of view collecting many versions of *Gerineldo* or *La condesita* can be important for the knowledge of those *romances* in a determined district not previously investigated, but rarely can they offer new aspects to the general knowledge of those themes given the thousands of versions already collected. It is of much greater interest to collect a single version, even though it is fragmentary, of *Lanzarote y el ciervo del pie blanco*, for example, since it is a very rare *romance*, and still more interesting to be able to determine that a ballad like *Río Verde* has survived until today in oral tradition after more than four centuries of anonymity; and it turns out to be a real challenge to come upon a traditional *romance* about which there do not exist any literary references, like the case of *El esclavo que llora por su mujer*.

Collecting *Romances* in the Canary Islands

It can be said that the Canaries were populated with *romances* when they were populated with Spaniards, that is, at the same time that they entered into history, which was the very moment in which the *romancero* was living its most splendid life in Spain. Incorporated into the crown of Castile in the fifteenth century, the Spaniards who went to the islands came from many different regions of the Peninsula, especially from Andalusia, Extremadura, Castile, and the Galicia-Asturias-León region. They arrived, just as when they went to America a short while later, with a multitude of epic-lyric songs in their memory and some little book or other in their pockets. Unfortunately, at that moment there was not any Martín Nucio in the Canaries to collect the texts that were then popular, for which reason we know nothing directly about the ballad repertory that populated and inhabited the Canaries in the first centuries following their conquest. Only an occasional indirect reference of some chronicler of the islands assures us of the existence of the genre in the seventeenth century.[4] The survival by oral means in the islands of a *romancero* with ancient roots guarantees, through textual criticism, the implantation of the *romancero* in the Canaries from a very early date, thereafter developing autonomously and coming to form one of the best defined branches of the Pan-Hispanic *romancero*. Alongside these minimal references of primitive chroniclers, the existence of an inquisitorial trial against a series of religious ballads at the end of the eighteenth century,[5] and very brief pieces of information left us by travelers to the islands in the eighteenth and nineteenth centuries (see Catalán 1969a:1:3-5), no *romance* text from the Canaries was known until the threshold of the twentieth century.

The history of ballad collecting in the Canaries is told by Diego Catalán in the introduction of what is to be the first part of the *Romancero general de las Islas Canarias: La flor de la marañuela* (1969a:1:3-46), a "collection of collections," which brings together all the texts, both published and unpublished, that were gathered by different people from 1920 to 1966. This collection, which is splendid (682 versions of 155 ballad themes of great interest), represents very disproportionately the tradition of the various islands of the archipelago.   Collecting efforts had concentrated on two islands, Tenerife and La Palma, and the other five had remained practically untouched.   Out of the total of 682 versions, some 400 are from Tenerife (the whole first volume), about a hundred from La Palma, 66 from Lanzarote, 54 from Gran Canaria, 23 from La Gomera, 11 from El Hierro, and only 3 from Fuerteventura.

The different islands of the Canaries have in many respects very defined and individual profiles as far as popular culture is concerned.   And this is true not only because certain ideological or pressure groups or even individuals fight to have each island display distinctive characteristics, which exist within the conglomerate, but also because geography and history have taken a different form in each one.   Thus it is that, although they comprise an archipelago in which all participate in the same common regional cultural coordinates, each island has its own cultural personality. Such being the case, one must not give up the search for the traditional *romancero* in the Canaries, as Diego Catalán very intelligently advised:

> This *Flor de la marañuela* simply hopes to be the first part of the *Romancero general de las Islas Canarias*. If what has been brought together up to this point suffices to demonstrate the richness and the rarity of the insular *romancero*, in no way does it exhaust the subterranean store of the Canaries' ballad tradition, which we should all help to bring forth. (1969a:1:vii).

The Canaries, Marginal Zone of the *Romancero*

In the last third of the nineteenth century, when there began to be a glimmering of the survival of the old Spanish *romancero* by means of oral transmission, a general belief was established among the students of the *romancero* that the tradition had been displaced to the more marginal zones of the Peninsula, that is, Portugal, Catalonia, Asturias, and, to a great degree, Andalusia. It was Menéndez Pelayo who most stoutly affirmed:

> Although the greatest and the best part of the Castilian *romances* have only come to us by written tradition (whether in Gothic broadsides or *romanceros* of the sixteenth century), it is not a small or insignificant fact that they still live on the lips of the people, especially in certain districts and population groups which, because of their relative isolation, have been able to retain this poetic store until today, which, apparently, has disappeared almost completely in the central regions of the Peninsula, in the provinces which by antonomasia we call Castilian, which was the cradle of the *romance* or, at least, where it attained its greatest degree of vitality and epic force (1945:9:151).

He appeared to have arrived at such a conclusion after the first explorations in the nineteenth century that were begun by the pioneers of the modern oral *romancero*: Almeida Garrett, Teófilo Braga, Milá y Fontanals, Mariano Aguiló, el Marqués de Pidal, and Menéndez Pelayo himself. If tradition as such was reluctant to come out into the light of day in peripheral geography, which was studied, why should it not be in the center, in Castile, where there had scarcely been any serious, perservering attempts. In the supplement that Menéndez Pelayo added to the *Primavera y flor de romances* of Wolf and Hofmann, he compiled *romances* collected from oral tradition in Asturias, Andalusia, Extremadura, Galicia, Catalonia, and Portugal together with ballads which had come from Judeo-Spanish communities in the East. This copious collection of more than two hundred texts was a harbinger of the extraordinary harvest which was to be confirmed years later. All in all, none or almost none of those *romances* came from the center of the Peninsula, old Castile. It was believed, therefore, that the *romancero*, engendered during the Middle Ages in Castile, with the passing of the centuries had abandoned its focal area to take refuge in the collective memory of the peripheral areas.

Menéndez Pidal would have to expend much effort to undo these beliefs and to forcibly demonstrate that Castile not only had

not forgotten its old epic minstrel songs, but also that it could
compete in abundance and elegance with those of the periphery.
The persistent silence of the *romancero* in Castile was only
apparent, for on inciting it skillfully, it could offer texts as
extraordinary and as archaic as those of any other region, even
including some that were unknown up to then outside of Castilian
territory.[6]

Field expeditions and studies about the *romancero* in Castile
multiplied from the twenties on to such an extent that in 1953 its
principal scholar, Ramón Menéndez Pidal, said: "It seems incredible
to us now how the ballad tradition of the center of Spain, which is
seen at present in such great abundance, could remain so unknown,
its existence so persistently denied for a whole century"
(1953:2:305). Exploration has continued and there has been an
intensification of the systematic character of the fieldwork. But in the same way exploration has also intensified in
other peripheral zones: the Canaries, Portugal and her Atlantic
islands, Asturias, the northern part of León, the mountain region of
Santander and Palencia, Galicia, Aragón, Catalonia, and,
exhaustively, the Sephardic communities of Spanish origin in
northern Africa and on the eastern shores of the Mediterranean.
The results in the form of *romanceros* and the experience of those
who have been collectors in the center as well as in the periphery
have always been the same: of course the *romancero* is alive in
Castile, but does it have the same vitality as in the periphery?
The most recent field expeditions through the plains of Segovia,
Valladolid, Soria, Burgos, Palencia, León, and Zamora offer much
poorer results than those obtained in the northwest, for example.
It is true that the mountainous region of León and, by extension,
the isolated zones of the northwest part of the Peninsula is a
privileged enclave in the preservation of the traditional *romancero*,
a crossroads where all the traditions converge, but the investigator
discovers, as he goes down to the plains, that the repertory
becomes poorer and shorter and that the tradition is known to a
smaller percentage of people. Recently published collections of
romances from the peripheral zones, Portugal, Madeira, the Azores,
northern León, and even the Canaries are superior in every respect
to those of the center in richness of repertory, in abundance of
versions, in the plenitude of texts, in rarer *romances*, and in more
archaic versions.

Therefore, simply because of the marginality of the Canaries

with respect to Castile, even before recognizing the special treasure
contained in the Canaries, the archaic and conservative character of
its *romancero* was already being predicted. Menéndez Pelayo
announced it at the end of the nineteenth century:

> I have already indicated my suspicion that in the
> Canaries there may exist old *romances* brought there in
> the fifteenth century by Castilian and Andalusian
> conquerers. If they should come to light, it would be a
> great find, because in analogous cases it has been
> observed that insular versions are more archaic and
> purer than those of the Continent, as has happened in
> Mallorca with relation to Catalonia, in Madeira and the
> Azores with relation to Portugal (1945:9:332).

And Menéndez Pidal repeated it again fifty years later when the
results of the first fieldwork in the Archipelago were already
beginning to be known:

> With respect to the Canaries, it is necessary to
> repeat what has been said for America. If its tradition
> appears very weak, it is because it has not had enough
> investigators. It is not clear, if the Portuguese insular
> tradition is strong and conservative, why it should not
> be the same in the Canaries as it is in Madeira
> (1953:2:356).

And then he evaluated the first fruits of this investigation:

> These archaisms assure us that the tradition of the
> Canaries is as dense as any. I hope that it will be
> explored deeply, because it will be an essential way to
> explain the oldest tradition that emigrated to America,
> since the importance of the Canary Islands in the
> colonization of America is very great (1953:2:357).

The prediction of one and the sound suspicions of the other
have come to be fully confirmed. In the Canaries a very archaic
and conservative branch of the ballad tradition took refuge. It is
even possible to hear today *romances* that have disappeared
everywhere else, the rarest *romances* in modern oral tradition, only
preserved outside of the Canaries by a few Sephardic communities
of North Africa or of Eastern Europe who have always proven
themselves to be the most zealous guardians of the old Spanish
epic-lyric patrimony. But not only the rarest *romances*; any
version of the Canarian *romancero* "presents an unmistakable seal

of antiquity; they are versions that have evolved little, close to those that are recorded in the oldest songbooks and *romanceros*" (Menéndez Pidal 1955:5).

Thus it is that the store of *romances* should never be considered exhausted, especially since, as in the Canaries, there remain so many *lacunae* that have not been explored in the studies carried out up to the sixties.

New Collecting Efforts

From 1966 (the year of the last field expeditions published in *La flor de la marañuela*) until 1980 there was a respite in ballad collecting in the Canaries, despite the fact that there was available a good fieldwork manual developed by M. Jesús López de Vergara and Mercedes Morales (1955), two of the best collectors in the Canaries whose findings, mostly in Tenerife, are included in *La flor de la marañuela*. It is with the decade of the eighties that field-work was begun again in several points on the islands by various people. It did not correspond to any systematic attempt at collecting, only to the desire to show examples of popular culture of a given zone wider in scope than just the *romancero* by gathering *romances* alongside of *canciones*, proverbs, riddles, stories, dances, and other folkloric genres, or just collecting what the informants would say to the generic question: "Do you know any old ballads?"

As far as we are concerned, it was in 1979 that we undertook the task in the Canaries. It coincided with a new phase of the Seminario Menéndez Pidal, the heir to the very rich ballad materials of the Menéndez Pidal family together with its aims and methods. Stimulated by the inexhaustible energy of its director, Diego Catalán, two objectives were proposed: one, the systematic exploration of certain peninsular zones which had produced nothing in former searches; and two, the formation of a group of young investigators who could initiate these explorations in their usual places of residence. The enterprise seemed to be, and in fact is, the last attempt to collect what oral tradition has amassed. The substantial changes that have affected Spanish rural life in recent years inevitably portend that the inherited traditional knowledge will die when its present possessors, the elders of the villages and towns, die, without having passed on this knowledge to the coming generations. There is no more oral transmission, and the younger generations know nothing at all about what remains of the

tradition in the older people.   Furthermore, the tradition exists as
a residual product in the oldest people, but not as a living
phenomenon.   In spite of everything, the new attempt to collect
ballads turned out to be providential because it did take place in
time.   With a great deal of effort and many difficulties it has been
possible to recover what one would have been able to recover at
the beginning of the century.   This means that up to the present
there has remained the bulk of what had been traditional for
centuries.   And thus it can be said that the Seminario Menéndez
Pidal in only five years has more than duplicated the ballad store
that had been formed in more than a century of collecting.   And
the same is true with respect to the second objective.   In the
Canaries, counting only our collections, the number of *romances*
brought together and published in *La flor de la marañuela* has
been tripled.

Our first investigation centered on a very limited zone in the
southeast of the island of Gran Canaria.   And the results were
astonishing (see Trapero 1982): in only four localities we managed
to collect 504 versions of 141 different *romances*.   It is true that
the figures do not distinguish between the religious ballads, those
from chapbooks, the *vulgares*, and the truly traditional ballads, but
it is an impressive lesson as to what extent anywhere in the
Canaries popular memory is capable of preserving such a fantastic
amount of collective knowledge.   What was collected in Gran
Canaria is, on the other hand, to a certain degree a living tradition
among the women workers packing tomatoes.   But it was not
limited to the southeast.   The investigation continued through the
whole island, with different characteristics in the various zones of
the south or the north, of the coast, the mountains, or what is in
between, and we amassed a collection of more than one thousand
versions, aside from those already published from the southeast, all
of which gives an idea of what is possible from a detailed and
persistent search.

After Gran Canaria came the island of Hierro, the smallest of
the archipelago and the least populated, which with only 6500
inhabitants gave us a harvest of 175 versions of 68 *romances*.
There the *romancero* is dead, pure archeology which is only
revived when someone asks for it.   An obvious example: in the
interval between carrying out the fieldwork (1982) and the
publishing of the book containing what was collected (Trapero
1985) in the summer of 1985, five of our best informants   had

died. Three years' delay in carrying out the fieldwork would have meant the loss of a third of what we gathered, with some of the best of the *romances*, including among them *Virgilios* and *La princesa peregrina*, both unknown in the Canaries up to that time and extremely rare in peninsular Spain.

La Gomera followed the island of Hierro and there we found paradise. We had written about Hierro in the prologue:

> The *romancero* that is still alive in the oral tradition of Hierro is extraordinary, so much so that it would be difficult to find another place with a similar geographical extension that is comparable in the wealth of its repertory.   Historic, geographic, and social conditions are unique and, along with them, their folkloric and literary traditions (Trapero 1985:37).

But after coming to know La Gomera, we had to rectify what we had said. La Gomera is not a lost paradise like so many places in Spain, Portugal, or the Hispanic world, but a paradise in which *romances* live today as they must have lived in the most favored places during the sixteenth and seventeenth centuries. It is an island where singing and dancing *romances* is a daily exercise of its whole population.   The island has at present about 25,000 inhabitants, and there we succeeded in collecting more than 400 versions of more than 140 ballad themes.   Among them appear some titles of ballads that are the rarest in modern oral tradition, including one that is unique: *Río Verde, El Cid pide parias al rey moro, Lanzarote, París y Elena, Fratricidio por amor.*

Our investigations are continuing, and now we are going on to Fuerteventura, an island about which we know absolutely nothing, and afterwards to other places until we obtain the complete map of the oral *romancero* of the Canaries.

An important aspect of our searches and studies has been music, a matter which had been completely ignored and which shows us the other face of the *romancero*. Diego Catalán had called attention to it already in the Primer Coloquio Internacional sobre el *Romancero*: "Another gap that we have to fill is that of music. No one of the collectors was a musicologist, and in the field expeditions they did not have the help of tape recorders" (1972:146). Today we have easily manipulable machines with high fidelity which make the collecting of materials in the field much easier.   Afterwards, in the tranquility of the study, we have

counted on the collaboration of a very capable musicologist, Lothar
Siemens Hernández, who has been fully aware of how neglected the
important reality of the music of the *romances* is, neglected not
only in the *romancero* of the Canaries but also in the *romancero*
in general.

But we are not alone.   Other collectors on their own
initiative have obtained new and always valuable versions in other
places on the islands: Talio Noda on the island of La Palma and
in the center of Gran Canaria, Francisco Eusebio Bolaños in the
northwest of Gran Canaria, Benigno León Felipe in the south of
Tenerife, Manuel J. Lorenzo Perera on the island of Hierro and in
the north of Tenerife, and others.   The interest in popular culture
awakened to a great degree by the political process of regional
autonomy widespread in Spain during the last few years also affects
the Canaries.   Today we are at a crossroads in which a radical
change of customs threatens to extinguish a whole traditional
culture.   In collecting what remains of those old popular
manifestions, welcome will be given to all who apply themselves to
the task of saving it for future generations—if not the tradition
itself, at least historical testimony to its existence.

The Canaries, a Heterogeneous Ballad Tradition

For those who know the Canaries from hearing or reading
about them, it may seem strange that each island has its cultural
peculiarities, its own signs of identity.   There are, of course,
characteristics common to all of them, recognized as such when the
Canaries are compared to other regions.   It could not be otherwise,
since it is a question of islands that belong geographically to Africa
and to the Atlantic but which are historically and culturally
European and Spanish.   But looking from within the Canaries
themselves, one cannot help observing the outstanding traits of
each island.   Geography began differentiating them, and history
continued the process.   The origin of the aborigines is not known,
nor even if the islands were all inhabited by the same people.
Archaeology has not even been able to come upon minimal remains
that guarantee communication among the islands, but, nevertheless,
it has demonstrated sufficiently the cultural and ethnic differences
among their inhabitants.   Incorporated into the crown of Castile in
the fifteenth century after a period of conquest that lasted almost
a century (from 1402 in Lanzarote and Fuerteventura to 1496 in

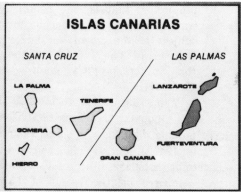

Tenerife), they were brought in on different terms. Some (Fuerteventura, Lanzarote, Hierro, and Gomera) became islands of *señorío*, that is, with an overlord, prolonging their dependency for several centuries; others (Gran Canaria, Tenerife, and La Palma) became islands of *realengo*, subject to the state, a situation which has prolonged to the present day certain socio-economic structures that had a determining effect upon the life of each one of them. To cap it all, nature also acted capriciously. To some it gave abundant water, like La Palma and Tenerife, and to others extremely dry conditions, like Lanzarote and Fuerteventura; some are high and mountainous, others low and sandy; some have abundant resources, others have scarcely any; some have easy access to the sea, for others it is almost inaccessible. Some have been in constant contact with other peoples and other cultures, with windows and doors open to every type of influence from abroad (Gran Canaria and Tenerife); others have been completely turned inward without any contact with the exterior world except that of their own inhabitants who left their island as emigrants, not to return (Hierro and Gomera). An English seaman, who came to know the islands well from his trips there in the middle of the eighteenth century, said of the latter:

La Gomera and El Hierro are so poor that no ship arrives there from Europe or America; nor are the inhabitants permitted any commerce with the Spanish West Indies, for they are not so completely under the jurisdiction of the Spanish crown as are [Gran] Canaria,

Tenerife, or La Palma since they have an overlord or proprietor, that is, the Count of La Gomera. But it would be very advantageous for them to be completely subject to the crown, for never was the saying so true that says "The rubbish of the king is more valuable than other people's grain," as in this case (Glas 1982:133).

It is not surprising, then, that the ballad tradition, which is one of the popular traditions established in its communities, should have notable differences. A few examples will serve.

In 1948 J. Pérez Vidal, one of the most knowledgeable people concerning popular culture of the Canaries and chief investigator of the *romancero* on the island of La Palma, published an article entitled "Romances con estribillo y bailes romancescos" (1948:197-241) in which he revealed the curious fact, unknown up to that time, that on La Palma *romances* were sung with a refrain called *responder* (answer), which was inevitably intercalated at the end of every four octosyllabic verses. Later critics generalized the phenomenon for all of the Canaries without investigating further, and caused the references to the Canaries in ballad studies to invariably report that on the islands *romances* are always sung with their corresponding *responderes.* (see Débax 1982:100-101). It was necessary to discover on Gran Canaria that each *romance* had its own melody and that the phenomenon of the *responderes* was unknown. Thus an important difference opened up: on Gran Canaria the *romancero* behaves, the same as any place on the Peninsula, like an individual song, while on La Palma, according to the information of Pérez Vidal, it is a genre that demands the help of a soloist to sing the ballad and a chorus for the *responderes.* Ballads are sung on Lanzarote and Fuerteventura just as they are on Gran Canaria, to judge by the few examples from the former that we have, that is, without a refrain and each one with its own melody. Conclusion—the phenomenon of the *responder* is not general in the *romancero* of the Canaries. Our investigations on the islands of Hierro and La Gomera clarified the situation: the phenomenon of the *responderes* of La Palma extends also to La Gomera and Hierro. It remains to be determined what happens on Tenerife where, paradoxically, despite its being the first and the best investigated in *La flor de las marañuela*, nobody has studied this matter. Thus, aside from the island of Tenerife, the Canaries are divided into two well-defined blocks, as far as the phenomenon of ballad refrains is concerned, which coincide with the present administrative division into two provinces: on the western islands or the province of Tenerife, all of the *romances* are sung with *responder*; on the eastern islands or the province of Las Palmas, the refrain is unknown.

A phenomenon parallel to refrains is that of music. Where the *romances* are sung with a refrain, the music is always the same and it has a specific name according to the island: *la meda* on Hierro and La Palma, *el tambor* on La Gomera, which is to say, with slight variation, the music is the same on all three islands. On the contrary, where the refrain does not exist, each *romance* has its own particular melody just as it does on the Peninsula and everywhere else.

The lack of knowledge about the *romancero* of Hierro and especially of La Gomera has deprived critics of a very unusual fact: the survival of a ballad dance, the *baile del tambor* on La Gomera, surely the last ballad dance of Spain and the last evidence we have of the *romancero* as a collective festive genre (Trapero 1986a).

A ballad like *Gerineldo*, perhaps the most popular in modern tradition everywhere, to judge by the lists in *La flor de la marañuela*, was exceedingly rare in the Canaries. New field expeditions, however, have shown that its role in insular tradition is very irregular, abundant in some (Gran Canaria), scarce in others (Tenerife), and unknown in still others (La Gomera). And the same happens with other very popular ballads like *Tamar*, very well known in Gran Canaria but undocumented up to now in the remainder of the islands. On the other hand, *El caballero burlado* (preceded by *La infantina* and with the conclusion of *La hermana cautiva*), which is quite rare in modern Spanish tradition, is the most frequent ballad on all of the Canary Islands. The *romances* of *Sildana* and *Delgadina* are abundant in the Canaries as independent ballads, but on Gran Canaria a new type predominates, the fusion of both themes in a unique *romance*, following the Portuguese model in this case.

Finally, new explorations have uncovered many new themes unknown before in the Canaries, some even completely unpublished in the modern Hispanic *romancero*, like *Río Verde*, *El Cid pide parias al rey moro*, *Pensativo estaba el Cid*, or *El esclavo que llora por su mujer*.

The Canaries were always the meeting point, a bridge between two continents, a shelter for all voyagers. The tradition

that lives on the islands is the heir of many influences, and with
it, of course, the *romancero*.   They received everything   from
Spain, the largest measure from the Andalusian *romancero*, but
also from the northwestern part of the Peninsula.   They also
received   a   great   deal   from   Portugal,   especially   from
Trás-os-Montes, and almost always by way of the archipelago of
Madeira.   Jewish influence is in evidence in the *romancero* of the
Canaries, although we do not know very well yet, because of the
lack of studies about the matter, how and when they reached
there.   And from America there returned what had previously
come from here, but americanized.   The Canaries are, with respect
to America, a round trip, a necessary bridge between the two
shores of the Atlantic which served to carry the culture of this
shore there and to bring it back again.   Therefore the *romancero*
of the Canaries is heterogeneous and unique.

The Rarest *Romances* of the Canaries

    It is difficult to know where to begin.   Diego Catalán, who
based his study of several individual ballads on the tradition of the
Canaries, in his introduction to the *Romancerillo canario* stated
that *Lanzarote y el ciervo del pie blanco* is the most extraordinary
one (1955:n.p.).   Before that Menéndez Pidal, when the tradition of
the Canaries was still not well known, had selected as being the
most outstanding the *Rapto de Elena* (or *Paris y Elena*) and *El
conde preso* (1953:2:357).   These three *romances* stood out for
being, if not unique versions, almost unique in the general
panorama of the modern *romancero*.   *Lanzarote*, which had only
been known in an Andalusian version collected in Almería in 1914,
presupposed the survival of a medieval European theme from the
Arthurian cycle by means of a process of oral transmission.   The
Rapto de Elena attested to the great archaism of the ballad
tradition in the Canaries and, at the same time, to the tie between
its *romancero* and the Sephardic, the only areas in which it has
been preserved.   As for *El conde preso*,   Menéndez Pidal's
attention was attracted by the primitive form of its versions,
comparable to those from Morocco, and so archaic that he said
that they had "visos de *chanson de geste*" (1953:2:357).
    Diego Catalán studied these three ballads extensively,
comparing the versions from the Canaries with the old tradition
and with other known modern traditions, and to them he added
three others, *El idólatra*, *El conde don Pero Vélez*, and *El poder*

del canto, as the most extraordinary and exotic ballads of the *romancero* of the Canaries (1970:82–117, 167–85, 270–80). Today, from the perspective of more extensive knowledge about the reality of the case and after many new discoveries, the list would have to be lengthened, its order changed and the previous data re-evaluated. The following order of ballads does not indicate order of importance. From those studied by Diego Catalán:

a. *El idólatra* is a *romance* with documentation that is abundant and widespread.

b. *Poder del canto* is one more version, although a very unusual one, of *El conde Niño*, a ballad which is very popular on the islands and everywhere (*Romancerillo* #10, *Flor* #439).

c. *El conde don Pero Vélez*, a very rare ballad of the sixteenth century, known in modern tradition in a single version from Tenerife (*Flor* #10), has not reappeared in the Canaries or elsewhere.

d. A new peninsular version of *Lanzarote* was collected in Beas del Segura (Jaén) a few years ago (Catalán 1979:229–32), but we now can offer many more from the Canaries. It seems as if the islands were the refuge sought by this *romance* in its modern life. To the three known versions from Tenerife, one must now be added from Gran Canaria and 119 from La Gomera—another good example of the arbitrary and capricious distribution of the *romancero* throughout Hispanic territory. What could cause *Lanzarote* to be forgotten everywhere while the inhabitants of La Gomera go on singing it as one of their favorites?

e. There were three Canaries' versions of *Paris y Elena* (aside from the Sephardic ones), one of them from La Gomera. And there we collected in 1983 a new version, which, however, was contaminated and somewhat defective.

f. *El conde preso* is today a ballad that is quite well known and documented in the Peninsula. In the Canaries new versions have appeared in Tenerife which maintain the epic style that Menéndez Pidal observed (Rodríguez Abad 1984:93–102).

Another series of rare *romances* that are rare in the general tradition and unpublished up to now in the Canaries are the following:

g. *Virgilios*, a novelesque *romance* of the sixteenth century which attributes to the Latin poet a courtly love affair in *romance* style. The protagonist is Virgil as he was popularized in the

Middle Ages.   The ballad was very widespread in olden times judging by the ballad lists we have, but today it is practically extinct in peninsular tradition although among the Sephardic Jews it is very popular.   We found it six times on the island of Hierro, and those versions clarified a very confused interpretation that had been given to the *romance* (Trapero in press).

h. *La princesa peregrina*, which is found only in the Sephardic tradition (in both the Northern Africa branch and that of Eastern Europe) and in the Portuguese tradition (on the continent and on its Atlantic islands), has also been collected on Hierro, where it is very well known.   It is a ballad that was not documented in the old tradition but which, nevertheless, given its present distribution and its configuration, appears to be old.

i. *¿Por qué no cantáis la bella?* is a *romance* which has been divinized, becoming one of the most frequent of the religious ballads but one which is very rare in its primitive form, being known by only a single peninsular version (from Huesca) and, of course, many Jewish ones.   In the Canaries it had been documented contaminating several versions of *Blancaflor y Filomena*.   Now we have succeeded in collecting it in its "divine" form, as well as quite a few times contaminating *Blancaflor y Filomena* (on Gran Canaria and La Gomera) and *Presagios del labrador* (on Gran Canaria), and twice as an autonomous ballad in its most primitive version.

j. Pérez Vidal tells us that among the unedited material he possesses from the island of La Palma collected in the forties, there is a version of *Isabel de Liar*, a historical ballad which is very rare in present-day oral tradition and was dispersed in such a way as to make its presence in the Canaries improbable.

Our investigations on the islands of Hierro and La Gomera have furnished us with a series of ballads about captives, among which there are four from the Canaries without any known documentation or reference.   We have entitled them: k. *Cautiva liberada por su marido*, l. *Cautiva y liberada*, m. *Rescate del enamorado*, and n. *Joven liberado por su enamorada* (Trapero 1985:#100, #102, #103, #110).   Judging by their narrative structure and their poetic language they appear to be late *romances*, possibly from the eighteenth century, popularized by means of broadsides and strongly traditionalized.

o. The last one in this group, the *Fratricidio por amor*, is a very rare *romance* collected by us on La Gomera and only known elsewhere by seven Sephardic versions (five from Tangier and two from Tetuán) and one Catalan version of the nineteenth century. It is a blind man's ballad from the end of the sixteenth century that relates an event that took place in Málaga: the execution of a woman convicted for having confessed to the murder of her sister whom she had killed out of love for her brother-in-law, hoping to supplant her sister in the conjugal bed. The old *romance* is to be found in the *Flor de varios romances nuevos* of Pedro de Moncayo (Barcelona, 1591) as a very clear example of the type of ballad about current events that circulated by means of broadsides. But it became traditionalized and attained an artistic excellence it did not have before, although to a different degree in each one of the three branches (Sephardic, Catalan, and Canaries) that preserve it.

We have left for the end the rarest of all, those that were unknown in the Canaries or in the *romancero* as a whole, those that have been documented for the first time in oral tradition, the last ones to appear, truly the four major trophies of the hunt. One is a frontier ballad, another a ballad about captives, and two are about the Cid: *Río Verde, El esclavo que llora por su mujer, El Cid pide parias al rey moro*, and *Pensativo estaba el Cid*.

p. *Río Verde* (or *Romance de Sayavedra*) is a frontier ballad from the end of the fifteenth century. It is based on a historical episode in which the Christian troops of Juan de Saavedra, mayor of Castelar de la Frontera, suffer a complete disaster in their attack on the Moors of Sierra Bermeja, along the Verde river in the present province of Málaga. The event occurred in 1448 and soon was turned into a *romance*. Its popularity must have been very great, since in the middle of the sixteenth century it was circulating in chapbooks with variants as notable as those offered by another version of the end of the century collected by Pérez de Hita in his *Guerras civiles de Granada* (Trapero 1986b). It had remained forgotten from that time on, dead as far as oral tradition was concerned, until we collected it in La Gomera in 1983. The story of its discovery and of its reconstruction as the result of several interviews is told elsewhere as an example of the decadence in which the modern *romancero* lives and the efforts demanded of the collectors in order to bring it to light (Trapero in press). The version from La Gomera begins as follows:

Sobre ti, Peña Bermeja,	Upon you, Red Mountain,
murió gran caballería,	many horsemen died,
murieron curas y condes	priests and counts died

y mucha gente moría,	and many people died,
murieron curas y condes	priests and counts died
en la ciudad de Valía,	in the city of Valía,
murió aquel que va juyendo	the one died who is fleeing
por un ramonal p'arriba.	up the sheep run.

q. *El Cid pide parias al rey moro* appeared in La Gomera, collected for the first time by Martha E. Davis when she was investigating its popular festivals in 1984, one year after our own investigations and from an informant who had been one of ours (surely the only informant from La Gomera who knows it, and he did not mention it to us). The *romance* is extraordinary for every possible reason: in the first place because it assures the survival in the modern *romancero* of one of the most famous of the old *romances* which were believed to be completely forgotten; in second place because it is a splendid, very complete version which seems to re-create the old text, even improving it as truly traditional literature always does. It is the same *romance* that with the title of *Por el val de las Estacas* is recorded in Durán (1849-51:#750) as coming from a sixteenth-century manuscript. In his note he says: "It belongs to the class of old ballads, and is one of the few that have been preserved without much alteration. We have not seen it in print, nor preserved by tradition anywhere else" (Durán 1945:1:492). It is also included in Wolf and Hofmann (1856:#31), citing Durán as the source. The version from La Gomera begins as follows:

Por las vegas de Granada	Across the plains of Granada
baja el Cid al mediodía	the Cid goes at noonday
con su caballo Babieco	with his horse Babieco
que a par del viento corría	who ran like the wind
y doscientos caballeros	and two hundred knights
que lleva en su compañía.	whom he has in his company.

r. We collected *Pensativo estaba el Cid* on Gran Canaria from the same informant who later gave us another very rare ballad, *El esclavo que llora por su mujer.* The Cid ballad is a new *romance* that has only literary, not traditional, antecedents. It appeared for the first time in *Flor de varios y nuevos romances* (Valencia, 1591, with a license of 1588); it is reproduced without any variation whatsoever in the *Cancionero general* of 1600 and in the *Romancero del Cid* of Escobar (Lisbon, 1605); it provided Guillén de Castro with the plot for his *Mocedades del Cid*, and it was included as an old ballad by Wolf and Hofmann (#28). Never have traditional versions of this ballad been collected, although there are a few of another ballad of the same cycle, *Rodriguillo venga a su padre* or *El Cid y el conde Lozano*, which has the same literary origin.   Although the Canaries' version is fragmentary, it offers unequivocal proof of its traditionalization.   It begins:

Pensativo está Rodrigo,	Rodrigo is thoughtful,
pensativo y enroñado	thoughtful and annoyed
por no poderse vengar	because he can't avenge
de su padre don Sagrario.	his father Don Sagrario.
Se va para el monte Olivo	He goes to Mount Olive
donde están los hortelanos,	where the gardeners are,
se ha hallado una espada vieja	he has found an old sword
del gran Román castellano.	of the great Castilian Román.

s. And finally a ballad of captives, *El esclavo que llora por su mujer*, which deserves special attention and poses many specific questions applicable to the entire *romancero*:   1.   Is it still possible to collect from oral tradition *romances* without either old or modern antecedents that are unknown to critics?   2.   Do the narrative structure and the language of the *romance* suffice to stamp it as old even without antecedents?   3.   We know that when a *romance* has been recorded by the Jews who were descendants of those who participated in the Spanish Diaspora it has the likelihood, if not the certainty, of being an old *romance*, but if this *romance* exists in some other place is it possible that it did not have a Spanish origin?   4.   How can one establish boundaries for the identification of a ballad theme when the textual discourse of their respective versions is so varied?   5.   Are two versions of the same theme but with maximum variation of discourse the product of individual re-creations from the same origin or, the other way around, despite having different origins and forms of discourse, has their thematic content become similar because of the presence of the same widely dispersed folkloric motif?

El esclavo que llora por su mujer: A *Romance* Unknown in the Canaries

As the fruit of one of these hunting expeditions for rare *romances*, we want to tell about one that is truly exceptional.   It is so completely unknown that it scarcely has a name; it is so rare that its character and origin are unknown; it is so challenging that it demands a more thorough study than we can dedicate to it here; and it is so beautiful that it is a joy to be able to present it. It goes as follows:

Peinándose está el cautivo
al pie de un verde naranjo,
peinándose está el cautivo
y lágrimas derramando.
5   En estas razones y otras
la morilla que ha llegado:
—¿Qué tienes, cristiano mío,
de qué te aflijes, mi esclavo?
—¿Para qué le digo nada
10 si no ha de ser remediado?
—Puede ser que se remedie
si se lo digo a tu amo.
—Tengo una mujer bonita,
niños chiquitos al lado.
15 —¿Habrá mujer en el mundo
que a mí se haya igualado?
—Tan bonita como vos,
sólo su rostro es más albo.
En estas razones y otras
20 el moro se ha presentado:
—En esta noche el gran perro
mi viña me irá cavando,
yo le daré con que crí(v)e
cien callos en cada mano,
25 la azada pesa cien libras,
el cabo pesa otro tanto.
En estas razones y otras
la noche que se ha acercado,
el moro se ha recogido,
30 la mora se ha recostado.
Allá a la medianoche
cuando la mora ha 'espertado:
—Cristiano mío, levanta
aunque estás muy bien echado,
35 quien tiene mujer bonita,
niños chiquitos al lado,
quien tiene mujer bonita
no duerme tan descuidado;
toma, mi bien, estas parias
40 con estas bolas colgando
y a tu mujer la bonita
dile que yo se las mando,
y en el bolsillo llevas
pa que vivas descuidado:
45 cuando pases entre moros
dirás paso entre paso,
que de moros has salido,
. . .
cuando pases por Turquía
50 dirás que eres turquesano,
cuando pases por las Indias
dirás que vienes de indiano
. . .

The captive is combing his hair
beneath a green orange tree,
the captive is combing his hair
and shedding tears.
While this is going on
the Moorish girl arrives:
"What's wrong, my Christian?
What upsets you, my slave?"
"Why should I tell you
if it can't be remedied?"
"Perhaps it can be remedied
if I tell your master."
"I have a pretty wife,
small children at her side."
"Is there any woman in the world
who is my equal?"
"As pretty as you,
only her face is whiter."
While this is going on
the Moor appears:
"Tonight the great dog
will dig in my vineyard,
I'll give him what makes
a hundred calluses on each hand,
the hoe weighs a hundred pounds,
the handle weighs as much."
While this is going on
night has come,
the Moor has gone to bed,
the girl has lain down.
There at midnight
when the girl awakened:
"My Christian, get up
even if you're resting well,
he who has a pretty wife,
small children at her side,
he who has a pretty wife
doesn't sleep so carefree;
take, my dear, this gift (?)
with these hanging balls
and to your pretty wife
say I'm sending them to her,
and in the purse you have
wherewith to live carefree:
when you pass among Moors
you will say as you pass,
that you are a Moor,

when you pass through Turkey
you'll say you're Turkish,
when you pass through India
you'll say you're Indian

(y el cristiano marchó para su casa para estar con su mujer la bonita.)
(and the Christian went home to be with his pretty wife.)

This version comes from La Gavia, a very primitive district in the outskirts of Telde on the island of Gran Canaria, and it was told to us by María Monzón, 87 years old, who, in her turn, had learned it when she was a child, along with many others (among them the previously mentioned *Rodriguillo*), from a little old woman from the nearby town of Santa Brígida who had died before the civil war. Since María Monzón's memory was weak and she had much to offer us, we repeated the interview on three separate occasions. The first time she did not even mention the *romance*; it was the second time when as she was repeating *Rodriguillo*, doubtless because of the similarity of the opening ("Pensativo está Rodrigo, / pensativo y enroñado"), she began to say: "'Pensativo está el cautivo', no, that's another one, but it didn't begin that way, it began: 'Peinándose está el cautivo / al pie de un verde naranjo.'"   And then she recited what she remembered of it, a few verses that kept increasing as the interview went on, and repeating them helped to put them in their place. Those verses had not been actualized in María Monzón's memory for many years, and it was necessary to give her time. It was at the third interview that she was able to complete the foregoing *romance*, which, even lacking a conclusion, loses none of its value.

The absence of literary antecedents obliges us to ask questions about its origin. Is it a traditional ballad or simply a learned re-creation that imitates the traditional genre? Does it belong to the oldest branch of the *romancero* or is it a more modern product from the new *romancero*? Does it exist elsewhere in modern oral tradition?   To the lack of older documentation is added its apparent absence among other modern versions that could serve as a counterpart.   It is not to be found in modern regional *romanceros* from any branch of the available tradition. It is also lacking in the bibliographical information we have about the old *romancero*.   And there is no reference to it in the critical bibliography on the modern *romancero*. In the mind of María Monzón it is one more *romance* alongside the aforementioned *Rodriguillo*, or *Gerineldo*, or the *Difunto penitente*, or various religious ballads, or those about modern crimes. According to her, they all came from the same source, the little old woman from Santa Brígida, and all of them have lived together as part of the

Maximiano Trapero with María Monzón

Domingo Medina being interviewed by Maximiano Trapero

traditional knowledge of María Monzón, who confesses herself to be completely illiterate. But from the investigator's point of view, is it truly a traditional *romance*? That is, is it a matter of an old text, created and reproduced according to traditional models, handed down in the family, which reached La Gavia and María Monzón by oral transmission? To affirm this opinion involves deducing an example of a very special type and genre, which are the genre and the language of the traditional *romancero*. And the *romance* of La Gavia is all of that without the slightest doubt. Furthermore, more than just any kind of an example, it is a true model, a precious paradigm of the language in which traditional epic-lyric knowledge is constructed. And if such a splendid example exists, how could it have passed unnoticed by the sixteenth- and seventeenth-century anthologists, supposing that it existed at that time? Why is it that it has not deserved the slightest reference in the very abundant literature about captives? How is it, in short, that it has not survived in other geographical areas of the *romancero*?

El esclavo que llora por su mujer in the Sephardic Tradition

Among the very rich materials of the Menéndez Pidal archives of traditional Judeo-Spanish poetry (more than two thousand poems aside, of course, from a great many more from other areas of Hispanism), there are two short poems that have an obvious connection to our *romance* (cf. Armistead and Silverman 1982:160). The two correspond to the eastern tradition. The first, from Salonika, was sent to Menéndez Pidal from Barcelona by Rosendo Serra in 1912. It is contaminated from verse 7 on with *¿Por qué no cantáis la bella?* and is published here for the first time:

	El día que yo nassí	The day I was born
	nassieron cien con mí.	a hundred were born with me.
	—¿De qué lloras, povre esclavo,	"Why are you weeping, poor slave,
	de qué llorache i vos quechache?	why are you weeping and complaining?
5	¿Non comes? ¿non durmiche?	Can't you eat? can't you sleep?
	¿o vos acossan en la vida?	or are you being tormented?"
	—Mucho bien como, mucho bien bevo,	"I eat very well, I drink very well,
	ni me acossan quando durmo,	nor am I tormented when I sleep,
	lloro yo por una amiga	I weep for a friend
10	que se llamava Marqueza,	who was called Marqueza,
	madre era de los mis hijos	she was my children's mother
	y también mi mujer primera.—	and also my first wife."

	Marqueza está en altas torres	Marqueza is in high towers
	lavrando sirma i perla,	embroidering with thread and pearls,
15	lavrando i una camisa	embroidering a shirt
	para el hijo de la reina,	for the queen's son,
	quando de la sirma le mancara	when she lacked thread
	de sus cabellos metía,	she put in her own hair,
	quando de la perla le mancara	when she lacked a pearl
20	de sus lágrimas ajuntava.	she added one of her tears.
	Reina, reina, reinadines,	Queen, queen, *reinadines*,
	por la ciudad de Marqueza.	in the city of Marqueza.
	Se subió en altas torres	She climbed the tall towers
	las que dan para la Marqueza,	that they give to Marqueza,
25	por allí passó un caballero	a knight passed by there
	que de las guerras vinía.	who came from the wars.
	—Hablar vos quero un secreto	"I want to tell you a secret
	que de mi tripa tenía.	that comes from within."
	. . . . .	
30	—Háblame como una hermana mía.	"Speak to me like a sister."
	Hablando y platicando	Talking and chatting
	a conocer se darían,	they recognized one another,
	se toman manos con manos,	they take each other's hands,
	onde los hijos la llevaría.	he led her to her children.

The second *romance*, from Smyrna, was collected from the lips of Leonor Israel by M. Manrique de Lara in 1911:

	—¿De qué lloras, probe esclavo?	"Why do you weep, poor slave?"
	¿De qué lloras? ¿Qué te quexas?	Why do you weep? Why do you lament?"
	¿U no comes u no bebes,	Can't you eat or drink,
	u t'azotan cuando duermes?	or do they whip you when you sleep?"
5	—Yo ya bien bebo, ya bien como,	"I drink well, I eat well,
	ni m'azotan cuando duermo.	nor do they whip me when I sleep.
	Lloro yo por una amiga,	I weep for a friend,
	una amiga bien querida;	a very beloved friend;
	madre es de los mis hijos,	she is the mother of my children,
10	mujer mía la primera.	my first wife."
	—Tú no llores, probe esclavo,	"Don't weep, poor slave,
	ni llores cuando te quexas.	don't weep when you lament.
	Si es por la tuya amiga muy querida,	If it is for your beloved friend,
	ya te la trajera a tus manos.	I will bring her to your hands.
15	Toma tú la[s] mis palabras	Take my word
	y vate a tus buenos estados.	and go to your good land."

Both versions are catalogued by Armistead (1978:1:305-6) among the *romances* of captives and prisoners with the numbers H20.1 and H20.2 respectively. He published the second of them, furthermore, in its entirety as one of the few that deserve the designation of very rare *romances* (1978:3:28). But its rarity is not only because of its lack of documentation—two unique versions in a single branch of the Sephardic tradition — but for other things as well: for its brevity, only eight verses if we discount the Salonika version with verses from *¿Por qué no cantáis la bella?*; for the inconsistent rhyme changes; for being a completely dialogued text, discounting again the contamination in the Salonika version. But even in the latter, which opens with a narrative verse, it functions like an exordium put into the slave's mouth. All of these features appear separately in other Sephardic texts, but not, of course, in combination.

In oral tradition everywhere, and naturally in the repertory of any "artisan" singer, various genres co-exist: *romances, canciones,* children's songs, prayers, magic spells and other poetic texts of related genres. In its Sephardic versions *El esclavo que llora por su mujer* would be difficult to classify. For that reason, on the manuscript of the version from Salonika that Rosendo Serra sent to Menéndez Pidal, the latter wrote a series of notes that reflect his uncertainty upon confronting an unknown text. Thus it is necessary to consider the origin and derivation of these texts.

Derivation

Armistead and Silverman have been the only ones who, although very briefly, have spoken about this *romance,* naturally before knowing about the Canaries' version, attributing to it an eastern origin. They believe that it comes from a neo-Hellenic ballad, a statement that Armistead makes again in his *Catálogo-Indice* (1978:3:28). They compare the text of our *romance* (in a new transcription with notable orthographic differences) with the neo-Hellenic ballad *Ho niópantros sklábos* (*El galeote recién casado*) on which they believe it to be based. The Spanish translation of the Greek ballad goes as follows:

> Cuarenta galeras éramos y sesenta y dos fragatas.
> Ibamos navegando con el viento del noroeste.
> Huimos del poniente y vamos al levante.
> También teníamos muchos esclavos, esclavos valientes.
> 5 Por el camino donde íbamos, por la vía donde pasábamos,
> el esclavo echó un suspiro y detuvo la fragata.
> Y nuestro Bey nos pregunta, nuestro Bey nos dice:
> —¿Quién echó un suspiro y detuvo la fragata?
> —Soy yo quien eché el suspiro e hice parar la fragata.
> 10 —¿Esclavo, pasas hambre; esclavo, pasas sed; esclavo, te falta ropa?
> —Ni paso hambre, ni sed, ni quiero ropa.
> Tres días estuve casado, por doce años esclavo.
> Pero hoy llegó una carta de mis padres:

Hoy venden mis casas; hoy podan mis viñas;
15   hoy casan a mi mujer con otro,
y mis niños huérfanos conocerán otro señor.
—Vete, mi esclavo, con lo bueno en buena hora
y que tu camino esté lleno de capullos y rosas. . . .
      (Armistead and Silverman 1982:161–62)

(We were forty galleons and sixty-two frigates. / We were sailing with the wind from the northwest. / We are fleeing from the west and going to the east. / We also had many slaves, valiant slaves. /5 Along the path we were going, along the way where we were passing, / a slave let out a sigh and stopped the frigate. / And our bey asks us, our bey says to us: / "Who let out a sigh and stopped the frigate?" / "I am the one who let out the sigh and made the frigate stop." /10 "Slave, are you suffering from hunger, or thirst, or do you lack clothing?" / "I am not suffering from hunger or thirst, nor do I want any clothing. / I was married for three days, I have been a slave for twelve years. / But today a letter arrived from my parents: / Today they are selling my houses; today they are pruning my vineyards; /15 today they are marrying my wife to someone else, / and my orphan children will know another master." / "Go, my slave, with good luck and good wishes, / and may your way be filled with buds and roses."/

There is no doubt about the similarities between the Greek ballad and the Sephardic songs, but how can one be sure that the latter derive from the former? The slave as the leading character, his sigh for his lost liberty, his beloved and his children who remain behind are all folklore motifs which appear in an infinity of popular, universal stories, whether *romances* or not. The greatest parallelism is between the questions and answers concerning the slave's sigh. In the Greek ballad the king is the captor, but who is in the Jewish texts? Furthermore, the question: "Why are you sighing, are you suffering from hunger or thirst, do you lack clothing?" is no more than a variant of the Jewish *romance*: "Why are you crying, what are you complaining about, can't you eat, can't you drink, can't you sleep?" Just as other *romances* or popular poetic forms contain similar questions that are topical formulas of discourse,[7] they do not indicate genetic derivation of one *fabula* from another. Armistead and Silverman themselves recognize that the Greek ballad incorporates, in its different versions, several traditional motifs that do not transcend the Judeo-Spanish *romance*: the supernatural effects produced by the sigh (v. 6); the slave or captive who gains his freedom by means of a magic song; and the motif of the interrupted wedding (v. 15) (1982:161).

To accept the fact that the *romance* of *El esclavo que llora por su mujer* is an adaptation of the ballad *El galeote recién casado* would mean that the Sephardic *romance* evolved until it reached the point of telling a story that is quite different from that of the Greek ballad and, of course, telling it in a very different manner. It would imply a long process of re-creation, not impossible, of course, that would demand a long period of time. Do these conditions correspond to the reality of the case? When the authorities we have cited say that the ballad is *neo*-Hellenic, what does that mean? To what time frame does the *neo* belong? If the Sephardic ballad did not show similarities with others of Hispanic tradition, the question would remain, but after considering the version from the Canaries, it seems to us that the question makes the foregoing explanation invalid.

Two Extreme Traditional Results

But the Canaries' version opens new questions when the two conservative traditions of this *romance* are compared. If the Sephardic texts are not considered *romances* in the strict sense, the text from the Canaries is one without the slightest doubt. Nobody would hesitate to affirm that the versions of Smyrna and Salonika tell the same *fabula* as that of La Gavia, but are they the same *romance*? Or rather, do they come from the same model? What poetic product are the Sephardic songs closest to—the *romance* of La Gavia or the Greek ballad? Modern oral poetic tradition of the Judeo-Spanish communities, especially those of the eastern branch, is nourished with materials of a very different origin. It is not to be doubted that the original bearers took with them from Spain a store of old *romances* in the first Diaspora of 1492, but it is also true that that old store was added to later and mixed with other texts: new *romances* and broadsides coming from Spain, *romances* born of Jewish inspiration in situ, stories and ballads turned into *romances* or similar forms which they took from the places where they settled, poetry and popular traditions of the Balkans (Turkey, Greece, Yugoslavia, Bulgaria, etc.). It seems astonishing to be able to produce evidence, as in this case, that a poetic re-creation that extended over centuries in places so distant and so different as the Canary Islands and eastern Europe could offer such extreme results starting from the same model. If we agree, however varying and diverse the forms may be, that it is a matter of the same *romance*, we also will have to accept that their origin was the same. The existence of a poetic theme, a *romance* in this case, in two places in which Hispanic tradition was established, ignoring distance, nationality, the culture of each place, even the language, is an unequivocal sign of the same Spanish origin. And if, as in this case, one of those places is the home of very old Judeo-Spanish communities, Salonika and Smyrna, we are almost entitled to say that the origin of that *romance* is very old, that it is, in fact, a *romance viejo* (cf. Menéndez Pelayo 1945:9:390 and Menéndez Pidal 1953:2:334, 338).

It seems obvious to us that the texts of Salonika and Smyrna are closer to and have more similarities with the text from La Gavia than the three have with the Greek ballad. In the former it is the same *fabula*: the weeping of a slave who is lamenting the absence of this wife and children and finds a remedy for his misfortune in the kindheartedness of his mistress who frees him. There is also similarity in the initial question:

> —¿De qué lloras, probe esclavo? ¿De qué lloras? ¿Qué te quejas?
> (Smyrna)
> —¿Qué tienes, cristiano mío? ?De qué te afliges, mi esclavo?
> (La Gavia)

and in the answer of the slave:

> —Madre es de los mis hijos, mujer mía la primera.
> (Smyrna)
> —Tengo una mujer bonita, niños chiquitos al lado.
> (La Gavia)

There is also the same narrative model, direct discourse, making it a *romance* of pure dialogue. In the Jewish versions (contamination aside) there is not a single verse of indirect narration, and in the twenty-six verses of the La Gavia version there are only seven, which serve to present the interlocutors, three of them using the same narrative formula (vv. 5, 19, 27). And finally there is the same structural development of the *fabula*, following the model of the *romance* as a scene, which is so characteristic of the old *romancero*, or rather, which was so pleasing to the ballad collectors of the sixteenth century (Menéndez Pidal 1953:1:63-64).

But the differences are also numerous and notable. In the first place, their length: the text from the Canaries, supposing that there are a few more verses in the conclusion which our informant forgot, has a length that is average for old traditional *romances*, between twenty and forty sixteen-syllable verses, but the Sephardic versions are abnormal in their brevity. The synthesis manifest in the *fabula* of the Smyrna version is astonishing, how an entire story is condensed into eight verses. Without narration and specific details in the dialogue, conditions and situations important for understanding the story have been lost, such as, for example, the identity of the interlocutors: one is the slave, but who is the other?   Instead, everything is condensed into a brief poetic sigh, the sigh of the slave who is weeping for his wife.   Nothing more is necessary to capture its quintessence. There is no shorter and at the same time no more intense scene in all of the Spanish *romancero*, whether ancient or modern.

In second place, the rhyme.   The monorhyme of the Canaries' tradition is in direct opposition to the Judeo-Spanish texts, which have no consistent rhyming pattern.

In third place, the *dramatis personae*.   There are two in the eastern texts, the slave and an unidentified master.   If tradition does not specify the latter, it is because the function of the second character is not affected by his condition.   Nevertheless, the condition of the second character is fundamental in the tradition of the Canaries since it offers a new and original reading of the *romance*.   The appearance of a third person in the Canaries clarifies, on one hand, the relation between slave and mistress and, on the other, complicates the structural relationship of the *dramatis personae*.   The kindness of the woman (v. 4) contrasts strongly with the cruelty of the man towards the slave (vv. 11–13). But why that attitude of the woman?   Why does the woman free the slave against her husband's will without his knowing it?   To say that she is moved by the slave's answer (v. 7) is not to say much, even though it is literally what the text says.   What it is necessary to understand, because the text is full of indications of this sort, is that the Moorish woman loves the slave and it is that "good love" that motivates his liberation, despite the fact that an absent wife and children are preferred to her.

And in fourth place, a very unusual fact.   The eastern texts only speak to us about a slave, and therefore make of it a story without place or time, a universal story that could be from anywhere.   On the other hand, the version from the Canaries hispanizes and christianizes the *fabula*, turning it into a story of Moors and Christians and the simple slave into a captive.   But was the original model the version of the Canaries or the eastern Jewish version?   That is, did the *romance* in its evolution pass from a period indifferent to religion, the eastern model (also represented by the Greek ballad), to a story of Christians and non-Christians, the Canaries model?   Or, on the contrary, did the

Spanish model, a story of captives, become universalized and lose the connotations that framed it in historical time and gave it a specified place? The Canaries model does not represent the result of an evolution of that type, but rather the type of *romances* of captives, one of the most characteristic and, of course, most preferred subgenres of the *romancero* of all time (Marco 1977:2:389-94). This is so because the identity of the characters—the Moor, his wife, and the Christian—and of the story—a story of captives—is not only made known by their being literally qualified that way, but also because the *romance* is full of topical allusions that characterize *romances* of captives: the cruelty of the Moor (vv. 11-13); the happy outcome thanks to the mediation of one of the characters who falls in love with the captive; the comparison between the beauty of the woman and the captive's beloved (vv. 8-9), including the mention of skin color; the precise utilization of the very archaic term *parias* (v. 20) to refer to a kind of coinage the Moors used to pay tributes to the Christians; or the mention of Turkey (v. 25) as an allusion to the destination of most of the Spanish Christian captives.

Whatever comparison one may make between the two conservative branches of the Hispanic tradition of *El esclavo que llora por su mujer*, the eastern Jewish and that of the Canaries, always inclines one toward a judgment in favor of the precedence of the latter. Not only has the Canaries model been able to preserve the primordial character of *romances* about captives, which was lost in the East where it was confused with stories about slaves and accommodated itself to a more universal ballad genre, but also the discourse-model *romance* is preserved intact and in unsurpassed shape in the Canaries but not among the eastern Sephardic peoples. The *romance* lives among the Jews in an unballad-like form, that is, it bears little resemblance to the splendid forms of the oral *romancero* of the Sephardic Jews; or else it is in a very decadent state, or it never came to be a true *romance*, that is, it was born as a *canción*, an allied genre, in order to narrate a Greek ballad in Spanish, according to Armistead and Silverman, and it remained as a brief narrative song. We would have been able to defend the second hypothesis before knowing of the existence of the *romance* in the Canaries, but now no longer. Thus there remains no other alternative than to speak of the decadence of this *romance* in eastern tradition, decadence that by now may be death (remember that the two versions were collected at the beginning of the century and have not reappeared in any of the numerous field expeditions that have been carried out in Sephardic communities during the course of this century). The version found in the Canaries, on the other hand, is splendid; it possesses all the characteristics that make of it an insuperable model of the genre of the single-scene *romance*, and within that category, of the dialogued *romance*, inherited from the medieval epics (Menéndez Pidal 1953:1:63–65). Even the failure of the memory of our informant, María Monzón, is allied in a special sense to the great poetic value of the *ex abrupto* conclusion, which, if it does not leave the listener in suspense (because the ending is announced in earlier verses), does leave the discourse without a conclusion, a situation which was so pleasing to the singers and collectors of the old *romances*.

Las Palmas
Canary Islands

Notes

[1]Translated from the Spanish by the editor.

[2]*La guarda cuidadosa, La fuerza de la sangre, Bodas de sangre,* and *La canción del huérfano,* all four unknown up to that time as autonomous *romances.*

[3]The *romancero vulgar* and that of blind men, transmitted by *pliegos sueltos* (chapbooks), have inundated and become mixed with oral tradition everywhere. The investigator who is a purist tries to avoid such texts, but they are precisely the ones the average informant most wants to communicate since they are the ones he appreciates the most.

[4]For example, Gómez Escudero in his *Historia de la conquista de Canarias* refers to the dances of La Gomera, and Diego Durón uses a refrain or a popular verse from *romances* in his works for the Capilla Musical of the cathedral of Las Palmas.

[5]Although the trial opens against eighteen religious *romances* taken from broadsides in the belief that they contain opinions contrary to church doctrine, it gives sufficient evidence of the popularity attained by the phenomenon of the *romancero*. At the present time we are working on a study of this matter.

[6]A paradigmatic example of this was the discovery in Burgo de Osma of the *romance* of *La muerte del príncipe Don Juan* in 1900 by Menéndez Pidal and his wife, a *romance* that until then had been completely hidden from old as well as from modern critics (Menéndez Pidal 1953:2:291–92).

[7]One example among many that could be cited here is from the ballad

of *La romería del pescador:*

Un día comiendo en la mesa
—¿Por qué suspiras, mi esposa,

(One day while eating at the table
"Why are you sighing, my wife,

suspiraba y no comía.
suspiras y no comías?

she sighed and did not eat.
sighing and not eating?")
(Trapero 1985:#89)

Collecting Portuguese Ballads[1]

Manuel da Costa Fontes

> A memória de meu tio Manuel
> Soares, (†1984), que tanto ajudou
> com a recolha do *Romanceiro da
> Ilha de S. Jorge.*

The Spanish began to publish extensive collections dedicated exclusively to their ballads in the middle of the sixteenth century (see Rodríguez-Moñino 1973). These collections included versions of many poems that had already become traditional, for they were being sung by common people throughout Spain. Although the Portuguese were also singing ballads at that time,[2] nothing of the sort was done in Portugal. This lack of ancient documentation renders the modern Portuguese tradition even more significant. Without the poems that have been transmitted from generation to generation throughout the centuries, our knowledge of the ancient Portuguese tradition would be very limited indeed.

The systematic collection of ballads was begun by Almeida Garrett in 1824. Having been forced into exile for political reasons, he was inspired by the example of the English Romantics, and made his early findings known through the publication of *Adozinda* while still abroad (London, 1828). Since he was the first to publicize the fact that ballads from the Middle Ages and the Renaissance were still being sung by common people in Iberia, he is the "father" of all subsequent fieldwork undertaken in Portugal, Spain, and in the other Pan-Hispanic traditions as well (see Costa Fontes 1983-84b:54-55).

My own fieldwork began among the Portuguese in California in 1970. Although I had heard ballads being sung within my own family since childhood, I became aware of their importance only when I took a course on the Spanish ballad from Professor Arthur

L.-F. Askins at the University of California, Berkeley in that year. I told him that my grandmother, Delfina Augusta da Costa, from the island of Terceira, who was then living with us in Tracy, California, knew *Bela Infanta, Febre Amarela,* and other "old songs." Advised by Professor Askins, I recorded everything that she knew, and began looking for more informants in Tracy and nearby communities in the San Joaquin valley. It was truly fascinating to discover that poems that could be traced to the Renaissance and even to the Middle Ages were still remembered by Portuguese immigrants in California.[3] The fieldwork in that state continued, on a sporadic basis, until 1975 (see *Cal* 1983b). In 1977 I explored practically every village on my father's island, São Jorge (see *SJ* 1983a), recording a few ballads on my native Terceira as well. In 1978 I was able to form two collections among the Portuguese settled in New England (Massachusetts and Rhode Island) (*NI* 1980) and Canada (Toronto) (*Can* 1979b) together with my wife, Maria-João. She had begun to accompany me during my fieldwork in California, and her collaboration became increasingly important as time went on. In the summer of 1980 we traveled to Portugal, forming a very large collection in the northern province of Trás-os-Montes (1987).[4] We also harvested a few ballads in Beira Alta and the Algarve at that time. In 1984 we returned to Canada, recording another 23 variants of 19 text types in Toronto and Montreal. In our efforts to salvage as many Portuguese ballads as possible before it is too late, we have interviewed more than 800 informants so far, gathering over 3,300 ballads and other traditional poems in the process. This paper will focus on the various methods of fieldwork that had to be devised for each area and on the functions of the ballads, as reported by the informants themselves, with emphasis on the province of Trás-os-Montes, where our largest collection was formed.

When I began to collect ballads in California, it did not take me long to find out that it was necessary to become thoroughly familiar with the Portuguese tradition in order to render my work as effective as possible. Since most of the immigrants were from the Azores, I put together a list of incipits taken from Teófilo Braga's *Cantos Populares do Arquipélago Açoriano* (1869). This list was used to elicit as many ballads as I could from my informants, for people are often unaware of the extent of their respective repertories. As a member of the Portuguese community in that state, I was in a privileged position to observe the so-called "natural ballad-singing situation," but such a course would have been utterly nonproductive. Had I followed it, I would still be trying to compile a collection in California today. I also learned very soon that the best informants are from villages, are advanced in years, illiterate or at most with an elementary education, and that, overall, women preserve the tradition much better than men. Since old people usually are very religious, a display of piety and asking for the rhymed prayers that they had learned from their mothers and grandmothers often helped to induce the most reticent ones to collaborate with us. Many thought very little of the rich tradition that they had inherited. When confronted with the tape recorder, a good number feared making mistakes, suspecting that what they knew was somehow "incorrect." To counter this situation, it was necessary to convince them of the great value of the ballad tradition and to encourage them with an effusive, constant display of appreciation for everything that they contributed. Old people are frequently lonely, especially in the English-speaking environment that surrounds them in North America. On many occasions we had to spend quite a few hours listening to the history of their illnesses and other endless stories with evangelical patience. Although we wanted to record their ballads, this was also the human thing to do.

The methods of fieldwork had to be constantly adapted to local conditions. Whenever possible, we began by seeking the help of relatives and friends. Besides recording what they themselves knew, they often indicated other informants who, in turn, would try to find more people for us to interview. Some even traveled with us to various cities in California and New England. In Massachusetts and Rhode Island, it was necessary to seek the help of Portuguese priests and community organizations for the first time. We had only two months for fieldwork, and it was imperative to proceed as quickly as possible. In Taunton, Father Américo Moreira announced our project after a Portuguese mass. Although no one volunteered to collaborate with us after the services, the announcement facilitated several interviews a few days later. In New Bedford, East Providence, and Providence, priests gave us lists with the names and addresses of prospective informants, accompanying us to their homes on some occasions. In Bristol, Jorge de Ávila Gonçalves, from the Center of Assistance to the Portuguese Worker, went with us from door to door. In Pawtucket, an employee from the Center of Assistance to the

Immigrant found several persons for us to interview.

These tactics were also used in Canada, where, rather than traveling constantly from city to city, we were able to stay in Toronto, where there was a community of more than 90,000 persons from many parts of Portugal (see Anderson and Higgs 1976:69). We began by renting a flat in the Kensington Park area, where most Portuguese used to live.[5] There are several Portuguese national churches in the city whose priests were most helpful. They would explain our project after one of the masses that were held throughout the week, reading three or four incipits of some of the most common ballads to insure that their parishioners understood what we were looking for. Those masses were attended mostly by old people. Besides praying for volunteers, Maria-João and I would plant ourselves by the door of the church as they were leaving, finding out which ones knew ballads, writing down their addresses, and setting up interviews. In this fashion we were able to discover many informants in front of churches such as Holy Cross, St. Helen's, and St. Agnes'. We also sought the help of organizations such as the Portuguese Community Center, a Catholic service housed in the basement of St. Helen's, Portuguese Free Interpreters, and the Portuguese department of the West End Y.M.C.A. St. Christopher's House, a social center for the aged, proved to be quite a find, for we recorded many ballads there. A few informants were discovered by less orthodox means. At times we would drive slowly through the streets trying to find old ladies to interview. The Portuguese ones usually dressed in black, but some of those we approached turned out to be Italian or Ukranian. The Italian ladies would reply with a swift "Non capisco!" that we understood, and the Ukranians probably answered the same thing, even though we did not really know what they were saying. During our second trip to Canada in 1984, we were more interested in recording folk tales. Since old men know many stories, we looked for informants in parks and malls where they gather to talk, to watch people go by, or to play cards. I even went into bars and barber shops while Maria-João waited in the car.

In North America we frequently appealed to the ethnic pride of prospective informants, pointing out that the ballads were, after all, Portuguese, and that they were condemned to disappear very soon. As they knew only too well, the young people, who often failed to learn the language of their ancestors properly, cared even less for their old songs. At times we took advantage of the fact that the Portuguese tend to be very clannish, preferring to socialize with people from their own region of origin. For example, we would tell some Azoreans how poorly their particular island was represented in our collection, and explain to continentals and Madeirans that most of our materials were of Azorean provenience. Whenever possible, we made our purposes clear by naming ballads according to their respective designations in the informant's home area.[6] We would also mention some of the most common ballads by their popular name or by incipit in order to get started. After a while, if the interviewee did not object too strenuously, we would go through our list in the hope of not leaving anything behind. Many people knew very little, but we also found a few outstanding informants.

This is how our three North American collections were formed. They reflect the fact that the majority of the Portuguese on this continent are from the Azores, for 208 of our 277 informants came from those islands, but we also interviewed 52 persons from the continent (Trás-os-Montes, Beira Alta, Beira Baixa, Beira Litoral, Estremadura, Baixo Alentejo) and 13 from the island of Madeira, collecting a total of 1209 ballads, rhymed prayers, and miscellaneous poems in the process. The task was not always easy. There were many days when, unable to find any informants, we were almost tempted to give up. In New England it was impossible to travel for several days because of the harshness of the winter. Although we were well received in most instances, that was not the case when we were suspected of belonging to the religious denominations whose representatives go from door to door trying to make new converts. Some people also seemed to fear that ballad collecting was a pretext to get into their homes in order to steal. In Modesto, California, an old lady who came to the door on crutches, upon discovering that I was looking for ballads, replied: "Songs? What do you want songs for, boy? Get yourself a job!" In Toronto, a woman from Figueira da Foz refused to grant a previously promised interview with the following words: "I really don't know anything and I do not have time to put up with you today!" It is only fair to emphasize, however, that cases of outright rudeness such as these were rare, for the vast majority of the Portuguese took great pride in preserving the hospitality which is so characteristic of their homeland.

The corpus of Portuguese balladry has been considerably

enriched by this fieldwork. The fact that the vast majority of our informants were from conservative lateral areas such as the Azores, Trás-os-Montes, and Madeira renders the three North American collections especially valuable (see Costa Fontes 1984b). Moreover, some of the poems that they preserve are extremely rare. The following version of *A Morte do Príncipe D. Afonso* was recited in Toronto on June 19, 1978 by Clementina Coelho, an immigrant from the island of São Miguel:

A princesa estava à janela,
casadinha d'oito dias;
por lá passa um pombo branco,
oh que novas le trazia!
5 —Que nova trago à senhora,
com vontade de chorar!
O vosso marido é morto
em reino de Portugal.
Caiu dum cavalo abaixo,
10 em cima dum lajeal;
arrebentou fel e bofes,
'tá em pontos de expirar.
A mulher, assim que soube disto,
logo tratou de mandar,
15 co'as suas aias atrás dela,
sem as poder apanhar;
co'as suas saiinhas nos braços,
sem as poder agüentar.
—Donde vindes, mulher minha?

20 Vens-me acabar de matar?
Tu ainda sedes criancinha,
ainda podeis casar.
—Casar é qu'eu já não caso,
'tou no mundo sem abrigo;
25 jà nã torno a encontrar
a prenda do meu marido.
—Chama-me aquele doutor
que vai pel'aquela rua,
qu'eu le quero preguntar
30 s'o mal de amor tem cura.
—O mal de amor nã tem cura,
qu'é um mal inviolado;
quem morre de mal de amor
não se enterra em sagrado;
35 enterra-se em campo verde
donde forem namorados.

The princess was at the window,
married for eight days;
a white dove passed by,
oh what news it brought her!
"The news I bring you
makes me feel like crying!
Your husband has died
in the kingdom of Portugal.
He fell off a horse,
on top of some flagstones;
bile and lungs burst out
and he is about to die."
His wife, discovering this,
left right away,
her ladies-in-waiting followed,
but couldn't keep up with her;
they lifted their skirts,
but couldn't hold them up.
"Where do you come from, my wife?
Do you want to finish me off?
You are still a child,
and you can marry again."
"I will not remarry,
I am alone in the world;
I will not be able to find
a husband such as you."
"Call me that doctor
who is walking on that street,
for I want to ask him
if lovesickness can be cured."
"Lovesickness has no remedy,
for it is an incurable disease;
whoever dies from it
can't be buried in holy ground;
only in the green meadows
where he fell in love."
(*Can* no.10)[7]

The princess who receives the sad news that her husband is about to die is Isabel, daughter of the Catholic Kings of Spain. Isabel had been married for eight months, not just eight days as stated in the ballad, to Prince Afonso, son and heir of John II of Portugal. The prince fell from his horse on the shores of the Tagus and died on July 13, 1491. At that time Ferdinand and Isabel were besieging Granada, which surrendered the following year. They asked their grieving daughter to join them immediately. According to Ramón Menéndez Pidal (1973:411), it was in the nearby town of Íllora that she asked Fray Ambrosio de Montesino, a well-known poet at the Castilian court, to write a poem about her husband's untimely death (see also Bénichou 1975; Nuno Alçada 1982-83). Nowadays this poem is remembered only in the insular Portuguese tradition. Our version concludes with *Não me Enterrem em Sagrado*, a separate ballad which in Portuguese survives only as an ending to other text types (see Costa Fontes 1983a:xx). Note that *A Morte do Príncipe D. Afonso* has lost its historical meaning for the people who still sing it. To them, it is merely the sad story of a girl who is widowed shortly after her marriage.

Many other rare ballads were harvested among the Portuguese immigrants, but I shall mention only a few. *Batalha de Lepanto*, which perpetuates the memory of the great naval encounter between the Christian forces commanded by John of Austria and the Turks at Lepanto in 1571, is exclusively Portuguese today (see Costa Fontes 1979a). We recorded a good version in California (*Cal* no.10) and a fragment in Stoughton, Massachusetts (*NI* no.2). *A Filha Desterrada (Dona Maria)*, which includes two verses from the epic *A Penitência do Rei Rodrigo*, is found only among Azoreans. Its third, fourth, and fifth published versions are from North America (*Cal* nos.33-34; *Can* no.65; see also Costa Fontes 1976). Before our work, there were only three known variants of *Lizarda*, which survives only in the Azores and Madeira. This ballad is derived from Gil Vicente's *Tragicomedia de Don Duardos* (c. 1525). We found two additional versions and a fragment in the United States and Canada (*Cal* nos.104-5; *Can* no.198; see also Costa Fontes 1978-79). As noted by Samuel G. Armistead and Joseph H. Silverman in their preface to the New England collection (1980:x), the initial verses of the Canadian fragment embody a contamination with the epic *As Ameias de Toro*. The longest versions of the religious ballad *Barca Bela*, which seems to have been preserved only in the Azores, are clearly related to the famous ballad of *Conde Arnaldos*, first documented by Juan Rodríguez del Padrón before the middle of the fifteenth century.

Thanks to the Azorean renditions, it was possible to demonstrate that *Barca Bela* in turn inspired *Remando vão remadores*, the poem composed by Gil Vicente to open his *Auto da Barca do Purgatório* (c. 1517) (see Costa Fontes 1983-84a). Seventy-nine-year-old Virgínia Valadão Serpa recited an excellent version in Stoughton, Massachusetts. Since the recording was accidentally erased, Mrs. Serpa was kind enough to repeat it on the telephone a few days later when we had already returned to Ohio (*NI* no.125). *A Morte do Príncipe D. João* is not as rare as previously thought (see Costa Fontes 1983-84b:54 and n.19), but this was not yet the case when Joaquim Martins, born in the province of Trás-os-Montes, recited the following version on May 27, 1978 in Toronto:

Tristes novas, novas tristes,	Sad news, sad news,
que têm vindo de Granada:	has arrived from Granada:
D. João estava doente,	Don João was ill,
com pena da sua amada.	and felt sorry for his beloved.
5 Foram chamar três doutores	They sent for three doctors
dos que havia em Granada;	that there were in Granada;
olhavam uns pelos outros,	they looked at each other,
mas nenhum dizia nada.	but not one said a word.
Disse o mais novo deles	Then the youngest of them said
10 daquela boca sagrada:	with his blessed mouth:
—Três horas tendes de vida,	"You have three hours to live,
e meia já vai passada.	a half-hour has already passed."
Depois a mãe perguntou-lhe:	(Then his mother asked him:)
—Tu deves alguma honra	"Do you owe a debt
a alguma menina honrada?	to any maiden of honor?"
15 —Devo-a à D. Isabel,	"I owe it to Dona Isabel,
que a deixo desgraçada.	I am leaving her dishonored."
Estando naqueles momentos,	At that moment,
D. Isabel chegara,	Dona Isabel arrived,
e, descalça e em cabelo,	barefoot, her hair uncovered,
20 seu rosto lumiava.	her face was shining.
—Tu que tens, D. Isabel,	"What's the matter with you, D. Isabel,
que vens tão atrapalhada?	for you seem so afflicted?"
—Venho de pedir a Deus	"I have been begging God
que te erga dessa cama.	to take you out of that bed."
25 —Se eu desta cama me erguesse,	"If I could rise from this bed,
eras mulher abençoada;	you would be truly blessed;
eu levaria-te à igreja	I would take you to church
a fazer-te mulher casada.	and make you a married woman."
	(*Can* no.13)

The hero of this ballad is Prince John, son and heir to the Catholic Kings of Spain, who died in October of 1497, not in

Granada, as the version above would have it, but in the city of Salamanca. Although this poem was not preserved in the ancient collections, there can be no doubt that it was composed soon after the prince's death (for bibliography see Armistead 1978:1:175). It is abundantly clear that these ballads, together with many other rare themes in North America, testify to the importance of conducting field work among immigrants whenever possible.

The *Romanceiro da Iha de S. Jorge (SJ)* was formed during the summer of 1977. My relatives on the island often accompanied me. I am especially grateful to my recently deceased uncle, Manuel Soares, who gave me a considerable amount of his time. When I was working by myself, it was usually sufficient to mention my family name for people to try to remember everything that they knew. The jewels of the collection, which includes a good number of rare poems, are *Perseguição de Búcar pelo Cid (SJ* no.1) and *Floresvento (SJ* no.2). Unfortunately, the lady who recited these epic ballads, while claiming to have learned them from two crazy old aunts who used to sing day and night, had also inherited a copy of what appeared to be T. Braga's *Cantos Populares do Arquipélago Açoriano* (1869).

Our fieldwork in Trás-os-Montes began in July of 1980. Upon arriving in Bragança, we went immediately to the bishop's residence, where we were kindly received by His Eminence, D. António Rafael, who had already been informed of our project. He indicated the best areas to explore in the district and gave us the names of priests interested in local history and ethnography, including some who were teachers at the seminary. On the following day (July 14) we went to the village of São Pedro dos Sarracenos by taxi. We were not very lucky. The only informant we could find on that day knew a version of *Barca Bela (TM* no.1241) learned in a school book and a fragment of *O Soldado + A Aparição (TM* no.203), but the rest of her repertory consisted of modern songs and rhymed prayers. Somewhat discouraged, we returned to the seminary the following day where we met Dr. Manuel António Gonçalves, whose name had been mentioned to us by the bishop. If my memory does not betray me, Dr. Gonçalves, who taught Portuguese at the seminary and at the high school, had put together a collection of local legends and proverbs, and was very much interested in the preservation of regional folk dances, which were in danger of disappearing. Thanks to him, our early investigations were rather successful. He took us to Rio de

Onor and to the Spanish half of that village, Rihonor de Castilla,[8] as well as to Varge, Sacóias, Guadramil, Deilão, Baçal, Vale-de-Lamas, São Julião, Palácios, and Gimonde. Our number of versions of rare or relatively rare ballads such as *Floresvento, O Conde Preso, Morte de D. Beltrão, O Prisioneiro,* and *Morte do Príncipe D. João* kept on increasing. Since Dr. Gonçalves could not continue accompanying us—in fact, we may have taken advantage of his generosity—we realized that it was absolutely necessary to rent a car in order to carry out the systematic fieldwork that we had planned. We went to Gimonde—it was already night—right after finding an old Volkswagen in Bragança. The car could barely move and, in addition, we lost the best cassette recorder that we had brought from the United States. When we explained the situation to the businessman who had rented us the car, he returned our money at once, and we sent for another car from Oporto. Then we went back to Gimonde, where we were told that the recorder had been found by the son of a "retornado"[9] and an Angolan mother. The boy gave us the machine with the best of good will. On July 26, armed with an excellent map of the district offered by Dr. Gonçalves, we left the "concelho"[10] of Bragança and went south towards Miranda do Douro, stopping to collect ballads along the way. We would look for a boarding house in a central area and explore the nearby villages during the day. Thus we covered the "concelhos" of Miranda do Douro, Vimioso, Macedo de Cavaleiros, Mirandela, Mogadouro, Alfândega da Fé, Vila Flor, Freixo de Espada-à-Cinta, Torre de Moncorvo, and Vinhais, recording ballads in a total of 114 towns and villages, but visiting a few more, for it was not possible for us to find informants everywhere. Of the "concelhos" that form the district of Bragança, Carrazeda de Anciães was the only one left out. On August 21 we collected our last ballads from Trás-os-Montes in Cabeça de Igreja (Vinhais). Although we had hoped to explore the whole province, we decided to relegate the district of Vila Real to another occasion, for we already had an excellent collection from Trás-os-Montes, and went south towards the Algarve. Since we found very little in that province, we drove to Beira Alta, where we were equally unfortunate. The chances are that we were simply unable to find good informants.[11] Be that as it may, there can be no doubt that the oral tradition of Trás-os-Montes is by far the richest in the country.

There was some difficulty in exploring the district of Bragança due to the poor roads, some of which were still unpaved. This lack of communications and the resulting isolation have probably played an important role in the preservation of the rich tradition of the province. On the other hand, it is lamentable that the poor roads that circle the mountains which abound in the district, besides hindering further development, also render access to areas of great natural beauty, such as Alfândega da Fé and Vinhais, more difficult than it should be.

Since the villages of northern Portugal give the impression of being deserted during the day because almost everyone leaves to work in the fields, the best occasions to find informants are around noon, when people return home for lunch, and at dusk. Naturally we kept looking for informants throughout the day because the time that we could spend in Portugal was limited. There are more people in the villages on Sundays, but even then many are unable to rest because of the labor shortage caused by emigration. This phenomenon is not new. Four of our oldest informants had been born abroad (Brazil, France, Argentina). We also interviewed three of the "retornados" who had been forced to abandon the properties acquired through many years of hard work in Angola and return to Portugal due to the recent, hasty decolonization. Some had married women from the former colonies. We owe versions of *Delgadinha* (*TM* no.607) and *As Filhas da Condessa* (*TM* no.1235) to an attractive girl of mixed Portuguese and African parentage who sang them with two white friends. A few persons who had come from France and from Canada to spend their vacation in their homeland also contributed to the collection. The labor shortage is such that many decided to forget that they had returned home to rest in order to help with agricultural tasks that could not be postponed.

The people of Trás-os-Montes are extremely hard-working. If the province is really as poor as we were told before arriving, this is due to the lack of industrial development, or perhaps because of the poor condition of the roads, or because the land simply refuses to produce more. The women also worked in the fields beside the men. The few exceptions that we noted were limited especially to the villages said to have a great percentage of New Christians (people descended from the Jews who became officially "converted" in 1497), such as Vilarinho dos Galegos (Mogadouro) and Campo de Víboras (Vimioso), where we saw groups of women tatting in the shade outside their homes. In Peso (Mogadouro) we interviewed seventy-seven-year-old Maria Loçana who, despite her advanced age, was traveling on her donkey from village to village in order to sell soap and other items. Although she resided in Azinhoso (Mogadouro), she was from Argozelo (Vimioso). After she left, we found out that the other informants considered her Jewish. This could very well be, for there are many Crypto-Jews in Argozelo. However, an informant from Carção, who had New Christians among his own ancestors, told us that some Old Christians were reputed to be Jewish just because they abandoned agriculture in order to dedicate themselves to commerce.

It did not take us long to realize that the people were so kind and hospitable that, in most instances, there was no need to seek the help of priests, although a few did assist us. As soon as we arrived at the center of a village and made our project known, everyone tried to help us with the best of good will. People were always offering us the famous ham and sausage of Trás-os-Montes as well as the excellent local wines. Although there were days of great discouragement when we could not find any informants, there were also days in which we recorded a great number of ballads. At times we would go from house to house, and on some rare and precious occasions a group of people would gather around us, each one awaiting his turn to recite or sing his repertory, while arguing with each other about the "correctness" of their respective versions. In some instances there were persons who refused to recite or sing a ballad because of having just heard someone else record a similar variant. On other occasions a ballad would be sung in chorus. Since we wished to harvest as many versions as we possibly could, Maria-João and I would separate, each with a recorder, when a group formed around us, so as to collect more ballads. If the group refused to divide, Maria-João would leave with a local woman in search of more informants. After a while we began to separate as soon as we reached a village. Our informants would frequently indicate others. In Constantim (Miranda do Douro) we found two former informants from Toronto, Albertina Esteves and Manuel Domingues, who had come to spend their vacation in Portugal. They helped us interview practically all the older inhabitants in the village. Some people went to considerable lengths to contribute to our collection. In Eiró (Vinhais) seventy-two-year-old Arminda do Nascimento agreed to be interviewed while ill in bed.[12] In São Julião (Bragança), Imperatriz dos Anjos Pires was very sad. She had just heard that her daughter, who lived in France, could not come to Portugal that summer because her house in Paris had been robbed. Nevertheless, she made an effort to collaborate with us. The three women whom we interviewed in Bemposta (Mogadouro) were very tired from working all day in the fields under the burning summer sun, but they recorded their respective repertories despite the fact that the husband of one of them kept calling her to make supper. She ignored him until she was finished. And so we recorded ballads in private homes, in village squares, in the fields when the farmers took a break, next to a house under construction when the workers stopped for a snack, in country stores, and even in taverns. In the city of Bragança we also collected a few ballads in the asylum.

Naturally we ran across some resistance at times. The interest of radio and television in various manifestations of regional folklore caused a small number of potential informants to suspect that we intended to commercialize what they told us, making money at their expense. Fortunately, it did not take long to convince them that our purpose was to preserve the ballads before it was too late, for, as they well knew, it would not take very long for them to be forgotten. Maria Augusta da Costa Lourenço (Carção, Vimioso), an excellent informant to whom we owe the only version of *A Filha do Ermitão* (*TM* no.1145; see also Costa Fontes 1982b) that we could find, helped to convince her neighbors to collaborate with us, exclaiming: "Although we tell them the ballads, they still remain with us!" We noted that the mistrust increased when we returned to a village for a second time. People probably began to speak with each other after our first visit, concluding that it was doubtful that anyone would expend so much energy to collect ballads out of mere dedication. Some informants who were in mourning also thought it inappropriate to collaborate with us. Ballads are to be sung on happy occasions. In Angueira (Vimioso), Adelina Ester Martins Afonso had forgotten most of her repertory because she had stopped singing after her husband's death seven years before. In other cases modesty constituted an additional obstacle. A few women refused to record poems or parts of poems they considered obscene, such as *A Filha do Imperador de Roma* and *A Tentação do Marinheiro*.

Contrary to the Azoreans, who usually prefer to recite their ballads because they are embarrassed to sing in front of strangers, the people of Trás-os-Montes love to sing and to listen to the recordings afterwards. We realized that this could constitute an inducement for them to collaborate with us, but we often had to ask them to recite the ballads, explaining that singing took a long time, especially when the harvesting melody ("moda da segada") was used, and that this would cause us to run out of tape and batteries. Moreover, since that melody was invariably the same, at least to our untrained ears, we had no interest in recording it time after time, wasting precious hours in the process. However, there were those who had to sing in order to remember the words of a ballad.

Leite de Vasconcellos lists some of the terms used to designate these poems in Trás-os-Montes: "trobos," "romances," "remances das segadas," "jacras," and "jacras das segadas" (l:1-2). I only recall hearing the words "jacra" and "jácara," but we did not make any effort to discover what ballads were called in the various locations listed.   As soon as we arrived anywhere, it was enough to ask for harvesting songs ("cantigas da segada") for everyone to understand what we were looking for. I believe that this name together with threshing songs ("cantigas das malhas") constitute the most common designations for ballads in the region.

Most of our collection was recorded, but we also used a reduced number of materials that had been written in popular notebooks as well as ballads collected by one of Dr. Gonçalves' students as part of an assignment.   Two other students of Dr. Gonçalves continued our fieldwork in Babe, offering us several ballads later. One of them is the only version of A Tecedeira (TM no.1224) in our collection. D. Clara Vitória Pires, a high school teacher in Bragança, besides sending for several aged ladies who came to record their respective repertories on the veranda of her house in Baçal, also offered us three ballads that she herself had collected.

We came upon some truly outstanding informants. Mariana Preto (about 75 years old of Guadramil, Bragança) contributed 32 poems to our collection. Ana Gouveia (62 years old of Gimonde, Bragança) recorded 38 poems. She had to be interviewed twice; since it was already late when we arrived at her home, there was not enough time for her to record her full repertory. Florinda dos Santos Rodrigues (63 years old of Nuzedo de Cima, Vinhais), a former informant of Father Firmino A. Martins (see Martins 1928-39), spent a good part of an afternoon reciting and singing 29 poems while baking bread.   In Carção (Vimioso) we were lucky to find António Albino Machado de Andrade (67 years old).   A shoemaker as well as "regedor" (alderman) of his village, he recorded more than 30 ballads while working at his bench.   Our best informant, however, was Cândida Augusta Ramos (Eiró, Vinhais), a beautiful and kind septuagenarian.   When we first interviewed her, the poor lady was in tears because her daughter, who had come to spend her vacation in Portugal, was about to return to   France.   Two days later we found her sitting in front of her house alone, as often happens with old people whose children emigrate.   Thoroughly studied, her 45 ballads would fill a thick volume.   We owe to her versions of rare poems such as *Perseguição de Búcar pelo Cid* (*TM* no.2), *Virgílio* (*TM* no.98), *Quem Quiser Viver Alegre* (*TM* no.99), *Abenámar* (*TM* no.113), *A Serrana Matadora* (*TM* no.547), *O Conde Preso* (*TM* no.52), *Canta, Mouro* (*TM* no.113), *A Morte Ocultada* (*TM* no.1024), *A Esposa de D. Garcia* (*TM* no.552), and *O Prisioneiro* (*TM* no.117). When we asked her from whom she had learned so much, she replied with great simplicity, as if she were still a young girl, that it had been from her mother and father.   We felt as if the years had not gone by, an impression that was repeated time after time in Trás-os-Montes upon hearing ballads that were already popular during the Middle Ages and the Renaissance, old parallelistic songs, or rhymed prayers in which a mother, invoking God with the name Adonai, begged Him to protect her children and keep them safe from the Inquisition and the irons of the king.[13]   It was as if time had not changed, people had remained the same, and the passing of the centuries were a mere illusion.   It is this impression which is felt with such force in Trás-os-Montes, the constant hope of coming upon "oceans never sailed before," making new but old discoveries, that has caused us to return to fieldwork repeatedly, despite the fact that, in the inevitable moments and days of great discouragement, we often swore that we would never again investigate oral tradition.

Although we collected many rare ballads in Trás-os-Montes, I shall limit myself to three examples of epic origin.   *A Perseguição de Búcar pelo Cid* is ultimately derived from the episode in the *Poema de Mio Cid* (vv. 2408-26) in which the Cid chases the Moor Búcar in front of the walls of Valencia, killing him as he reaches the ocean (see Armistead 1978:1:97).   Our version was recited   twice   by   the   aforementioned   septuagenarian   Cândida

Augusta Ramos on August 16, 1980 in Eiró (Vinhais):

Bem se passeia o mourinho
de calçada em calçada,
olhando para Valência,
o qu'está d'enmuralhada!
5 —Ó Valência, ó Valência,
de fogo sejas queimada!
Ainda ontem eras dos mouros,
agora estás cautivada.
Quando eras dos mouros,
10 eras de prata lavrada;
agora que és da cristandade,
és de pedra mal talhada.
E o rei, que aquilo ouviu
d'altas torres dond'estava,
15 chamou pela sua filha,
pela sua filha Bernarda.
—Entretem-me esse mourinho
de palavra em palavra;
as palavras sejam poucas,
20 d'amores venham tomadas.
—Como o hei-de entreter,
    meu pai,
se eu d'amores não sei nada?

The little Moor was walking
from street to street,
looking at Valencia,
oh how strongly walled it is!
"Oh Valencia, oh Valencia,
may you be burned with fire!
Yesterday you were still Moorish,
now you have been captured.
When you belonged to the Moors,
you were of wrought silver;
now that you are Christian,
you are of poorly carved stone."
The king, who heard those words
from the tall towers where he was,
called for his daughter,
his daughter Bernarda.
"Entertain that little Moor for me
with conversation;
let the words be few,
but as if you were in love."
"How can I entertain him, father,

when I know nothing of love?"

E o pai foi-s'embora.   E ela esperou o mourinho:
(Her father left and she waited for the little Moor:)

—Vai-te daí, ó mourinho,
que vem o meu pai e te mata;
25 os cavalos d'el-rei, meu pai,
já tropelam na calçada.
—Não tenho medo ao teu pai
nem à sua gente armada,
que o teu pai não tem cavalos
30 como a minha égua Paira,
a não ser um filho dela,
que não sei por onde ele pára.
—Vai-te daí, ó mourinho,
não digas que eu te sou falsa;
35 esse cavalo, mourinho,
meu pai tem-le dado cevada.
Palavras não eram ditas
e o cavalo rochinava,
e o mourinho, qu'aquilo ouviu,
40 ele fugia que voava;
por a clara vinha fora,
bem s'ele maniava.

"Get away, oh little Moor,
my father will come and kill you;
the horses of my father, the king,
are galloping along the street."
"I do not fear your father
nor his armed men,
for he doesn't have horses
like my mare Paira,
unless it be a son of hers
whose whereabouts I don't know."
"Get away, oh little Moor,
don't say that I deceive you;
to that horse, little Moor,
my father has fed barley."
These words were barely said
and the horse began braying,
hearing this, the little Moor
ran so fast he seemed to fly;
through the good vineyard,
he moved as fast as he could.
    (*TM* no.2)

Unlike some other Portuguese versions (cf. Leite de Vasconcellos 1:no.4), ours fails to state that the Cid manages to kill the Moor.

A Morte de D. Beltrão is ultimately derived from the

Chanson de Roland. The following version preserves the reference to Roncevaux ("Rocesvale"), where the massacre of the rear guard of the French army occurred (for bibliography see Armistead 1978:1:104). It was recited by Mariana Preto (about 75 years old) in Guadramil, Bragança on July 18, 1980:

—Quedos, quedos, cavaleiros,
dos que el-rei mandou contar.
Contaram e recontaram,
só um le vem a faltare;
5 era esse o D. Beltrão,
tão forte no pelejare.
Sete vezes que contaram,
. . . .
todas sete lhe caíram
10 ao bom velho de seu pai.
—Volta atrás, velho triste,
sem mais dizer nem falar;
se a sorte não caísse,
não teria d'ir buscare.
15 De dia vai pelo monte,
de noite vai pelos vales.
Chegou àquela mortaldade
onde fosse Rocesvale.
Os braços já tem cansados
20 de tanto morto virare;
vira todos os franceses
e D. Beltrão não pôde achare.
Viu estar um perro mouro
num ar a ver velare.
25 —Diz-me lá, meu pobre mouro,
que me digas sem m'enganare:
Cavaleiro d'armas brancas,

seu cavalo sem igual,
na ponta da sua lança
30 traz um branco cendal,
que le bordou sua dama,
bordado a ponto real?
—Esse cavaleiro, amigo,
morto está naquele fragal,
35 co'as pernas entre as águas(?)
e os corpos no areal,
com três feridas no peito,
qual delas seja a mais mortal:
por uma l'entra o sol,
40 por outra l'entra o luar;
pela mais pequena delas
um gavião a voar.
—Não torno a culpa ao meu filho
nem aos mouros de le matar;
45 torno a culpa ao seu cavalo

"Be still, oh knights, be still,
the king wants you counted."
They counted and recounted,
only one was missing;
it was D. Beltrão,
who was such a brave warrior.
They drew lots seven times,
. . . .
and each time the lot fell
to his father, a good old man.
"Go back, sad old man,
without saying another word;
if the lot hadn't fallen to you,
you wouldn't have to look for him."
By day he travels in the mountains,
by night in the valleys.
He arrived at the massacre
that took place at Roncesvaux.
His arms are already tired
from turning over so many corpses;
he looks at all the French
and can't find D. Beltrão.
Then he saw a Moorish dog
standing guard on a battlement.
"Tell me, my poor Moor,
let me know without deceit:
Did you see a knight with white arms,
and an unequalled horse,
on the tip of his lance
a white sendal,
embroidered by his lady,
with royal stitches?"
"That knight, friend,
is dead on those cliffs,
with his legs in the water
and his body on the sand,
three wounds in his chest,
each of which is mortal:
the sun shines through one,
the moon through another;
through the smallest one
a hawk flies."
"I do not blame my son,
nor the Moors for killing him;
I blame his horse

de não o saber retirar.

Milagre, quem tal diria,
quem tal pudesse contar!
O cavalo quase morto
50 ali se pôs a falare:
—Não me torne a mim a culpa,
que ma não pode tornar.
Três vezes o retirei,
três vezes para o salvare;
55 três vezes encurteu—me a rédea
e alargou o peitoral;
três vezes me deu espora
co'a sanha de pelejare;
a terceira fui a terra
60 co'esta ferida tão mortal.

for not withdrawing him from
        battle."
And then a miracle happened,
who would think of such a thing!
The horse almost dead
began to speak right then:
"Do not blame me for it,
you have no right to do so.
Three times I withdrew him,
three times so as to save him;
three times he pulled my reins back
and loosened my girth;
three times he gave me the spurs
such was his fury to fight;
the third time I fell to the ground
with this mortal wound."
        (*TM* no.9)

Floresvento has its origin in the twelfth-century French
Floovent. Since the published Galician version (Catalán 1979:241,
n.63) depends on the Portuguese variants from Trás-os-Montes,
and the Sephardic verses, although precious documents in
themselves, constitute fragments (see Costa Fontes 1982a), this
ballad, which is absent from all the early collections, is essentially
Portuguese today. A comparison of the versions from the Azores
and Trás-os-Montes with the French *Floovent* and its Italian prose
derivative, *Fioravante*, made it possible to determine to some
extent what the lost Iberian prototype, without which the existence
of the ballads cannot be explained, must have been like (Costa
Fontes 1985). The following version was recited by António Albino
Machado de Andrade in Carção, Vimioso on August 1, 1980:

—Cruel vento, ó cruel vento,
roubador maioral!
Roubaste as três igrejas,
as melhores de Portugal.
5 —Se roubei as três igrejas,
dinheiro tenho para as pagare.
—Cruel vento, ó cruel vento,
derrubador maioral!
Roubaste as sete fortunas,
10 as melhores de Portugal.
—Se roubei as sete fortunas,
com elas m'hei-de governare.
—Cruel vento, ó cruel vento,
roubador maiorale!
15 Roubaste as três meninas
mais lindas de Portugal
—Pois se roubei as meninas,
dinheiro tenho p'r'às pagare.

"Cruel wind, oh cruel wind,
you are the biggest thief!
You have robbed three churches,
the best in Portugal."
"If I robbed the three churches,
I have money to make amends."
"Cruel wind, oh cruel wind,
you are the biggest thief!
You have robbed seven fortunes,
the best in Portugal."
"If I robbed the seven fortunes,
I'll manage my affairs with them."
"Cruel wind, oh cruel wind,
you are the biggest thief!
You have abducted three maidens,
the prettiest in Portugal."
"If I abducted the maidens,
I have money to make amends."

—Cruel vento, cruel vento,	"Cruel wind, cruel wind,
20 a honra das meninas	the honor of the maidens
com dinheiro não se paga.	cannot be restored with money.
. . . .	. . . .
Tu hás ir a pagare	You'll pay for your crimes
mas é às cadeias de Portugal.	in the jails of Portugal."

Depois foi preso. E acabou.
(Then he was imprisoned. That's all.)

(*TM* no.62)

Since the very beginning of our fieldwork in California, we were acutely aware of the fact that the Portuguese ballad, at least in the form in which it has survived for centuries, was condemned to disappear very soon.   Therefore, our main purpose was to collect as many ballads as possible, thus preserving and making them available for future studies.   Given these objectives, I repeat, it would have been utterly nonproductive to remain in a given area over a long period of time in order to make a detailed study of their role at the individual and community levels.   Such investigations can be undertaken by those who have the training and the inclination to do so.   What I have to report on the functions of the ballads is largely based on what the informants themselves told us, for we never waited for the so-called "natural ballad-singing situations" to arise.

Having been born into an Azorean family where the tradition was preserved, I can confirm the obvious fact that the main function of the ballad is to entertain.   My grandmother used to sing them to herself during her domestic chores whenever she felt like it, and so did my mother, together with other lyrical and church songs that they knew.   Some women reported that, besides helping to while away the hours during endless domestic chores, ballads could be extremely useful when the time came to put children to sleep.

In the Azores these poems were transmitted from generation to generation, especially at the family level, but that was not always the case.   Women also sang ballads when they got together to embroider and to card and spin wool during winter evenings, or to shuck corn, an occasion when the men also worked at their side. Some were sung to the viola during dances that used to be held in private homes.   On the island of São Miguel, a reduced number of ballads seemed to play a role in the popular theater of some villages.   In Toronto, Lígia Almeida reported that *Bela Infanta* (*Can* no.37) and her second version of *Rico Franco* (*Can* no.170) formed part of plays. According to Manuel Moniz Graça, *Paixão do Redentor* (*Can* no.426) was one of the ballads sung during the penitential pilgrimages in which groups of men would travel on foot around the island of São Miguel in eight days, stopping to pray in chorus in front of each church. On the island of Graciosa, men and women perform a type of narrative folk dance, "o bailado das espadas" (the dance of swords) during Carnival (see Fagundes 1976). The ballad *Veneno de Moriana* formed the basis for the dance entitled "A Juliana," the usual name for the protagonist in the Azorean versions who poisons the faithless lover who invites her to his wedding with another woman. *Nau Catrineta*, a poem about hunger at sea, was sung in "Os Marujos" (The Sailors). Another ballad-singing situation was provided by the ancient festivities held yearly in honor of the Holy Ghost. Groups of men dressed as "foliões" (buffoons, jesters) sang religious ballads such as *O Lavrador da Arada* and *Barca Bela*. Joanne Purcell also heard them singing *Bernal Francês* in Ponta Delgada (Flores) (1970:236-37). Since *Bernal Francês* is a profane ballad about adultery, it is difficult to explain how it came to form part of their repertory. This is not the case with the rare *As Queixas de Ximena*, known in the Portuguese tradition through a single Azorean version.[14] That epic ballad became integrated into those festivities because Ximena begs the king for justice, complaining that the Cid has killed her best doves.[15] The dove, which is represented on top of the silver crowns worn by selected participants (usually three, at least in my village of Altares, Terceira) during the festivities in question, constitutes a symbol of the Holy Ghost.

In Trás-os-Montes, where ballad-singing is intimately related to agriculture, there were two melodies for several poems: one when they were sung in groups while harvesting, and another for more intimate occasions. As some informants told us, a ballad can also be adapted to any melody but, according to our recordings, this must not happen very frequently. The melody used while harvesting was rather slow. The goal was to pass the time, relieving the tedium of the work. The alternate melodies are much more lively in comparison.

Ballads sung during threshing were usually short. The fact that men and women would divide into two groups, alternating the verses and the act of threshing, may help to explain the survival of the medieval parallelistic structure of some ballads and songs (see

Costa Fontes 1982b). After one group sang a particular verse or strophe, the other group would repeat it in an alternate rhyme. The ballads used to while away the hours during the harvest were frequently lengthier, and some were reserved for a particular time of day, often in accordance with their opening verses. *A Fonte Clara* was sung in the morning because it began:

Manhãninha do S. João,	On the morning of St. John's Day,
pela manhã d'alvorada,	in the morning at dawn,
Jesus Cristo se passeia	Jesus Christ was walking
ao redor da fonte clara.	around the clear fountain.

(*TM* no.895)

Mothers also probably sent their daughters to the fountain for water in the morning, for that is when *A Fonte da Salgueirinha* was sung:

Minha mãe mandou-me à fonte,	My mother sent me to the fountain,
à fonte do salgueirinho;	to the fountain of the willow;
mandou-me lavar a cântara	she told me to wash the jar
com a flor do romeirinho.	with flower of rosemary.

(*TM* no.1215)

During the morning some people also sang *Indo Eu por Aí Abaixo*, at times on their way to work:

Indo-m'eu por aí abaixo	I was going down the road
em busca dos meus amores,	looking for my beloved,
encontrei um laranjal	and found an orange grove
carregadinho de flores	loaded with flowers.

(*TM* no.1251)

Alta Vai a Lua, Alta was reserved for noon:

Alta vai a lua, alta,	The moon is high, even higher
mais que o sol ao meio-dia;	than the sun at midday;
mais alta vai a Senhora	the Blessed Mother was even higher
quando p'ra Belém partia.	when she left for Bethlehem.

(*TM* no.945)

Around two o'clock people would sing *A Branca e a Morena*:

Indo-m'eu a passear	I was taking a walk
pela tarde, às duas horas,	at two in the afternoon,
encontrei numa janela	and found in a window
duas donzelas formosas.	two pretty maidens.

(*TM* no.1165)

When it was time for the mid-afternoon snack, the workers paradoxically would sing *Veneno de Moriana*, a ballad whose heroine poisons her faithless lover with a glass of wine:

—Apeia-te, ó cavaleiro,	"Dismount, oh knight,

darei–t'eu de merendar.
—D. Augénia, ó D. Augénia,
que é que tens para me dare?

I will give you something to eat."
"Dona Augénia, Dona Augénia,
what do you have to offer me?"
(*TM* no.481)

At dusk everyone would return home singing *Agora Baixou o Sol*:

Agora baixou o sole
lá p'ra trás daquela serra;
capinha leva vermelha,
que lha deu a Madanela.

The sun had just set
behind that mountain range,
wearing a little red cape
offered by Madanela.
(*TM* no.1287)

Many other poems were interspersed throughout the day. Naturally, ballads were also sung during other agricultural tasks such as picking olives, as well as on most of the occasions reported by the Azoreans: when women embroidered or were busy with their housework, when people gathered to work together in the evening, and so on. Ballads such as *A Loba Parda* (*TM* no.1030) and *As Três Comadres* (*TM* no.1107) were integrated into the repertory of the "pauliteiros," the famous folk dancers from Miranda do Douro who perform with sticks (see Mourinho 1984:448–518). This folk group was duplicated by the Portuguese in Toronto.

Although we were especially interested in ballads, we recorded a good number of poems of other genres with fairly specific functions in Trás-os-Montes. Some rhymed prayers were said when going to bed and upon arising, while entering church, when the priest came from the sacristy, during communion, and at the end of the mass. There were prayers for the sake of the souls in purgatory, beggars' songs such as *À Porta das Almas Santas* (*TM* no.1419), spells with various purposes, from those thought to help in finding lost items, to those that supposedly cured infirmities such as toothaches, and those employed to undo the effects of the evil eye and to confuse one's enemies. *Pela Rua da Amargura* (*TM* no.1416) and *As Doze Palavras* (*TM* no.1232; Aarne, Thompson 2010) were used during the vigils held for someone who was about to die. According to one informant, it was important to avoid errors with the latter: "If one makes a mistake, the soul will not go to a good place." Some Azoreans also seemed to believe this. A few poems were reserved for cyclical festivities such as Christmas and Twelfth Night. *Vinde e Adoremos* (*TM* no.1402) was sung from house to house in Gimonde (Bragança) during Christmas, but the custom has been reportedly abandoned.

Quando os Santos Reis Souberam (*TM* no.1550) was reserved for Twelfth Night.   When the workers arrived home at dusk, they sang *Esta Rua é Comprida* (*TM* no.1601) in chorus.   In Rio de Onor, a local poet would even compose verses to celebrate weddings (cf. *TM* no.1666).   Those poems were declaimed before the newlyweds and their guests at the door of the church after they were married.

Although I know that ancient historical ballads such as *Morte do Príncipe D. Afonso* are completely devoid of any historical value among the people, being remembered because of the universal human situations portrayed, I am not in a position to discuss what single ballad themes may represent to individual informants.   Once again, our main objective was to collect as many ballads as possible, for the ancient and noble tradition that has preserved them across the centuries will soon disappear.   In North America Portuguese balladry will die with those who brought it from their homeland.   Young people seldom care for ballads in an environment in which the language of their ancestors must be relegated to a secondary position.   It is true that many have to use Portuguese to communicate with their parents and grandparents, who frequently know little or no English.   However, young people prefer to use English among themselves, even while in the presence of their elders, and there are some who emphatically refuse to speak any Portuguese.

The situation is not much better in Portugal itself.   Many prospective informants told us that they had not cared to learn the old songs, preferring the modern ones that were more popular during their youth.   One of the reasons why the oral tradition of Trás-os-Montes is the richest in the country is the fact that ballads were associated with agriculture, being sung by groups of people especially while harvesting and threshing, but these customs have almost disappeared today.   Machines have been substituted for the sickle, the mallet, and the paved areas previously used for threshing and drying cereals.   The groups of laborers who used to go from village to village in the North, at times crossing the Spanish border in order to follow the harvest, are practically extinct today.   Those laborers used to learn and transmit new ballads while working in the fields.   The other ballad-singing occasions are becoming rarer and rarer due to the influence of radio, television, the spreading of literacy, the increasing urbanization of the countryside, and other pressures of modern life.

To sum up, progress will cause the ballads that have survived, thanks to the aged, to be almost forgotten when those people die. Fortunately, a great effort is being currently undertaken in Portugal to preserve as many ballads as possible. The "Grupo de Estudos Dr. José Leite de Vasconcellos," directed by Pere Ferré, has already given us a splendid collection from the archipelago of Madeira (1982), and there are several more in preparation: District of Vila Real (Trás-os-Montes, over 1,000 variants), Madeira (416 versions harvested by Pere Ferré and Vanda Anastácio in 1983), Beira Alta and Beira Baixa (more than 300 versions recorded during carnival in 1985). José Joaquim Dias Marques has formed a monumental collection of about 1,100 ballads in the "concelhos" of Bragança and Vinhais, of which he has already given us a stimulating preview (1984-85). Recently he visited the Alentejo with Ana Maria Martins, recording about 100 poems. Working with Maria Angélica Reis da Silva, Dias Marques has also been able to find several ballads in the "concelho" of Loures, near Lisbon. José António Falcão and Maria de Lurdes Gonçalves das Dores have been exploring the Alentejo and the Algarve. Maria Aliete Farinho das Dores Galhoz's fundamentally important *Romanceiro Popular Português*, which draws from several sources—theses, other poems gathered by Leite de Vasconcellos, as well as ballads collected in various parts of the country by the editor herself and by others—is now in print. I would like to express my gratitude to these good friends for keeping me abreast of their crucially important investigations and hope that all the results will be made available as soon as possible.

Kent State University

Notes

[1]The fieldwork summarized in this paper was undertaken thanks to the generous support of the Luso-American Education Foundation (1975, 1977), the Office for Research and Sponsored Programs, Kent State University (1977), the National Endowment for the Humanities (1978, 1980), and the John Simon Guggenheim Memorial Foundation (1984). Some of the notes that follow first appeared in the introductions to the ballad collections that I have published: *Romanceiro Português dos Estados Unidos 2: Califórnia (Cal)*; *Romanceiro Português do Canadá (Can)*; *Romanceiro Português dos Estados Unidos 1: Nova Inglaterra (NI)*; *Romanceiro da Ilha de S. Jorge (SJ)*, but I have drawn more heavily from the introduction to my recent *Romanceiro da Província de*

Trás-os-Montes (*TM*).   My observations must be read in conjunction with Joanne B. Purcell's indispensable "Ballad Collecting Procedures in the Hispanic World" (1979).   A short version of this paper was read at the Tenth International Congress on Patristic, Medieval, and Renaissance Studies, Villanova University, September 1985.

[2]C. Michaëlis de Vasconcelos (1934) was able to document over eighty *romances* that were cited or partially quoted in works written by about fifty Portuguese medieval and Renaissance writers.

[3]In 1970 I also found out, thanks to Professor Askins, that Joanne B. Purcell had already investigated this tradition in 1967 and 1968 (Purcell 1968; 1969).   I met her in 1973 when I transferred to the University of California, Los Angeles.   What she had done in California and the splendid collection she had put together during eighteen months of fieldwork (1969-70) in the Azores, Madeira, Minho, Beira Alta, Beira Baixa, Alto Alentejo, and Trás-os-Montes (see Purcell 1970; 1972) constituted an important stimulus to me.   (Her *Romanceiro Português das Ilhas Atlânticas*, which was transcribed by Isabel Rodríguez García, is now out.)   Joanne's work had originally been inspired by Professors Samuel G. Armistead and Joseph H. Silverman, with whom she had studied in Los Angeles.   In 1975 Joanne introduced me to them and to Diego Catalán.   Their distinguished example and constant encouragement strengthened my resolve to go on collecting as many Portuguese ballads as I could.   Unfortunately, Joanne is no longer with us.   For an evaluation of her momumental contribution, see Armistead and Costa Fontes (1984).

[4]For a preliminary report, see Costa Fontes (1984a).

[5]When we returned in 1984, many had begun moving to other areas within the city as well as to surrounding communities such as Mississauga.

[6]On São Jorge the word "oravia" or "aravia" is preferred throughout most of the island, but in the village of Beira, where it means "joke" or "rubbish," there are people who simply refer to them as "histórias."   The term "oravia" also appears on the island of Flores, but the word "trova" is much more common there.   Throughout the Azores, ballads are also known as "décimas" and "casos," designations which are also used to identify the modern narrative poems transmitted by the so-called "literatura de cordel" (chapbooks).   Although the ancient and standard word "romance" appears in some of the old ballads (cf. Costa Fontes 1983a:98, 102), it is no longer used with that meaning on the islands.   With informants from Madeira and continental Portugal, we merely asked for old songs that told stories.

[7]Please note that, since this ballad and the ones that follow were transcribed from recordings as faithfully as I could, grammatical errors and inconsistencies on the part of the informants were not corrected.

[8]Although Rio de Onor is half Portuguese and half Spanish, it really constitutes a single village, for the inhabitants choose to ignore the border. Since there is a great deal of intermarriage, there are Portuguese who inherit property in Spain and vice versa.   When we were trying to conduct interviews in the small country store ("venta") on the Spanish side, eighty-one-year-old Caetana Fernández López, upon discovering that we were Portuguese, insisted on speaking to us in our own language, for she had learned it from her mother.   Someone said that at one time a Portuguese officer tried to separate the two halves of the village by blocking the main road with a chain along the border, but the inhabitants simply pretended that there was another road

next to it. There is an important monograph about this village (Dias 1981).

[9]Term used to designate settlers from the former colonies who saw themselves forced to return to Portugal after their hasty, poorly planned independence.

[10]Portuguese provinces are divided into districts which are subdivided into "concelhos." The closest English translation is "county."

[11]I interviewed 15 informants from that province in New England, and Pere Ferré and his team were able to collect over 300 ballads in Beira Alta and Beira Baixa in 1985 (personal communication from Pere Ferré of May 8, 1985).

[12]She recited *Gerineldo* (*TM* no.636) and a variant of *O Velho Viúvo + A Fonte Clara* (*TM* no.1070), but, although she tried very hard, she was unable to remember her version of the rare *Persequição de Búcar pelo Cid*. Fortunately, she recorded it for Dias Marques (4:533–34) two years later (1982). This, together with the splendid results obtained by Pere Ferré and his team in the two Beiras, shows how important persistence is to successful fieldwork.

[13]I have alrady studied a selection of these prayers in "Crypto-Jewish Prayers from Rebordelo," a paper read at the 39th annual meeting of the Rocky Mountain Language Association, Provo, Utah, October, 1985. The final version of this paper, entitled "Four Portuguese Crypto-Jewish Prayers and their 'Inquisitorial' Counterparts," will be submitted to the *Mediterranean Language Review*. The other seven prayers we recorded will be presented in a separate article.

[14]Although Braga presents this ballad as if he had two different variants, the second of which is reported to be from two islands (!), they practically repeat each other word for word (Braga 1906–09:2:249 [Pico]; Braga 1911–13:2:56–57 [Flores and Corvo]). According to Pere Ferré (personal communication), who has investigated Braga's sources in detail, he merely published the same version twice.

[15]The hero is not specifically named in the Azorean rendition, but his name appears in the ancient and in the Sephardic traditions (see Armistead 1978:1:82).

The Living Ballad in Brazil:
Two Performances

Judith Seeger

Many approaches have been devised to study the elusive art form known as the oral traditional ballad, to try to reach an understanding of the interplay between memory and creativity in its transmission from one generation to another over several centuries. In this paper I will add yet another approach: a close analysis of two oral performances I recorded in rural Brazil in 1978.

Since an oral traditional ballad in order to survive must be intelligible, meaningful to its listeners, and aesthetically pleasing, it is evident that problems will be raised by performing ballads of medieval Iberian origin in a contemporary rural Brazilian context. Some of these problems are linguistic, brought about by evolution of the spoken language. Others arise from changing socio-economic and historical conditions. Attempts by singers to resolve these problems lead sometimes to inspired innovations and sometimes to strained accommodation between the received text and the singer's desire to bring it to life for contemporary listeners. At every moment in each variant the desire to maintain tradition confronts the necessity for innovation. Sometimes tradition takes precedence; sometimes innovation. A ballad requires both to survive. Each rendering of a living ballad is the sum of the varying resolutions of its vital conflicts.

It was in order to observe such conflicts and their resolutions that during 1977 and 1978 I spent a year living in the coastal town of Conceição da Barra, Espírito Santo, Brazil, searching for oral traditional ballads in performance contexts.[1] Conceição da Barra is the center of a rural region settled by fishermen and small farmers, which has had a relatively stable population for most of its history. I chose to work there after reading and talking with Brazilian ballad scholars including Bráulio do Nascimento and

175

Guilherme Santos Neves.   Neves, though he was far from sanguine about the vitality of the oral traditional ballad, had collected ballads in the region; so I knew a tradition had existed there.

My field project grew from the conviction that a legitimate and interesting way to approach questions of creativity, transmission, aesthetics, and meaning in oral traditional balladry would be to seek out the singers to discover how, when, where, and to whom they performed.   My specific goal was to hear ballads performed for others, not for my microphone alone.   I knew this approach would preclude collecting a large corpus of variants, but I expected the extratextual information obtained would compensate for the small number of texts.   By remaining in one place over an extended period, I would give myself time to learn about the singers and listeners, their way of life and the entire oral tradition they shared.   From the vantage of this general context I wanted to observe how an individual in a given performance intellectually and artistically interprets a traditional piece to the satisfaction of all involved.

In my fieldwork I confronted the problems faced by any collector of oral traditional ballads.   Experience confirmed the warning that asking for a *romance* would lead to nothing.   The word, which in Brazil denotes a narrative song, a narrative poem written for the *literatura de cordel*, and a novel, had absolutely no eliciting value.   Incipits (the first lines of a ballad) and plot synopses were scarcely more effective at first, though they later led to recordings of *O cego (The Blind Man)* and *Juliana e dom Jorge (Juliana and Don Jorge,* known to collectors of Spanish ballads as *El veneno de Moriana).*   When exhaustive searching for ballads proved nearly fruitless, I turned my attention to the local storytelling tradition. This tradition, though it too is less vital than it once was, continued to exist around Conceição da Barra and to involve both sexes and all ages. In sessions attended by a number of individuals I hoped to gain contextual and performance information that would be applicable to a discussion of the apparently defunct ballad tradition.

I began with the help of local people to organize storytelling sessions of the type Kenneth Goldstein in his book *A Guide for Fieldworkers in Folklore* has called "induced-natural."[2]   Such sessions, though convened by me, were modeled on what people had told me about traditional events.   Since the ideal of effacing myself and hiding my recording equipment was clearly impossible, the sessions could never be entirely unselfconscious. Their quality as traditional events varied, but at some point during the best of them tellers would invariably turn away from the microphone to interact with living people—verbally by inserting them into the story, visually by eye contact, sometimes by touch. The unresponsive microphone would lose its initial appeal, and the session would take on a dynamic of its own in which individuals would swap stories and anecdotes, each one suggesting another.

As time passed I found myself working almost exclusively with the poorer inhabitants of the region, who were richer in oral traditions. Some sessions were held in houses in the dark back streets of Conceição da Barra. Some were convened on isolated small farms. Most gatherings took place in the nearby settlement of Itaúnas. To correspond to the needs of the participants, almost all the sessions were held on Saturday nights. The get-togethers were relegated to nighttime by local custom, reinforced by the belief, particularly prominent among the men, than anyone who told stories during the day would grow a tail. The few daytime sessions I recorded involved women and a few men who allowed themselves to be convinced that it was all right to tell stories during the day on weekends. One of the best male tellers, however, retorted to some women who insisted nothing would happen to him if he told stories during the day that it was all right for them because they could hide their tails under their skirts. Saturday was the chosen night because it was the only time people were not faced with having to rise early to work the next morning.

Twice I was surprised when within the context of storytelling sessions unsolicited ballads were performed. The bulk of the rest of this paper will be devoted to describing the settings and analyzing those two spontaneous performances, both versions of the ballad *El conde Claros de Montalbán (Count Claros of Montalbán)*, whose first published texts date from sixteenth-century Spain.[3] One woman performed the version known to collectors of Hispanic ballads as *Conde Claros en hábito de fraile (Count Claros in Monk's Attire)*, the other *Conde Claros y la infanta (Count Claros and the Princess)*. In my analyses I will comment on musical, linguistic, social, and aesthetic characteristics of each performance.

In considering the music of the ballad, I am departing from the mainstream tradition of ballad studies. Musicological studies of Hispanic ballads do exist, notably those of Israel Katz.[4]

Nevertheless, scholars in the field have never examined relationships between the text and the tune of a ballad, and most published ballad variants in any tradition are not accompanied by their melodies.   Though it is true that traditional texts may be sung to different tunes and that the same tune may be adapted to different texts, it does not follow that searching for relationships between a given text and its tune is in vain.   The typical ballad melody has distinctive generic characteristics, two of which are particularly significant in terms of the text.   These are its shortness and its internal organization.

The shortness of the ballad melody has important implications.   A ballad tune is typically a four-phrase unit to which are sung texts whose lengths, though they vary, always exceed four phrases.   An obvious consequence of the wedding of brief tune and lengthy tale is the necessity of repeating the melody.   The ballad scholar and musicologist, Bertrand Bronson, has commented suggestively on what he perceived to be a fundamental conflict between the narrative ballad and its essentially lyric melodic vehicle:

> Upon reflection, we must perceive that the very idea of narrative, or progress from point to point in a story, is inimical to its statement in identical units of simple melody, repeated as many times as need requires.   The melodic form, an integrated succession of a given number of short phrases, has powerfully imposed itself on the verse form to mutual advantages; but the inherent demands of *narrative* [Bronson's emphasis] songs are for a freer and more dramatic vehicle; . . . clearly, the traditional ballad music operates against the narrative effect and acts to reinforce the level impassivity of the characteristic style.   And this is a source of its peculiar power.   Although it intensifies the emotional (and lyric) effect of the words as they pass, it deindividualizes and objectifies their stated content.   It regularizes and levels out the hills and valleys of narrative interest and reduces the varying speeds of travel to its own constant pace.   (1979:128-29)

Of course the description of ballad narrative as "progress from point to point in a story" is not strictly accurate.   As Bronson surely knew but chose not to emphasize here, near repetition, called parallelism, is a fundamental device of ballad organization on the structural and verbal levels as well as on the musical level. For example, the often-doubled questions posed by the father to his pregnant daughter in the Hispanic ballad known as the *Mal encanto* (*Evil Spell*) illustrate verbal and structural parallelism, as does the often-tripled test of the princess in *Count Claros in Monk's Attire*. In either case, a single question or proposition would suffice to advance the narrative. The predominance of dual and triple figures in these and other ballads shows that parallelism is an important feature of the genre. There is a difference between voluntary parallelism and obligatory, essentially unaltered melodic repetition. Nevertheless, the gulf between the narrative character of the ballad text and the repetitive nature of its musical realization is not so wide as Bronson might lead us to believe. On the contrary, the repetitive structure of the music, with all the power Bronson ascribes to it, reinforces a fundamental characteristic of the organization of the text. A ballad, even stripped of its tune, is not simply a linear narrative, but rather a narrative structured in a particular and characteristic way.

The second point to be considered with regard to the ballad tune is its internal organization. A typical ballad melody has an identifiable structure: four musical phrases which reach a mid-cadence at the end of the second phrase and terminate with a final cadence at the end of the fourth. Roger Abrahams and George Foss describe the traditional tune type of the Anglo-American ballad thus:

> As the verbal rhyme brings a sense of repose and finality to the stanza, so are the melodic cadences arranged to produce tension at the mid-cadence and repose at the final cadence. This is done musically by placing a tone other than the final at the mid-cadence, the final tone representing to the traditional singer the tone of greatest repose within the scale. (1968:161)

It will immediately be objected that the Hispanic ballad does not traditionally employ stanzaic verbal rhyme. And, in fact, the unchanging assonance characteristic of the Hispanic tradition does seem to allow a degree of melodic freedom not available to the Anglo-American ballad. If we letter each phrase, the generic ballad tune can be represented by ABCD. Repetition of the final two phrases, though not the rule in Hispanic balladry, is by no means unknown. Unlike in the Anglo-American ballad, there is no verbal restraint against singing a strophe representable by ABCDCD, or some variation thereof, if the singer feels that the extra verses complete a thought rather than begin a new melodic and verbal unit. This phenomenon has been documented for the Brazilian ballad by Jackson da Silva Lima and Antônio Lopes, and I have examples of it in a ballad corpus I collected in northern Spain.[5]

Such flexibility, however, is not usually needed. The typical sung Hispanic ballad, like its Anglo-American congener, is sung to a four-phrase tune and thus expresses the repeated pattern of tension resolving in at least temporary repose that is built into the music. Close examination of ballad texts reveals that the musical relationship between the mid-cadence and the final cadence reinforces a hierarchical relationship between two lines of verse (or two units of thought) which may be described as unfinished leading (at least temporarily) to finished. Though this relationship may not be immediately evident in written representation of a ballad that does not employ strophic rhyme, it is nonetheless an important element of the sung (the heard) ballad.

Indeed, the strophic character of a ballad melody seems to be an important influence on the organization of the text. Both ballad variants to be discussed in this paper adhere to traditional assonance schemes, though they in fact employ rhyme. Yet their organization is clearly stanzaic. Each group of four hemistichs is a unit, and is regarded as such by the singer. The prose intercalations that introduce each four-hemistich unit are the most obvious indication of strophic division. But even if they were removed, the unity of each group (hereafter called stanza) would be evident. The two verse lines that comprise each four-phrase stanza are always related to each other in terms of the hierarchy "unfinished → finished" that corresponds to the musical organization "tension → repose." A stanza may consist, for example, of a question and its answer, a statement and its elaboration, a sentence opened by a dependent clause, two parallel verse lines, or a description of a scene in which the second verse is consequent to the first. Though the specific intra-stanzaic relationships differ, each stanza is structurally a unit. The hierarchical nature of this unity—which replicates on the level of the stanza the hierarchical relationship between hemistichs— coincides with the organization of the ballad melody.

THE LIVING BALLAD IN BRAZIL

The variants to be discussed here present the particular
renderings of two traditional performers. The melding of text with
tune is one level on which we shall observe the singers' craft.
Each segment of text will be printed separately and discussed
before moving on to the next. Segments that are particularly
interesting musically are accompanied by musical transcriptions.
The transcriptions, written using the conventions of writing
Western erudite music, are not perfect representations of what was
sung. Even inexact representations, however, demonstrate the
reciprocal influences between text and tune that interest us here.[6]

Count Claros in Monk's Attire: Dona Branca

I do not know what prompted Maria da Conceição, a
forty-two-year-old resident of the town of Itaunas, Espírito Santo,
to sing the story of *Count Claros in Monk's Attire*. It was
Saturday night, May 20, 1978. I had met Dona Conceição three
months earlier, presented by her seventy-three-year-old mother,
who had first invited me to Itaunas after approaching me on the
street one day in Conceição da Barra and introducing herself. The
two women were much alike. Short, swarthy, and stoutly-built,
they were outgoing and cheerful. Both had welcomed me into
their homes and had told me some of the stories they remembered
from the time when they used to pass Sunday afternoons and long
evenings trading tales with others. I had tried in every way I
could imagine to discover whether they knew any ballads, to no
avail. Since both women were clearly trying out of sheer good will
to help me, I assumed they knew no ballads.

That evening we were in a small house at a storytelling
session very much like others held in the town. Itaunas was at
the time a settlement of some three hundred people linked to
Conceição da Barra by a narrow dirt road, which regularly became
impassable during and after heavy rains. The town was separated
from the sea by the Itaunas River, known locally as the River of
the Poor because it provided abundant fish for people who could
not afford to buy meat. The original town, located on the seaward
bank of the river, had been literally buried by sand. All that
remained of it were a few nearly-interred trees and a mast stuck
in the towering dunes to mark the place where the church perhaps
still stood. The inhabitants of the new Itaunas were those who
had decided not to leave the region when the fine sand—carried
by the prevailing northeast winds and no longer impeded by the

receding forest—gradually invaded and then covered their homes. One reason oral tradition survived in Itaunas was that it had electricity for only three hours a night, when there was enough fuel to run the town generator.

Our host for most Itaunas storytelling sessions was a man named Pulquério Aldo dos Santos, known to all as Seu Antero. He had built himself and his family a small house and adjacent store where he sold inexpensive sugarcane liquor and cups of weak but sweet coffee as well as other assorted goods: bananas, coconuts, home-made sweets, beer, soft drinks, cheese. A typical storytelling session in Seu Antero's living room would begin after nightfall. I would be seated on the bed that served as a couch when no one was sleeping. The rest of the furniture consisted of a low bookcase on which were arranged school books and knick-knacks; rough wooden benches lining two walls, brought in especially for the session; a clay water filter and glass high on a corner shelf; and on a square table at one end of the bed/couch a small candle-lit shrine to Saint Benedict the Moor ornamented with plastic flowers, rosaries, medals, and ribbons. The whitewashed walls were decorated with colorful pictures cut from magazines.

The front doorway and glassless window, its shutter left open, would be crowded with people of all ages coming to see what was going on. Passage through the back doorway, which led to the bedroom and outside to the kitchen behind the store, was reserved for the family. Seu Antero's wife would appear in that doorway to listen to the proceedings when she was not needed in the kitchen or the store. Seu Antero himself would disappear through the doorway from time to time and return fortified by a drink of sugarcane liquor. Occasionally he passed a glass of liquor to adult men sitting on the benches, "to help warm up their memories." Women stood leaning against the walls and sat on the floor with children beside them and in their laps. Older boys scaled and balanced on the top of the interior wall behind me, which, as in most rural Brazilian homes, did not reach the ceiling.

The session of May 20, except for the unexpected appearance of Count Claros, was not one of the better ones. A *jongo*, the local circle dance, was being held nearby. Drumming and singing could be heard in the background, and there was an extraordinary amount of coming and going from one event to the other. Our host, a leading singer and drummer as well as storyteller, was distracted. The call of the drums was finally too much for us; the session dissolved earlier than usual, and we all went to join the dance.

Dona Conceição began to perform abruptly, after complaining about the noise of people entering and leaving, stepping on the feet and hands of those seated on the floor, begging pardon. She was sitting on the floor facing me near the center of the room. Spectators were as usual crowding into the open doorway and leaning on the windowsill. Dona Conceição spoke and sang rapidly, but clearly, in her usual manner. During the first segment of the ballad, until she recounted the midwife's verdict on Dona Branca's condition, there was talking in the background as new arrivals searched for places to sit or stand. Thereafter the audience was listening and silent except for occasional murmurs, laughter, and Seu Antero's comments on the story. His remarks are noted in brackets in the following transcription.

Dona Conceição began:

"Disse que tinha uma moça, que ela ficou gorda em casa."

(It was said that there was a girl, who "got fat" at home.)

In the style that has become typical of many Brazilian ballads she begins with a prose introduction. The prose, as well as the storytelling performance context, indicate that she regards the ballad primarily as a tale. Her style of presentation is appropriate to a piece performed for entertaining a group. It is distinctly not that of a lullaby, for example, or a song sung to lighten solitary work.

I recorded many stories beginning with the formula "disse que . . . ." In the region of Conceição da Barra it was more popular than the more formal "era uma vez . . . ." The expression "dizem que . . . ," is often used in everyday conversation to absolve the teller of a fantastic story from responsibility for the truth of repeated hearsay. It would precede the recounting of abnormal or inexplicable happenings—werewolves, for example, or other strange beings said to roam the surrounding eucalyptus forests. Pronounced emphatically it would indicate incredulity on the part of the teller, who, nevertheless, was not willing to go so far as to deny out of hand the verity of what was being told. The conventional "disse que" has a parallel effect in formal oral narrative. Singular, but impersonal, preterite, it is a distancing device. It separates what is to follow from ordinary discourse, promising that the narrative will be interesting, structured, and

possibly incredible. The narrator, merely passing it on, assumes no
responsibility but to tell it well.

The rest of the opening phrase puts the central transgression
in a nutshell. The expression "ficou gorda" is a vernacular
euphemism for becoming pregnant. The word *gorda*, phonetically
close to the forbidden *grávida*, suggests the condition without
actually saying it. In popular speech, people of northern Espírito
Santo as in much of Brazil tend to reduce trisyllabic words whose
accent falls on the first syllable to two syllables. *Sábado*, for
example, typically becomes *sabo*; *lámpada* becomes *lampa*.
Metathesis of an "r" and its preceding or following vowel is also
common. And the word *gorda*, in addition to being nearly
derivable from *grávida* by the rules of vernacular sound change
alone, has the further advantage of pointing out the salient
characteristic of the pregnant woman's changing figure. Saying
that the girl became pregnant "em casa" means that she was living
in her natal house at the time. She was not married.

"Entaõ o pai dela falou assim . . . cantou assim:"

(So her father said thus . . . sang thus:)

The phrase is incomplete, leading into the sung dialogue that
is to follow. Dona Conceição hesitates as the style of delivery is
about to pass from that of spoken narrative to that of sung ballad.
She seems suddenly to be caught short by the significance of her
own words. Obviously the father did not sing to his daughter.
Yet Dona Conceição is going to sing his question. She is briefly
undecided, then resolves to use the verb that really describes what
is going to happen. For a moment the narrator is more conscious
of her manner of recounting the story than of what is being
recounted. She thus prepares the audience for the change from
speaking to singing.

=144 (very irregular)

2-- O que tendes minha filha que 'tas tão a-ma-re-la?

(What's the matter, my daughter? Why are you so yellow?)

The first question is typical of *Count Claros in Monk's Attire*
variants that begin with the *Evil Spell*, as do most Brazilian texts.

The second is not. I have discussed its Brazilian origin and significance in my article "Notes on Traditional Creativity: Examples of Innovation in Two Brazilian *Romances.*" Suffice it to say here that it is an innovation with respect to the traditional language of the ballad.

"Aí, ela falou p'r'o pai assim:"
(So she said to her father thus:)

This prose intercalation, like most of those that follow, identifies another speaker. Traditionally singers who regard ballads as songs have felt no need to indicate differing speakers. There is a strong tendency in contemporary Brazil, however, to identify them unless actual singers alternate as they do in dramatic representations (these days usually by children) of such ballads as *Juliana and Don Jorge* and *The Blind Man,* or unless the ballad is sung as a lullaby or to accompany work, situations in which the absence of a critical audience precludes the need for clarification.

The language of the prose segments is always colloquial. The "aí" that introduces this phrase is a typical discourse marker in informal narrative style. Dona Conceição uses it to begin almost every prose segment. Here, as in the following intercalations, her verb indicates speech, not song. Now that she has introduced the switch to song once and become involved in her story, she no longer hesitates over the discrepancy between her singing and the character's saying.

4-- De co-mer go-ia – ba ver¹ dei-ta-da na som-bra de-la.

(It's from eating green guavas, lying in the shade of the tree.)

The young woman's most common excuse in the *Evil Spell* is that drinking cold water has caused the change in her complexion. Dona Conceição's green guavas, in contrast, are unknown to published texts. As I have already discussed these unusual lines in the work cited above, I will not linger over them here. The music, however, merits a closer look.

Like any traditional singer, Dona Conceição sang in a natural voice, choosing a comfortable range. Though I have transcribed the piece to end on the note G above middle C in accordance with norms of ballad transcription, each stanza actually terminates about a quarter tone above F# below middle C. The melody rises to its highest pitch in the first hemistich where key words are often located: "filha" in hemistichs 1 and 5, "pai" in 9 and 13, "carta," "beijo," "abraço" in later hemistichs. The mid-cadence falls on the second, a definite point of tension in the major scale of this tune. The third phrase, nearly recapitulating the preceding one, maintains the tension by ending on the same note as the mid-cadence. The last phrase is a four-step cadence descending to the final, which is also the tonic of the scale.

Though Dona Conceição did not noticeably employ either volume or tone quality to heighten her delivery, she did, without departing from the general contour of the received tune, manipulate pitch distribution in accordance with the demands of the text. In the third phrase of the tune, for example, the first pulse always falls on the highest note (the C above middle C in my transcription). Usually two leading tones precede it:

não é na-da

But the pitch pattern may be altered to correspond to another stress pattern, as, for example in hemistich 15:

nu-ma ca-ie-ra

The same technique may be observed in the fourth phrase, where the tonal pattern of hemistichs 8 and 28:

differs from that of the others:

The first stress of this phrase normally falls on the note B. Exceptions are found in the first and seventh stanzas, in which Dona Conceição elides the last word of the third hemistich to the first word of the fourth, and the stress falls on the second C. Similar variations may be observed throughout the ballad. They demonstrate how changing tonal distribution molds the music to fit the words.

I have not barred the musical transcriptions, since barring would indicate metrical rigidity that does not exist here. Though the four phrases, each comprising eight beats, are in principle of equal length, they in fact differ slightly. The second and fourth phrases are as a rule longer than the first and third because their last notes, corresponding to the mid and final cadences, are briefly extended. Additionally, timing with a stopwatch shows that phrase duration is not fixed. Thus, although the metronomic tempo indication suggests the speed of the singing, it does not describe accurately the tempo of even two contiguous phrases. Rather, Dona Conceição consistently departs from the tempo and returns to it. In those stanzas where the rhyme scheme is á-a for example, the first "a" is lengthened while the second is scarcely touched. The word "pai" in hemistichs 9 and 13 is briefly extended, thereby receiving a rhythmic accent that reinforces the importance of the word. The subtlety of most of Dona Conceição's rhythmic alterations, perceived as metrical irregularity, defies representation in words or transcription.

Each phrase has two principal pulses, indicated with accents above the musical staff. Varying locations of these pulses within the metric scheme of the phrases are determined by the interaction of text with melody. There are phrases (notably hemistichs 39 and 43: "Boca/corpo que dom Carlos beija/abraça," where the first musical pulse falls on the word "que") in which melodic stress cannot be made to coincide with verbal stress. Such moments, common in balladry and discussed by Charles Seeger in his study (1977) of the Anglo-American ballad *Barbara Allan*, create a

counterpoint between words and music, which enriches the texture
of the piece by calling attention to the occasionally uneasy
accommodation between words and music. Moments where musical
and verbal stress do not coincide are probably more common and
less significant in Hispanic than in Anglo-American balladry
because English poetic meter is based on stress and Hispanic meter
is based on syllable count. Yet they are striking here, since it is
clear that Dona Conceição makes an effort to have the stress of
her music and words coincide as much as possible.

"Aí o pai foi, falou assim:"
(So her father went and said thus:)

The spoken interruption takes the form adopted by most of
the succeeding intercalations: "Aí [. . .] foi, falou assim." The
phrase, though not inverse, is formulaic in this variant of the
ballad. It may be expanded or contracted, but its structure is
always the same.

6   "—O que tendes, minha filha, que 'tas tão desmudada?
8   —Não é nada, senhor pai, é a saia mal talhada."
(What's the matter, my daughter? Why are you so changed?
It's nothing, father sir. It's my badly tailored skirt.)

This stanza adopts the characteristic assonance and the second
most common excuse of the *Evil Spell*. "Desmudada" is a regional
pronunciation of the rarely used adjective *demudada*. The young
woman blames her badly-tailored skirt for her altered appearance
in many variants of this ballad from Brazil, Spain, Portugal, and
Catalonia, as well as in its tragic Hungarian counterpart, sometimes
called *Barbara Angoli*, and the German *Ritter und Magd* and
Schwabentöchterlein. The motif of the shortened skirt, which also
appears in the sixteenth-century Spanish *Tiempo es, el caballero*
seems to float freely within the ballad tradition of the dishonored
maiden.

"Aí o pai dela mandou fazer uma roupa diferente . . . .
Aí mandou chamar a parteira. A parteira falou assim:
"Dona Branca não sente febre nem 'defruço'. Olhe o
bucho!"

(Then her father had some different clothes made . . . .
Then he had the midwife called. The midwife said:
"Dona Branca doesn't have fever or the flu. Look at her
gut!")

Usually the excuse of the ill-tailored skirt prepares for a neat reversal in which tailors summoned by the father point out to him that the young woman is responsible for the change in the skirt rather than the other way around as she has claimed. That segment of verse has been either forgotten or intentionally omitted here. The pause after the first sentence replaces stating of the obvious: that different clothing will make no difference. The father calls the midwife.

Dona Conceição had evidently memorized the midwife's short speech. Months later when I asked her the meaning of the word I have spelled "defruço" she said, and others confirmed, that it meant what Brazilians normally call *gripe*, or flu. The word *defruço* is probably derived from *defluxo*, defined as a head cold. Its phonetic transformation follows standard unwritten rules. In Brazilian vernacular "l" is often replaced by "r." Pronunciation of intervocalic "x" is not fixed: it may sound as "ks," "z," "s," or "sh." *Defruço* is a euphemism whose creation was motivated by fear. It was used by older people, Dona Conceição explained, to avoid naming the dread influenza for fear of summoning it. After defining the word for me, Dona Conceição repeated the midwife's declaration word for word, laughing heartily. The diagnosis is decidedly coarse. Using the word "bucho," which usually denotes the stomach of an animal, to refer to the womb of a young woman is unflatteringly suggestive.

"Aí foi, o pai dela foi, falou assim:
(So he went, her father went and said thus:)
10   —Filha que faz iss' ao pai merece ser degolada,
12   cõ'a navalha de arpaõ, um arpaõ bem amolada."
(A daughter who does that to her father deserves to be beheaded, with the blade of a harpoon, a well sharpened harpoon.)

The father, typically, is outraged at what his daughter has done *to him*. His suggestion that her head be cut off (or her throat be slit), however, is unknown to published texts of *Count Claros in Monk's Attire*, where immolation is always the selected method of execution. The choice of a harpoon as the weapon to carry out the beheading gives the rendering a local flavor. Much of the Brazilian coast, including northern Espírito Santo, was once whaling country.

The fourth hemistich of this stanza includes the first of three cases in this variant in which demands of the rhyme scheme supersede grammatical rules. The word "amolada" modifies "arpão." But *arpão* is masculine, so the concording adjective would be *amolado*. At a moment of conflict the singer chooses to sing "amolada" to rhyme with "degolada."

> "Aí o irmão dela foi, falou assim:
> (So her brother went and said thus:)
> 14 —Filha que faz iss' ao pai merece ser requeimada
> 16 numa caieira de fogo, com lenha bem atiçada."
> (A daughter who does that to her father deserves to be thoroughly burned in an oven of clay tiles, with well lit wood.)

I have seen no other variant of the *Count Claros* beginning with the *Evil Spell* in which a brother is introduced. In this respect Dona Conceição's rendering recalls the Portuguese texts of *Count Claros in Monk's Attire* in which the wayward woman's brothers debate forms of execution. The intervention of the brother here probably stems from the incorporation of the previous anomalous stanza, rather than from influence by those variants, which are otherwise quite distinct. Need for identifying a second speaker arises from the presentation of alternative methods of execution. Since the brothers of an unmarried woman traditionally share with her father responsibility for her sexual honor, a brother is a logical interlocutor at this point.

The "caieira" is either an oven for baking lye or a kiln made of the clay tiles it is to fire. Its appearance, reinforced by the emphatic "requeimada," meaning well or excessively burned, suggests that Dona Branca in this variant is not merely to be scorched on a pyre; she is to be baked to a crisp.

> "Aí ela foi, pegou a passear na varanda, chorando."
> (So she went and started walking on the balcony, crying.)

This prose intercalation, like that revealing the truth about Dona Branca's condition, condenses a narrative juncture which in the tradition of the Iberian Peninsula appears in verse. It rarely appears in any form in the Brazilian tradition, where Dona Branca's wish for a messenger usually follows directly upon her father's sentence. Dona Conceição describes her as crying, a necessary modifier to show that her action, "passear na varanda," is not the pleasurable stroll it might otherwise appear. The sentence has narrative, visual, and dramatic value. It locates Dona

Branca on the marginal territory from which she will summon the messenger, as well as describing in concrete ballad style, despite the prose, her movement and emotional state.

"Aí ela foi, falou assim:
(So she went and said thus:)
18 —Se tivesse um criado que fizesse meu mandar,
20 eu mandava uma carta a Carlos de Montevar.
(If I had a servant who would do my bidding,
I would send a letter to Carlos de Montevar.)
O nome do rapaz chamava-se Carlos de Montevar."
(The name of the fellow was Carlos de Montevar.)

The characteristic -á assonance of the *Count Claros* begins in hemistich 18, though not without some violence to the language, for "mandar" makes an awkward noun in this context. Claros' name in the ballad tradition can take many forms. The name in this rendering is remarkably close to the original. Claros, where it has been retained, has universally become Carlos. The surname Montevar fits the -ar rhyme scheme, which will be maintained from now on.

Hemistich 20, almost halfway through the ballad, is the first to mention the male protagonist. Such delay is typical of *Count Claros* variants that begin with the *Evil Spell*, and is to some extent a consequence of the joining of the two ballads. Though the plan in hemistichs 13-16 to burn the misbehaving daughter strongly hints at imminent transition to *Count Claros in Monk's Attire*, the ballad at that point is still within the assonance scheme of the *Evil Spell*. The transformation to the dominant ballad is completed only in hemistich 20.

This delay might appear to be a case like those proposed by Ruth House Webber in her 1979 article "Ballad Openings: Narrative and Formal Function," in which an ambivalent opening could serve as a device to pique the curiosity of the audience, to make the listeners pay closer attention. The *Evil Spell*, after all, is a ballad in its own right, whose outcome may be either marriage or death. There are thus at least three directions in which such a beginning might go, and it is not unreasonable to postulate that an audience might listen carefully to discover which one will be chosen.

For contextual reasons I doubt that any such suspense was generated during Dona Conceição's performance. Part of the appeal of traveling storytellers and singers was undoubtedly novelty. In such cases a ballad opening like that of the *Evil Spell* might indeed generate suspense. Familiar repetitions by accomplished performers were also appreciated, however, and the variant under discussion clearly falls into that class. The ballad performed by Dona Conceição was recognized as being the rendering of a recently deceased local storyteller named Benedito Duarte. Only if Benedito Duarte knew more than one ballad with this same beginning could any doubt as to its ending arise. More likely he took advantage of the ambiguous *Evil Spell* opening to exercise a ribald sense of humor, with no thought of creating narrative tension. The situation as it is presented here is altogether too light-hearted to lead credibly to tragedy for the lovers, particularly in a ballad tradition like the Luso-Brazilian in which young love, even erring young love, is more often exalted than punished.

If it does not create suspense, however, the delay in mentioning the name of the man responsible for Dona Branca's condition does have the effect of focusing almost half the ballad on the central struggle between the father and his daughter. Their conflict is further stressed in the text by the alternating "filha," "pai," "filha," "pai," at places of emphasis in the first two stanzas (—O que tendes, minha filha, . . .; —Não é nada, senhor pai . . .) subsequently compressed into the initial "filha" and final "pai" of hemistich 9 (—Filha que faz isso ao pai . . .), repeated in hemistich 13.

The verb form "mandava" in hemistich 19, though strictly speaking ungrammatical in this context, is characteristic of colloquial speech, not limited to Espírito Santo or to any socio-economic group. In informal conversation the imperfect tense is almost always used following an imperfect subjunctive "if" clause, in preference to the grammatically correct conditional.

In an aside, which may have been directed specifically to me, Dona Conceição explains the sudden appearance of Carlos de Montevar. To her he is an ordinary fellow, a "rapaz." The old story has been recast in local contemporary idiom. Claros' sixteenth-century nobility, like that of his lover, has been forgotten.

"Aí foi, apareceu o demônio. Aí foi, falou assim:
(So the demon appeared. So he went and said thus:)
22   —Dona, faça a carta, que eu mesmo vou levar.

24   Viagem de quinze dias   eu tiro só num jantar."
      (Lady, make the letter.   I'll take it myself.
      A fifteen-day trip I'll make in the time it takes to eat
      dinner.)

The first hemistich of this stanza is curious because it is missing two syllables. The deficiency could easily be remedied by having the speaker address Dona Branca as "Minha dona," just as Claros in the first hemistich of the last stanza addresses "Meus senhores." I suspect this was not done here because the speaker is a demon in whose mouth the courteous formula "My lady" might be taken literally. At the minor expense of two syllables he is kept properly obsequious and safely distant from the young woman, who must not be suspected of seriously trafficking with infernal powers. His form of address parallels that of the disguised Claros in hemistichs 37 and 41 (—Dona, me dê um beijo/abraço . . .), who must also not be allowed to get too close. But the function of the formal address in the second case is different. It establishes an ironically comic contrast between the friar's very proper language and his very improper propositions.

Though a messenger who can inform Claros of his lover's peril is indispensable in *Count Claros in Monk's Attire*, the identity of the messenger varies greatly. In the Peninsular tradition of the ballad the messenger may be a relative, a servant, a bird or an angel. In the Brazilian tradition it is sometimes a demon. When I asked Dona Conceição why a demon suddenly appeared to serve as Dona Branca's messenger, she merely laughed and said that was the way it was. Since Dona Branca is no longer, as on the Iberian Peninsula, the daughter of a count, calling on a servant, though possible, is not specifically supported by her situation. The elaborate family background that justifies the predominance of the brother or cousin messenger in certain Portuguese variants is absent. As far as people in the region of Conceição da Barra were concerned, a demon would be at least as likely a messenger as any, a service requiring fast travel being precisely the sort of task a demon would be capable of performing. Dona Conceição and her audience live in a world inhabited by spirits, and they are familiar with their behavior and powers. The boast in the third and fourth hemistichs of the stanza is to be taken literally.

"Aí ela foi, fez a carta, entregou a êle, falou assim:
(So she went and made the letter, gave it to him, and said
thus:)

2b-- Se ê-le 'ti-ver jan-tan-do dei-xa ê-le a-fin-dar.

(If he's having dinner let him finish.)

2c-- Se ê-le 'ti-ver dor-min-do dei-xa ê-le a-cor-dar.

(If he's sleeping let him wake up.)

Instructions, frequent in the Portuguese variants of *Count
Claros in Monk's Attire* when the woman addresses a young
brother or cousin, are vestigial in the Brazilian tradition, where
they appear only but not always when the messenger is
supernatural, whether angel or demon. The complex social and
family context that justifies instructing a young brother or cousin
in the etiquette of approaching a count has not survived
transmission to the ex-colony.

"Afindar" is a nonstandard form of "findar." It probably
appears here by analogy with its rhyming word "acordar." The
added syllable, by extending the first line and making it exactly
parallel to the second, serves a poetic purpose.

The musical transcription of this stanza illustrates a
partnership between musical and literary meter. Since Hispanic
ballad meter requires phrases whose penultimate syllable is stressed
to have eight syllables and those whose final syllable is stressed to
have seven, it is clear that in a literary ballad these lines would be
lacking syllables. If we follow the customary practice of
synaloepha, the first and third hemistichs contain an insufficient
seven syllables each, the second and fourth a severely deficient five.
As sung, however, each syllable receives its own note. Hemistichs
25 and 27 are properly awarded eight sung beats, 26 and 28 are
awarded seven. The music expands the verse.

Throughout this variant the relationship between syllable and
note is almost uniformly one to one. Dona Conceição occasionally

elides or apocopates words (as, for example, "iss' ao pai" in hemistichs 9 and 13). But apocopation in such contexts is characteristic of everyday speech. Equally, her omission of the first syllables of *estás* and *estiver* is consecrated by nearly universal usage. Dona Conceição reduces the word *para* to *pa* in hemistichs 40 and 42, but nobody says *para* in normal conversation. More noticeable is her pronouncing the entire word in the final hemistich of the ballad ("para seu pai se queimar"), where she needs both its syllables to fill the line. On the whole Dona Conceição tends to give words their full syllabic value.

"Aí quando chegou lá, chamou, disse assim:
(So when he arrived there he called and said thus:)
30   —Abr' aqui portas de vidro, janelas de Montevar,
32   que aqui tem uma carta que Dona Branca mandar.—"
(Open the glass doors, the windows of Montevar,
because there is a letter here which Dona Branca sent.)
[Seu Antero: E-e-i-i-i. . . .]

The implied grandeur of Claros' mansion is one of the two remaining traces of his original nobility. The other is the *dom* preceding his name in hemistichs 39 and 43 ("boca/corpo que dom Carlos beija/abraça"). Though every mature woman is called *dona* in contemporary Brazil, *dom* has been almost entirely replaced by *seu*, a contraction of *senhor*. The nobility of the characters is vestigial in the Brazilian tradition of *Count Claros in Monk's Attire*. It has been retained to a greater degree in the Brazilian *Count Claros and the Princess* tradition for internal reasons to be discussed below.

The infinitive "mandar," used instead of "mandou" in hemistich 32, marks the third concession of grammatical rules to the higher-ranked demands of rhyme.

"Aí êle pegou a carta; aí êle falou assim:
(So he took the letter; so he said thus:)
34   Quando leu esta cartinha se pôs logo a chorar.
36   Vestiu-se em traje de padre; coroa mandou botar."
(When he read this little letter he began to cry.
He dressed as a priest; he had a crown put on.)

This is the only verse segment of the ballad that is not dialogue. It is prefaced, however, with the same formula announcing dialogue that introduces the other segments. The error underlines the formulaic character of the prose intercalations.

The "esta" of the stanza's first hemistich suggests unexpected immediacy. It is as if the singer were holding the letter in her hand. Dona Conceição seems briefly to merge her own perspective with the otherwise distanced narrative. The very Brazilian diminutive "cartinha" contrasts to the archaic tone of most of the rest of the stanza. The construction in the second hemistich, "se pôs a . . . ," is unusually formal, as is the "vestiu-se" of the third hemistich. Though accurate in terms of grammatical rules, "vestiu-se" is a departure from the colloquial tone that characterizes the rest of the variant. Contemporary vernacular rarely employs the reflexive pronoun with this verb. Just as "esta cartinha" of hemistich 34 abruptly brings the ballad into our midst, the rest of the stanza abruptly removes it. At this moment of conflict between tradition and innovation, tradition has imposed itself.

Hemistich 36 is a good example of a clash between tradition and innovation whose resolution is less than satisfactory. Dona Conceição's "coroa mandou botar" seems to be an attempt to reinterpret an action whose significance has been lost. Forms of the phrase *raspar coroa* meaning "to tonsure" appear frequently in the Brazilian *Count Claros in Monk's Attire*. But someone involved in the transmission of this particular variant apparently did not understand what it meant to shave one's crown, and chose to replace it with the more intelligible "put on a crown." Unfortunately, the result in the context of the narrative is nonsense.

It is significant that the rendering's only narrative verse segment should include both its most archaic forms of expression and its least successful innovation. Narrative verse has tended to disappear from Brazilian ballad tradition, being either omitted altogether or replaced by prose. The ability to create and innovate, even to recall, that can be observed in dialogue segments does not seem to extend to narrative verse.

"Aí quando êle chegou, ela estava chorando. Aí êle foi, falou assim:
(So when he arrived she was crying. So he went and said thus:)
38   —Dona, me dê um beijo, qu' eu não lhe deixo matar.
(Lady, give me a kiss, and I won't let them kill you.)
Ela foi, falou assim:
(She went and said thus:)

40 —Boca que dom Carlos beija não é pa' padre beijar.
    (The mouth that don Carlos kisses is not for priests to kiss.)
    Ela não conheceu mais êle.
    (She didn't know him any more.)
[Seu Antero laughs.]
    "Aí êle foi, falou assim:
    (So he went and said thus:)
42 —Dona, me dê um abraço, qu' eu não lhe deixo matar.
    (Lady, give me a hug, and I won't let them kill you.)
    Aí ela falou:
    (So she said:)
44 —Corpo que dom Carl' abraça não é pa' padre abraçar."
    (The body that don Carlos hugs is not for priests to hug.)
[Seu Antero: "Viu!" (See!) Unintelligible comments and murmurs
from the audience, now entirely involved in the story on the side
of Dona Branca.]

Claros' journey is another narrative segment that apparently
has not survived in the Brazilian *Count Claros in Monk's Attire*.
A feeling that some preparation for the temptation scene is lacking
may have led Dona Conceição to explain in an aside that Dona
Branca did not recognize her lover. Clarification is particularly
necessary since the detail of the crown, which originally helped
describe the disguise, in its form here actually subverts it.

The variant returns to dialogue in hemistichs 37–44, divided
as at the beginning of the ballad into challenges and ripostes.
Dona Branca shows as much wit and presence of mind in fending
off her disguised lover as she did in answering her father.

These stanzas are entirely traditional. The test is the heart
of *Count Claros in Monk's Attire*, and thus is much less open to
significant alteration than any other segment. In contrast to its
end, the beginning of this variant has been doubly altered. The
Evil Spell opening has itself been modified by a singer about whose
name we may only speculate. Nevertheless, the rendering is a
well-constructed unit. The father's questions parallel the lover's
propositions. And Dona Branca's second set of responses, as
compared to the first, concisely demonstrates that she has grown
into assuming responsibility for her actions. The test in *Count
Claros in Monk's Attire* may comprise from one to three challenges.
Its doubling here does not indicate forgetfulness or structural
weakness. On the contrary, by exactly paralleling the doubled
questions at the beginning, it reinforces the melding of the *Evil*

Spell and the *Count Claros* into a single ballad.

 "Aí êle foi, falou assim:
 (So he went and said thus:)
46 —Meus senhores, me desculpem. Todos queiram desculpar;
48 A fogueira fica feita para seu pai se queimar."
 (Gentlemen, excuse me. All of you excuse me please.
 The pyre has been made for her father to be burned.)

Such violent revenge is unusual but not unique among published Brazilian variants of *Count Claros in Monk's Attire*. In published Peninsular texts Claros' revenge is limited to his carrying off his lover without her father's consent, sometimes daring any of her relatives to try to stop him, sometimes remarking ironically on the "dowry" the father planned to give his daughter, occasionally consigning dogs or old women to the flames so as not to waste a perfectly good pyre. In Dona Conceição's variant the father is explicitly the guilty party. Claros, with extreme politeness begging the pardon of those who have gathered to watch the execution, suggests that the fire can be used to burn the father. The narrator agrees:

 "A fogueira estava feita para ela. O pai
 dela—*pã!*—caiu dentro da fogueira, morreu queimado.
 (The fire was made for her. Her father—pow!—fell in the
 fire and burned to death.)
 [Seu Antero: "Ei!"]
 E êle casou com ela. Estão vivendo até hoje."
 (And he married her. They're still living today.)
 [Seu Antero (laughing): "Ai, meu Deus do céu!"] (Oh, my
 God in heaven!)
 Unintelligible comments and laughter from the rest of the
 audience.
 [Seu Antero: "Essa estória é muito bonita. . . . Boa, boa . . ..
 E boa essa estória."]
 (That story is very pretty. . . . Good, good . . . It's good,
 that story.)

This gruesome ending was told with a smile and received with approving laughter. The *pã* represents the sound of the father falling into the fire. From the perspective of total identification with the lovers his impromptu immolation is morally, socially, and poetically justified.

The terminating "estão vivendo até hoje" is similar to the conventional tale ending, "and they lived happily ever after." It is more immediate, however. The narrator specifically brings the end of the story into the present, for a moment locating these characters in everyday reality. This final sentence could serve as a metaphor for the oral traditional ballad itself, a medieval creation which through generations of transmission is still living today.

Count Claros and the Princess: Claralinda

Dona Preta, whose real name is Maria Eulália de Jesus, was sixty years old when I met her in 1978. Born and brought up in rural southern Bahia, she had traveled extensively within the region comprising southern Bahia, northeastern Minas Gerais, and northern Espírito Santo. She moved to Conceição da Barra while I was there, and established a *terreiro*, a center for Afro-Catholic ritual as practiced in her native Bahia, known as *candomblé*.

By profession Dona Preta was a *mãe-de-santo*, a medium. During the weekly sessions at her *terreiro* spirits were called down through singing, dancing, and the beating of drums to possess her and her followers. Part of her office, for which, unlike the *candomblé* sessions, she was paid, was to seek the occult sources of people's spiritual, emotional, or financial difficulties, and to perform services to right wrongs. Dona Preta insisted she worked only toward good ends; unlike others of her profession, she claimed to shun the powers of evil, though she knew how to deal with them when they appeared unsummoned. She also sold cloth and women's clothes her adult children bought cheaply in São Paulo and brought to Conceição da Barra. Dona Preta's prices were high, but her followers paid them more or less willingly, partly to help her make a living and partly to gain and retain her good graces.

I first recorded Dona Preta at one of her *candomblé* sessions, and I began to get to know her when I took the tape to the center a few days later for her to hear. I was told Dona Preta was a good storyteller, and could well believe it, for her dominating and dramatic manner transformed even the most banal of conversations into a performance; but when I approached her on the subject of telling me stories she demurred. In Bahia, she said, people had gathered often to tell stories, but she had not told a story in years. Alienated from her natural storytelling context, she had lost all interest in the pastime. I never asked her specifically about ballads, since she clearly lived and worked more in the Afro-Brazilian than in the Luso-Brazilian tradition.

I continued to visit Dona Preta with friends who had become involved in her spiritist center. It was after I had done a few favors for her—disinterested favors because I had abandoned hope that she might perform for me—that she suddenly volunteered to tell some stories for me to record. At her invitation I took my tape recorder to the *terreiro* one Sunday afternoon. The room looked strangely small and bare without the usual crowd of magnificently attired dancers. The floor was clear, but the benches that lined the walls began to be occupied by others who had been invited or had dropped in to see what was going on.

Dona Preta first invited my good friend Niva and me to come into the tiny kitchen adjoining the center. There she offered us coffee and sweet bread. When we had eaten and drunk all we wanted, we returned to the main room. Dona Preta seated herself on a nearby chair while I set up the tape recorder on a small table she had provided. She told three stories for me that afternoon. Another woman and a man contributed with one story apiece.

Dona Preta later told me she had learned most of her stories and ballads from a man she called her stepfather. He did not live with her family, but spent most of his time "up north"—she could not tell me exactly where. Whenever he returned to Bahia families would vie for his presence, for he was an accomplished storyteller and singer. In return for food and hospitality, and the pleasure of telling a good story to an appreciative audience, he would spend the night entertaining. He was not paid for these evenings. Dona Preta's stepfather was a traveler, and thus a diffuser of stories and songs. Dona Preta recalled a few of these for me, including the *Donzela guerreira* (*The Warrior Maiden*). I am certain she had known many more, for, unable to read, she had a prodigious memory and the true traditional performer's love of telling a good tale.

To my astonishment the first story Dona Preta told was a variant of *Conde Claros y la infanta* (*Count Claros and the Princess*). She began in prose:

> Disse que era um reis que tinha uma filha. Bom . . .
> Como êle era . . . era um reis, muito rico, né? Tinha
> uma filha. Bem . . . essa filha já vivia quase

escondida.

Então tinha um moço. Também não era gente muito ruim, não, gente bem de vida também, mas não era reis, né? Então intentou de casar com essa . . . com essa dona. Conversaram namoros escondidos [smiling] d'aqui, d'ali, namoros escondidos.

Quando era um dia êles trataram, foram para a praia. Quando êles estão lá conversando, batendo um papo numa bancada, vai passando . . . um sujeito trabalhava p'r'o reis, né? Era de lá. Era acho que empregado lá da fazenda, da casa. Aí vai passando . . . [emphatically] que quando ela avistou o reis . . . quando ela avistou . . . avistou o sujeito longe, ela levantou e ficou logo em pé. Aí quando êle vem passando *pa-pa-pa* . . . aí ela gritou . . . [long pause] . . . Hm . . .

Aí ela falou assim:

(It was said there was a king who had a daughter. Well . . . Since he was . . . he was a king, very rich, right? He had a daughter. Well . . . that daughter lived almost hidden away.

Then there was a young man. He wasn't very poor. He was well off, too. But he wasn't a king, right? So he tried to marry that . . . that lady. They got together in secret to talk about love. Here, there. Secret love talks.

One day they decided, they went to the beach. While they are there talking, having a talk on a long bench, here comes . . . a fellow who worked for the king, right? He was from there. He was, I think, an employee of the ranch, of the house. So here he comes . . . and when she saw the king . . . when she saw. . . she saw the fellow far away, she got up and stood. So when he comes by *pa-pa-pa-pa-pa* . . . she yelled . . . Hm . . .

Then she spoke thus:)

Dona Preta begins with the same formula as does Dona Conceição. She describes at greater length the relationship between the very rich king and his nubile daughter, whom he keeps almost hidden. After establishing this inherently unstable narrative situation, she introduces the suitor. Typical of the Brazilian tradition of *Count Claros and the Princess*, nothing remains of Claros' amorous anguish, so greatly emphasized in the sixteenth-century Spanish text of this ballad. His nobility has been abandoned as well. Whereas Dona Conceição's Claros was a *rapaz*, Dona Preta's is a *moço*. There is no significant difference between the terms; Claros is merely a young man. For cogent narrative reasons he has not, however, been demoted to servant, peasant, or fisherman. If Claros worked for the princess or her father, the tale type suggested would be the ballad of *Gerineldo*, which treats the particular difficulties raised by sexual congress between mistress and servant. If he were a peasant or fisherman, the tale type, very popular in the region of Conceição da Barra, would be that of the young man who wins a princess by wit and resourcefulness despite his poverty and humble lineage. Neither of these tale types corresponds to *Count Claros and the Princess*. If Dona Preta's protagonist has lost his medieval pedigree, he nonetheless retains the substantial fortune that in contemporary Brazil puts him in a social class from which he may aspire to woo a princess despite her father's objections.

The location of the tryst may be an innovation by Dona Preta. The archaic pleasance (*vergel*), occasionally modernized in Brazil into a garden (*jardim*), is inappropriate here since the king lives on a ranch. Its replacement by the beach may have been determined by local characteristics. We were living in a town very much dominated by the sea, whose beach was far more hospitable to dalliance than its insect-infested tropical forest.

Dona Preta's description of what the two young people were doing at the beach is no more than mildly suggestive. The young man's intentions are explicitly honorable. Though *conversas* are often a colloquial euphemism for sexual relations (and Dona Preta's smile at "namoros escondidos" hints that something is left unspecified), there is nothing in the narrator's tone when the two are discovered that might force a double meaning. On the contrary, her appositive "batendo um papo" seems designed to defuse the sexual charge of this sensitive moment. Unlike in some other variants of *Count Claros and the Princess*, the two are not caught *in flagrante*. The princess sees the approaching servant and stands while he is still far off. Then, as he is passing, she calls to him.

Though I have transcribed all Dona Preta's hesitations and

repetitions as well as her minor errors and their rectifications, it should be remembered that such mistakes are hardly perceived in an oral performance. I had to listen attentively several times to the recording before I could represent them faithfully. What is perceived is the informal tone of the telling. This prose introduction—divided into a narrative background recounted in the past tense and a narrative present describing the meeting of the lovers with the passerby—is typical of Dona Preta's storytelling style. Highly colloquial, pronounced in her heavy Bahian accent, it contains the interjections, "bom . . . ," "bem . . . ," as well as pauses for dramatic effect and the question tag "né?" at the end of sentences, designed to involve the audience. Dona Preta, apparently uncertain of the passerby's identity, enters the narrative with the first person "I," a device that lends the impression of authenticity and immediacy to the telling.

The ranch, like the beach, is a Brazilian feature. Locally, the authority of the rich rancher would be the palpable analogue of that of a remote king. King and rich rancher have here been merged into a single powerful figure. But if a rancher can stand in for a king, we might reasonably wonder why the father's royalty has been retained at all. Claros' nobility in both *Count Claros and the Princess* and *Count Claros in Monk's Attire* has gone the way of his lover's virginity; and in the Brazilian *Count Claros in Monk's Attire* the young woman's father (who in contemporary Peninsular variants is usually a count) has lost his nobility as well.

There are both narrative and social reasons for the retention of the father's royalty in *Count Claros and the Princess.* In narrative terms Dona Preta's variant has been subsumed into the group of ballads and tales that open with the father's imprisoning his daughter to prohibit her contact with men. Often the man who performs such an act is a king. In contrast, the *Evil Spell* opening, which has become the most common beginning of the Brazilian tradition of *Count Claros in Monk's Attire*, is neutral regarding the social status of the father.

Further, royalty, which has never been essential in *Count Claros in Monk's Attire*, is indispensable in *Count Claros and the Princess.* The significant difference in this respect between the two versions of the *Count Claros* story is that the father in *Count Claros in Monk's Attire* threatens to kill his daughter, whereas the father in *Count Claros and the Princess* threatens to kill her lover, and often has the informer killed. Only a person of legitimate social authority may order the execution of another, unless (*Count Claros in Monk's Attire* seems to be saying) that other is his own daughter.   The credibility of *Count Claros in Monk's Attire* depends on the belief that any father in questions of honor has life-and-death authority over his own daughter.   It is important to note, however, that *Count Claros in Monk's Attire* does not support this belief. Despite the notorious variability characteristic of any oral traditional ballad throughout its secular career, the young woman in *Count Claros in Monk's Attire* is never actually burned, and some variants (including Dona Conceição's) go so far as to condemn her father to the flames.   Thus, the real moral to be drawn from *Count Claros in Monk's Attire* is that there are laws higher than those of the honor code.   According to them the father's assumption of power belonging only to God is a potentially mortal illusion.   *Count Claros and the Princess* does not deal with such questions.   Kingship must be retained because the social and political authority it affords is required for the unfolding of the narrative.

Dona Preta, unlike Dona Conceição, supported her performance by gestures. Her onomatopoeiac *pa-pa-pa-pa-pa* was accompanied by chopping hand movements to indicate the passerby's rapid pace.   This attracted the attention of the listeners, who in this recital were also spectators.

After announcing that the princess called out to the passerby, Dona Preta paused and stared at the floor.   Even more pointedly than Dona Conceição she seemed to be contemplating the imminent switch to a musical mode.   Perhaps she was silently recalling the tune; perhaps she was pausing for effect.   The final prose line—whose verb, unlike Dona Conceição's at the parallel juncture of her performance, indicates speech—leads into the singing after only a short pause.

As in Dona Conceição's variant, prose segments introduce changing speakers.   "Aí ela falou," and "aí éle disse," have become part of the ballad.   Dona Preta's delivery was more calculated and dramatic than that of Dona Conceição; her prose intercalations were slightly more varied. Greater conscious control over the nuances of presentation is to be expected from a singer whose profession involves performance, even if her usual sphere is not the oral traditional ballad.

= 96 (rubato)

2 -- Ca-va-lei-ro   Cai —fai,   a meu pai —   não vá con- ta

(Gentleman Caifai, don't go tell my father.)

4 -- Qu'eu te dou no-ve fa-zen-da' en- cos-ta —— d'a bei - ra   mar.

(I'll give you nine ranches along the seacoast.)

The first hemistich is an abrupt break from Dona Preta's informal spoken style. The princess uses the peculiar, and to my knowledge unique, address "Cavaleiro" to call the passerby. In most Brazilian variants of this ballad, as in much of the Peninsular tradition, the passerby is a hunter, and is addressed as "Caçador."

"Caifai" is also anomalous. Since I have discussed its significance in my article "Notes on Creativity," I will merely observe here that the name carries connotations of betrayal, which intimate from the outset that the princess is wasting her time trying to convince him not to tell on her. Following the *Count Claros* tradition, however, she makes three offers in exchange for his silence.

Offering land seems to be rare in the Brazilian tradition of this ballad. In the only published variant to offer land (Lima 1977:151–53), the princess tries to buy the passerby's silence with lands in France. Dona Preta's bribe is more Brazilian and far more vivid: nine ranches, which, to increase their value, are located along the coast. The number nine is fitting in this variant sung by a woman accustomed to dealing with mystical numbers. The *uma* that would fit both metrical and concordance schemes perhaps does not convey with sufficient force either the princess's wealth or her desperation. *Tres* does not have sufficient syllables to fill the line; and *sete*, though it would provide internal rhyme with *fazenda*, is less sonorous than *nove* with its nasal and voiced consonants.

Alliteration and internal rhyme in this stanza and throughout
the rendering suggest that Dona Preta is unusually sensitive to
sounds. The labio-dental voiced/unvoiced fricative sequence v...f of
"nove fazenda" replicates that of "Cavaleiro Caifai," whose first
syllables are themselves nearly identical. In "nove fazenda" the
v...f sequence is pleasingly framed by two sonorant "n's." I am not
claiming that Dona Preta constructed her ballad on the level of
individual sounds. But I do believe that certain sound sequences
would prove more satisfying than others to her practiced ear.
Dona Preta, as *mãe-de-santo*, was a composer as well as a singer.
Like the spirits her music summoned, she was highly attuned to
the nuances of sounds.

Dona Preta distinctly sang "nove fazenda." The lack of
noun/adjective concordance presents no problem to her. Omission
of the final "s" that in grammatically correct speech indicates
plurality is characteristic of the vernacular, the plural number alone
being considered sufficient. Absence of the "s" of "encostada" in
the final hemistich of this stanza is, moreover, functional, for its
presence would create syllabic excess. Though both Dona Preta
and Dona Conceição are tolerant of hemistichs that lack syllables,
neither ever exceeds the correct number.

Dona Preta's tune, which actually began and ended on B-flat
below middle C, is slower, more chant-like than Dona Conceição's.
The first phrase ("Cavaleiro Caifai") is divided musically as well as
verbally into two parts based on nearly repeated ascending major
thirds. The second phrase begins a fourth above the last note of
the first phrase. This is the highest pitch of the tune, to which it
does not return. It is an anacrusis, corresponding neither to
musical nor to verbal stress. Nonetheless it is an important
moment, where the princess begins her plea and where in reply the
passerby emphatically rejects it.

The functional importance of the verb "contar" ("to tell") in
the second phrase is underlined by its position at the mid-cadence,
the extended point of greatest musical tension. The significance of
the phrase's other important word, "pai," is emphasized musically
through the extension of the word's single syllable into three beats
and two pitches. No comparable phenomenon was observed in
Dona Conceição's almost conversational rendering, where each
syllable received a single beat and pitch. The major third is the
principal interval of the second phrase as it was of the first. But
it is now descending rather than ascending.

The third phrase, though on different pitches, essentially repeats the contour of the second. The fourth phrase consists basically of four steps descending to the final. Yet it, too, is patterned in descending thirds. The final of the melody is not the tonic of its implied major scale, but rather the third of that scale. The tonic itself is never touched, though its octave serves as the initial pitch of the second phrase. Absence of the tonic reinforces the chantlike, continuous quality of the melody, with its confined yet restless alternation between ascending and descending notes at the interval of a third. The pattern of the music mirrors the movement of the ballad's first segment: back and forth, back and forth, back and forth between the princess and the passerby.

In terms of rhythm Dona Preta's rendering is more regular than Dona Conceição's. The phrases, however, are of different lengths. Phrases 1 and 3 have eight beats each and two principal pulses, which fall on their third and seventh beats. The second and fourth phrases are longer than the first and third, and seem to have a secondary pulse as well as two principal musical pulses. Musical pulses correspond to verbal stresses in stanzas 1, 3, 5, 7, and 9. They differ in 2, 4, 6, and 8.

"Aí êle falou assim:
(So he said thus:)

6 -- Tu-as fa-zen-d'eu não que-ro. Nem p'ra el— eu que-r' ol-har.

(Your ranches I don't want. I don't even want to look at them.)

8 -- Se eu for con-tar ao rei— mui-to mais— e' de gan-har.

(If I go tell the king I will gain much more.)

When Dona Preta is speaking she uses the vernacular pronunciation "reis" for the word she pronounces "rei" in the sung portions of the ballad. In this instance sung verse resists the inroads of colloquial alteration.

Again Dona Preta omits the final "s" of "fazendas," the

plural having been adequately represented by "tuas." She is then able, as in the first stanza, to drop the now-final unstressed "a," thus avoiding an excess syllable. Apocopation and elision, characteristic of this variant, will be represented in the transcriptions from now on, but not mentioned in the text. Together with the slow, repetitive tune, the tendency to join words gives this variant a flowing sound that may be contrasted with the more staccato rendering sung by Dona Conceição.

In view of the predominance of vowel elision in this performance, the lack of it in the third hemistich of this stanza ("Se eu for contar ao rei") is worthy of note. In the corresponding hemistich of the first stanza, the first two syllables comprising three words ("qu'eu te") established the principal adversaries, the princess assuming the role of subject and the passerby that of object. In this stanza the roles are reversed. The action pivots on the potential betrayal contemplated in the third hemistich of the stanza. This hemistich names the individuals involved: the potential informer ("I" in this stanza) and the king. Focus on the former is sharpened by the avoidance of vowel elision, while emphasis on the latter is provided by its location at the end of the hemistich and reinforced by the music: two pitches for a single syllable.

With the exception of hemistich 19 (a special case to be discussed below), hemistichs 7, 15, and 23 ("Se eu for contar ao rei") are the only ones in this position to have fewer than eight syllables. Despite this, the music continues to have eight beats. The final word of the hemistich, "rei," like "pai" in the second hemistich of the first stanza, is awarded an extra beat and two pitches. "Pai" and "rei" are, of course, the same person seen from crucially different perspectives. The third hemistich of the second stanza, "Se eu for contar ao rei," is like a distorted echo of the second hemistich of the first stanza: "A meu pai não vá contar." As if to emphasize this, the music lingers over the word "rei" in the second stanza as it did over "pai" in the first.

Similarly, the music lingers lovingly over the word "mais" in the final hemistich of this stanza. Its three beats and two pitches follow the same pattern as the corresponding moment of the second hemistich. They thus constitute musical rhyme, whose significance can be seen when we return to the first stanza, specifically to the already-mentioned "pai" of its second hemistich. The words "pai" and "mais" are in assonance, which is supported by the musical rhyme. These two features in turn reinforce the fundamental unity of each pair of stanzas. Within each pair the princess's varying offer and the passerby's corresponding rejection of it are preceded by her unvarying plea and followed by his equally unvarying speculation that telling the king will be worth more to him than anything she can offer. Essentially unchanging lines framing each pair of stanzas define the principal conflict, which in this version of the *Count Claros* is not between the father and his daughter but rather between the princess and the informer:

Cavaleiro Caifai, a meu pai não vá (vai) contar
....
....
Se eu for contar ao rei muito mais hei (é) de ganhar.
"Aí ela falou:
(So she said:)

| 10 | —*Cavaleiro Caifai*, a meu *pai* não *vai* contar; |
| 12 | Eu te dou *minha* s*obrinha* para voc*ê* s*e* c*as*ar." |

(Gentleman Caifai, don't go tell my father.
I will give you my niece for you to marry.)

This is a traditional offer, not substantially different from Claros' sixteenth-century offer of his first cousin as wife. Dona Preta's rendering is, however, consistent with the tendency in the Brazilian tradition for the woman to take the initiative. Claros is certainly necessary in both versions of the *Count Claros* ballad, but in neither of them does he have a central role in the conflict.

When she needs the syllable to complete the hemistich, Dona Preta, like Dona Conceição, avoids her customary apocopation of the word *para*. The anomalous "você" in a context where the pronoun "tu" has been and will henceforth be employed seems also to be a means of fulfilling syllabic requirements.

Dona Preta in this stanza sings "vai" in the second hemistich instead of "vá." This contributes to the unusual amount of internal rhyme, alliteration, and near alliteration (indicated by italics) in an otherwise undistinguished stanza.

"Êle respondeu:
(He answered:)

| 14 | —Sua sobrinh' eu não quero, nem p'ra el' eu quer'olhar; |
| 16 | Se eu for contar ao rei, muito mais é de ganhar." |

(Your niece I don't want. I don't even want to look at her.
If I go tell the king I will gain much more.)

The second response parallels the first. "Sua" used here in place of the "tua" of the second stanza and the "teu" of the sixth may have been suggested by the "você" of hemistich 12 or the initial "s" sound of "sobrinha."

"Aí ela disse:
(Then she said:)

18 -- Ca-va-lei-ro Cai-fai, a meu pai— não vá con - tar.

(Gentleman Caifai, don't go tell my father.)

20-- Qu'eu te dou ou - ro'em pó en-quan-to po —ssa ca-rre-gar.

(I will give you gold dust. As much as you can carry.)

The arrangement of words and music underlines the seductiveness of this final offer. The first syllable of "ouro" is drawn out for two notes, and its second syllable is not dropped but rather pronounced and elided to the following word. If the third hemistich were recited it would have only six syllables (a mere five if "dou" were elided to "ouro"), while the fourth hemistich would have eight, an unacceptable number for a masculine rhyme. As sung, however, the third hemistich is immediately linked to the fourth by the device of singing the first syllable of "enquanto" on what is usually the final note of the preceding phrase. Music and words work together to form a line without the customary caesura. It is as if the princess did not want the passerby to have time to stop and think.

This is the culminating offer. In other Brazilian variants it typically takes the generic form "gold and silver." Dona Preta's image of "all the gold dust you can carry" is, in contrast, particularly vivid.

"Ele falou:"
(He said:)

22   —Não quero teu ouro em pó, nem p'ra el' eu quer' olhar;

24   Se eu for contar ao rei,   muito mais é de ganhar."
     (I don't want your gold dust.   I don't even want to look at
     it.   If I go tell the king I will gain much more.)
     But the greedy passerby wants still more.   Just as the
finality of the last offer was indicated by altered phrasing, the
finality of the refusal is reinforced by a change in the word order
established in the preceding stanzas.   The "não quero," previously
located at the end of the first hemistich, is placed at the
beginning.   This emphatic refusal closes the tripartite series of
offers and rejections, and the first section of the ballad.

     Bom . . . Então ela . . . não pôde fazer mais nada, né?
     Saiu.   Que ligeiro viajou, mais o moço também: "Vam'
     'bora p'ra lá!"   E êle se mandou, *pa-pa-pa-pa-pa-pa.*
     Foi chegando lá, bateu palmas [claps hands] entrou aí,
     foi chegando, foi dizendo . . . :
     (Well . . . then she . . . couldn't do anything else,
     could she?   She left.   And she traveled fast, with the
     young man, too: "Let's get going!"   And he went in a
     hurry, *pa-pa-pa-pa-pa-pa.*   He was arriving there.   He
     clapped his hands.   He went in.   He was arriving, he
     was saying . . . :")
     Return to prose narrative underlines the closure of the first
part of the ballad.   Again in her conversational narrative style
Dona Preta appeals to the audience to agree that the princess had
done all she could.   All three abandon the beach, racing to the
palace.   The informer is the fastest.   The *pa-pa-pa-pa-pa-pa,*
accompanied as at the beginning by a chopping hand gesture, again
represents his rapid pace.   In rural Brazil people clap their hands
to attract the attention of those inside a house.   Dona Preta
accompanied the narration with the action.   The final phrase of
this segment, composed entirely of verbs of action and present
participles, emphasizes the informer's haste.   Waiting for nothing,
he gains entrance to the palace, simultaneously approaching the
king and speaking.

26   "—Deus salve, senh . . . doutor rei,   sua coroa sagrada;
28   Que eu vi a dona Lira   mai' dom Carl' a conversar."
     (God save, Mr. . . . Doctor King, your sacred crown;
     I saw Dona Lira talking with Don Carlos.)
     The singer's almost involuntary intervention can be seen in
the first hemistich of this stanza.   In those Brazilian variants that

have retained this segment in verse, the informer's address ranges from the highly formal to the relatively informal. The narrators of three variants published by Jackson da Silva Lima (1977) are content to have the informer address the king as "senhor rei," an address probably derived from reversal of the greeting "rei senhor" found in Portuguese variants and an early twentieth-century Brazilian text. "Senhor rei," however, is not quite equivalent to "rei senhor" in terms of respect. The English equivalent of the former, "Mr. king," is a far cry from the latter, "king (my) lord." The distinction between the two forms of address in Portuguese, though less glaring, seems to have distressed Dona Preta.

Dona Preta begins to have the informer greet the king as "senhor rei." Then suddenly she hesitates, evidently judging the greeting insufficiently respectful. Quickly searching her memory, and almost without breaking stride, she substitutes the more respectful "doutor" for the "senhor" her sense of fitness has rejected. The term *doutor* is often used in Brazil to address any man of higher social and economic rank than the speaker.

This correction, made on the spur of the moment, illustrates one way in which contemporary patterns may be inserted into archaic niches of the traditional ballad. Somewhere in the history of this variant an old form of address had been replaced by a modern form Dona Preta found inadequate. Unable to reinvent the original formula, she replaced the faulty formula with one that seemed better to her. Her replacement, based on her own experience, manifests a specific instance of the openness that allows ballads to survive in contemporary oral tradition.

Whereas Dona Conceição consistently altered word endings in order to accommodate them to the rhyme scheme, Dona Preta refuses to do so. Though the second syllable of "sagrada" in hemistichs 26 and 34 is elongated and the third barely touched, the entire word is pronounced clearly despite its lack of coherence with the -*ar* rhyme scheme of the rest of the ballad. Addressing the "coroa sagrada" of the king lends an archaic tone to the rendering, which is particularly striking after "doutor rei." For a moment the ballad reaches back centuries to the time when the literally sacred honor of a king, represented metonymically by his crown, could be sullied by the sexual misbehavior of his daughter.

In this stanza the denouncing word "conversar" takes on shades of the double meaning Dona Preta seemed to mitigate in the prose introduction. The "mais" of hemistich 28 is the typical vernacular replacement of "com" in this context. Now that the ballad is nearly over we have the first mention of the protagonists' names. "Lira" and "Carl" are recognizably related to Claralinda (as she is called most frequently in the Portuguese *Count Claros and the Princess* tradition) and Claros. Here, as in Dona Conceição's rendering of *Count Claros in Monk's Attire*, calling Claros "dom" is a vestige of his former nobility.

> "Aí o reis falou assim:
> (Then the king said thus:)
> 30   —Se tu me contass' oculto   muito haveras de ganhar;
> 32   Como tu contou ao largo,   vou mandar te degolar."
> (If you had told me in secret you would have gained a lot.
> Since you told in public I am going to have you beheaded.)

It is clear that the informer is to be executed for the crime of indiscretion. The first two hemistichs indicate he was possibly right in thinking he would gain more by telling the king than by keeping the secret. The second two show that his telling in public has led to his downfall. This reasoning is typical of the kings in the Luso-Brazilian tradition of *Count Claros and the Princess*, where the informer, for his sins, has been elevated to the status of a major character.

The absence of subject/verb concordance in the first and third hemistichs is characteristic of popular speech. The second person singular verb form (retained in hemistich 30 in the archaic "haveras") has virtually been lost. The corresponding pronoun, *tu*, is occasionally used in everyday conversation, as it is here, with the third person singular verb form.

> [Rapidly, and laughing throughout]   Aí salta ese moço
> lá p'ra cima. Se viu lá p'ra cima. *Pá!* [claps hands
> once] os pescoço . . . o pescoço "avoou" p'ra lá!
> (So that fellow jumps way up in the air. He found
> himself way up in the air. *Pow!* His neck . . . his neck
> flew that way!)

This climactic segment, despite being in prose, contains a substantial amount of repetition, and was recited rhythmically. The informer's come-uppance, related with laughter, reinforced by clapping, was greeted by smiles and nods from the audience.

Dona Preta's variant, like some Portuguese and all other known Brazilian variants of *Count Claros and the Princess*, has undergone significant structural change from the sixteenth-century

version, which focuses on the lovers.   The powerful moral and
narrative motif of greed and its punishment has drawn *Count
Claros and the Princess* into its orbit.   This transformation of the
ballad has assured its survival, in modified thematic form.

> "Aí ela foi entrando [claps hands once] mais o noivo, né? . . .
> mais o rapaz. Aí ela falou:
> (So she was coming in, with her fiancé, right? . . . with the
> young man. Then she said:)

34   —Deus salve, meu pai rei, sua coroa sagrada;
36   Que dom Car' é meu marido, com ele hei eu é de casar."

> (God save, my father king, your sacred crown;
> Don Carlos is my husband. I have to marry him.)

The fourth hemistich seems to incorporate both "hei" and
"é."

Nothing is said about punishing the lovers.   In this variant,
consistent with the contemporary Luso-Brazilian tradition of *Count
Claros and the Princess*,   the   original   transgression,   though
motivating the action, has ceased to pose an important problem.
By   the   princess's   single   word,   "marido,"   the   young   man   is
transformed   from   illicit   lover   into   husband.   Though   hemistich   36
makes it clear that his status as husband is *de facto* rather than
de jure,   this   potentially   inflammatory   statement   provokes   not   a
murmur of protest from the king.   On the contrary, he is delighted
to   engineer   a   quick   resolution   of   the   dilemma   posed   by   the
informer's public proclamation of his shame:

> Foi nada, não, minha gente.   [laughing] Na mesma da
> hora . . . com êle fez a festa.   Chamou o pai, chamou
> o juiz, casou . . . e as   meninas [gesturing with her
> chin toward the kitchen] estão terminando de beber
> cafezinho no instante. Já foi o fim, o fim da festa.
> (It was nothing, my friends. At that very moment . . .
> he made a celebration. He called the father, he called
> the   judge,   he   got   married . . .   and   the   girls   are
> finishing drinking coffee right now.   That was the end,
> the end of the party.)

Closing   a   story   with   a   wedding   or   party   where   one   fits   the
narrative is traditional, as is linking the party, and thereby the
narrative itself, to the circumstances of the telling.   I recorded a
story from another woman in Conceição da Barra with a slightly
different   and   more   conventional   form   of   the   same   ending.   The

party to which that tale's characters had adjourned had just ended, and the teller (who had attended) told me she was just bringing me a piece of cake when she slipped and fell and dropped it. Dona Preta's closing, like Dona Conceição's, but more vividly and specifically, brings the ballad into the present. She has modified the formula in accordance with the actual event. The girls to whom she referred in word and gesture were some of the members of her spiritist center who, just as she was finishing the ballad, were finishing what remained of the coffee and sweet bread Dona Preta had offered Niva and me before the session began.

Thus far, the discussion of Dona Preta's variant has followed segment by segment the narrative of the ballad. The structure of the ballad, however, merits a closer look. A very brief analysis of its superficial structure shows both dual and triple organization. Its nine stanzas are divided into two parts, the first part comprising six stanzas and the second three. The first part of the ballad moves slowly, back and forth between the princess and the passerby. There is no action, only talk. In contrast, each stanza of the rapidly moving second part describes or implies an action: betrayal, execution, marriage.

Further divisions may be perceived within the sections. The first six stanzas are divided by parallelism into three pairs, each comprising an offer and its rejection. This segment's primary disposition may thus be considered to be three times two. Another factor is introduced, however, by variation within the stanzas. The first two pairs vary minimally, only as much as is required by changing the offer. The greater variation of the culminating third pair sets it apart from the others. From the perspective of verbal parallelism the three pairs of stanzas may be divided into two plus one, a division that mirrors the organization of the ballad itself.

The three stanzas of the second part may also be divided into two plus one. The first stanza expresses the confrontation between the informer and the king, the second its resolution. The third compresses into four hemistichs the confrontation between the princess and her father and the resolution of the situation that has motivated the ballad. Yet the finality of this disposition is denied by the verbal parallelism between the first and third stanzas of the segment ("Deus salve [. . .] rei, sua coroa sagrada"), a parallelism that emphasizes the section's fundamental unity.

I do not mean to imply that anyone in Dona Preta's audience was counting stanzas, much less pondering their interrelationships.   Nevertheless, dual and triple figures are so widespread within oral tradition that they may reasonably be considered fundamental organizing principles.   The aesthetic value of such patterns lies in the satisfaction afforded when the completion of a series fulfills expectations raised by its beginning and sustained by its continuation.

The presence of overlapping patterns like those we have seen here adds another dimension to the variant.   At one moment the ballad may be perceived to have a certain form.   Then, looking from another angle, we see that it also has another.   The ballad, like an optical illusion, may simultaneously incorporate distinct patterns.   This capability, even if not consciously perceived, adds to its texture.   A sung oral traditional ballad cannot be reduced to a mere chain of events.   Organizing principles are at work on every level of its composition and performance.   Narrative structure is expressed through superficial and verbal structures as informed by musical structure.   Inconsistent interaction among the elements that comprise a traditional ballad traditionally performed creates a dense counterpoint that enriches its presentation.

The variants considered here, with all their flaws and successes, represent complete narrative structures convincingly performed.   Every moment of each rendering manifests a resolution of the inevitable, indeed life-giving, conflict between tradition and actuality, just as each text manifests a given moment in the lifetime of the ballad.   The oral traditional ballad is not a museum piece.   In order to survive, it must be able to incorporate change on every level—structural, thematic, verbal, musical—without disintegrating.   The variants examined here demonstrate this capacity.   They provide specific examples of ballad survival through the interplay of retention and adaptation, evident in two captured instants of the *Count Claros* tradition.

Indiana University

Notes

[1]My fieldwork in Brazil was supported by a joint grant from the Fulbright/Hays Commission and the Social Science Research Council.

[2]Bibliographical information on this work and all others to which I refer can be found in the list of references at the end of the volume.

[3]Both of these, and a third version of the "Count Claros" story, known as "Count Claros and the Emperor," can be found in Wolf and Hofmann's *Primavera y flor de romances*, nos. 190–92.

[4]See, for example, Katz 1972–75.

[5]Five months I spent collecting ballads in the province of León, Spain, were supported by a grant from the Council for International Exchange of Scholars and the Comité Conjunto Hispano–Norteamericano para la Cooperación Cultural y Educativa.

[6]Recordings of these ballads and the other material I recorded in Espírito Santo are available for consultation at the Instituto Nacional do Folclore, Rua do Catete, 179, Rio de Janeiro, RJ, Brazil and the Archives of Traditional Music, Indiana University, Bloomington, IN, 47405 USA.

The Traditional *Romancero*
in Mexico: Panorama[1]

Mercedes Díaz Roig

A traditional genre possesses two principal characteristics: its power of conservation and its power of variation. Thanks to the first, it can preserve up to the present time themes, plots, motifs, and texts that were born centuries ago. Thanks to variation, the texts are able to adapt themselves to the place where they are received and to the people that adopt them. In this game of change and preservation is the reason for the long life of *romances*, *canciones*, proverbs, sayings, and stories.

The reasons that these texts take root in foreign lands are more difficult to explain, but it is evident that among the most important are their undeniable attractiveness, whether aesthetic or conceptual (or both); their language (if not always simple, at least within the capacity of everybody); and their style (topical and therefore familiar). When a traditional genre is accepted, it becomes a part of the culture of those communities, and its possessors do not feel that it is something foreign. Only the specialist is able to recognize the origin of the texts and place them within a broader cultural frame (Hispanic culture, Western culture, etc.), but for those who sing, recite, and tell traditional genres, the texts are as much their own as those created in their community, and they feel absolutely free to use them and to vary them as they choose.

Inherent in everything traditional is its diffusion, both spatial and temporal (and generally social as well). The *romancero*, as a traditional genre, has acquired broad diffusion in both of these aspects: several centuries of age and a vast territory that includes Spain, Portugal, Ibero-America, the Sephardic communities all over the world, and the nuclei of Spanish and Portuguese speakers within other countries. Although it is among the least privileged

218

classes socially that it circulates most widely, we also find it among the middle and even the upper classes. This is very noticeable as far as children's ballads and religious ballads are concerned, but texts of other kinds have been collected quite frequently among those classes.

The presence of the *romancero* in America today has not been studied in its totality, but there is proof of its existence in almost all of the American countries.[2] The American tradition is very similar to the Peninsular tradition, with logical adaptations to the speech of each region and to the idiosyncrasies of each human group as well as to each individual. It can be said, then, that the American *romancero*, with the characteristics that emanated from its different possessors, represents a series of manifestations of the same common phenomenon, which, together with the manifestations, also individual, of other communities of speakers of Hispanic languages, make up what Ramón Menéndez Pidal called in the title of his (1953) book: *El Romancero hispánico (hispano-portugués, americano, y sefardí)*.

We understand by traditional *romances* those narrative songs with forms and themes common to the whole Hispanic tradition that have strong textual similarities. In this study of the Mexican *romancero*, I will not, of course, take into account narrative songs, whether traditional or not, created in Mexican territory or in Chicano nuclei, nor those that clearly do not derive directly from the Hispanic *romancero*, that is, songs for which there are no textual marks that relate them to a particular *romance*. Nevertheless, taking variation into account, which is characteristic of the *romance*, I shall consider as such texts of Hispanic origin interpolated with national motifs or formal influences of the same kind, or, and this is most important, texts with additions made by Mexican re-creators.[3]

The *romancero* came to the American continent with the *conquistadores*, and precisely the first piece of evidence comes from Mexico. Bernal Díaz de Castillo relates that in San Juan de Ulúa (Veracruz) in 1519 Alonso Hernández Portocarrero recited to Cortés these verses from an old *romance* (1928:1:113):

Cata Francia, Montesinos,	Look at France, Montesinos,
cata París la ciudad,	look at the city of Paris,
cata las aguas del Duero	look at the Duero's waters
do van a dar en el mar.	where they enter the sea.

The colonists must also have brought the traditional

romancero with them, at least during the sixteenth century when
it enjoyed great popularity in Spain among all social classes.
Books of *romances* were also imported, as well as broadsides
destined for sale in the Colony (cf. Leonard 1953). When interest
became centered on the new *romancero* toward the end of the
century, it undoubtedly diminished the introduction of *romances* by
the upper classes, who followed the literary fashion of the period,
but not among the lower classes since the *romances* formed part of
their cultural patrimony. After Independence, the influx of
Spaniards did not cease, and it continues up to the present. The
immigrants are usually country people, and we know that even
today the *romancero* is alive for them. In addition to these
emigrations, one must not forget the massive emigration that took
place between 1939 and 1942 of Spanish Republicans defeated in
the civil war of 1936–39, who had been brought up with an
appreciation and liking of what was folkloric.

Thus from the earliest days ballad texts could have circulated
among Spaniards and Creoles and later among the Mexicans who
spoke Spanish. As the use of the Spanish language spread, the
different manifestations of traditional literature also spread, were
absorbed, adopted, and, in this case, adapted by the Spanish-
speaking Mexicans. The *romancero*, which was an important part
of the aforesaid manifestations, continued its traditional life in these
lands based on repetition and variation of what was received,
nourished constantly by what emigrants from Spain brought in,
and, above all, renourishing itself with the product of its own life
in the country. All of that resulted in the *romancero*'s being
deeply rooted today in the new land and forming part of the
cultural stock of the Mexican.

The collection and study of this *romancero* has stimulated the
interest of a number of folklorists and investigators since the
beginning of the century. Menéndez Pidal, a pioneer in this field
as in so many others, was the first to publish a Mexican version of
a *romance*, *Hilitos de oro* (1906:72–111). Some years later, Pedro
Henríquez Ureña included another in an article about the American
romancero (1913:347–66). Antonio Castro Leal published two
romances, *Las señas del esposo* and *Gerineldo + La condesita*
(1914:237–44),[4] and in 1922, according to Mendoza (1939:349), the
Universidad Nacional Autónoma of Mexico published a pamphlet
with a version of *Delgadina*. The most important set of ballads of
the twenties was prepared by Pedro Henríquez Ureña and Bertram

D. Wolfe for the *Homenaje ofrecido a Menéndez Pidal*, which
contains twelve versions of five *romances* and several fragments of
others (1925:2:375-90).   Several folklorists continued to publish
Mexican versions, for example, Manuel Toussaint (1927:101-104),
Higinio Vásquez Santa Ana (1931), Gabriel Saldívar (1934), and
Hector Pérez Martínez (1935).   On the other hand, commercial
publishers of popular music, like the Casa Vanega Arroyo, from the
end of the nineteenth century, and Eduardo Guerrero, from the
beginning of the twentieth, went on publishing broadsides for
popular consumption which contained *romances*.   In 1939 the
volume by Vicente T. Mendoza came out, *El romance español y el
corrido mexicano*, which brings together everything that had been
published together with many versions collected by the author.
The book contains fifty-five versions and several fragments of
fifteen traditional *romances*, together with several *romances vulgares*
and information about their publication in the eighteenth century.
It has great importance, not only for the richness of its content,
but also because it demonstrated without a shred of doubt the
traditionality of the Hispanic *romancero* in Mexico.   In addition,
Mendoza's publication provided an impulse for those interested in
the genre.   From 1940 on, collections by folklorists, scholars, and
amateurs multiplied, and publications followed one upon another
until the middle of the century.   Among them we can cite those of
the aforementioned Mendoza (1951, 1952, 1956), of Andrés
Henestrosa (1977), who collected versions published in periodicals or
other works, and of Celedonio Serrano (1951).

The zeal for ballad collecting diminished during the following
years, not only in Mexico but also in other countries, and
publications were sporadic although they never completely ceased.
The Seminario Menéndez Pidal (which has now become a
university institute) did not give up, however, the publication of
the thousands of versions from its archives (among them many
from America) in its series of the *Romancero tradicional de las
lenguas hispánicas* and, under the direction of Diego Catalán,
organized several congresses for specialists[5] which have given a new
impetus to ballad collecting and to ballad studies in Spain and
have encouraged American scholars as well to continue their work.
In Mexico a team of investigators from the Universidad Nacional
Autónoma under my direction prepared a compilation of everything
published up to 1980.   This compilation, *El romancero tradicional
de México* (designated henceforth *RTM*), to which was added a

number of versions collected directly by university investigators, came out in 1986. The book contains two hundred eighty-five versions (some very fragmentary) of twenty-nine *romances* collected in twenty-five states of Mexico, thus comprising an important addition to the general Hispanic corpus and, furthermore, enabling us to have at hand the results of several decades of ballad collecting.

In this rapid panorama of collecting in Mexico, it is unfortunately necessary to say that a part of the texts have been gathered and published by various folklorists who lack adequate scientific knowledge. Thus some texts have been retouched, others lack information about the informants, and in others this information is confused or erroneous. Even Mendoza himself occasionally presents texts with some of these signs of carelessness. All of this, naturally, affects the value of the collections, but it does not invalidate them since trustworthy texts surpass in number those that are not.

Studies on the *romance* in Mexico have been scarce and generally have served as a point of departure for the study of the *corrido*, for which reason little attention has been paid to the *romance* for its own sake. Mendoza himself attaches more importance to the music of the *romance* than to the texts (1939: 4-8, 15-32, 35, 39-57, 61).

Romances and Texts in Mexico according to the Latest Compilation and their Relationship with other American Countries

Out of the twenty-nine *romances* collected in Mexico based on the *RTM*, we must exclude a few that are not truly traditional for one reason or another or because we do not have complete versions of them.

La conquista de Sevilla and *La batalla de Roncesvalles*, in addition to being fragments, are more closely related to the new *romancero* than to the old; only the second has two verses from an old *romance*. *La mala suegra* and *El conde Olinos* have been taken from books; the same is true of *Gerineldo* + *La condesita*. *Los versos de la Parca* was built upon a text from the *Flor nueva de romances viejos* of Menéndez Pidal (1928), as Diego Catalán has demonstrated (1970:51-54); in any case it is semi-learned. For its part, *Román Castillo* is a *romance* created in Mexico without Spanish antecedents, although it is very interesting for the influence of the *romancero* on its opening, rhyme, and form. *Doña Blanca*, although perhaps coming from a *romance* that is now lost, from the seventeenth century on has been a game song without a developed story (see Rodrigo Caro 1978:2:161). We have only four octosyllables of *El conde preso*, three of *La doncella guerrera*, and two of *Fontefrida*, all collected before 1940, and no further mention of these *romances* has been found. On the other hand, we have a two-verse fragment of *El conde Olinos* and two fragments of *Gerineldo* (of four and six verses respectively), but the only complete versions, as we have already said, are from books. Nevertheless, we can perhaps consider these last two *romances* as possibly having taken hold in Mexico.

Aside from those already mentioned, which we excluded for the reasons indicated above, we have seventeen *romances* in complete versions (fragments are not counted unless they fully reflect the plot and the gaps are minor). We have a single version of *La malcasada*, *La muerte de Prim*, *El marinero*, *La Virgen y el ciego*, *La buenaventura de Cristo*. There are not many examples of *La aparición*, *La dama y el pastor*, and *La monjita*. I believe, nevertheless, that this lack of versions is not so much because these themes did not have a foothold in Mexican territory as it is the result of scarce and sporadic searches by the also scarce and occasional collectors.[6] Nine *romances* exist that have circulated widely: *Hilitos de oro* (42 versions), *Delgadina* (29 versions), *Las señas del esposo* (21 versions), *Don Gato* (18 versions), *Mambrú* (15 versions), *Bernal Francés* (14 versions), *La adúltera* (13 versions), *La búsqueda de la Virgen* (5 versions), and *Alfonso XII* (5 versions). In addition to the foregoing there are two floating motifs, that is, motifs composed of several verses of traditional *romances* that are used, with slight variation, in the creation or re-creation of other *romances*: "No me entierren en sagrado . . ." (9 versions linked to different texts) and "De la corva al carcañal" (2 versions).[7]

This corpus of the *RMT*, which is the most complete, is, I believe, representative in that it contains religious ballads, children's as well as "adult" ballads; on the other hand, although the majority are texts that we can classify as novelesque, we also find among them one historical *romance* (*La muerte de Prim*) and another that is historical-novelesque (*Alfonso XII*). As far as their antiquity is concerned, we can say that four of the *romances* had already been collected in the sixteenth and seventeenth centuries

(*La aparición*, *Las señas del esposo*, *La adúltera*, and *Gerineldo*). Others were documented during those centuries, although we do not have complete texts from that period, as is the case of *Bernal Francés*, *Hilitos de oro*, and *La malcasada*. Likewise, we have versions of the first *romance* documented in writing in the fifteenth century (1421), *La dama y el pastor*, and one of the last *romances* to be created (1878), *Alfonso XII*.

Our seventeen *romances* do not correspond exactly to the *romances* that are most widespread in America.[8] Only seven of them coincide with witnesses from the other American countries: *Hilitos de oro*, *Delgadina*, *Las señas del esposo*, *Bernal Francés*, *Mambrú*, *Don Gato*, and *La adúltera*. Although much less widespread than in the rest of the American continent, six others exist in Mexico: *La búsqueda de la Virgen*, *Alfonso XII*, *La aparición*, *La dama y el pastor*, *El marinero*, and *La Virgen y el ciego*. Still no trace has been found in Mexico of *Blancaflor y Filomena* or *Santa Catalina*, and only fragments of *Gerineldo* and *El conde Olinos*; these four are, on the other hand, common in the rest of the Americas. Mexico coincides with other countries in the scarcity of *La malcasada* and *La muerte de Prim* and also *La monjita*, which is found in only a few countries, albeit with an average number of versions.

It seems appropriate to note that there still have not been found in Mexico versions of *La bastarda*, *Carabí*, *Silvana*, *Las hijas de Merino*, *La muerte de don Juan*, *Isabel*, *La bordadora*, and *La mala yerba*, which exist in some countries of the American continent, although in a reduced number. Neither do we have versions of *El conde Alarcos*, *La muerte ocultada*, *El quintado*, *Las tres cautivas*, *La infantina* + *La hermana perdida*, *La condesita*, *El duque de Alba*, *Misa de amor*, *La muerte de Elena*, or several more of which there are examples in the rest of America. Nevertheless, we have a version of *La buenaventura de Cristo*, which apparently is not to be found in any other American tradition.

The two floating motifs deserve special mention, the first of which, "No me entierren en sagrado . . ." (Don't bury me in a cemetery), is very widespread in all of the Americas as well as in Mexico. It is in our country where, apparently, it has been integrated into a greater number of songs (not texts), since it is found in one traditional *romance* (*Don Gato*), in one *romance vulgar* (*La cantada de Isabel*), in a *corrido* (*El hijo desobediente*), and in a folkloric dance (*El caballito*). About the second motif,

"De la corva al carcañal" (From the back of the knee to the heel of the foot), which comes from the old *romance* of *La muerte de don Beltrán*, for the moment we can say that it appears to be the only example on the American continent.

As for the number of texts collected (176), Mexico is high on the list among the various American countries and, as far as traditional *romances* are concerned, it is also important since it is only surpassed by Argentina, Colombia, Chile, and Santo Domingo. If one takes into account the aforementioned fact that ballad collecting has been carried out in Mexico only in a sporadic way by a few folklorists, we can say that the foregoing statistics seem to indicate that there exists in Mexico a great wealth of ballads waiting to be brought to light.

Mexican Versions[9]

In the corpus that we mentioned there are three principal types of versions: (1) those that are very similar to the common Spanish versions; (2) those that have strong points of contact with the former but show some form of local adaptation; and (3) those that have crossings, signs, and national re-creations of importance, whether because of their frequency or because of their significance.

Among the first we can cite the only versions collected of *La Virgen y el ciego*, *El marinero*, *La muerte de Prim*, and *La buenaventura de Cristo*, all the versions of *La monjita*, *La aparición* and *La búsqueda de la Virgen*, just as almost all the versions of *Mambrú* of the type "Mambrú se fue a la guerra . . ." and several versions of *Alfonso XII*, *Don Gato*, *Hilitos de oro*, and *Mambrú* of the type "En Francia nació un niño . . . ." These versions are an example of the phenomenon of textual repetition, which preserves with little or no variation a text that has been received.

The versions of the second type faithfully follow the inherited model; nevertheless, among the slight variations that they present are to be found lexical changes that consist of replacing some words with similar local terms. This does not affect the story or its narrative presentation, but it reveals a certain liberty in the handling of the text and constitutes a visible sign of its belonging to a specific community. This type of version is scarce, since the handling of the text generally brings with it, in addition to lexical changes, re-elaborations of different kinds (type 3). From type two we have several versions of *Las señas del esposo*, *Hilitos de*

oro, *Mambrú*, *Don Gato*, and the version of *La malcasada* that
includes words like *zaragüato* (a kind of monkey), *Hernán Cortés*,
sarape, *desconchinflado* (disjointed), *tapanco* (a large platform that
forms a small room between the roof and part of an interior room),
boruca (noise), *pelona* (a pejorative term), *chile*.

Within this same class, there are two cases that stand out,
which are versions of *Mambrú* ("Un niño nació en Francia . . .")
and of *Hilitos de oro*, both having national re-creations that do
not disturb the story.   In fact, in *Mambrú* the local re-creations
are in the refrain, an imitation of a burlesque refrain of other
Spanish versions, but slightly different, and which, in addition,
contain some expressions like *trompudo* (large-nosed), *babosa*
(idiot), *zonceses* (stupidities), etc.   The re-creation places the
versions in Mexico, but it does not affect the text, which is a quite
faithful reproduction of the Spanish text.

Hilitos de oro also has, at times, specific traits that one could
consider to be outside of the story even though related to it.   It is
a matter of an enumerative amplification (often repetitive and
generally parallelistic) which presents maternal recommendations
and makes profuse use of local terms, for example:

No me la siente en el suelo siéntemela en un cojín que aunque la ve trigueñita es hija de un *gachupín*.	Don't have her sit on the floor seat her on a cushion for though she is fair-skinned she is the daughter of a Spaniard [pejorative].
No me la siente en el suelo siéntemela en un *petate* que aunque la ve trigueñita es hija de un *pinacate*. (*RTM* XVI. 34)	Don't have her sit on the floor seat her on a mat for though she is fair-skinned she is the daughter of a smelly black bug (i.e., mulatto).

I have said that the elaboration is outside of the story because it
is a game of rhymes that has to do with the childish, playful
character of the *romance* and in no way modifies what was
inherited.   It is a kind of appendix stemming from the use to
which the *romance* was put, and not from the *romance* itself. It
could be said that these two cases are halfway between versions of
the second and third types.

The third class of versions, that is, those that have important
re-creations, can be divided into four groups: (a) those that do not
modify the plot but which present it differently from the majority
of the Spanish versions; (b) those that do not change the theme or
the nucleus of the plot, but amplify it; (c) those that affect the

story;[10] and (d) those made in a way that differs from the usual one, since they do not use traditional style and language but instead the more polished style and language of the urban middle classes.   It is in this third category of versions (and in all of its four groups) that national re-creation is exercised with most vigor, for which reason I shall examine some of these texts more closely in order to give an idea of what they are like.

Group a: Different Presentation of the Same Plot

   In this section there are included texts with the same narrative sequence as the common versions and a similar outcome. The variants are to be found in the details, in abundant use of the national lexicon, and, at times, in the re-creation of an episode or scene without change of meaning within the story.

   For example, in *La adúltera* we have two types of openings that differ from those of the common Hispanic versions.   The latter present a lady on the balcony who accepts the proposition of a passer-by, or even solicits it.   A variant that abounds in the Canaries presents first a suitor who adorns the lady's doorway with branches.   In Mexico the beginning of the story is put in the lover's mouth.   In the oldest versions a man tells about his encounter with a woman "a las orillas del mar" (along the seashore), her invitation to go to her house, and the husband's arrival while they are chatting (a common euphemism); afterward the usual dialogue between husband and wife follows.   In more modern versions, products of a re-creation made by a singer of *rancheras*, it is the husband who tells us the story of the betrayal of his wife—

Quince años tenía Martina	Martina was fifteen
cuando su amor me entregó	when she gave me her love
a los dieciséis cumplidos	when she became sixteen
una traición me jugó.	she betrayed me.

—and the scene continues between the married couple.

   In the majority of the versions of *Delgadina*, the traditional opening "Un rey tenía tres hijas . . ." (A king had three daughters) has changed to present Delgadina walking "de la sala a la cocina" (from the living room to the kitchen) showing off her figure: "con un vestido de seda / que su pecho lo ilumina" (in a silken dress / which highlights her breast).   Before the incestuous paternal proposition, a small scene has been created in which the

father asks her to get ready to go to mass, and it is after mass
that the proposition takes place.   The *romance* goes on in the
usual way with the variants of the Hispanic versions except that in
some there is no answer from the mother to her request for water,
a variant that is not found in any other version that I know of
(cf. Díaz Roig 1986:202-3).   Although the same story is being told,
all of these details separate these texts from the more common
ones.   To the foregoing one must add the many national words
like *nagüas*, *Morelia*, *pápa*, *máma*, etc., which give these versions
characteristics of a specific milieu.   Also in *Hilitos de oro*   the usual
Spanish opening, "De Francia vengo, seõra, / de por hilo
portugués" (I come from France, my lady, / for Portuguese thread)
is changed to "Hilitos, hilitos de oro, / que se me vienen
quebrando" (Little threads, little golden threads, / which are
always breaking for me) or "Angel de oro, / arenitas de un
marqués" (Golden angel, / sands of a marquis) and their variants,
but similar openings are found in other regions of Spain and in
several American countries.

Individual versions of *Mambrú*, *Alfonso XII*, and *Don Gato*
include the Mexican motif of the burial taken from "La cucaracha"
(see note 7), which, without changing the plot, gives the version a
burlesque tone that is incompatible with the meaning of the text
(except for *Don Gato*).   We can consider it to be a crossing
provoked by the mention of a burial in the text which the
informant included automatically without considering the text itself,
or a burlesque addition appropriate to children for whom the
romance is sung.   In my opinion, the first case would apply to
Alfonso XII, in which, in addition to being a version re-created in
romantic language, the burlesque tone is even more out of place,
and the second case to *Mambrú*, a children's ballad.   In *Don Gato*
its inclusion does not stand out since it is a *romance* with animal
protagonists.   This version then enters perfectly into the group 3a,
but the other two would constitute a special case of tone change
more in accord with group 3c.

Group b: Significant Amplification of the Plot

This is not very common.   Nevertheless, one of the most
widespread *romances* in Mexico, *Bernal Francés*, presents this
phenomenon.   Here it has to do with a preliminary scene or
episode that relates the suspicions of the husband and his

determination to prove them:

Su marido maliciaba	Her husband suspected
que Elena era preferida	that Elena was wanton
que cuando ausente él estaba	that when he was away
de un francés era querida.	she was courted by a Frenchman.
5 Su marido fingió un viaje	Her husband feigned a trip
para poderla agarrar	in order to catch her
en el hecho en que se hallaba	at what she was doing
y poderla asegurar.	and to ensnare her.
Al punto de medianoche	At exactly midnight
10 a su casa se acercó,	he approached his house,
con bastante sentimiento	with great passion
a Elena la recordó:	he woke Elena up:
—Abre las puertas, Elena,	"Open the doors, Elena,
ábrelas sin desconfianza,	open them without fear,
15 que soy Fernando el francés	for I am Fernando the Frenchman
que vengo desde la Francia.	who has come from France."
(*RTM* VII. 1)	

The structure is altered in the foregoing since the final surprise is removed and the public is informed about what really is going on, while in the common versions the listener is deceived as well as the wife.   This little scene is enlarged in many versions to create an entire episode in which the husband meets the lover, kills him, and afterwards goes home to entrap his wife.

With all of these elaborations the plot, in fact, has not been changed, since what has been created corresponds to what is not specifically said in other versions, that is, the suspicions and intentions of the husband.   The addition of the lover's death does not change the nucleus of the story, but it does enrich it.   The lover's punishment lies within the possible variations of a *romance* about adultery, and so it is not surprising that it can be found in many versions of *La adúltera*   (cf. Martínez-Yanes 1979:132-53).

We do not know for sure if these important variations in the ballad of *Bernal Francés* are of Mexican origin, since they are also found in other American texts (from Texas, New Mexico, Guatemala, and Nicaragua), but the predominance of that structure in Mexico is notable (14 out of 21 complete texts), suggesting that it probably is Mexican.

Group c: Re-creations that Affect the Story

Despite what is generally thought, this is a phenomenon found with some frequency in the Hispanic *romancero*.   A careful examination of the versions of a single *romance* shows us that in some cases crossings, elisions, re-creations, and truncated endings change the meaning of the story being told and even its theme. *Delgadina* without an incestuous proposal turns into a *romance* about parental cruelty (cf. Díaz Roig in press); *Las señas del esposo* without the identification of the husband sometimes causes the theme of the faithful wife to become that of the unfaithful wife (cf. Díaz Roig 1979:121–31); *La infantina* and *El caballero burlado* are transformed when the ending of *La hermana cautiva* is included, and the original stories either are lost or become diluted; *El conde Olinos* in a truncated version changes its theme from that of "love that is more powerful than death" to the much more common "death for love" (see Díaz Roig 1986:118, 126).

In Mexico there are versions of other *romances*, which, like *La adúltera*, when they have a truncated ending (perhaps as a result of the bad memory of the informants) and conclude with her excuses, present the story of adultery that is not found out. In fact, when there is no answer given to the wife's words, it would seem that the husband has allowed himself to be deceived, accepts the invented excuse, and has his suspicions dispelled. This ballad of successful deception, the product of truncated versions, is completely realized in other versions in which it is made explicit that the adulterous wife convinces her husband and, in addition, flaunts it (see *RTM* VI. 8 and Espinosa 1953:64).

The two versions that we have of *La dama y el pastor* have an important elaboration also found in the Chicano versions. It is a question of the final motif, which affects the plot since the shepherd does not finally reject the lady; rather it is the lady who rejects the shepherd in vengeance for the insult she received:

—Oye, pastor adorado,	"Listen, dear shepherd,
bien te puedes retirar,	you may well retire,
mis palabras no comprendes,	you don't understand my words,
tú te puedes ir allá.	you may go away."
5 —Oye, joven blanca y bella,	"Listen, fair maid,
tus palabras no entendí,	I didn't understand your words,
mi ganado está en la sierra,	my flock is in the mountains,
pero yo me quedo aquí.	but I'm staying here."
—No hay perdón para el que yerra,	"There is no pardon for one who errs,
10 mucho menos para ti,	much less for you,
tu ganado está en la sierra,	your flock is in the mountains,
bien te puedes ir de aquí.	be gone from here."

(*RTM* III. 1)

Finally, it is necessary to take note of the fact that the

versions of *Las señas del esposo* follow the above-mentioned model, that is, they accept the death of the husband and, in some of them, the wife is presented as lascivious because she is thinking only about marrying again (Díaz Roig 1979:121-31).   As I indicated, this changes the theme of the ballad.

All of these re-creations have their own characteristics, either because they are crossed with texts of other Mexican songs like "Juana Luna" (*La adúltera*), "La mujer abandonada" (*Las señas del esposo*), or because of the very high frequency of vocabulary of Mexican origin.   One version of the latter *romance* can be cited as an example in which the following terms appear within ten verses: *güero* (blond), *costeño* (coast dweller), *Cuautla*, *tápalo* (shawl), *café* (brown), *me vi* (I looked at myself), *chula* (pretty).

Group d: Re-creations in Non-Traditional Style

Two *romances* present versions with re-creations in a style that is different from that of the base text.   One is a version of *Don Gato*, which has characteristics of a learned version: an abundance of adjectives, unusual nouns, careful syntax, detailed story, perfect sequence.   Nevertheless, the text has maintained its traditional air in that the re-creator has kept all the motifs, has added no new ones, uses a good part of the original vocabulary, and is discreet in his work.   In this way, the text turns out to be only slightly different from the usual ones, and perhaps only a specialist can detect the learned hand of the re-creator.

This is not the case in two versions of *Alfonso XII* in which the re-creators intercalate verses with a completely different style, verses which are out of character:

Ella, triste y solitaria,	She, sad and lonely,
dicen que de amor murió	they say died of love
pues tu rango y tu nobleza	for your rank and nobility
ella nunca ambicionó.	she never coveted.
5 Hoy la cantan los troveros	Today troubadours sing of her
como ejemplo de un amor	as an example of love
y recuerdan a Mercedes,	and they recall Mercedes,
muerta ya como una flor.	now dead like a flower.
¿Dónde vas, Alfonso XII,	Where are you going, Alphonso XII,

10 dónde vas, triste de ti?	where are you going, poor you?
Vas muy triste, vas muy solo,	You go very sad and all alone,
llevas muerto el corazón.	the heart you bear is dead.
(*RTM* IX. B. 3)	

Porque la bella reposa	Because the beauty reposes
donde no se puede amar.	where one can't love.
(*RTM* IX. B. 5)	

As can easily be appreciated, the style is that of a romantic song and completely inappropriate for the *romancero*. It is very likely that when the *romancero* circulates among the middle and upper classes, it may come upon re-creators in whom semi-cultured poetic tastes predominate over traditional ones. Naturally this stylistic tendency comes forth in their re-creations. It is necessary to emphasize that today, in general, these learned characteristics seldom appear, whereas in the sixteenth century poets and printers often left their mark on the *romances* that they reworked.

Besides the variations of a thematic type that have been seen, one must not fail to mention a variation in form that occurs quite frequently in Mexico: the use of strophes and the loss of monorhyme. Both tendencies can be observed in Spanish ballad texts and represent the influence of the lyric song, which is much more widespread than its narrative counterpart. In Mexico added to this influence is that of the *corrido* (a narrative song, but with a lyrical form), for which reason the variations in form of the *romances* are much more frequent. I do not mean that all the *romances* are *corridos* in form, but rather that many texts are in almost perfect quatrains with a partial loss of monorhyme, although rarely does a text systematically change rhyme every four verses. The texts that show the most lyric influence are naturally the ones that are most often re-created, since the re-creations are usually done in the common form, eight-syllable quatrains with the same rhyme. This is as valid for the new parts (crossings, creations) as for the inherited parts that are re-elaborated. Nevertheless, not all the versions of a given *romance* present this problem. For example, there are versions of *Las señas del esposo* that completely rhyme in *é*, or versions with one or two distichs in a different rhyme, or polyrhymed versions with a predominance of the original rhyme, and versions in which the original rhyme has a frequency similar to that of the rest. In addition to the *romance* mentioned, there are others that present similar rhyme schemes like *La*

adúltera, Alfonso XII, Delgadina, Hilitos de oro (with predominance
of the original rhyme), *Don Gato* (in which monorhymed versions
predominate), *La búsqueda de la Virgen,* and *Bernal Francés*
(without the predominance of any particular rhyme).   Also, some
romances keep their monorhymed versions: *La malcasada, La
aparición, Mambrú,* and *La Virgen y el ciego.*

The influence of the lyric song and the *corrido* also manifests
itself in the direct intervention of the singer who addresses the
public at the beginning or at the end.   This presence is noteworthy
in the versions of *Bernal Francés,* less frequent and only at the
end of *Delgadina,* and occasional in *La adúltera* and *Don Gato.*

There are, of course, many other characteristics that deserve
mention and are part of the phenomenology of the traditional song:
fragmentary texts, texts with a changed structure (this occurs quite
frequently in *Bernal Francés*), texts with badly integrated crossings,
texts reworked with more or less coherency, and so forth.   Here I
have only wanted to present a few examples of the most
outstanding examples of *romances* from the Mexican tradition and
show how the handling of the texts confirms that they have been
propagated and taken root in this country.   The particular
characteristics of these versions present to us some of the many
forms that textual re-creation can adopt in the open road of its
traditional life.

El Colegio de México

Notes

[1] Translated from the Spanish by the editor.

[2] Up to now, as far as I know, no *romance* texts have been published
from Bolivia, Honduras, Panama, or Paraguay, but their existence is assumed.

[3] That is to say, I shall not take into account *corridos, bolas, valonas,*
etc., but I shall consider, for example, the versions of *Bernal Francés* that
have been re-created both formally and thematically.

[4] The latter, however, was taken from the *Almanaque de la Ilustración*
(1888). See *Romancero tradicional* (1976:8:312).

[5] Madrid, 1971; Davis, CA, 1977; Madrid, 1982; and a meeting during the
congress of the Asociación Internacional de Hispanistas (Venice, 1980).   These
congresses stimulated in turn other international meetings like the one
organized by the University of California (Los Angeles, 1984) and by the
Rijkuniversiteit (Utrecht, 1985).

[6]For example, in recent months, Professor Aurelio González has collected several texts, among them two versions of *El marinero*, of which there is only one in the *RMT*, and I have just collected a new version of *La Virgen y el ciego* which reinforces my comment about the lack, not of tradition, but of ballad collecting.

[7]There is another floating motif that is strictly Mexican which did not come from a *romance* but from a popular song, *La cucaracha*: ". . . ya lo llevan a enterrar / entre cuatro zopilotes / y un ratón de sacristán," (they are taking him off to be buried / between four buzzards / and a rat as sacristan), which is intercalated in versions of three *romances*: *Don Gato*, *Mambrú*, and *Alfonso XII*.

[8]These are: *Las señas del esposo, Delgadina, Hilitos de oro, La búsqueda de la Virgen, Don Gato, La adúltera, Bernal Francés, Mambrú, El marinero, La dama y el pastor, Alfonso XII, El conde Olinos, Blancaflor y Filomena, La Virgen y el ciego, La aparición, Santa Catalina*, and *Gerineldo*. For this and other data about the American tradition, I base my remarks on some eight hundred texts from the principal collections. It is clear that, even though the corpus is important, my conclusions should not be taken as definitive.

[9]I have treated the Mexican tradition in several studies (1983:44–47; 1986:159–223); likewise in a paper presented in the XXIII Congreso del Instituto Internacional de Literatura Iberoamericana (Madrid, 1984), and I have touched upon the subject in several articles and notes.

[10]Generally the versions of groups a, b, and c are apt to present a high percentage of lexical variants from Mexican speech, not only in the re-created parts but also in the inherited ones.

The Judeo–Spanish Ballad Tradition

Samuel G. Armistead and Joseph H. Silverman

As the repertoire of an isolated, archaizing minority, which
has lived for centuries in contact with Balkan, Near Eastern, and
North African cultures, the ballad tradition of the Spanish-speaking
Sephardic Jews constitutes one of the most . distinctive and
interesting branches of the Hispanic *romancero*. In regard to its
archaism, Judeo-Spanish balladry is comparable, perhaps, to that of
other Hispanic lateral areas, such as the Portuguese tradition of
Trás-os-Montes, the Azores, and Madeira or the Castilian
repertoires of León and Zamora Provinces and of the Canary
Islands.[1] In a Pan-European perspective, one could compare the
Sephardic tradition with that of Iceland and the Faroe Islands;[2] of
the German speech-island of Gottschee (Slovenia) and, to a lesser
degree, of other, more recently settled "East German"
communities;[3] or again with the folksongs of French Canada and
Louisiana, or even, perhaps, with certain features of
Anglo-American balladry.[4]

Exiled from Spain in 1492, the Spanish Jews (Sephardim)
settled in various Mediterranean areas, but their Hispanic language
and culture have only survived down to the present at two
geographic extremes: on one hand, in the Balkans, Turkey, and
the Near East and, on the other, in various towns in Northern
Morocco. Apart from these modern traditions, we have only
limited documentation of Sephardic balladry at earlier stages in its
development. As far as narrative themes are concerned, we can
form a certain idea of what the early Eastern Sephardic ballad
repertoire was like during the first century of the Diaspora, in that
numerous first verses (incipits) or key internal verses were used as
tune indicators in collections of Hebrew hymns (*piyûtîm*) dating
from as early as 1525.[5] On the basis of such evidence,
sixteenth-century Eastern balladry turns out to have been

somewhat different and significantly richer in narrative themes than its modern counterpart. The contrafact hymn tradition continued up through the nineteenth century, and there is also limited evidence of such incipits for Morocco in the late 1700s and early 1800s, thus giving us at least a fragmentary glimpse of the North African tradition at an earlier stage in its traditional trajectory.[6] The first full text of a Sephardic ballad to be discovered so far was sung by the false Messiah, Shabbethai Zevi, and written down in a Dutch translation at Izmir (Turkey) in 1667.[7] We also have versions of three traditional ballads, transcribed in a characteristic mixture of Spanish and Portuguese, from the Sephardim of Holland in a manuscript miscellany dated 1683.[8] There is equivocal evidence of Spanish ballads being sung by a Sephardic Jew (or a Morisco?) in Tunis in 1746, but no Tunisian texts survive and no modern Tunisian Jews speak Spanish as their native language.[9] From Eastern areas, however, handwritten Judeo-Spanish ballads first appear in the early 1700s and become relatively abundant by the end of the eighteenth century. By that time, the texts have become quite similar to those that will begin to be collected in large numbers from the late 1800s until the present.[10]

Today the Eastern and North African traditions have quite distinctive characteristics. In the East, the repertoire has experienced a radical transformation vis à vis its Hispanic origins; texts have become shorter and lyric elements tend to be emphasized; ballad music has been assimilated to the Balkan-Near Eastern musical idiom; narrative themes and stylistic features have also been borrowed from Greek, Turkish, and Arabic traditional poetry; contacts with the modern Spanish ballad are minimal or essentially non-existent; and ballad language has remained archaic, preserving many phonological features in common with medieval Spanish.[11] In Morocco, on the other hand, ballad texts are still remarkably close to their sixteenth-century Peninsular congeners; obviously, they have also undergone their own evolution, but an overall impression of textual conservatism is striking; the music is essentially Hispanic and Western in character; the language has been largely assimilated to a slightly substandard modern Andalusian colloquial Spanish, with features of the earlier Judeo-Spanish dialect (ḥakitía) surviving only as an occasional substrate influence; and there has been a massive infusion of modern Peninsular ballads, which imparts to the basically archaic Moroccan repertoire a decidedly mixed, eclectic character.[12]

It is difficult, if not impossible, to identify specific Peninsular regional characteristics in the Sephardic subtraditions that might indicate the ballads' origin in one or another area of Spain. Just as in the language (Révah 1980-84), the ballad repertoire has been reformed into a local *koine*, in which early regional variations seem to have been largely obliterated by subsequent developments. Even so, a number of Moroccan texts show particular affinities to Peninsular traditions of the South and East.[13] (But do such characteristics go all the way back to the fifteenth-century Diaspora?) In the East, various text-types are known today on the Peninsula only in Catalonia,[14] but such data tell us little about the origins of the tradition as a whole, which, like the Jewish exiles themselves, must have originated in almost every region of the Iberian Peninsula.

The Sephardic repertoire includes narrative types from almost all the thematic categories present in the other Hispanic subtraditions. The only obvious exception is, of course, the abundant Peninsular and Hispano-American balladry concerned with events in the New Testament and the Apocrypha. In all other thematic categories, the Judeo-Spanish tradition is richly representative and includes many early (fifteenth- and sixteenth-century) text-types that survive nowhere else in the modern tradition. The role of Sephardic balladry as an aid to reconstructing earlier stages of the Hispanic tradition is, of course, crucial. A number of Sephardic ballads perpetuate narratives that were current in the medieval Castilian and French traditional epic, and a majority of the epic-based songs derive, in direct oral tradition, from such medieval poems. There are, then, Sephardic ballads ultimately related to the *Cantar de Mío Cid* (*Poem of the Cid*), to the *Mocedades de Rodrigo* (*Early Adventures of the Cid*), to *Roncesvalles* (the Spanish adaptation of the *Roland*), to *La Mort Aymeri de Narbonne*, to *Beuve de Hantone*, and to other epic narratives as well.[15] Many Sephardic ballads concern events in Spanish and Portuguese history, and some that can be dated after 1492—*The Death of the Duke of Gandía*, *The Exile of the Jews from Portugal*, and *The Death of Prince John* (all three reflecting events of the year 1497)—point to post-diasporic contacts between the Jewish exile communities and the Iberian Peninsula, most probably through late emigration of *cristianos nuevos* (New Christians), eager to reembrace their Jewish faith rather than endure further inquisitorial persecution.[16] The Sephardic repertoire attests to the continued function of ballads as a record of current events (*noticierismo*): *The Death of King Sebastian* (1578), *Philip II's Testament* (1598), or even the modern Moroccan *Revolt of the Beni Ider*.[17] Biblical ballads—at least with respect to songs in "authentic" octosyllabic *romance* meter—are less frequently encountered than might be expected. With a few exceptions, all these songs are (or were) also known in the Christian Spanish tradition: *Sacrifice of Isaac, Rape of Dinah, David and Goliath, Thamar and Amnon, David Mourns Absalom, Solomon's Judgment.* Two *romances* about Moses and another on the martyrdom of Hannah's sons appear to be exclusively Sephardic. *The Crossing of the Red Sea* is unique, in that it is sung only in Greece and Turkey, on one hand, and, on the other, for ritual purposes by a Crypto-Jewish remnant population in northeastern Portugal. There are a number of Judeo-Spanish ballads concerned with classical antiquity: *Paris' Judgment, The Abduction of Helen, The Death of Alexander, Tarquin and Lucrece,* and *Virgil* (who is imprisoned for seducing the king's niece). Such ballads doubtless ultimately derive from medieval adaptations of classical narratives.

There are numerous Judeo-Spanish *romances* concerning a great variety of novelesque themes: prisoners and captives; the husband's return; faithful or unhappy love; the unfortunate wife; the adulteress; female killers; rape and abduction; incest; seductive or seduced women; other amorous adventures; tricks and deceptions; religious themes; death personified; animals; and various other subjects. A number of these narratives are clearly of medieval provenance: *The Sisters: Queen and Captive* (from *Fleur et Blanchefleur*); *Don Bueso and his Sister* (the *Kudrun* story); the *é* assonant *Husband's Return* (with a French balladic precursor dating from the fifteenth century); *The Weeping Knight* (from an erudite ballad written before 1498); the *ó* assonant *Adulteress* (ultimately related to an Old French *fabliau, Le Chevalier à la robe vermeille*); *The Beauty in Church* (brought from Greece to Spain, through Catalonia, during the fourteenth-century Catalan occupation of Athens); *The Lady and the Shepherd* (derived from the first known Hispanic ballad, written down in 1421); among other narratives that could be cited. The presence of numerous Christian elements (the Virgin, the Pope, priests, nuns, churches, crosses, mass, baptism, pork as food, and many others), in evidence even in the long-isolated Eastern tradition, also clearly bespeaks the Sephardic ballads' medieval Hispanic ancestry.[18] Other songs,

The ballad of *Virgil*, from an eighteenth-century Bosnian Sephardic manuscript (J.N.U.L., MS Heb. 8° 2946) (Armistead and Silverman 1971b).

for a variety of reasons—style among them—are obviously of late origin: *The Child Murderess; The Girl who Killed her Sister for Love of her Brother-in-law; The Rag Merchants' Bonnet Maker; The Miserly Sister* (blood flows from the bread denied to an impoverished sibling).   Many modern Spanish ballads reached Morocco quite recently, as we have seen, and in exile the Sephardim, both in the East and in North Africa, continued to compose narrative songs in *romance* meter.   Such are Eastern *romances* like *Condemned by the Pasha, The Renegade Girl,* and *The King's Favorite,* with their clearly Oriental ambience,[19] or the equally Moroccan *Carnations and Beatings, The Jealous Christian,* and *The Revolt of the Beni Ider.*[20] *The Death of King Sebastian,* celebrating, from a Jewish perspective, the disaster of Alcazarquivir in 1578, was also obviously composed by Moroccan Sephardim.

Many narrative types current among the Spanish Jews recall ballads known throughout Europe.   Some of these similarities seem to be coincidental (*Moriana's Poison* and the Anglo-Scottish *Lord Randal,* for example), but a majority certainly imply genetic relationships.   There are, for instance, probable (though distant) Sephardic congeners of the following ballads in the Anglo-Scottish tradition: *Lady Isabel and the Elf-Knight* (Child 4); *Hind Horn* (17); *Clerk Colville* (42); *Twa Magicians* (44); *Young Beichan* (53); *Fair Annie* (62); *Lady Maisry* (65); *Lord Thomas and Fair Annet* (73); *Maid Freed from the Gallows* (95); *Baffled Knight* (112); *Mother's Malison* (216); *Our Goodman* (274); and possibly several others.   Similar correlations can be established with Scandinavian, German, Italian, and French balladry, as well as with repertoires even further afield, such as that of Rumania.[21]   France doubtless links Iberia to the Continent and the sources of many Hispanic ballads are certainly to be found in French *chansons populaires.*

One of the most striking features of Eastern Sephardic balladry is embodied in a variety of narrative themes adapted from modern Greek *tragoúdia.*   Such Judeo-Spanish *romances* as *The Bottomless Well, The Daughter's Dream, The Newly Married Galley Slave,* and *Death and the Girl* have close, sometimes even verbal, correspondences with Greek ballads.[22]   *The Cursed Son's Return* embodies a particularly apt characterization of the Judeo-Spanish tradition in its intricate juxtaposition of medieval Spanish elements—in the initial and concluding segments—with a narrative adapted from the modern Greek ballad of *The Evil Mother.*[23]   To offer our readers at least one example of a Sephardic ballad, here

is a version of *The Cursed Son's Return*, as sung by Mrs. Leah
Huniu, from the Island of Rhodes (in Los Angeles, July 31, 1959):

—¿Di qué yoráx, Blancailiña,
de qué yoráx, Blancaiflor?
2 —Yoru pur vos, cavayeru,
que vos vax y me dixáx.
Mi dixáx niña y muchacha,
chica di la poca idat.
4 Me dixáx hijos chiquetos,
yoran y dimandan pan.—
Mitió la mano al su pechu,
sien liras li fue a dar.
6 —¿Estu para qué m'abasta,
para el vino o para'l pan?
—Vendiréx viñas y campus,
media parti de sivdat.
8 —¿Estu para ké m'abasta,
para el vino o para'l pan?
—Vendiréx los mis vestidus
sen sudar i sen manchar.
10 —¿Y esto para qué me abasta
u para el vinu, para'l pan?
—Si estu nu vus abasta,
vus prometu pur cazar.—
12 Esto que sintió su madri,
maldisión le fue a'char:
—Todas las navis dil puertu
vaigan i tornin sin sar.
14 La nave de el me hiju
vaiga y no torn'atrás.—
S'aparósi a la vintana,
la qui da para la mar.
16 Vido vinir navis francas,
navigando pur la mar:
—Así viva'l capitañu
que me digas la virdat.
18 Si's que vitis al mi hiju,
al mi hiju carunal.
—Yo lu vide a tu hiju
ichadu en l'arinar;
22 una piedra pur cavesal,
l'arena pur covyirtal.—
Estu que sintió su madri,
eya si mitió a yurar.
—No yoréx vos, la mi madre,
que so tu hiju carunal.

"Why are you weeping, Blancalinda?
Why are you weeping, Blancaflor?"
"I'm weeping for you, my lord,
for you are leaving me.
You leave me a young girl,
only a child in years.
You leave me with little children,
who weep and beg for bread."
He put his hand in his pocket
and gave her a hundred liras.
"What good is this to me
for buying bread or wine?"
"You can sell fields and vineyards
and half of all the city."
"What good is this to me
for buying bread or wine?"
"You can sell my clothes,
neither sweated nor soiled."
"And what good is this to me
for buying bread or wine?"
"If this is not enough,
I promise to marry you off."
When his mother heard this,
she put a curse on him:
"May all the ships in port
go and return without grief.
And may my son's ship
go and never return!"
She stood by the window,
the window that looks out to sea.
She saw foreign ships come,
sailing across the sea:
"Long may you live, my captain,
if you will tell me the truth.
Have you seen my son,
that son so dear to my heart?"
"Yes, I have seen your son,
he was lying on the sand,
with a stone for a pillow
and the sand for a coverlet."
When his mother heard this,
she began to weep.
"Don't weep, my mother,
for I am your dear son."

Verses 1-11 and 21-22 are based on the early Spanish ballad
of *Count Dirlos*, first printed around 1510, but the rest, the core of
the narrative, closely parallels a modern Greek ballad, *The Evil*

רומאנסה 6

דולסי אירמאש לה יו ונאדרי, לי אה טאן דולסי אין איל אבֿאבֿאר.
דיא בֿזיקוֿש אֿש פֿידרדו, לי טֿירֿס לי קואֿבֿרו אינבֿיינדו אֿדאֿר .

לי 2 בֿזיקוש אֿש פֿידרדן, לי טֿירֿס לי קואֿשבֿרו אינבֿיינדו אֿדאֿר
בֿוק דוק אירחֿן ד אֿמֿרים, לי לֿוש דוק די צֿ'ילֿוֿנשֿאד: קי טֿורֿנֿה.
ייודחֿבֿֿה בֿה בֿלאֿנֿקֿה כֿינֿייה , לאֿהֿגֿרֿימֿאֿש די צֿ'ילֿוֿנֿשֿאֿד .
די קי ייודאֿש בֿלאֿנֿקֿה בֿינֿייה , לאֿהֿגֿרֿימֿאֿש די צֿ'ילֿוֿשֿאֿד .
ייורו בֿור צֿוש קאֿבֿֿאֿבֿֿיֿירו , קי צֿוֿש בֿֿאֿש אֿי ונֿי דֿיֿשֿֿאֿש .
ונֿי דֿיֿשֿֿאֿש כֿינֿייה אֿי טֿוֿבֿֿאֿבֿֿת, אֿי גֿֿיֿקֿה די לֿה פֿוקֿה אֿיֿדֿאֿד .
ונֿי דֿיֿשֿֿאֿש אֿחֿוֿם בֿֿיֿקֿיֿטֿוֿש, ייורֿאֿן אֿי דֿיֿמֿאֿנֿדֿאֿן פֿאֿן .
אֿיֿסֿטֿו סֿיֿנֿטֿיֿו אֿיֿל קאֿבֿֿאֿבֿֿיֿירֿו, דֿיֿשֿֿו טֿוֿד אֿי טֿוֿרֿנֿו אֿבֿֿֿרֿאֿס .
ונֿטֿיֿיֿו לֿה עֿנֿבֿֿו אֿיֿן קֿו פֿיֿגֿֿו , קֿיֿןֿ דֿוֿבֿֿלֿוֿנֿיֿס לֿי דֿאֿרֿה .
פֿאֿרֿה קֿי ונֿי בֿֿאֿסֿֿﬠֿה אֿיֿסֿטֿו , פֿאֿרֿה צֿיֿמֿו אֿו פֿאֿרֿה פֿאֿן .
סֿי אֿיֿסֿטֿו כֿו צֿוֿש אֿבֿֿאֿסֿֿﬠֿה, צֿ'ינֿדֿיֿרֿש וֿמֿדֿֿייֿה קֿיֿצֿֿדֿאֿד .
צֿ'ינֿדֿיֿרֿש לֿוֿש וֿרֿס צֿֿיֿסֿﬠֿיֿדֿוֿק, סֿין מֿאֿבֿֿאֿל אֿי קֿן קֿוֿדֿאֿר .
סֿינֿה טֿרֿס אֿנֿייֿוֿש ﬠ' אֿיֿסֿﬠֿירֿאֿש. אֿלֿוֿש קֿוֿאֿטֿרֿו בֿֿוֿש קֿאֿבֿֿאֿש.

The *Cursed Son's Return*, from the Hebrew-letter chapbook, *Güerta de romansas antiguas de pasatiempo* ([Salonika?], before 1908), belonging to the Menéndez Pidal Archive in Madrid (Armistead and Silverman 1971a).

Mother. Entire narratives are not the only Balkan or Near Eastern features present in the Eastern Sephardic repertoire. Turkish, or rather Pan-Balkan, exclamations (*amán, ğanim, vay*) punctuate many songs, and Eastern ballad music has, as we have seen, been assimilated to Oriental norms. Imagery, too, is sometimes of Eastern origin, as when a young man's stature is compared to a cypress tree, using the Turkish word *selvi*, as also in Greek (*kyparíssa*) and other Balkan languages.[25] Some Eastern Sephardic ballads have, demonstrably, been translated from French or Italian; such are *The Diver, Fishing for a Ring*, and *The False Pilgrim*.[26] Thus, from the perspective of its many and variegated extra-Hispanic elements, the Sephardic *romancero* can be characterized not only as a precious treasury of medieval survivals, but also as a richly eclectic tradition, to which all the many peoples—Hispanic, Mediterranean, Balkan, Near Eastern, Christian, and Muslim—with whom the Sephardim came into contact have made their distinctive contributions.

Modern collecting of Judeo-Spanish balladry began in the East in the late nineteenth century and in Morocco during the first decade of the twentieth. Emigrant populations in Israel and in North and South America have also been a major source of texts.[27] The most ample and significant collections for the Eastern tradition are those of Attias (1961), Benmayor (1979), Crews (1979), and Hemsi (1932-73), as well as the various sources we have edited.[28] For Morocco, the collections of Bénichou (1968b), Larrea Palacín (1952), Librowicz (1980), Martínez Ruiz (1963), and Nahón (Armistead, Silverman, and Librowicz 1977) are indispensable. The Benardete collection (Armistead and Silverman 1981b), formed among immigrants in New York in 1922-1923, and Isaac Levy's four volumes (1959-1973), collected in Israel, include texts from both the East and Morocco, as do the massive collections—still largely unedited—of the Menéndez Pidal Archive in Madrid (some 2,150 texts) and Armistead, Silverman, and Katz (some 1,485 texts).[29] Today, a corpus of several thousand texts, both edited and unedited, makes possible detailed comparative studies of the traditional development of individual themes, of thematic differences between various regional repertoires, and of creativity in oral tradition, among many other subjects. Ultimately, Sephardic balladry can only be studied as but one component of the Pan-Hispanic tradition, in conjunction with ballads from Castilian areas of Spain and from the Canary Islands and Spanish America;

from Portugal and Galicia, the Atlantic Islands, and Brazil; and from Catalonia, in its various regional subtraditions.[30] In such a Pan-Hispanic perspective, the Judeo-Spanish tradition has played and will continue to play a crucial role in the diverse research orientations currently being developed by ballad studies as a burgeoning subdiscipline of Hispanism: historical and source work, comparative studies of European congeners, ballad geography, music, bibliography and cataloguing, literary criticism, oral creativity, sociological perspectives, formulism, semiotics, and computerized investigations.[31]

The most recent fieldwork on both branches of the Sephardic tradition, but especially among Eastern singers, reveals a steadily decreasing repertoire, in which in general only the more common themes continue to be sung by an increasingly aged and diminishing group of singers. The Judeo-Spanish tradition is clearly in the final stages of a critical decline. Even so, there are surprising exceptions and, from time to time, excellent ample versions and notable rarities still continue to come to light.[32] But time is running out and all efforts must be bent to saving for future study the surviving vestiges of this venerable tradition.

University of California, Davis
University of California, Santa Cruz

Notes

[1]For Trás-os-Montes, see Costa Fontes (1984a and 1987); also Dias Marques (1984–85); Armistead (1982a); for Azores, Costa Fontes (1983a); for Madeira, Ferré et al. (1982); for León and Zamora, Petersen et al. (1982) and Armistead (1983a); for the Canaries, Catalán et al. (1969a) and Trapero et al. (1982; 1985).

[2]For Iceland, see Olason (1982); for the Faroes, Wylie and Margolin (1981), particularly on the functions of ballad dancing; note the exhaustive catalog of Icelandic and Faroese text-types in Jonsson et al. (1978).

[3]For Gottschee, see Brednich and Suppan (1969) and, for "East German" settlements, Künzig and Werner (1975).

[4]For the archaism of Anglo-American ballads, see, for example, Combs (1967:57–60); Barry et al. (1929). We know of no specific comparative study of the survival in Canada of narrative themes which have died out in France. For a sampling of the Canadian tradition, see, among others, Gagnon (1925); Barbeau's many collections (e.g. 1962); d'Harcourt (1956); for Louisiana, Whitfield (1939:34–36, 56–59, for example); Oster (1962).

[5]See Avenary (1971) and Armistead and Silverman (1981a).

[6]See Armistead and Silverman (1973); Armistead, Hassán, and Silverman (1974).

[7]See Menéndez Pidal (1948); Armistead and Silverman (1971a:101-2); Scholem (1973:400-1).

[8]See Armistead and Silverman (1980a; 1980b).

[9]See Armistead (1979d). A fragment of a Judeo-Spanish ballad—obviously of Moroccan origin—has been collected on the island of Jerba (Fiore, 1969), but this cannot be counted as an authentic Tunisian text.

[10]See González Llubera (1938); Attias (1959; 1973); Armistead, Hassán, and Silverman (1978).

[11]For a detailed characterization of the Moroccan tradition, see Bénichou (1968b:307-59; 1983).

[12]On the transformation of Eastern texts, see Catalán (1970-71:5-14); on Near Eastern music, Katz (1972-75; 1980-84); on Balkan and Near Eastern textual features, Benmayor (1978); Armistead (1979-81); Armistead and Silverman (1982; 1983-84).

[13]See, for example, Menéndez Pidal, Catalán, and Galmés (1954:114-15, 198-201); Catalán (1969b:195-97); Armistead, Silverman, and Katz (1986:270-73).

[14]See, in Armistead (1978:nos. I3, L12), the ballad types *Husband's Return* (á-a) and *Married to an Old Man* (é).

[15]See Armistead and Silverman (1971a:56-67; 1982:35-42); Armistead, Silverman, and Katz (1986).

[16]For bibliography on these *romances* (and others cited below by their English titles), see Armistead (1978), where ballads are indexed under both their Spanish and English titles.

[17]See Armistead (1989);   Armistead and Silverman (1979:50-59); Larrea Palacín (1958:61-63).

[18]See Armistead and Silverman (1965; 1982:127-48).

[19]Concerning these ballads, see Benmayor (1979:no. 13); Armistead (1978:nos. H23, U5); and Armistead and Silverman (1971b:no. C21; 1979:no. A11).

[20]See Armistead, Silverman, and Librowicz (1977:nos. 52-57); Larrea (1958:61-63).

[21]See Armistead (1979b); Armistead and Katz (1978); Rechnitz (1978; 1979).

[22]See Armistead (1979-81); Armistead and Silverman (1982:151-78; 1983-84). Some of these Eastern ballads have migrated to Morocco.

[23]See Armistead and Silverman (1971a:306-14; 1982:163-68).

[24]This version was included in Menéndez Pidal and Goyri de Menéndez Pidal (1957-85:3:125-26). In v. 13b, the word *sar* is from Hebrew *tsa^{c}ar* "anguish, affliction."

[25]See Armistead and Silverman (1982:194-99, 208-27).

[26]See Armistead and Silverman (1982:229–39); Armistead (1978:no. I9).

[27]For the history of Judeo-Spanish ballad collecting in Morocco, in America, and elsewhere, see Armistead, Silverman, and Librowicz (1977: 15–22); Armistead and Silverman (1981b:4–11).

[28]See Armistead and Silverman (1971a; 1971b; 1982); Armistead, Silverman, and Hassán (1981c).

[29]For the Nahón and Bernadete collections, see Armistead, Silverman, and Librowicz (1977); Armistead and Silverman (1981b); for the Menéndez Pidal Archive, Armistead (1978); for our own collection, Armistead and Silverman (1983); Armistead, Silverman, and Katz (1986).

[30]On the Pan-Hispanic character and distribution of the *romancero*, see Menéndez Pidal (1953:2:358–59).   Such publications as the *Romancero tradicional de las lenguas hispánicas* (*RT*, 1957–85) and the *Catálogo general* (*CGR*, 1982–88) are Pan-Hispanic in scope.

[31]For recent surveys of Sephardic and Pan-Hispanic ballad research, see Armistead (1982a; 1982b; 1983b; 1985).   For fundamentally important Pan-Hispanic ballad studies, in which Sephardic balladry has played a crucial role, note, among others, Bénichou (1968a, Catalán (1969b; 1970), and the *CGR* (1982–88).

[32]For the most recent collecting, see Benveniste (1986), Merrill–Mirsky (1984), Noga–Alberti (1984), W. Hamos (1982), Weich-Shahak (1984).   For an example of a recently collected ballad's making a crucial contribution to our knowledge, see Armistead, Librowicz, and Silverman (1986).

The Structure and Changing Functions
of Oral Traditions

Beatriz Mariscal de Rhett

> Not graven on tablets was this law, nor sealed
> Within papyrus rolls, but in plain speech
> Delivered to thee from a dauntless tongue.
> (Aeschylus, *The Suppliants*)

The transmission of knowledge by means of oral literary forms, so strongly attacked by Plato in the fourth century B.C., has not disappeared completely.[1] Throughout the many centuries of supremacy of the written word over non-written communication, many non-literate communities have retained literary traditions that rely on being memorized and orally transmitted by members of that community. Oral traditions that have been able to adapt themselves to the changes in their environment have been able to survive to our day in coexistence with forms of literate origin, although mostly relegated to marginal social groups.

One of the oral literary genres that still retains great vitality is the Hispanic *romancero*. Field research begun at the end of the nineteenth century in several regions of the Iberian Peninsula and, since the turn of the century, expanded to other Spanish and Portuguese peninsular and insular areas, to Africa and the Near East where Sephardic communities settled, and to some Latin American countries, proved that the traditional *romancero* was alive in practically all of the Spanish- and Portuguese-speaking world.

During the past few years, interest in this type of literature has increased considerably. Field research in Latin America and among Sephardim and Portuguese residing in Canada and the United States has complemented the somewhat sketchy picture we had of the *romancero* tradition on this continent. Concerning the Peninsular tradition, individual researchers as well as a number of

247

research groups directed by the Instituto Menéndez Pidal of the Universidad Complutense of Madrid and sponsored by United States, Spanish, and Portuguese institutions have carried out extensive field trips in Spain and Portugal to collect *romances*. These field trips have been very successful; several thousand *romance* texts, some of them quite rare, have been collected from oral tradition during the last decade.[2]

Romances, like all other oral traditions that live in the collective memory of the people, must fulfill some social function within the communities that retain them in order to survive the overpowering intrusion of the more prestigious literary forms, and they must be structured in such a way that they can be memorized not only by especially gifted people, but by practically anyone in the community.[3] As the environment changes, *romances* adapt structurally and functionally to those changes in order to remain in the tradition. My observations will center on these two aspects of the adaptation of oral traditions to their dynamic environments.

Since the sixteenth and seventeenth centuries, when the *romancero* was most popular both at court and among the common people, the occasions for the singing of *romances* have become fewer as the genre has been relegated mostly to rural communities. What for centuries were "natural" occasions for the singing or reciting of *romances* have been practically eliminated within the past four or five decades. Traditional *romances* are still being sung during some communal tasks, such as the harvesting of olives in the south of Spain, during festive occasions mostly of a family nature (christenings or weddings), or during summer afternoons when small groups of women get together to knit or sew outside their homes (an occasion that has proved very fruitful in our collecting work). However, other occasions such as the *filandones*, where women of different generations could sing *romances* as they got together to spin wool, are no longer common, and the noise of tractors has effectively eliminated the singing of *romances* that used to accompany different agricultural chores. The collective nature of the creative process of this type of literature remains, nevertheless, unchanged.

In spite of the more limited occurrence of *romance* singing, *romance* narratives continue to function as a means of transmitting social values or commenting on social problems. Whether they talk about "el príncipe don Juan" (Prince John, son of the Catholic

Kings) or "el novio de Ricardina" (Ricardina's boyfriend), two alternative characterizations of the protagonist of *La muerte del príncipe don Juan*, *romances* are understood by their interpreters as dealing with what happens in life, "cosas de la vida," as was very clearly stated by a *romance* singer. When the narratives, which may have originated several centuries ago, or even in another culture, are adopted by a community, they become a part of its particular culture as a result of the capacity of this type of structure to adapt to the world in which it lives.

Unlike other traditions, the *romancero* is, in general, not transmitted by special singers, although the individual who has a good voice or a good memory will most likely retain a greater number of *romance* themes. Any member of the community can participate in the transmission/creation of this traditional art. Both young and old have memorized and sung *romances* for hundreds of years without any differentiation being made between the "producer" or performer of the text and the "consumer" or receiver, since the latter will in turn become the producer.

When in response to our inquiries someone sings or recites *romances*, either because they concede spontaneously that they know *romances* or because others who have heard them prompt them to do so, there is always some intervention on the part of others present, even if they claimed they did not know any *romances*. Non-singing bystanders not only help the person singing or reciting to remember certain lines or passages they might have forgotten, they also tend to reject anything that does not correspond to what they learned or think is right. The singer will sometimes modify her or his version to conform to what the other members of the community perceive to be either correct or superior. As a consumer of *romances*, anyone can be as much a part of the productive process as the person in charge of the performance, even though not every contribution has aesthetic value.

The non-specialized character of *romance* singers assures the possibility of a wide participation by the members of the community in their "appropriation" of the text. Whatever change occurs within the narrative structure is consensual and the result of the natural process of adaptation of the text to its dynamic environment and to changing communication needs of the community. In contrast, texts transmitted by professional interpreters are as "closed" as any "cultured" text, even if they are intended for popular consumption. The prestige of the professional interpreter and of the media that transmits such texts (radio, television, tapes, records, etc.) effectively prevents the appropriation and reinterpretation of the model by the public. Traditional literature, on the other hand, is conceived by its consumers as belonging to them; it is a product of their culture and thus remains open to transformation as changes in the referent require new interpretations.

This "openness" of oral texts constitutes one of the main differences between popular and traditional literatures, a difference that is seldom made evident when popular traditions are considered, since it is not the nature of the texts that is taken into consideration, but merely the fact that the consumers of both these types of artistic products are members of the popular classes.

I have insisted on the non-specialized character of *romance* singers because it is central to my discussion of variation and adaptation of *romance* functions and narrative structures. *Romance* singers have no desire either to entertain their audiences with innovation or to perfect the text they are reproducing; in fact, their main concern is to render the text exactly the way they learned it. And yet, variation is precisely what characterizes oral traditions. In the course of the life of a *romance* there is a slow but irreversible change that affects not only the superficial levels of organization of the text, the level of the discourse or of the plot, but also the deeper levels, such as the level of the *fabula*, where the narrative's causality responds to its referent, the social reality, or even the functional level.[4]

When we compare the different versions of a *romance* and observe how the same structure or model can be manifested in many varying forms, the relationship between the different levels of organization of the narrative becomes evident. Any variation at a superficial level of the text can affect a deeper level, which in turn can generate change in the more superficial one. The signified generates its signifier or signifiers, but the signifier(s) can, in turn, regenerate the signified each time the sign is interpreted. Given the openness of oral structures, the new signifieds tend to generate new signifiers that express better or more efficiently those regenerated signifieds.[5]

If, as we have observed, innovation does not occur at a conscious level at the moment of the oral production of a *romance*, we must look into other stages in the process of transmission of the text in order to understand the creative processes of oral traditions. I will discuss some of them briefly.

Oral transmission of a text requires its memorization by the receiver, who will in turn become its transmitter. Memory thus plays a central role in oral traditions; the retention/variation process of oral transmission of texts is closely connected with the way the human mind processes information for long-term memorization.

In recent years many psychologists, linguists, and other specialists in the cognitive sciences have shifted their interest from minimal signifying units to connected discourse as the basis for their studies on memory. Their observations on the relationships between discourse structures and thought processes help us to understand particular narrative structures.[6]

Lexical Variation

Research has demonstrated that soon after input subjects do not normally retain the precise wording of discourse segments unless they concentrate on that wording.[7] In the case of *romances*, the poetic mode plays a crucial mnemonic role; wording is central to memorization of the narrative. Whether *romances* are sung or recited, their expression is just as important as their narrative content. Nevertheless, a comparison between two different versions of a *romance*, even if its known versions are not very abundant, reveals an important degree of lexical and syntactical variation.[8] The opening lines of five versions of *Belardo y Valdovinos* collected from modern oral tradition can serve as an example:

De las guerras ven Bernardos	From the wars came Bernardos
de las batallas venía,	from the battles he came,
cien caballos trae delante	a hundred horses he drives before him
todos ganados do un día.	all won in one day.
(Lugo)	
Don Belardo fue a la guerra	Don Belardo went to war
la cosa que él más quería;	the thing he liked best;
cien caballos trai adiestros,	a hundred horses he leads,
todos los ganó en un día.	he won them all in one day.
(Oviedo)	

Bem se passeia Bernardo pela ribeira de Umbria, leva duzentos cavalos, todos ganhou num dia. (Vinhais, Portugal)	Bernardo was riding along the shore of Umbria, he leads two hundred horses, he won them all in one day.
Alta vai a lua alta com'o sol de mediodía cuando don conde Belardos de la batalla salía; sacó ciento cien caballos todos a rienda perdida. (Orense)	High is the moon high like the noonday sun when Count Belardos left the battle; he took away a hundred horses all swiftly running.
Alta, alta va la luna como el sol del mediodía cuando el conde don Belardo de la campaña salía; seis mulas lleva de rienda, todas las ganó en un día. (Zamora)	High, high is the moon like the noonday sun when Count Belardo left the campaign; six mules he leads by the rein, he won them all in one day.

Linguistic Competency

Given the ephemeral nature of an oral text, the receiver must have the competency to decodify the message at the time of its performance; he must be able to anticipate the meaning of each narrative element as well as the relationships between them as they are being expressed orally. Familiarity with the language utilized in the text, that is, familiarity with the paradigmatic meanings of the narrative units that come together in the narrative, is therefore essential to its understanding and memorization.

Most, if not all, of the poetic language of the *romancero* is formulaic, that is, it is composed of discourse units of varying lengths that convey a unitary meaning. The use of formulaic language in oral traditions and the role this type of language plays in the structuring of oral texts has been studied by specialists not only in the field of literature, but in fields such as folklore, linguistics, and anthropology as well. The specific nature and use of formulas in the *romancero* has also been the subject of important studies such as R. H. Webber's (1951). I will thus insist on only one point, on the fact that what is essential to the process of transmission of oral narratives is not the ability of the producers/consumers of oral texts to use formulas in different contexts, but rather their comprehension of the unitary meaning of formulas.[9]

Let us consider the following discourse formulas that appear in two *romances*, *Juan Lorenzo* and *El prisionero*:

Entrar quiere el mes de mayo salir quiere el mes d'abril, cuando el trigo está en grano, las flores quieren salir. (*Juan Lorenzo*)	The month of May is coming in the month of April is going out, when the wheat is ripe, the flowers are coming out.
Mes de mayo, mes de mayo, mes de las fuertes calores, cuando los toritos bravos, los caballos corredores, cuando los enamorados gozaban de sus amores. (*El prisionero*)	Month of May, month of May, month of severe heat, when the brave bulls, the running horses, when lovers were enjoying their love.

Although there are few lexemic and syntactic coincidences between them, they do have an obvious equivalence. The second formula, through a more elaborate description, makes explicit what the first one only insinuated, the surging of sexual plenitude. The arrival of summer with its connotation of sexual plenitude which these formulas express serves in *Juan Lorenzo* to refer to the protagonist's deprivation of his natural sexual life because another man will take his wife away from him.   In the case of *El prisionero*, the formula is part of the lack of a natural life on the part of the protagonist who, imprisoned, is unable to fulfill his (or her) sexuality. The meaning of the formula is made explicit with the mention of brave bulls ("toritos bravos"), running horses ("caballos corredores") and lovers who were enjoying their love ("enamorados que gozaban de sus amores").

At the next level of semantic organization of the text, where the plot constitutes the signifier of the *fabula*, narrative motifs, which are also formulaic, are likewise adjusted to the varying needs of communication of the *romance* singers.

In *La muerte ocultada*, a young couple is expecting their first child when the husband is mortally wounded. The tradition presents several possibilities for the encounter of the hero with death. In a version from Salamanca, for example, the hero goes hunting and is killed by a lioness:

Salía don Bueso a cazar un día, la brava leona de morderle había.	Don Bueso went out to hunt one day, the savage lioness was to bite him.

In the Moroccan branch of the tradition, he encounters death personified:

Levantóse Ueso	Ueso arose
lunes de mañana,	one Monday morning,
alzara sus armas	he took up his arms
y a la caza iría.	and went out hunting.
5 En un prado verde	In a green meadow
se sentó a almorzar,	he sat down to lunch,
vio venir a Huerco	he saw Huerco coming
las aguas pasar.	across the waters.
—Así Dios te deje	"Thus may God let you
10 con Alda vivire	live with Alda
que tú ya me dejes	[and] may you now let me
las aguas bullire.	stir up the waters."
—Así Dios me deje	"Thus may God let me
con Alda folgare,	take pleasure with Alda,
15 que yo no te deje	[and] may I not let you
las aguas pasare.	cross the waters."
Hirió Ueso a Huerco	Ueso wounded Huerco
en el calcañale;	in his heel;
hirió Huerco a Ueso	Huerco wounded Ueso
20 en la voluntade.	in his will.

And in the following version from Cáceres, as in the majority of versions collected from modern oral tradition, war is the cause of death:

Estando don Pedro	When Don Pedro was
sentado a la mesa,	seated at the table,
le vino la orden	there came to him the order
para ir a la guerra.	to go to war.
Ya viene don Pedro	Now Don Pedro is returning
de la guerra herido,	from the war wounded,
y doña Teresa,	and Doña Teresa,
cuanti había parido.	who had already given birth.

The plot segments, "the hero goes hunting" and "the hero goes to war," are not the same, nor is the battle between Huerco (death personified in Judeo-Spanish) and the hero, who tries to prevent Death from crossing the barrier of water that separates the world of the living from the world of the dead, the same as the hero's being mauled to death by a lioness. The unitary signification of the narrative motif, "the hero is mortally wounded as he encounters death," is reinterpreted in terms of the social environments of the *romance* singers. As man no longer encounters death in a direct confrontation with other-world forces or with wild beasts, man himself becomes his natural enemy, and he dies in battle against man.[10]

The substitution of discourse or plot formulas for others of equal semantic value demonstrates the capacity of *romance* singers to understand their unitary meaning. Memorization of formulas implies their decodification. Familiarity with the language of the text with the signifying units utilized in the narrative is not only essential to its understanding and memorization, but it also helps in the memorization of other similar texts, other *romances*.

Semantic Cohesiveness of the Text

Comprehension and retrieval of memorized information at the time of its rendition requires strong semantic cohesiveness of the text. In order to achieve cohesiveness, all the elements that comprise its discourse must be integrated with one another (see Bransford and MacCarrell 1974). The orally transmitted text can retain global coherence throughout time and space only if the receiver/transmitter can comprehend the causal relationships between the actions and situations presented in the narrative. The capacity of the *romance*'s narrative to adapt semically and lexemically to its changing referent makes possible its continued semantic coherence.

In order to strengthen the semantic coherence of a text, while at the same time helping the receiver to anticipate the signification of the elements that comprise the narrative, *romances* count on the use of indices (see *CGR* 1.A, 1984). An index is a narrative element of varying complexity (it can be a single word or a formula comprising several verses) which refers not to what happens in the narrative, but rather to what is. It is not a part of the syntagmatic chain of events. The signification of an index is paradigmatic; it cannot be completed within the syntagma where it appears (see Barthes 1966:1-27). Indices help to understand the actions of characters by pointing to their traits or to the nature of events. Although they are often redundant expressions of the narrative content, they are essential to the understanding of the *fabula*, where the narrative's causal relationships are established.

The *romancero* utilizes different types of indices, some of them a part of its particular semantic system, for example, specific occasions when an event might occur, like St. John's Day, the summer solstice, or Monday, signaling something ominous. The listener can anticipate the death of the protagonist when *romances* include formulas like: "Un lunes por la mañana / don Pedro de caza salía" (One Monday morning, Don Pedro went out hunting) and "Don Diego salió de caza / un lunes por la mañana" (Don Diego went out hunting one Monday morning). Likewise in *La esposa de don García*, which begins with "Yo me levantara un lunes / un lunes muy de mañana" (I got up one Monday, one Monday very early). Monday presages the ill fortune of the protagonist who is to be kidnapped by the Moors.

Other indices are semantic clichés that belong to a universal mythical tradition, such as the water that separates the world of the living from the world of the dead in *La muerte ocultada*, or the *locus amoenus* where encounters occur signaling the amorous nature of the encounter. For example, the maiden going on a pilgrimage or to her brother's wedding in *La fatal ocasión* will successfully escape her pursuer until they reach a cool fountain, the *locus amoenus*:

El correr y ella correr,	He was running and she was running,
alcanzarla no podía;	he could not overtake her;
quiso Dios que la alcanzó	God willed that he should overtake her
al pie de una fuente fría.	at the foot of a cool spring.

or:

Mucho corre el caballero,	The knight runs hard,
tanto y más corre la niña,	the girl runs even harder,
se llegaron a encontrar	they came together
al pie de una fuente fría.	at the foot of a cool fountain.

Given the place of the encounter, the lad's intentions become obvious:

—Si viniera a quitarme honra,	If you came to take away my honor,
Dios le quitare la vida.	may God take away your life.

Other sites such as a green meadow ("en un verde prado") or the shade of an olive tree ("al pie de una verde oliva") are also understood as indices that a love encounter, whether natural or forced, is going to take place.

Indices also play an important part in the *romancero* in providing coherence in texts where events are not presented in their logical place within the narrative. For example, in *Bernal Francés*, a *romance* of adultery, the husband pretends to be his wife's lover in order to test her. As the narrative begins with the arrival of the disguised husband, several indices are used to help the listener understand what is happening before it is made evident: the candlelight which would reveal the identity of the supposed lover is blown out when he enters the room, providing a clue that something is not right. The wife is also called wretched ("la güitada") when she is getting ready to go to the arms of her lover, making the listener aware that tragedy will befall her, thus helping to decodify the seemingly discordant elements of the narrative.

Social Competency

The decoding of information is an active process that requires the invoking of previously acquired information. Comprehension and memory are sensitive to contextual constraints, to the way in which referential, semantic, and pragmatic environments direct the processing of the information that has been received.[11]

Participants in the chain of transmission of oral texts decodify the narratives in terms of their own social structures. The types of relationships they establish between the actions and situations narrated and the world as they perceive it will not only determine their comprehension and memorization of the text, but in addition it will necessarily play a part in their restructuring of the narrative when the information is retrieved in a future oral performance of the text.[12]

Our experience of several years of collecting *romances* from oral tradition in Spain and Portugal confirms something that has been observed by previous generations of collectors but has not been analyzed in all its consequences: the fact that the majority of our informants, and therefore the principal depositaries of oral traditions, are women. I would also point out that the phenomenon is not limited to the Hispanic *romancero*. In the works of Latin American authors who utilize materials from oral traditions, we have testimonies that their sources are almost invariably feminine. Such is the case, for example, of Miguel Angel Asturias, Gabriel García Márquez, and José Emilio Pacheco.[13]

A statistical study of *Gerineldo*, one of the most widespread *romances* in the modern oral tradition, reveals the following: for the 819 versions published by the Seminario Menéndez Pidal in the *Romancero tradicional de las lenguas hispánicas*, we have the names of 668 informants of whom 549 are women, more than 82% of the total. Interestingly, many of these women were not old: 277 of them were under fifty years of age, and 42 of them were under twenty (*Gerineldo* 1975-1976).

Feminine transmission of oral literature is not merely a sociological fact since, given the openness of this type of literature, the active role played by women in the creative processes of oral traditions has necessarily been a determining factor in their function and structure. In several centuries of traditional life,

women's voices and their world views have been incorporated into
these forms inherited from the past.

The *romance* of *Las quejas de doña Urraca*, which we know
both in its sixteenth-century tradition and in versions collected
from modern oral tradition, provides us with an example of how a
text that originally offered a political commentary on a historical
event, i.e., which had had a more or less journalistic function, has
been able to survive by adapting its narrative structure to convey
a message relevant to its twentieth-century transmitters.[14] *Las
quejas de doña Urraca* is an episode taken from the *Cantar de la
muerte del rey don Fernando*, a medieval epic poem which we
know only through prose passages that appear in thirteenth and
fourteenth-century chronicles: the *Primera crónica general*, the
Crónica de veinte reyes, and the *Crónica de 1344*.

When Fernando I was on his deathbed, he divided his
kingdom among his three sons, Sancho, Alfonso, and García,
leaving his daughters, Urraca and Elvira, out of his will. Urraca
accuses her father of unjustly disinheriting her and gets him,
through threats of dishonoring him, to make a new partition of the
kingdom, granting Zamora to her and Toro to Elvira. As he
changes his will, the king also demands that his sons take an oath
that they will abide by his last will. The partitioning of the
kingdom had widespread political repercussions in which the Cid, a
partisan of Sancho, the oldest son, was to play an important role.
The rivalry between the three brothers resulted in a series of
betrayals followed by bloody revenge, which included the
well-known hostility between the Cid and Alfonso because of
Sancho's murder during the siege of Zamora.

Although the Cid is a hero of almost eternal popularity in
most of the Hispanic world, he is not a protagonist of the *romance*.
His role as mediator between father and daughter and his defense
of Urraca's rights of inheritance, mentioned by the chronicles and
therefore by the *Cantar de Mio Cid*, is not mentioned in the
modern *romance*. The protagonists are King Fernando and
Princess Urraca, two historical figures who are not easily recognized
by the people who sing the *romance* in our day.[15]

Both characters, King Fernando I and Princess Urraca, the
same as any character appearing in a *romance* narrative, are
defined in terms of their roles as actants in the narrative, in
Greimas'   terminology: *sujet/objet*;   *destinateur/destinataire*;
adjuvant/opposant, and as representatives of the narrative's referent,

the social reality. This double definition is essential to the renovation of a text. Because the relationships between the two characters are defined in terms of the referent, they will be adapted to the new contexts in which the *romance* is sung.

The *romance* of *Las quejas de doña Urraca* as was registered in sixteenth-century *cancioneros* and broadsides is a brief dialogue between the princess and the king. I will use the version published in the sixteenth-century *Cancionero de romances* (1550, 1967:213-14) as an example of that tradition:

	Morir vos queredes padre	You are about to die father
	san Miguel vos aya el alma	may Saint Michael have your soul
	mandastes las vuestras tierras	you gave away your lands
	a quien se vos antojara	to whomsoever you chose
5	a don Sancho a Castilla	to Don Sancho Castile
	Castilla la bien nombrada	renowned Castile
	a don Alonso a Leon	to Don Alonso León
	y a don Garcia a Bizcaya	and to Don García Vizcaya
	a mi porque soy muger	because I am a woman
10	dexays me deseredada	you leave me disinherited
	yrme yo por essas tierras	I shall go through those lands
	como vna muger errada	like a sinful woman
	y este mi cuerpo daria	and give this body of mine
	a quien se me antojara	to whomsoever I choose
15	a los Moros por dineros	to Moors for money
	y a los Christianos de gracia	and to Christians free
	de lo que ganar pudiere	what I can earn
	hare bien por la vuestra alma.	I will offer for your soul.
	Alli preguntara el rey,	Then the king asked,
20	Quien es essa que assi habla?	Who is it that is speaking this way?
	Respondiera el arçobispo	The archbishop answered
	Vuestra hija doña Vrraca.	Your daughter Doña Urraca.
	Calledes hija calledes	Be silent daughter be silent
	no digades tal palabra	don't say such a thing
25	que muger que tal dezia	for a woman who said such a thing
	merescia ser quemada	would deserve to be burned
	alla en Castilla la vieja	there in old Castile
	vn rincon se me oluidaua	[is] a corner I forgot about
	çamora auia por nombre	Zamora is its name
30	çamora la bien cercada	well-encircled Zamora
	de vna parte la cerca el Duero	on one side the Duero surrounds it
	de otra peña tajada	on another a steep cliff
	del otro la moreria	on another the Moorish district
	vna cosa muy preciada	a very prized thing
35	quien vos la tomare hija	whoever takes it from you daughter
	la mi maldicion le cayga.	upon him may my curse fall.
	Todos dizen amen amen	All say amen, amen
	sino don Sancho que calla.	except Don Sancho who is silent.
	El buen rey era muerto	The good king was dead
40	çamora ya esta cercada	Zamora is now encircled
	de vn cabo la cerca el rey	on one side the king surrounds it

	del otro el Cid la cercaua	on the other the Cid surrounded it
	del cabo que el rey la cerca	on the side that the king surrounds
	çamora no se da nada	Zamora does not yield at all
45	del cabo que el Cid la cerca	on the side that the Cid surrounds
	çamora ya se tomaua	Zamora was already taken
	Assomose doña Vrraca	Doña Urraca appeared
	assomose a vna ventana	she appeared at a window
	de alla de vna torre mocha	from there from a flat tower
50	estas palabras hablaua.	she spoke these words.

The sixteenth-century singers of the *romance* were perfectly familiar with the obligations and prerogatives of kings and princesses and with the social codes of the nobility omnipresent in the narrative.   In that context the protagonist, a princess, could forcefully claim her part of the kingdom by reminding her father that not only male children were the depositaries of the king's honor, but that she, equally an inheritor of his blood, could also jeopardize his honor.   In spite of being a woman, she thus had the right to demand the means necessary to maintain that honor.

The threat of prostituting herself used by Doña Urraca as a way of forcing her father to change his will, obviously an exaggerated recourse in the case of a princess, in more current contexts has been interpreted literally.   Prostitution, although an extreme measure, constitutes, in fact, one of the few possibilities for a woman without any means whose horizon is limited to prostitution or to the undertaking of lowly tasks:[16]

E eu vou-me por 'qui fora	And I'm going out from here
como triste desgraçada,	as a sad wretched woman,
nem de preto, nem de branco	neither by black, nor by white
de ninguem serei guardada,	nor by anyone will I be protected,
com a minha roca a cinta,	with my distaff girded on,
mulher não tem outra arma.	a woman has no other weapon.

As reality changed and the codes that ruled the causality of the tale became obsolete, the narrative had to adjust the causality of the events to the new reality in order to retain its semantic coherence.   The drama of a young woman condemned by her father to a life of poverty and dishonor demanded an explanation more in accord with the world view of the *romance* transmitters, an explanation they found in another narrative that deals with the conflict between a father and a daughter, the *romance* of *Silvana*, which tells of such a conflict arising out of her rejection of his incestuous advances.

In the modern Portuguese insular tradition *Las quejas de doña Urraca* begins with *Silvana* or with a combination of *Silvana* and *Delgadina*, another *romance* with a father-daughter incest theme:[17]

Passeava Dona Silvana
por sua corredor acima
se ela canta, melhor bailha,
melhor romances fazia.
5 Seu pai andava-a mirand'
todas as horas do dia.
—Bem podias, Silvana,
seres minha pel' um dia.
—Serei um, e serei duas,
10 do papai sou toda a vida;
mas as penas do inferno,
papai, quem as passaria?
—Sou eu, Dona Silvana,
que as passo toda a vida.
15 —Vá, meu pai, para o seu quarto,
p'a á sua fresca camilha,
que eu vou-me para o meu quarto,
vestir minha alva camisa.—
Foi Silvana para o seu quarto,
20 mais triste que a noite o dia;
chamava por sua mãe,
há sete anos falecida.
—O que queres, minha filha
o que queres, filha minha?

25 Empresta-me os teus vestidos,
teus fatos de cada dia,
que eu quero ir ver teu pai,
o ladrão o que te queria.
Como podes conhecer honra
30 a quem três filhos [pariu]?
Um foi Dom Pedro de Castro,
outro João de Castilhas,
outra foi Dona Silvana,
filha que nunca teria.
35 —Oh que vozes são estas
que eu oiço tão desmudadas?
—E a nossa filha Silvana,
chora que 'ta desgraçada.

—A João deixo-lhe as casas,
40 a Pedro terras lavradas.
—A nossa filha Silvana,
essa não lhe deixas nada?
—Lá lhe deixo aquela boia
e aquela boia dourada.
45 Pel' uma banda corre ouro,
por outra a prata lavrada.
—Quando ela nasceu no mundo,
já a boia i-era tomada

Dona Silvana was walking
along her corridor,
if she can sing, she can dance better,
[and] make better *romances*.
Her father kept watching her
all the hours of the day.
"You could, Silvana,
be mine for a day."
"It would be one, and it'd be two,
my whole life belongs to my father;
but hell's torments,
father, who would endure them?"
"I am the one, Dona Silvana,
who has endured them all my life."
"Go, my father, to your room,
to your fresh bed,
for I'm going to my room,
to put on my white chemise."
Silvana went to her room,
sadder than night or day;
she called for her mother,
dead for seven years.
"What do you want, my daughter,
what do you want, daughter of
    mine?

Lend me your clothes,
your everyday things,
for I want to go and see your father,
the thief who loves you.
How can you know honor
[you] for whom I bore three children?
One was Don Pedro de Castro,
another João de Castilhas,
another was Dona Silvana,
a daughter [I wish] I never had."
"Oh what cries are these
I hear that are so distraught?"
"It is our daughter Silvana,
she weeps because she is
    dishonored."

"To João I leave the houses,
to Pedro cultivated lands."
"To our daughter Silvana
don't you leave anything?"
"To her I leave that *boia* there,
that *boia* of gold.
Along one side runs gold,
along another wrought silver."
"When she was born into the world,
already the *boia* was taken

entre duques e marqueses,
50 todos de espada dourada.
   —Rei que 'tas para morrer,
   diste tu m'a parte n'alma;
   repartistes os teus bens
   e a mim não me destes nada.
55 —Lá te deixo aquela boia,
   e aquela boia dourada,
   pel' uma banda corre ouro,
   por outra prata lavrada.
   —Quando eu nasci neste mundo,
60 já a boia i–era tomada,
   entre duques e marqueses,
   todos de espada dourada.—
   Vai Silvana por ali fora
   como pobre desgraçada,
65 c'a sua roca à cintura,
   mulher não tem outra arma.

by dukes and marquis,
all with golden swords."
"King who are about to die
you gave up my part of your soul;
you divided up your possessions
and didn't give me anything."
"I leave you that *boia* there,
that *boia* of gold,
along one side runs gold,
along another wrought silver."
"When I was born into this world,
the *boia* was already taken,
by dukes and marquis,
all with golden swords."
Silvana goes away from there
as a poor dishonored woman,
with her distaff at her waist,
a woman has no other weapon.

The tale of a princess' right to her part in the partition of the Spanish kingdom has become, without losing an important number of historical details, a commentary on woman's dependency and subordination to her father, her powerlessness before his whims, and the limited possibilities she has to provide for herself if she loses her father's support.

The theme of incest, adopted by *Las quejas de doña Urraca* in order to clarify the antagonism between the protagonists, is the subject of several *romances* collected from modern oral tradition.[18] Also with a historical reference we have versions of *Las almenas de Toro*, dramatized by Lope de Vega in his comedy of the same name. In the latter *romance* the king's fury because the woman he admires and wants to make either his wife or his mistress, depending on her social rank, turns out to be his sister and he is therefore banned from having her, drives him to have her killed by his men.[19] Among folkloric *romances* we have the already mentioned *Silvana* and *Delgadina*, and of Biblical inspiration, *Tamar*, a *romance* that has been collected in practically every region of Spain as well as among Moroccan Sephardim. The more than two hundred versions of *Tamar* collected from modern oral tradition offer us a wide range of positions adopted by its transmitters/creators towards this problem of such vital concern to women. *Tamar* was also registered in the sixteenth century, but that tradition, very close to the Biblical story (2 Sam. 13-14), has little to do with the modern oral tradition.[20]

The *romance* narrates the rape of Tamar (or Altamara) by

her brother when, at her father's request, she goes to her brother's room where he lies in bed claiming to be sick. Her cries of grief and desperation are heard by her father, whose response to her plight varies from one branch of the tradition to another. One of the few versions in which the father shows a concern for his daughter is from Vich (Catalonia), which bases his reaction on the fact that he is first of all a king and must act as a ruler.[21] Incest is considered a social crime that must be punished according to the law. The king, after hearing from his daughter what she claims to have occurred, confronts his son with his sister's accusation. When the son accepts his guilt, he condemns him to be burned as an example for all his subjects:

—Posa 't en confesion,	"Go to confession,
que promptament ets de cremar–ne;	for soon you are to be burned;
que si el rei permetia allo,	for if the king permitted that,
que farien los vassalls!	what would the vassals do!"

More common is the little concern shown by the father towards Tamar's plight after having sent her, his own daughter, to "comfort" his son. In spite of her distress, the father is only interested in his son:

—¿Cómo queda mi hijo,	"How is my son,
cómo queda en la cama?	how is he in bed?"
—El su hijo queda bueno,	"Your son is well,
pero yo vengo enojada.	but I am outraged."
—Como mi hijo quede bueno,	"As long as my son is well,
por tus enojos no hay nada.	your outrage doesn't matter."
(Zamora, Albacete, Lugo, Portugal, Cuba)	

Not only is the king not concerned with the victim, but the solutions he proposes treat lightly the violence committed against his daughter. In Albacete and Zamora, for example, the father suggests that the whole thing be kept quiet by shutting her up in a convent:

—No llores mi Altamarita,	"Don't cry my Altamarita,
no llores mi Altamarada,	don't cry my Altamarada,
que yo te meteré a monja	for I will place you as a nun
convento de Santa Clara.	[in the] convent of Santa Clara."

In Lugo and Santander he proposes that she quietly marry:

—Calla, calla, el Altamar,	"Be quiet, be quiet, Altamar,
de ti no se sepa nada,	let nothing be known about you,
que en lo que tu padre vive	for as long as your father lives
estarás tú bien casada.	you will be well married."

Both solutions require that the whole incident be kept secret. But a marriage to her own brother, suggested in a version from Lugo, demands more than discretion; it requires the Pope's intervention:

—Cala, Tamariña, cala,
que con él serás casada.
—¿Cómo ha de ser eso, mi padre,
siendo yo su propia hermana?
—Hay un Padre Santo en Roma
que a todos purificaba.

"Be quiet, Tamariña, be quiet,
for you will be married to him."
"How can that be, my father,
since I am his own sister?"
"There is a holy father in Rome
who purifies everyone."

Every one of the solutions proposed by the father are acceptable only in social terms; they have little to do with the forced woman's grief, and she rightly rejects them:

—¡Vaya un consuelo de padre

para buena deshonrada!

"What a consolation from a father
for a dishonored girl!"

or:

—No se me da que me oigan,
ni tampoco ser casada,
dáseme por la mi alma,
no la quería manchada.

"I don't care if they hear me,
nor if I am to be married,
what I care for is my soul,
I did not want it stained."

Her father's indifference and his inability to come up with an acceptable solution leave her with the alternative of either appealing to higher forces, God (or the Devil), or to her own. As an example of the first instance, we use a version collected in Havana, Cuba in 1912:

—El su hijo bueno queda
¡si el demonio lo llevara!—
Aun la palabra no es dicha
ya la casa está rodeada;
5   unos entran por la puerta
otros entran por ventanas.
—Devuelve tú, la mi hija,
devuelve tú la palabra.
—Palabra que yo dijese
10   no sería redoblada.
—Ya quedarías a gusto,
ya quedarías vengada.
—Aun no he quedado yo a gusto,
aun no he de quedar vengada
15   mientras no le vea arder
y l'arramble la cernada.

"Your son is well
may the devil take him!"
The word is not even said
the house is already surrounded;
some enter by the door
others enter by windows.
"Take back, my daughter,
take back the word."
"The word that I said
won't be revoked."
"Now you must be pleased,
now you must be avenged."
"I am still not pleased,
I still won't be avenged
until I see him burn
and cover over his ashes."

The second solution appears in versions from Albacete, León, and Guadalajara:

La niña pidió un puñal
y en el pecho se lo clava.

The girl asked for a dagger
and stabs it in her breast.

—Que quiero morir con honra	"I want to die with honor
y no vivir deshonrada.	and not live dishonored."

The Andalusian tradition, which is strongly influencing other regional traditions, suggests another type of solution: the birth of a child, a solution which overrides the affront in favor of the woman's natural instinct as a mother:

De los siete pa los ocho	From seven to eight
los pañalitos bordaba,	she embroidered diapers,
de los ocho pa los nueve	from eight to nine
las camisinas bordaba	she embroidered little shirts
con un letrero que dice:	with a phrase that says:
hijo de hermano y hermana.	son of brother and sister.

The growing protagonism of Tamar in the *romance*, which has left behind the original Biblical tale's concern with Amnon's death at the hands of his avenging brother, Absalom, resulting in the rise of Solomon, Amnon's younger brother, to the throne, has not altered the structure of the *fabula* although it has altered the message conveyed by the narrative.

The young woman's rejection of any solutions to the rape by her brother that subordinate her to social considerations, reveals, in my opinion, a defiant feminine viewpoint which brings to light the active role of women in the creative process of oral traditions. The women who were transmitting a narrative that deals with the problem of incest could not be indifferent to its solution, and their views on the subject have been incorporated into the *romance*'s narrative structure.

It is dangerous and somewhat contradictory to speak of authorship when dealing with collective poetry, but the multisecular, active participation of women in the process of transmission/re-creation of orally transmitted poetry has necessarily had a determining influence on it. The complete picture of how a prevalently feminine transmission of *romances* has, in fact, shaped the composition of the genre as well as the development of individual *romance* narrative structures requires not only a consideration of the total inventory of the themes that are still present in modern oral tradition, but a comparative analysis of all the individual versions of each *romance* theme as well, a very complex task that would require the effort of many researchers interested in the *romancero*.

The hundreds of hours of recordings of *romances* collected from oral tradition in the last ten years have produced, as I have noted, thousands of *romance* texts which add to the already considerable materials from the unedited collections of the Menéndez Pidal archive and other private collections. Paradoxically, it is the abundance of materials that makes difficult any attempt to undertake a comprehensive study of modern oral tradition.   The results, however, should be of interest, in my opinion, not only to *romancero* specialists, since they could also serve as an example of the behavior of oral traditions in general.

The *romances* of *Las quejas de doña Urraca* and *Tamar* are but two examples of *romances* whose functions and messages have changed quite radically in the course of their traditional lives. They serve to underline the fact that themes that have been able to adapt themselves in order to convey commentaries on subjects of importance to women have been able to survive while others are disappearing, their social function having expired.

New approaches in *romancero* studies have brought forth the creative aspect of modern oral tradition.   Although there has been a reduction in the number of *romances* with a historical referent that have been retained by the tradition, there has also been important creativity on the part of *romance* transmitters as they have adapted forms and themes inherited from the past to their own needs of communication.[22]

The functions and structures of the traditional *romancero* have changed in the course of several centuries of traditional life. The projection of heroes who exemplified political behavior has been adapted to present more personal or individual modes of behavior.   The creativeness of many generations of "common" people has not only kept alive an archaic literary form, but it also continues to produce poetic narratives of great beauty.

El Colegio de México

Notes

[1]Eric A. Havelock (1963) explains Plato's seemingly exaggerated rejection of Greek traditional poetry and his attack on the poets in terms of his overall plan for the reform of the educational system within the ideal state proposed in *The Republic*. It was because of its effectiveness in transmitting values that Plato wanted to banish the oral performance of poetry which, in his mind, was laden with dangerous ideals.

[2]The texts collected during the Seminario Menéndez Pidal field trips are

at this time being transcribed and edited for publication; the task, however, is monumental and will require some time to complete.   As for *romances* contained in articles and books, Armistead's extensive bibliography (1979a) and its update to 1987, now in press, together with the *Bibliography of the Hispanic Ballad in Oral Tradition* (1980) include over 2,000 entries.

[3]Havelock (1963:166-67) insists on the fact that traditional Greek poetry was remembered in varying degrees by the whole population and not only by its performers since this is the only guarantee for the stability of an oral tradition.   *Romances* are short narratives and therefore easily remembered by many.

[4]This division into four levels of semantic organization corresponds to Cesare Segre's (1974).   Segre's division, however, is considered by him to be only a means of analyzing texts while we believe that the relationship between the different levels is a generative one.

[5]René Thon (1973:85-106) compares signs with biological forms in which the descendant, the signifier, can become the parent, the signified, within the lapse of a generation.

[6]The specialized bibliography on this topic is very abundant, but the collection of articles on the understanding of stories edited by Teun A. van Dijk (1980a), which represents different approaches to this subject, can be of special interest to oral literature specialists.

[7]In spite of the important progress that has been made in understanding thought processes, current scientific theories cannot fully explain how the semantic system of a speaker-hearer is used or how it is learned.   Cf. Fodor, Bever, and Garret (1974:141-220).

[8]Diego Catalán and Suzanne Petersen undertook a pioneering computer-aided analysis of the large corpus of *La condesita*, which revealed, among other things, that important variation occurred even in verses that seemed more stable within the tradition.   Cf. Petersen (1976a) and Catalán (1976:55-77).

[9]For a discussion of the narrative units of the *romancero* taking into consideration the different levels of semantic organization of oral texts, see Beatriz Mariscal de Rhett (in press).

[10]The corpus of published and unpublished texts of this *romance* as well as a study with a semiotic approach has been published by Beatriz Mariscal de Rhett (1984-1985).

[11]Interdisciplinary approaches to cognitive processes are becoming more and more common, as is the case with Teun van Dijk's work (1980a).   Earlier studies like Maurice Halbwach's (1925, re-ed. 1975) dealt with such issues as the relationship between memory and social class and memory and religious groups.

[12]In his discussion of semantic macrostructures, Teun van Dijk proposes that, since the general and conventional information that speakers use to create the frames needed to understand discourse is historical and therefore culturally variable, the coherence of a text can only be attained within a given context (1980b).

[13]Gabriel García Márquez recounts how *One Hundred Years of Solitude* took shape when he remembered the way his grandmother would tell him

stories: "I had to tell the story just like my grandmother told me hers" (1982:80). Miguel Angel Asturias dedicates his *Leyendas de Guatemela* (1930): "To my grandmother, who told me stories." Likewise in conversations following his lectures at the University of California at San Diego (January 1985), José Emilio Pacheco talked about his grandmother as his source of tales and legends.

[14]This *romance* was studied by Joanne B. Purcell (1976). The versions of the *romance* collected by the author from oral tradition in the Azores, as well as the two unpublished versions from the Menéndez Pidal archive, are included in this dissertation.

[15]Apart from a version from Santa Cruz de los Cuérragos, Zamora, collected by Tomás Navarro Tomás, and a fragment collected in Seville by Manuel Manrique de Lara, both in the Archivo Menéndez Pidal, all the known versions from modern oral tradition are Portuguese from Madeira, the Azores, and the Algarve.

[16]Doña Urraca's threat is used by several seventeenth–century authors like Cervantes in the second part of the *Quijote* (2:ch.5), Quevedo in his *Romance XCIV* of the *Musa IV*, and Ruiz de Alarcón in *El semejante a sí mismo* (III.vi).

[17]The following version is from Sitio de Pontes, Porto Santo in the Madeira Archipelago. It was sung by Juliana d'Oliveira, 41 years of age, and collected by Joanne B. Purcell (1976).

[18]The incestuous marriage between Urraca and Alfonso, which is not mentioned in the Castilian chronicles, is ratified by more than one testimony: a twelfth–century chronicle by Ibn al–Sayrafi and by the Franciscan Juan Gil de Zamora's "De praeconis civitas Numantinae" of 1282. Cf. Lévi-Provençal and Menéndez Pidal (1948:157–66).

[19]Both in the *romance* and in Lope's play, the incestuous relationship between Doña Urraca and her brother Alfonso is transferred to Doña Elvira and her brother Sancho.

[20]Armistead and Silverman demonstrate (1974:245–59; 1982:96–101) that the *romance* published in the sixteenth century is not the origin of the *romances* of modern oral tradition. They propose that the various published *romances* from that period simply attest to the popularity of the theme in the sixteenth–century *romancero* tradition.

[21]Marguerite M. Morton studies this conflict between the roles that Tamar's father must play (1979). She proposes that the king in fact has three conflicting roles: the role of king, the role of father, and that of a mother who has to look after a sick son.

[22]Paul Bénichou (1968a) challenged Ramón Menéndez Pidal's theory of an "aedic" or creative period in the *romancero* tradition, the fifteenth and sixteenth centuries, followed by a "rhapsodic" period or age of decadence in which there has been little creativity, roughly since the beginning of the seventeenth century. Menéndez Pidal's theory, however, was directly related to his interest in *romances* with Spanish historical themes at the time he wrote his important series of essays, "Poesía popular y romancero" (1914–16; 1973), in which he set forth that theory.

References

Aarne and Thompson 1973
   Antti Aarne and Stith Thompson. *The Types of the Folktale: A Classification and Bibliography.* FFC 184. 2nd rev. Helsinki: Academia Scientiarum Fennica.

Abrahams and Foss 1968
   Roger D. Abrahams and George Foss. *Anglo-American Folksong Style.* Englewood Cliffs, N.J.: Prentice-Hall.

Aitken 1945
   Robert Aitken. "Routes of Transhumance of the Spanish Meseta." *Geographical Journal,* 106: 59–69.

Almeida Garrett 1963
   João Baptista de Almeida Garrett. *Romanceiro.* Ed. by Fernando de Castro Pires de Lima. 3 vols. Lisbon: Fundação Nacional para a Alegria no Trabalho.

Alves 1934
   Francisco Manuel Alves. "Cancioneiro Popular Bragançano." In *Memórias Arqueológico-Históricas do Distrito de Bragança: Arqueologia, Etnografia e Arte.* Vol. 10. Porto: Tip. da Empresa Guedes. Pp. 347–585.

Anderson and Higgs 1976
   Grace M. Anderson and David Higgs. *A Future to Inherit: The*

Portuguese Communities of Canada. Toronto: McClelland and Stewart.

Armistead 1978

Samuel G. Armistead. *El romancero judeo-español en el Archivo Menéndez Pidal: Catálogo-índice de romances y canciones.* 3 vols. Madrid: Cátedra-Seminario Menéndez Pidal.

Armistead 1979a

————. "A Critical Bibliography of the Hispanic Ballad in Oral Tradition (1971–1979)." In *El romancero hoy: Historia, comparatismo, bibliografía crítica.* Pp. 199–310.

Armistead 1979b

————. "Judeo-Spanish and Pan-European Balladry." *Jahrbuch für Volksliedforschung,* 24: 127–38.

Armistead 1979c

————. "Recent Field Work on the Hispanic Ballad in Oral Tradition." In *El romancero hoy: Nuevas fronteras.* Pp. 53–60.

Armistead 1979d

————. "Spanish *Romances* in Tunisia in 1746." *Neophilologus,* 63: 247–49.

Armistead 1979–81

————. "Greek Elements in Judeo-Spanish Traditional Poetry." *Laografía* (Athens), 32: 134–57.

Armistead 1980

————. "Recent Developments in Judeo-Spanish Ballad Research." In *Studies in Jewish Folklore.* Ed. by Frank Talmage. Cambridge, Mass.: Association for Jewish Studies. Pp. 21–32.

Armistead 1982a

————. "Una encuesta romancística: Trás-os-Montes, julio 1980." *Quaderni Portoghesi,* 11–12: 67–85.

Armistead 1982b

———. "New Perspectives in Judeo-Spanish Ballad Research." In *The Sephardi and Oriental Jewish Heritage.* Ed. by Issachar Ben-Ami. Jerusalem: Magnes. Pp. 225–35.

Armistead 1983a

———. "The Ballad of *Celinos* at Uña de Quintana." In *Essays . . . in Honor of Edmund L. King.* Ed. by Sylvia Molloy and Luis Fernández Cifuentes. London: Tamesis. Pp. 13–21.

Armistead 1983b

———. "Estudios sobre el romancero en los Estados Unidos." *Arbor,* 116. 451–54: 37–53.

Armistead 1985

———. "Hispanic Ballad Studies: Recent Trends in Criticism." In *Narrative Folksong. New Directions: Essays in Appreciation of W. Edson Richmond.* Ed. by Carol L. Edwards and Kathleen E. B. Manley. Boulder, Colo.: Westview Press. Pp. 106–30.

Armistead 1989

———. "Romancero e historia: *La pérdida de don Sebastián.*" In *Actas del Congreso Romancero—Cancionero UCLA (1984).* Ed. by E. Rodríguez Cepeda, with S. G. Armistead. Vol. 2. Madrid: Porrúa.

Armistead and Costa Fontes 1984

——— and Manuel da Costa Fontes. "In Memoriam Joanne Burlingame Purcell." *La Corónica,* 13: 151–54.

Armistead, Hassán, and Silverman 1974

———, Iacob M. Hassán, and Joseph H. Silverman. "Four Moroccan Judeo-Spanish Folksong *Incipits* (1824–1825)." *Hispanic Review,* 42: 83–87.

Armistead, Hassán, and Silverman 1978

———. "Un nuevo testimonio del romancero sefardí en el siglo XVIII." *Estudios Sefardíes,* 1: 197–212.

Armistead and Katz 1978
——— and Israel J. Katz. "The New Edition of *Danmarks gamle Folkeviser.*" *Yearbook of the International Folk Music Council*, 9: 89–95.

Armistead, Librowicz, and Silverman 1986
———, Oro A. Librowicz, and Joseph H. Silverman. "El rey don García en el romancero: Un nuevo testimonio." *La Corónica*, 14. 2: 293–95.

Armistead and Silverman 1965
——— and Joseph H. Silverman. "Christian Elements and De-Christianization in the Sephardic *Romancero.*" In *Collected Studies in Honour of Américo Castro's Eightieth Year*. Ed. by Marcel P. Hornik. Oxford, Eng.: Lincombe Lodge Research Library. Pp. 21–38.

Armistead and Silverman 1971a
———. *The Judeo-Spanish Ballad Chapbooks of Yacob Abraham Yoná*. Folk Literature of the Sephardic Jews, 1. Berkeley: University of California Press.

Armistead and Silverman 1971b
———. *Judeo-Spanish Ballads from Bosnia*. Philadelphia: University of Pennsylvania Press.

Armistead and Silverman 1973
———. "El cancionero judeo-español de Marruecos en el siglo XVIII (*Incipits* de los Ben Çûr)." *Nueva Revista de Filología Hispánica*, 22: 280–90.

Armistead and Silverman 1974
———. "Una contraparte antigua de *Tamar y Amnón.*" Annali [Istituto Universitario Orientale, Naples], 16: 245–59. Rpt. in *En torno al romancero sefardí: Hispanismo y balcanismo de la tradición judeo-español*. Pp. 96–101.

Armistead and Silverman 1977
———. With the collaboration of Oro Anahory Librowicz. *Romances*

judeo-españoles de Tánger (recogidos por Zarita Nahón). Madrid: Cátedra-Seminario Menéndez Pidal.

Armistead and Silverman 1979

——. *Tres calas en el romancero sefardí (Rodas, Jerusalén, Estados Unidos)*. Madrid: Castalia.

Armistead and Silverman 1980a

——. "El romancero entre los sefardíes de Holanda." In *Etudes . . . offerts à Jules Horrent*. Ed. by Jean Marie d'Heur and Nicoletta Cherubini. Liège: Gedit. Pp. 535–41.

Armistead and Silverman 1980b

——. "Three Hispano-Jewish *Romances* from Amsterdam." In *Medieval, Renaissance and Folklore Studies in Honor of John Esten Keller*. Ed. by Joseph R. Jones. Newark, Del.: Juan de la Cuesta. Pp. 243–54.

Armistead and Silverman 1981a

——. "El antiguo romancero sefardí: Citas de romances en himnarios hebreos (Siglos XVI-XIX)." *Nueva Revista de Filología Hispánica*, 30: 453–512.

Armistead and Silverman 1981b

——. *Judeo-Spanish Ballads from New York (collected by Maír José Benardete)*. Berkeley: University of California Press.

Armistead and Silverman 1981c

——. With the collaboration of Iacob M. Hassán. *Seis romancerillos de cordel sefardíes*. Madrid: Castalia.

Armistead and Silverman 1982

——. *En torno al romancero sefardí: Hispanismo y balcanismo de la tradición judeo-española*. Madrid: Seminario Menéndez Pidal.

Armistead and Silverman 1983

——. "The Traditional Balladry of the Sephardic Jews: A Collaborative Research Project." *La Rassegna Mensile di Israel*, 49. 9–12: 641–67.

Armistead and Silverman 1983–84
———. "Sephardic Folkliterature and Eastern Mediterranean Oral Tradition." *Música Judaica*, 6. 1: 38–54.

Armistead and Silverman 1986
———. With musical transcriptions and a study by Israel J. Katz. *Judeo-Spanish Ballads from Oral Tradition: I. Epic Ballads*. Folk Literature of the Sephardic Jews, 2. Berkeley: University of California Press.

Asturias 1930
Miguel Angel Asturias. *Leyendas de Guatemala*. Madrid: Ediciones Oriente.

Attias 1959
Moshe Attias. "Ha-rômansah Tarkînôs wĕ-Lûkreçîah bi-kĕthāb-yād shabĕtha'î." *Shevet va'Am*, 3: 97–101.

Attias 1961
———. *Romancero sefaradí: romanzas y cantes populares en judeo-español*. 2d ed. Jerusalem: Ben-Zewi Institute.

Attias 1973
———. "Çĕrôr rômansôth bĕ-kth'y shel Sarayevo." *Shevet va'Am*, 2(=7): 295–370.

Avenary 1971
Hanoch Avenary. "Cantos españoles antiguos mencionados en la literatura hebrea." *Anuario Musical*, 25: 67–79.

Barbeau 1962
Marius Barbeau. *Le Rossignol y chante*. Ottawa: Musée National du Canada.

Barry 1929
Phillips Barry et al. *British Ballads from Maine*. New Haven: Yale University Press.

Barthes 1966
    Roland Barthes. "Introductions à l'analyse structurale des récits."
    Communications, 8: 1–27.

Bénichou 1968a
    Paul Bénichou. *Creación poética en el romancero tradicional*. Madrid:
    Gredos.

Bénichou 1968b
    ———. *Romancero judeo-español de Marruecos*. Madrid: Castalia.

Bénichou 1975
    ———. "El romance de la muerte del príncipe de Portugal en la
    tradicíon moderna." *Nueva Revista de Filología Hispánica*, 24: 113–
    24.

Bénichou 1983
    ———. "Sobre una colección de romances de Tánger." *Hispanic
    Review*, 51: 175–88.

Benmayor 1978
    Rina Benmayor. "A Greek *Tragoúdi* in the Repertoire of a Judeo-
    Spanish Ballad Singer." *Hispanic Review*, 46: 475–79.

Benmayor 1979
    ———. *Romances judeo-españoles de Oriente: Nueva recolección*.
    Madrid: Cátedra-Seminario Menéndez Pidal.

Benveniste 1986
    Grace Benveniste. "Five Sephardic Ballads Collected in Los Angeles."
    La Corónica, 14. 2: 258–62.

Bibliografía 1980 *(BRO* 1)
    *Bibliografía del romancero oral (Bibliography of the Hispanic Ballad
    in Oral Tradition)*, 1. Compiled by Antonio Sánchez Romeralo,
    Samuel G. Armistead, Suzanne H. Petersen. Madrid: Cátedra-
    Seminario Menéndez Pidal.

Braga 1869
Teófilo Braga. *Cantos Populares do Arquipélago Açoriano*. Porto: Livraria Nacional.

Braga 1906–9
———. *Romanceiro Geral Português*. 2d ed. 3 vols. Lisbon: Manuel Gomes (1, 2), J. A. Rodriques (3).

Braga 1911–13
———. *Cancioneiro Popular Português*. 2d ed. 2 vols. Lisbon: J. A. Rodrigues.

Bransford and MacCarrell 1974
J. D. Bransford and N. S. MacCarrell. "A Sketch of a Cognitive Approach to Comprehension." In *Cognition and the Symbolic Process*. Ed. by W. B. Weimer and D. S. Palermo. New York: Wiley.

Brednich and Suppan 1969
Rolf Wilhelm Brednich and Wolfgang Suppan. *Gottscheer Volkslieder*. I. *Volksballaden*. Mainz: B. Schotts' Söhne.

Bronson 1979
Bertrand Harris Bronson. *The Ballad as Song*. Berkeley: University of California Press.

Cancionero 1914
Cancionero de romances impreso en Amberes sin año. Ed. by Ramón Menéndez Pidal. Madrid: Centro de Estudios Históricos. 2d ed. Madrid: Gráfica Comercial, 1945.

Cancionero 1967
Cancionero de romances (Anvers, 1550). Ed. by Antonio Rodríguez-Moñino. Madrid: Castalia.

Caro 1978
Rodrigo Caro. *Días geniales o lúdicros (1625)*. Ed. by Jean-Pierre Etienvre. 2 vols. Clásicos Castellanos 212–13. Madrid: Espasa-Calpe.

Carré Alvarellos 1959

Lois Carré Alvarellos. *Romanceiro popular galego de tradizón oral.* Porto: Junto de Província do Douro Litoral.

Castro Leal 1914

Antonio Castro Leal. "Dos romances tradicionales." *Cuba Contemporánea* 6. 3: 237–44.

Castro Rey and García Bermejo 1981

Javier Castro Rey and Francisco García Bermejo. "Romance de la loba parda (Cuatro versiones de la provincia de Segovia)." In *Cultura tradicional y folklore: I. Encuentro en Murcia.* Ed. by Manuel Luna Samperio. Murcia: Editora Regional.

Catalán 1959a

Diego Catalán. "A la caza de romances raros en la tradición portuguesa." In *Actas del III Colóquio Internacional de Estudios Luso-Brasileiros (Lisboa, 1957).* Vol. 1. Lisbon: Imprensa de Coimbra. Pp. 445–77. Rpt. in *Por Campos del romancero.* Pp. 228–69.

Catalán 1959b

———. "El 'motivo' y la 'variación' en la transmisión tradicional del romancero." *Bulletin Hispanique,* 61: 149–82.

Catalán 1959c

———. "Un nuevo romance fronterizo." *Ibérida,* 1: 69–79. Rpt. in *Siete siglos de romancero.* Pp. 83–99.

Catalán 1969a

———, ed. *La flor de la marañuela: Romancero general de las Islas Canarias.* 2 vols. Madrid: Seminario Menéndez Pidal-Gredos.

Catalán 1969b

———. *Siete siglos de romancero (Historia y poesía).* Madrid: Gredos.

Catalán 1970

———. *Por campos del romancero: Estudios sobre la tradición oral moderna.* Madrid: Gredos.

278 REFERENCES

Catalán 1970–71
———. "Memoria e invención en el romancero de tradición oral." *Romance Philology*, 24: 1–25, 441–63.

Catalán 1972
———. "El Archivo Menéndez Pidal y la exploración del romancero castellano, catalán y gallego." In *El romancero en la tradición oral moderna*. Pp. 85–94.

Catalán 1975
———. "Análisis electrónico de la creación poética oral: El programa Romancero en el Computer Center de UCSD." In *Homenaje a la memoria de Don Antonio Rodríguez-Moñino (1910–1970)*. Madrid: Castalia. Pp. 157–94.

Catalán 1976
———. "Análisis electrónico del mecanismo reproductivo en un sistema abierto: El modelo *romancero*." *Revista de la Universidad Complutense*, 25. 102: 55–57.

Catalán 1978
———. "Los modos de producción y 'reproducción' del texto literario y la noción de apertura." In *Homenaje a Julio Caro Baroja*. Ed. by Antonio Carreira et al. Madrid: Centro de Investigaciones Sociológicas. Pp. 245–70.

Catalán 1979
———. "El romancero de tradición oral en el último cuarto del siglo XX." In *El romancero hoy: Nuevas fronteras*. Pp. 217–56.

Catalán 1986
———. "Conflictiva descodificación de las fábulas romancísticas." In *Culturas populares: Diferencias, divergencias y conflictos*. Madrid: Casa de Velásquez-Universidad Complutense. Pp. 93–113.

Catalán in press
———. "Poética de una poesía colectiva."

Catalán and Armistead 1973
    ——— and Samuel G. Armistead, eds. With the collaboration of
    Antonio Sánchez Romeralo. *El romancero en la tradición oral
    moderna: 1er coloquio internacional.* Madrid: Cátedra-Seminario
    Menéndez Pidal-Universidad de Madrid.

Catalán and Cid 1975–76
    ——— and Jesús Antonio Cid, eds. *Gerineldo: El paje y la infanta.*
    3 vols. Romancero Tradicional de las Lenguas Hispánicas, 6–8.
    Madrid: Seminario Menéndez Pidal-Gredos.

Catalán and Galmés 1954
    ——— and Alvaro Galmés. "La vida de un romance en el espacio y el
    tiempo." In *Cómo vive un romance: Dos ensayos sobre
    tradicionalidad.* Madrid: Consejo Superior de Investigaciones
    Científicas. Pp. 143–301.

CGR 2, 3 1982–83
    See *El romancero pan-hispánico: Catálogo general descriptivo.*

CGR 1. A 1984
    See *Teoría general y metodología del romancero pan-hispánico.*

CGR 1. B 1988
    See *General Theory and Methodology of the Pan-Hispanic Ballad.*

Checa Beltrán 1981
    José Checa Beltrán. "A propósito de una nueva recolección de
    romances en la provincia de Jaén." Diss. Universidad Complutense
    de Madrid, Facultad de Filología.

Cid 1979
    Jesús Antonio Cid. "Recolección moderna y teoría de la trasmisión
    oral: *El traidor Marquillos*, cuatro siglos de vida latente." In *El
    romancero hoy: Nuevas fronteras.* Pp. 281–359.

Combs 1967
    Josiah H. Combs. *Folk-Songs of the Southern United States.* Trans. by
    D. K. Wilgus. Austin: University of Texas Press.

Corominas and Pascual 1980–83
    Joan Corominas and José A. Pascual. *Diccionario crítico etimológico castellano e hispánico.* 5 vols. Madrid: Gredos.

Correas 1967
    Gonzalo Correas. *Vocabulario de refranes y frases proverbiales (1627).* Ed. by Louis Combet. Bordeaux: Institut d'Etudes Ibériques et Ibero-Américaines de l'Université de Bordeaux.

Cortés Vázquez 1976
    Luis Cortés Vázquez. *Leyendas, cuentos y romances de Sanabria: Textos leoneses y gallegos.* Salamanca: Gráficas Cervantes.

Cossío and Solano 1933–34
    José María de Cossío and Tomás Maza Solano. *Romancero popular de La Montaña: Colección de romances tradicionales.* 2 vols. Santander: Sociedad Menéndez y Pelayo.

Costa Fontes 1976
    Manuel da Costa Fontes. "*Dona Maria* and *Batalha de Lepanto*: Two Rare Luso-American Ballads." In *Portuguese and Brazilian Oral Traditions in Verse Form.* Pp. 147–57.

Costa Fontes 1978–79
    ———. "*Lizarda:* A Rare Vicentine Ballad in California." *Romance Philology*, 32: 308–14.

Costa Fontes 1979a
    ———. "The *Batalha de Lepanto* in the Portuguese Oral Tradition." *Hispanic Review*, 47: 487–503.

Costa Fontes 1979b (*Can*)
    ———. *Romanceiro Português do Canadá.* Preface by Samuel G. Armistead and Joseph H. Silverman. Acta Universitatis Conimbrigensis. Coimbra: Universidade.

Costa Fontes 1980 (*NI*)
    ———. *Romanceiro Português dos Estados Unidos: 1. Nova Inglaterra.* Preface by Samuel G. Armistead and Joseph H.

Silverman. Acta Universitatis Conimbrigensis. Coimbra: Universidade. Parallel ed. in Fuentes para el Estudio del Romancero: Serie Luso-Brasileira, 1. Madrid: Cátedra-Seminario Menéndez Pidal.

Costa Fontes 1982a
———. "A Sephardic Vestige of the Ballad *Floresvento.*" *La Corónica,* 10: 196–201.

Costa Fontes 1982b
———. "Três Romances Raros: *Quem Dever a Honra Alheia, A Condessa Traidora e A Filha do Ermitão.*" *Quaderni Portoghesi,* 11–12: 87–103.

Costa Fontes 1983a (*SJ*)
———. *Romanceiro da Ilha de S. Jorge.* Preface by Samuel G. Armistead and Joseph H. Silverman. Musical transcriptions by Halim El-Dabh. Acta Universitatis Conimbrigensis. Coimbra: Universidade. Parallel ed. in Fuentes para el Estudio del Romancero: Serie Luso-Brasileira, 3. Madrid: Cátedra-Seminario Menéndez Pidal.

Costa Fontes 1983b (*Cal*)
———. *Romanceiro Português dos Estados Unidos*: 2. *Califórnia.* Preface by Samuel G. Armistead and Joseph H. Silverman. Acta Universitatis Conimbrigensis. Coimbra: Universidade. Parallel ed. in Fuentes para el Estudio del Romancero: Serie Luso-Brasileira, 2. Madrid: Cátedra-Seminario Menéndez Pidal.

Costa Fontes 1983–84a
———. "*Barca Bela* in the Portuguese Oral Tradition." *Romance Philology,* 37: 282–92.

Costa Fontes 1983–84b
———. "*Voces nuevas:* A New Spanish Ballad Collection." *Journal of Hispanic Philology,* 8: 49–66.

Costa Fontes 1984a
———. "Um Novo Romanceiro Transmontano: Introdução, Índice Temático e Antologia." *Arquivos do Centro Cultural Português,* 20: 331–90.

Costa Fontes 1984b
———. "The Portuguese Immigrant *Romanceiro* in America." *La Corónica*, 12: 219–27.

Costa Fontes 1985
———. "The Ballad of *Floresvento* and its Epic Antecedents." *Kentucky Romance Quarterly*, 32: 309–19.

Costa Fontes 1987 (*TM*)
———. *Romanceiro da Província de Trás-os-Montes (Distrito de Bragança)*. With the collaboration of Maria-João Câmara Fontes. Preface by Samuel G. Armistead and Joseph H. Silverman. Musical transcriptions by Israel J. Katz. Acta Universitatis Conimbrigensis. 2 vols. Coimbra: Universidade.

Covarrubias 1611
Sebastián de Covarrubias. *Tesoro de la lengua castellana o española*. Madrid: Luis Sánchez.

Crews 1979
Cynthia M. Crews. With an editorial note by Iacob M. Hassán. "Textos judeo-españoles de Salónica y Sarajevo con comentarios lingüísticos y glosario." *Estudios Sefardíes*, 2: 91–258.

Dantín Cereceda 1942
Juan Dantín Cereceda. "La cañada ganadera de la Vizana o real cañada coruñesa en el reino de León." *Publicaciones de la Real Sociedad Geográfica*. Series B, 114: 1–15 (with a detailed map).

Débax 1982
Michelle Débax. *Romancero*. Madrid: Alhambra.

Devoto 1955
Daniel Devoto. "Sobre el estudio folklórico del romancero español: Proposiciones para un método de estudio de la trasmisión tradicional." *Bulletin Hispanique*, 57: 233–91.

Devoto 1969
———. "Un no aprehendido canto: Sobre el estudio del romancero

tradicional y el llamado 'método geográfico.'" *Abaco: Estudios sobre literatura española*, 1: 11–44.

d'Harcourt 1956
Marguerite and Raoul d'Harcourt. *Chansons folkloriques françaises au Canada*. Québec: Laval University Press.

Dias 1981
Jorge Dias. *Rio de Onor: Comunitarismo Agro-Pastoril*. 2d ed. Lisbon: Presença.

Dias Marques 1984–85
José Joaquim Dias Marques. "Romances dos Concelhos de Bragança e de Vinhais." *Brigantia* (Bragança), 4: 527–50, 5: 43–62.

Díaz 1982
Joaquín Díaz. *Romances, canciones y cuentos de Castilla y León*. Valladolid: Ediciones Castilla.

Díaz, Delfín Val, and Díaz Viana 1978
———, José Delfín Val, and Luis Díaz Viana. *Catálogo folklórico de la provincia de Valladolid: Romances tradicionales*. 2 vols. Valladolid: Institución Cultural Simancas.

Díaz del Castillo 1928
Bernal Díaz del Castillo. *Historia verdadera de la conquista de la Nueva España*. 2 vols. Madrid: Espasa-Calpe.

Díaz Roig 1979
Mercedes Díaz Roig. "Sobre una estructura narrativa minoritaria y sus consecuencias diacrónicas: El caso del romance *Las señas del esposo*." In *El romancero hoy: Poética*. Pp. 121–31.

Díaz Roig 1983
———. "Algunas observaciones sobre el romancero tradicional de México." In *Sabiduría popular* (Zamora, Mich.). Pp. 44–47.

Díaz Roig 1986
———. *Estudios y notas sobre el romancero*. México: El Colegio de México.

Díaz Roig in press
———. "Los romances con dos núcleos de interés." In *Tercer Coloquio Internacional sobre el Romancero*.

Díaz Roig and González 1986
——— and Aurelio González. *El romancero tradicional de México*. Mexico: Universidad Nacional Autónoma de México.

Díaz Viana 1982
Luis Díaz Viana. "Tres versiones sorianas del romance tradicional de *La loba parda*." *Revista de Folklore*, 3. 18: 185–88.

Díaz Viana 1983
———. *Romancero tradicional soriano: Folklore de la provincia de Soria*. Vol 1. Soria: Diputación Provincial de Soria.

Diccionario 1969
Diccionario de autoridades (1726). Fac. ed. Madrid: Gredos.

van Dijk 1980a
Teun A. van Dijk, ed. *Story Comprehension*. In *Poetics*, 9. 1–3: 1–332.

van Dijk 1980b
———. *The Structures and Functions of Discourse: An Interdisciplinary Introduction to Text-Linguistics and Discourse Studies*. Span. trans. *Estructura y funciones del discurso*. Mexico: Siglo XXI.

Di Stefano 1967
Giuseppe Di Stefano. *Sincronia e diacronia nel Romanzero*. Istituto di Letteratura Spagnola e Ispano-Americana, 15. Pisa: Università di Pisa.

Durán 1849–51
Agustín Durán. *Romancero general o Colección de romances*

castellanos anteriores al siglo XVIII. 2 vols. Biblioteca de Autores Españoles 10, 16. Madrid: M. Rivadeneyra. Rpt. 1945.

Espinosa 1953
Aurelio M. Espinosa. *Romancero de Nuevo México.* Madrid: Consejo Superior de Investigaciones Científicas.

Fagundes 1976
Francisco Cota Fagundes. "As Danças Carnavalescas na Terceira e na Califórnia." In *Portuguese and Brazilian Oral Traditions in Verse Form.* Pp. 117–27.

Farinho das Dores Galhoz 1987
Maria Aliete Farinho das Dores Galhoz. *Romanceiro Popular Português.* Lisbon: Centro Nacional de Investigação Científica.

Ferré, Anastácio, Dias Marques, and Martins 1982
P. Ferré, V. Anastácio, J. J. Dias Marques, and A. M. Martins. *Subsídios para o Folclore da Região Autónoma da Madeira: Romances Tradicionais.* Funchal: Câmara Municipal.

Ferreira [1975]
Aurélio Buarque de Holanda Ferreira. *Novo Dicionário da Lingua Portuguesa.* Rio de Janeiro: Editora Nova Fronteira.

Fiore 1969
Silvestro Fiore. "Les Similitudes littéraires médiévales au carrefour des religions et un texte inédit de l'Espagne séphardique." *Revue Belge de Philologie et d'Histoire,* 47: 885–905.

Flor 1969
La flor de la marañuela: Romancero general de las Islas Canarias. Ed. by Diego Catalán. 2 vols. Madrid: Seminario Menéndez Pidal-Gredos.

Fodor, Bever, and Garret 1974
J. A. Fodor. T. G. Bever, and M. F. Garret. *The Psychology of Language: An Introduction to Psycholinguistics and Generative Grammar.* New York: McGraw-Hill.

Foster 1968
    John Wilson Foster. "The Plight of Current Folklore Theory."
    Southern Folklore Quarterly, 32. 3: 237–48.

Fribourg 1910
    André Fribourg. "La Trashumance en Espagne." *Annales de
    Géographie*, 19. 105: 231–44.

Fuero Juzgo 1815
    Fuero Juzgo en latín y castellano. Madrid: Ibarra.

Gagnon 1925
    Ernest Gagnon. *Chansons populaires du Canada*. 7th ed. Montreal:
    Beauchemin.

García Márquez 1982
    Gabriel García Márquez. *El olor de la guayaba: Conversaciones con
    Plinio Apuleyo Mendoza*. Bogotá: La Oveja Negra.

García Matos 1951–60
    Manuel García Matos. *Cancionero popular de la provincia de
    Madrid*. Ed. by Marius Schneider, José Romeu Figueras, and Juan
    Tomás Parés. 3 vols. Barcelona and Madrid: Consejo Superior de
    Investigaciones Científicas.

General Theory 1988 (*CGR* 1. B)
    *General Theory and Methodology of the Pan-Hispanic Ballad:
    General Descriptive Catalogue*. Trans. from the Spanish by
    Suzanne H. Petersen. Madrid: Seminario Menéndez Pidal.

Gerineldo 1975–76 (*RT* 6–8)
    Gerineldo: El paje y la infanta. Ed. by Diego Catalán and Jésus
    Antonio Cid. 3 vols. Romancero Tradicional de las Lenguas
    Hispánicas, 6–8. Madrid: Seminario Menéndez Pidal-Gredos.

Glas 1982
    G. Glas. *Descripción de las Islas Canarias (1764)*. Ed. by Constantino
    Aznar. Tenerife: Instituto de Estudios Canarios.

Goldstein 1964
Kenneth Goldstein. *A Guide for Field Workers in Folklore*. Memoirs of the American Folklore Society, 52. Hatboro, Pa.: Folklore Associates.

Gomarín Guirado 1981
Fernando Gomarín Guirado. "Nuevas versiones del romance de 'La loba parda' en la cañada soriana occidental." In *Cultura tradicional y folklore: 1. Encuentro en Murcia*. Ed. by Manuel Luna Samperio. Murcia: Editora Regional. Pp. 169–73.

González-Llubera 1938
Ignacio González-Llubera. "Three Jewish Ballads in MS *British Museum Add.* 26967." *Medium Ævum*, 7: 15–28.

Goyri de Menéndez Pidal 1906–7
María Goyri de Menéndez Pidal. "Romances que deben buscarse en la tradición oral." *Revista de Archivos, Bibliotecas y Museos*, 10: 374–86, 11: 24–36. Rev. ed. in Eduardo Martínez Torner. *Indicaciones prácticas sobre la notación musical de los romances*. Madrid: Centro de Estudios Históricos, 1929.

Gutiérrez Esteve 1978
Manuel Gutiérrez Esteve. "Sobre el sentido de cuatro romances de incesto." In *Homenaje a Julio Caro Baroja*. Ed. by Antonio Carreira et al. Madrid: Centro de Investigaciones Sociológicas. Pp. 551–72.

Halbwachs 1925
Maurice Halbwachs. *Les Cadres sociaux de la mémoire*. Paris-La Haye: Mouton. 2d ed. Paris: Presses Universitaires de France, 1952. Rpt. New York: Arno Press, 1975.

Hamos 1982
Andrea Warren Hamos. *The Crisis in the Sephardic Ballad Tradition in the United States: An Analytic Documentation*. Diss. University of Pennsylvania, Philadelphia.

Havelock 1963
  Eric A. Havelock. *Preface to Plato.* Cambridge, Mass.: Harvard University Press.

Hemsi 1932–73
  Alberto Hemsi. *Coplas sefardíes (Chansons judéo-espagnoles) [pour chant et piano].* 10 fascicles. Alexandria: Edition Orientale de Musique; Aubervilliers (privately printed).

Henestrosa 1977
  Andrés Henestrosa. *Espuma y flor de corridos mexicanos.* Mexico: Porrúa.

Henríquez Ureña 1913
  Pedro Henríquez Ureña. "Romances en América." *Cuba Contemporánea,* 3–4: 347–66.

Henríquez Ureña and Wolfe 1925
  ——— and Bertram D. Wolfe. "Romances tradicionales en México." In *Homenaje ofrecido a Menéndez Pidal.* Vol. 2. Madrid: Hernando. Pp. 375–90.

Horrent 1957
  Jules Horrent. "Comment vit un romance." *Les Lettres romanes,* 11: 379–94.

Jonsson 1978
  Bengt R. Jonsson et al., eds. *The Types of the Scandinavian Medieval Ballad: A Descriptive Catalogue.* Stockholm-Oslo: Svenskt Visarkiv-Universitetsforlaget.

Jovellanos 1846
  Gaspar Melchor de Jovellanos y Rámirez. *Informe sobre la ley agraria* (1795). In *Obras de Don Gaspar Melchor de Jovellanos.* Nueva ed. Vol. I. Logroño: D. Domingo Ruiz. Pp. 33–306.

Katz 1972–75
  Israel J. Katz. *Judeo-Spanish Traditional Ballads from Jerusalem: An*

Ethnomusicological Study. 2 vols. New York: Institute of Medieval Music.

Katz 1980–84
    ———. "The Musical Legacy of the Judeo-Spanish *Romancero.*" In *Hispania Judaica.* Ed. by Josep M. Sola-Solé, S. G. Armistead, and J. H. Silverman. Vol. 2. Barcelona: Puvill. Pp. 45–58.

Klein 1920
    Julius Klein. *The Mesta: A Study in Spanish Economic History, 1273–1836.* Cambridge, Mass.: Harvard University Press.

Kundert 1962
    Hans Kundert. "Romancerillo sanabrés." *Revista de Dialectología y Tradiciones Populares,* 18: 37–124.

Künzig and Werner 1975
    Johannes Künzig and Waltraut Werner. *Volksballaden und Erzähllieder: Ein Reportorium unserer Tonaufnahmen.* Freiburg im Breisgau: Institut für ostdeutsche Volkskunde.

Lacoste 1981
    Camille Lacoste. "Tradición oral." In *Utiles de encuesta y de análisis antropológicos.* Ed. by Robert Creswell and Maurice Godelier. Madrid: Fundamentos.

Larrea Palacín 1952
    Arcadio de Larrea Palacín. *Romances de Tetuán.* 2 vols. Madrid: Consejo Superior de Investigaciones Científicas.

Larrea Palacín 1958
    ———. "Sobre literatura judeo-española." *Cuadernos Hispanoamericanos,* 97: 57–70.

Leader 1967
    N. A. M. Leader. *Hungarian Classical Ballads and their Folklore.* Cambridge, Eng.: The University Press.

Leite de Vasconcellos 1958–60
   José Leite de Vasconcellos. *Romanceiro Português*. Acta Universitatis
   Conimbrigensis. 2 vols. Coimbra: Universidade.

Leonard 1953
   Irving A. Leonard. *Los libros del conquistador*. México: Fondo de
   Cultura Económica.

Lévi-Provençal and Menéndez Pidal 1948
   E. Lévi-Provençal and Ramón Menéndez Pidal. "Alfonso VI y su
   hermana la infanta Urraca." *Al-Andalus*, 13: 157–66.

Levy 1959–73
   Isaac Levy. *Chants judéo-espagnols*. 4 vols. London: Fédération
   Séphardite Mondiale; Jerusalem: Edition de l'auteur.

Librowicz 1980
   Oro A. Librowicz. *Florilegio de romances sefardíes de la diáspora
   (Una colección malagueña)*. Madrid: Cátedra-Seminario Menéndez
   Pidal.

Lima 1977
   Jackson da Silva Lima. *O folclore em Sergipe: 1. Romanceiro*. Rio de
   Janeiro: Livraria Editora Cátedra and Instituto Nacional do Livro
   (Mistério da Educação e Cultura, Brasilia).

Lopes 1967
   Antônio Lopes. *Presença do romanceiro: Versões maranhenses*. Rio
   de Janeiro: Civilização Brasileira.

López de Vergara and Morales [1955]
   M. Jesús López de Vergara and Mercedes Morales. *Romancerillo
   canario (Catálogo-manual de recolección)*. La Laguna: Universidad.

Lord 1960
   Albert B. Lord. *The Singer of Tales*. Cambridge, Mass.: Harvard
   University Press.

Marco 1977
Joaquín Marco. *Literatura popular en España en los siglos XVIII y XIX: Una aproximación a los pliegos de cordel*. 2 vols. Madrid: Taurus.

Mariscal de Rhett 1984–85
Beatriz Mariscal de Rhett, ed. *La muerte ocultada*. Romancero Tradicional de las Lenguas Hispánicas, 12. Madrid: Seminario Menéndez Pidal-Gredos.

Mariscal de Rhett in press
———. "Hacia una definición de las unidades narrativas en el romancero." In *Tercer Coloquio Internacional sobre el Romancero*.

Martínez Ruiz 1963
Juan Martínez Ruiz. "Poesía sefardí de carácter tradicional (Alcazarquivir)." *Archivum* (Oviedo), 13: 79–215.

Martínez-Yanes 1979
Francisco Martínez-Yanes. "Los desenlaces en el romance de Blancaniña: Tradición y originalidad." In *El romancero hoy: Poética*. Pp. 132–53.

Martins 1928–39
Firmino A. Martins. *Folclore do Concelho de Vinhais*. 2 vols. Coimbra: Universidade; Lisbon: Imprensa Nacional.

Mendoza 1939
Vicente T. Mendoza. *El romance español y el corrido mexicano: Estudio comparativo*. Mexico: Universidad Nacional Autónoma.

Mendoza 1951
———. *Lírica infantil de México*. Mexico: El Colegio de México.

Mendoza 1956
———. *Panorama de la música tradicional de México*. Mexico: Imprenta Universitaria.

Mendoza and Rodríquez de Mendoza 1952
——— and Virginia R. Rodríguez de Mendoza. *Folklore de San Pedro Piedra Gorda (Zacatecas)*. Mexico: Congreso Mexicano de Historia.

Mendoza Díaz-Maroto 1980
Francisco Mendoza Díaz-Maroto. "Para el romancero albacetense: 2. Romances rústicos (Primera parte)." *Al-Basit: Revista de Estudios Albacetenses*, 2d series, 7: 183–214.

Menéndez Pelayo 1945
Marcelino Menéndez Pelayo. *Apéndices y suplemento a la "Primavera y flor de romances" de Wolf y Hofmann*. Antología de poetas líricos castellanos, 9 (Obras completas, 25). Santander: Consejo de Investigaciones Científicas.

Menéndez Pidal 1906
Ramón Menéndez Pidal. "Los romances tradicionales de América." *Cultura Española*, 1: 72–111. Rpt. in *Los romances de América y otros estudios*. Madrid: Espasa-Calpe, 1939. Pp. 13–46.

Menéndez Pidal 1914
———, ed. *Cancionero de romances impreso en Amberes sin año*. Madrid: Centro de Estudios Históricos. 2d ed. Madrid: Gráfica Comercial, 1945.

Menéndez Pidal 1914–16
———. "Poesía popular y romancero." *Revista de Filología Española*, 1: 357–77, 2: 1–20, 105–36, 3: 233–89. Rpt. in *Estudios sobre el romancero*. Obras completas, 11. Madrid: Espasa-Calpe, 1973. Pp. 85–216.

Menéndez Pidal 1920
———. "Sobre geografía folklórica: Ensayo de un método." *Revista de Filología Española*, 7: 229–338. Rpt. in *Cómo vive un romance: Dos ensayos sobre tradicionalidad*. Pp. 1–141; rpt. in *Estudios sobre el romancero*. Pp. 217–323.

Menéndez Pidal 1928
———. *Flor nueva de romances viejos*. Madrid: La Lectura. 2d ed.
Madrid: La Lectura, 1933. (All subsequent eds. based on the 2d.)

Menéndez Pidal [1945]
———. *Cómo vivió y cómo vive el romancero*. Valencia: La
Enciclopedia Hispánica. Rpt. in *Estudios sobre el romancero*. Pp. 403–
62.

Menéndez Pidal 1948
———. "Un viejo romance cantado por Sabbatai Ceví." In *Mediaeval
Studies in Honor of Jeremiah Denis Matthias Ford*. Ed. by Urban T.
Holmes, Jr., and Alex J. Denomy. Cambridge, Mass.: Harvard
University Press. Pp. 183–90.

Menéndez Pidal 1953
———. *Romancero hispánico (Hispano-portugués, americano y
sefardí): Teoría e historia*. 2 vols. Madrid: Espasa-Calpe. 2d ed. 1968.

Menéndez Pidal 1955
———. "El romancero tradicional en las Islas Canarias." *Anuario de
Estudios Atlánticos*, 1: 3–10.

Menéndez Pidal 1973
———. *Estudios sobre el romancero*. Obras completas, 11. Madrid:
Espasa-Calpe.

Menéndez Pidal, Catalán, and Galmés 1954
———, Diego Catalán, and Alvaro Galmés. *Cómo vive un romance:
Dos ensayos sobre tradicionalidad*. Madrid: Consejo Superior de
Investigaciones Científicas.

Merrill-Mirsky 1984
Carol Merrill-Mirsky. *Judeo-Spanish Song from the Island of Rhodes:
A Musical Tradition in Los Angeles*. Diss. University of California,
Los Angeles.

Merrill-Mirsky 1986
———. "Three Judeo-Spanish Ballads from the Island of Rhodes Collected in Los Angeles." *La Corónica*, 14. 2: 263–67.

Michaëlis de Vasconcelos 1934
Carolina Michaëlis de Vasconcelos. *Estudos sobre o Romanceiro Peninsular: Romances Velhos em Portugal.* 2d ed. Coimbra: Universidade.

Morton 1979
Marguerite M. Morton. "*Tamar:* Variation on a Theme." In *El romancero hoy: Poética.* Pp. 305–11.

Mourinho 1984
António Maria Mourinho. *Cancioneiro Tradicional e Danças Populares Mirandesas.* Vol. 1. Bragança: Escola Tipográfica.

Muerte ocultada 1984–85
La muerte ocultada. Ed. by Beatriz Mariscal de Rhett. Romancero Tradicional de las Lenguas Hispánicas, 12. Madrid: Seminario Menéndez Pidal-Gredos.

Noga-Alberti Kleinbort 1984
Eleonora Noga-Alberti Kleinbort. "Tres romances de la tradición oral judeo-española: Algunas versiones recogidas en Buenos Aires." *Incipit*, 4: 145–55.

Nuno Alçada 1982–83
João Nuno Alçada. "Teatralidade e Intertextualidade do Tema da Morte do Príncipe D. Afonso de Portugal nas Literaturas Culta e Popular." *Revista Lusitana, Nova Série*, 3: 69–101.

Olason 1982
Vésteinn Olason. *The Traditional Ballads of Iceland: Historical Studies.* Reykjavík: Stofnun Arna Magnússonar.

Olmeda 1903
Federico Olmeda. *Folk-lore de Castilla o Cancionero popular de Burgos.* Seville: María Auxiliadora.

Oster 1962
    Harry Oster. "Notes on Some Classic French Folk Ballads Recently
    Collected in Louisiana." In *Studies in Comparative Literature*. Ed. by
    Waldo F. McNeir. Baton Rouge: Louisiana State University Press.
    Pp. 239–58.

Palencia 1490
    Alonso de Palencia. *Universal vocabulario en latín y en romance.*
    Seville: Pablo de Colonia.

Panadero Moya 1976
    Miguel Panadero Moya. *La ciudad de Albacete.* Albacete: Caja de
    Ahorros Provincial.

Parry 1971
    Milman Parry. *The Making of Homeric Verse: The Collected Papers
    of Milman Parry*. Ed. by Adam Parry. Oxford: Clarendon Press. Rpt.
    New York: Arno Press, 1980.

Pérez Martínez 1935
    Héctor Pérez Martínez. *Trayectoria del corrido.* 2d ed. Mexico: n. p.

Pérez Pastor 1891–1907
    Cristóbal Pérez Pastor. *Bibliografía madrileña o descripción de obras
    impresas en Madrid (1566–1625).* 3 vols. Madrid: Huérfanos.

Pérez Vidal 1948
    José Pérez Vidal. "Del folklore canario: Romances con estribillo y
    bailes romanescos." *Revista de Dialectología y Tradiciones Populares*,
    4: 197–241. Rpt. in *Poesía tradicional canaria.* Las Palmas: Cabildo
    Insular de Gran Canaria, 1968. Pp. 11–43.

Petersen 1976a
    Suzanne H. Petersen. "El mecanismo de la variación en la poesía de
    trasmisión oral: Estudio de 612 versiones del romance de *La condesita*
    con ayuda de un ordenador." Diss. University of Wisconsin, Madison.

Petersen 1976b
    ———. "Representación cartográfica de datos complejos mediante

ordenador." *Revista de la Universidad Complutense* (Madrid), 25: 205–19.

Petersen 1978
———. "A Computer-Aided Analysis of the Problematic Relationship between Rhyme and Lexical Stability in the Traditional Hispanic *Romancero.*" In *Ballads and Ballad Research.* Ed. by Patricia Conroy. Seattle: University of Washington. Pp. 88–100.

Petersen 1979
———. "Computer-generated Maps of Narrative Affinity." In *El romancero hoy: Poética.* Pp. 167–228.

Petersen 1982
———, ed. *Voces nuevas del romancero castellano-leonés.* 2 vols. AIER 1, 2. Madrid: Gredos.

Petersen 1985
———. "A Computer-Based Research Project on the *Romancero.*" In *Narrative Folksong. New Directions: Essays in Appreciation of W. Edson Richmond.* Ed. by Carol L. Edwards and Kathleen E. B. Manley. Boulder, Colo.: Westview Press. Pp. 195–238.

Pliegos poéticos 1960
Pliegos poéticos en la Universidad de Praga. Prologue by Ramón Menéndez Pidal. 2 vols. Joyas Bibliográficas 7, 8. Madrid: Centro de Estudios de Bibliografía y Bibliofilia.

Poema 1960
Poema de Mio Cid. Ed. by Ramón Menéndez Pidal. 9th ed. Clásicos Castellanos, 24. Madrid: Espasa-Calpe.

Portuguese . . . Traditions 1976
Portuguese and Brazilian Oral Traditions in Verse Form (As Tradições Orais Portuguesas e Brasileiras em Verso). Ed. by Joanne B. Purcell et al. Los Angeles: University of Southern California.

Purcell 1968
    Joanne B. Purcell. "Portuguese Traditional Ballads from California."
    Diss. University of California, Los Angeles.

Purcell 1969
    ———. "Traditional Ballads among the Portuguese in California."
    Western Folklore, 28: 1–19, 77–90.

Purcell 1970
    ———. "A Riqueza do Romanceiro e Outras Tradições Orais nas Ilhas
    dos Açores." *Atlântida*, 14: 223–52.

Purcell 1972
    ———. "Sobre o Romanceiro Português: Continental, Insular e
    Transatlântico. Uma Recolha Recente." In *El romancero en la
    tradición oral moderna*. Pp. 55–64.

Purcell 1976
    ———. "The *Cantar de la muerte del rey don Fernando* in Modern
    Oral Tradition: Its Relationship to Sixteenth-Century *Romances* and
    Medieval Chronicles." Diss. University of California, Los Angeles.

Purcell 1979
    ———. "Ballad Collecting Procedures in the Hispanic World." In *El
    romancero hoy: Nuevas fronteras*. Pp. 61–73.

Purcell, Rodríguez García, and Saramago 1987
    ———, Isabel Rodríguez García, and J. das P. Saramago. *Romanceiro
    Português das Ilhas Atlânticas*, I. Acta Universitatis Conimbrigensis.
    Coimbra: Universidade. Parallel ed. in Fuentes para el Estudio del
    Romancero: Série Luso-Brasileira. Madrid: Seminario Menéndez
    Pidal.

RAE *Diccionario* 1726–37
    Real Academia Española. *Diccionario de la lengua castellana*. 6 vols.
    Madrid: Francisco del Hierro.

Rechnitz 1978
    Florette M. Rechnitz. "Hispano-Romanian Ballad Relationships: A

Comparative Study with an Annotated Translation of A. I. Amzulescu's *Index of Romanian Ballads.*" Diss. University of Pennsylvania, Philadelphia.

Rechnitz 1979
———. "Hispano-Romanian Ballad Correspondences." In *El romancero hoy: Historia, comparatismo, bibliografía crítica.* Pp. 141–49.

Révah 1980–84
Israel S. Révah. "Les Parlers des juifs d'Espagne avant l'expulsion de 1492." In *Hispania Judaica.* Ed. by Josep M. Sola-Solé et al. Vol. 3. Barcelona: Puvill. Pp. 63–82.

Rodríguez Abad 1984
Ernesto Rodríguez Abad. "El Conde Grifos Lombardo: Versiones de Teno Alto y Los Silos." In *Gaceta de Daute.* Vol 1. Santa Cruz de Tenerife. Pp. 93–102.

Rodríguez-Moñino 1973–78
Antonio Rodríguez Moñino. *Manual bibliográfico de cancioneros y romanceros. I. Impresos durante el siglo XVI.* 2 vols. Coord. by Arthur L. -F. Askins. Madrid: Castalia.

Romancerillo 1955
Romancerillo canario (Catálogo-manual de recolección). Ed. by Jesús López de Vergara and Mercedes Morales. La Laguna: Universidad.

Romancero . . . oral moderna 1973
El romancero en la tradición oral moderna: Primer coloquio internacional. Ed. by Diego Catalán and Samuel G. Armistead. With the collaboration of Antonio Sánchez Romeralo. Madrid: Cátedra-Seminario Menéndez Pidal-Rectorado de la Universidad de Madrid.

Romancero hoy: Historia 1979
El romancero hoy: Historia, comparatismo, bibliografía crítica (The Hispanic Ballad Today: History, Comparativism, Critical

Bibliography). Ed by Samuel G. Armistead, Antonio Sánchez Romeralo, and Diego Catalán. Madrid: Cátedra-Seminario Menéndez Pidal.

Romancero hoy: Nuevas 1979
   El romancero hoy: Nuevas Fronteras (The Hispanic Ballad Today: New Frontiers). Ed. by Antonio Sánchez Romeralo, Diego Catalán and Samuel G. Armistead. Madrid: Cátedra-Seminario Menéndez Pidal.

Romancero hoy: Poética 1979
   El romancero hoy: Poética (The Hispanic Ballad Today: Poetics). Ed. by Diego Catalán, Samuel G. Armistead, and Antonio Sánchez Romeralo. Madrid: Cátedra-Seminario Menéndez Pidal.

Romancero pan-hispánico 1982–83 *(CGR 2, 3)*
   El romancero pan-hispánico: Catálogo general descriptivo (The Pan-Hispanic Ballad: General Descriptive Catalogue). Dir. by D. Catalán et al. Vols. 2, 3. Madrid: Seminario Menéndez Pidal-Gredos.

RT 1957–85
   Romancero tradicional de las lenguas hispánicas. Collection of texts and notes of María Goyri and Ramón Menéndez Pidal. 12 vols. to date.
   1. *Romanceros del rey Rodrigo y de Bernardo del Carpio.* Ed. by R. Lapesa et al. Madrid: Gredos, 1957.
   2. *Romanceros de los condes de Castilla y de los infantes de Lara.* Ed. by D. Catalán. Madrid: Gredos, 1963.
   3–5. *Romances de tema odiseico.* Ed. by D. Catalán. 3 vols. Madrid: Gredos, 1969–72.
   6–8. *Gerineldo: El paje y la infanta.* Ed. by Diego Catalán and Jesús Antonio Cid. 3 vols. Madrid: Gredos, 1975–76.
   9. *Romancero rústico.* Ed. by Antonio Sánchez Romeralo. Madrid: Gredos, 1978.
   10–11. *La dama y el pastor: Romance, villancico, glosas.* Ed. by Diego Catalán. 2 vols. Madrid: Gredos, 1977–78.
   12. *La muerte ocultada.* Ed. by Beatriz Mariscal de Rhett. Madrid: Gredos, 1984–85.

RTM 1986
   El romancero tradicional de México. Ed. by Mercedes Díaz Roig and Aurelio González. Mexico: Universidad Nacional Autónoma de México.

Salazar and Valenciano 1979
   Flor Salazar and Ana Valenciano. "El romancero aún vive. Trabajo de Campo de la CSMP: 'Encuesta Norte-77.'" In *El romancero hoy: Nuevas fronteras.* Pp. 361–421.

Saldívar 1934
   Gabriel Saldívar. *Historia de la música en México (Epocas precortesiana y colonial).* Mexico: n. p.

Sánchez Romeralo 1978
   Antonio Sánchez Romeralo, ed. *Romancero rústico.* Romancero Tradicional de las Lenguas Hispánicas, 9. Madrid: Gredos.

Sánchez Romeralo 1979a
   ———. "El romancero oral ayer y hoy: Breve historia de la recolección moderna (1782–1970)." In *El romancero hoy: Nuevas fronteras.* Pp. 15–51.

Sánchez Romeralo 1979b
   ———. "El Valle de Alcudia, encrucijada del romancero." In *El romancero hoy: Nuevas fronteras.* Pp. 267–79.

Scholem 1973
   Gershom Scholem. *Sabbataí Seví: The Mystical Messiah (1626–1676).* Princeton: Princeton University Press.

Seeger 1977
   Charles Seeger. "Versions and Variants of 'Barbara Allen' in the Archive of American Songs to 1940." In *Studies in Musicology 1935–1975.* Berkeley: University of California Press. Pp. 273–320.

Seeger in press
   Judith Seeger. "Notes on Traditional Creativity: Examples of

Innovation in Two Brazilian *Romances*." In *Tercer Coloquio Internacional sobre el Romancero.*

Segre 1974
Cesare Segre. *Le strutture e il tempo: Narrazione, poesia, modelli.* Torino: Einaudi.

Serrano Martínez 1951
Celedonio Serrano Martínez. "Romances tradicionales en Guerrero." *Anuario de la Sociedad Folklórica de México,* 7: 7–72.

Teoría general 1984 (*CGR* 1. A)
Teoría general y metodología del romancero pan-hispánico: Catálogo general descriptivo. Dir. by Diego Catalán. Madrid: Seminario Menéndez Pidal-Gredos.

Tercer coloquio in press
Tercer Coloquio Internacional sobre el Romancero y Otras Formas Poéticas Tradicionales. Madrid: Seminario Menéndez Pidal.

Thon 1973
René Thon. "De l'Icône au symbol: Esquisse d'une théorie du symbolisme." *Cahiers internationaux de symbolisme,* 22–23: 85–106.

Toussaint 1927
Manuel Toussaint. "La Canción de Mambrú: Folklore histórico." *Revista Mexicana de Estudios Históricos,* 1: 101–4.

Trapero 1982
Maximiano Trapero. With the collaboration of Lothar Siemens Hernández. *Romancero de Gran Canaria.* I. *Zona del Sureste: Agüimes, Ingenio, Carrizal y Arinaga.* Las Palmas de Gran Canaria: Mancomunidad de Cabildos.

Trapero 1985
———. With the collaboration of Elena Hernández Casañas and Lothar Siemens Hernández. *Romancero de la Isla de Hierro.* Madrid: Seminario Menéndez Pidal and Cabildo de Hierro.

Trapero 1986a
———. "Los bailes romancescos y el 'baile del tambor' de La Gomera." *Revista de Musicología*, 9.

Trapero 1986b
———. "En busca del romance perdido *Río Verde*." *Revista de Dialectología y Tradiciones Populares*.

Trapero 1987
———. With the collaboration of Elena Hernández Casañas and Lothar Siemens Hernández. *Romancero de la Isla de La Gomera*. Cabildo Insular de La Gomera.

Trapero in press
———. "El romance de *Virgilios* a la luz de nuevas versiones canarias." In *Tercer Coloquio Internacional sobre el Romancero*.

Trapero in press
———. "El romance *Rio Verde:* Cuatro siglos de tradición ignorada." In *Homenaje a A. Zamora Vicente*. Madrid: Castalia.

Vásquez Santana 1931
Higinio Vásquez Santana. *Historia de la canción mexicana: Canciones, cantares y corridos*. Vol. 3. Mexico: Talleres Gráficos de la Nación.

Vicuña Cifuentes 1912
Julio Vicuña Cifuentes. *Romances populares y vulgares recogidos de la tradición oral chilena*. Santiago de Chile: Imprenta Barcelona.

Voces 1982
Voces nuevas del romancero castellano-leonés. Ed. by Suzanne H. Petersen. 2 vols. Archivo Internacional Electrónico del Romancero 1, 2 (AIER). Madrid: Seminario Menéndez Pidal-Gredos.

Webber 1951
Ruth House Webber. *Formulistic Diction in the Spanish Ballad*. University of California Publications in Modern Philology, 34. Berkeley: University of California Press.

Webber 1979
———. "Ballad Openings: Narrative and Formal Function." In *El romancero hoy: Poética.* Pp. 55–64.

Webster's 1949
[Noah Webster]. *Webster's New International Dictionary of the English Language.* 2d ed. Springfield, Mass.: Merriam.

Weich-Shahak 1984
Susana Weich-Shahak. "Mazal Tov's Repertoire of Songs: Genres in Judeo-Spanish Songs" (in Hebrew). *Jerusalem Studies in Jewish Folklore,* 5–6: 27–56.

Whitfield 1939
Irène Thérèse Whitfield. *Louisiana French Folk Songs.* University, La.: Louisiana State University Press.

Wolf and Hofmann 1856
Fernando José Wolf and Conrado Hofmann. *Primavera y flor de romances, o Colección de los más viejos y más populares romances castellanos.* 2 vols. Berlin: Asher. Rpt. in M. Menéndez Pelayo. *Antología de poetas líricos castellanos,* 8 (Obras completas, 24). Santander: Consejo Superior de Investigationes Científicas-Aldus, 1945.

Wylie and Margolin 1981
Jonathan Wylie and David Margolin. *The Ring of Dancers: Images of Faroese Culture.* Philadelphia: University of Pennsylvania Press.

About the Authors

Samuel G. Armistead (University of California, Davis) is the leading American scholar in the field of the Spanish epic and ballad. His many books and articles on the Sephardic ballad in collaboration with Joseph Silverman are models of their kind. He has also published, among other works, a three-volume catalogue of the Judeo-Spanish ballads in the Menéndez Pidal Archives as well as several valuable bibliographies of the *romancero*.

Diego Catalán is director of the Seminario Menéndez Pidal, an institute of the Universidad Complutense of Madrid dedicated to *romancero* studies. In addition he is Professor at both the Universidad Autónoma in Madrid and the University of California, San Diego. His long and distinguished list of publications includes studies of the Spanish epic and ballad together with the chronicles and other medieval texts, as well as studies in linguistics and textual analysis.

Manuel da Costa Fontes is Professor of Spanish and Portuguese at Kent State University. His interest in the Portuguese ballad had its origin in his own roots. He has been an extraordinarily successful collector of Portuguese ballads both on this side of the Atlantic and abroad, resulting to date in five volumes of ballad texts from different localities. He is now working on the Portuguese folk tale.

Mercedes Díaz Roig was a distinguished professor at the Colegio de México, where she has become the expert in the study of the *romance* in Mexico. She recently completed the definitive collection of the traditional Mexican ballad and was at work on a Pan-American *romancero* study at the Seminario Menéndez Pidal before she died. Her many books and articles treat various aspects of the ballad and the popular lyric.

Beatriz Mariscal de Rhett is Professor at the Colegio de México as well as a member of the staff of the Seminario Menéndez Pidal. She has published *La muerte ocultada*, the latest volume in the series of the *Romancero tradicional* put out by the Seminario Menéndez Pidal. It includes a semiotic study of the ballad narrative, a topic in which she is particularly interested.

Suzanne H. Petersen (University of Washington) is at present one of the most innovative scholars working on the *romancero*. She has carried out extensive studies both of the mechanism of variation in ballads and of ballad geography by means of new computer techniques. In addition she has edited several volumes for the Seminario Menéndez Pidal.

Antonio Sánchez Romeralo (University of California, Davis) has been an active collaborator and editor of various volumes published by the Seminario Menéndez Pidal. One of them, *Romancero rústico*, was the product of his own special interest, that of searching for *romances* along shepherds' routes. In addition, he is the author of an important study on the *villancico*, a traditional lyric song type.

ABOUT THE AUTHORS 305

Judith Seeger is a writer, musician, anthropologist, and sometime teacher as well as ballad collector. She undertook a protracted search for traditional ballads in Espíritu Santo, Brazil in an effort to record *romances* sung under natural conditions. Recently she has carried out a similar project in the mountains of León in Spain.

Joseph H. Silverman (d.1989, University of California, Santa Cruz) joined with Samuel Armistead to form an outstanding team. They have collected Sephardic ballads in many parts of the world and published them in volumes of great scholarly value. Professor Silverman had also written several important studies on the Golden Age in Spain.

Maximiano Trapero is Professor at the Colegio Universitario de Las Palmas in the Canary Islands. He has devoted the last several years to systematically collecting Spanish ballads throughout all the islands of the archipelago, where he has recorded some rare *romances*. He has published three important collections of ballads up to the present as well as a number of articles. He has also been carrying out investigations on the popular theater in Castile and León.

Ana Valenciano is a veteran member of the permanent staff of the Seminario Menéndez Pidal whose name appears as collaborator on most of the volumes the Institute has published. One of her chief responsibilities has been to direct the Seminario's field expeditions, an activity which has involved all the organizational work, training the fieldworkers, and taking active part in the expeditions themselves.

Ballad Titles

The titles of ballads are alphabetized according to the first important word.

Spanish Ballads

Ballad titles in Spanish are accompanied by an English title or translation in parentheses and followed by page and note numbers. Occasionally, the Portuguese title is given.

Portuguese Ballads

Portuguese ballad titles are accompanied whenever appropriate by the corresponding Spanish title, under which they are also listed above, and are followed by an English translation in parentheses and by page and note numbers.

Ballad Titles in English

Ballad titles give in English are followed by the Spanish and/or Portuguese titles, under which page and note numbers are listed.

The Abduction of Helen (El rapto de Elena)
The Adulteress (La adúltera)
The Beauty in Church (La bella en misa)
The Blind Man (O Cego)
The Bottomless Well (El pozo airón)
Carnations and Beatings (Claveles y bofetadas)
The Child Murderess (La infanticida)
Condemned by the Pasha (El sentenciado del bajá)
Count Claros and the Emperor (El conde Claros y el emperador)
Count Claros and the Princess (El conde Claros y la infanta)
Count Claros in Monk's Attire (El conde Claros en hábito de fraile)
Count Claros of Montalban (El conde Claros de Montalbán)
Count Dirlos (El conde Dirlos)
The Crossing of the Red Sea (El paso del mar rojo/O Passo do Mar Vermelho)
The Cursed Son's Return (La vuelta del hijo maldecido)
The Daughter's Dream (El sueño de la hija)
David and Goliath (David y Goliat)
David Mourns for Absalom (David llora a Absalón)
Death and the Girl (La moza y el Huerco)
The Death of Alexander (La muerte de Alejandro)
The Death of King Sebastian (La muerte del rey don Sebastián)
The Death of Prince John (La muerte del príncipe don Juan)
The Death of the Duke of Gandía (La muerte del duque de Gandía)
The Diver (El buceador)
Don Bueso and his Sister (Don Bueso y su hermana)
Evil Spell (El mal encanto)
The Exile of the Jews from Portugal (La expulsión de los judíos de Portugal)
The False Pilgrim (El falso peregrino)
Fishing for a Ring (La pesca del anillo)
The Girl who Killed her Sister for love of her Brother-in-Law (La fratricida por amor)
The Husband's Return (Las señas del esposo)
The Jealous Christian (El cristiano celoso)

Juliana and Don George (Jiuliana e D. Jorge/El veneno de Moriana)
The King's Favorite (La favorita del rey)
The Lady and the Shepherd (La dama y el pastor)
Married to an Old Man (Casada con un viejo)
The Miserly Sister (La hermana avarienta)
Moriana's Poison (El veneno de Moriana)
The Newly Married Galley Slave (El galeote recién casado)
Paris' Judgment (El juicio de París)
Philip II's Testament (El testamento de Felipe II)
The Rag Merchants' Bonnet Maker (El bonetero de la trapería)
The Rape of Dinah (El rapto de Dina)
The Renegade Girl (La conversa)
The Revolt of the Beni Ider (La rebelión de los Beni Ider)
The Sacrifice of Isaac (El sacrificio de Isaac)
The Sisters: Queen and Captive (Las hermanas reina y cautiva)
Solomon's Judgment (El juicio de Salomón)
Tarquin and Lucrece (Tarquino y Lucrecia)
Thamar and Amnon (Tamar/Tamar y Amnón)
Virgil (Virgilios)
The Warrior Maiden (La doncella guerrera/A Donzela Guerreira)
The Weeping Knight (Gritando va el caballero)

Ballads from Other Traditions

The Baffled Knight (Child 112) 240
Barbara Allan (Anglo-American, Child 84) 187
Barbara Angoli (Hungarian) 188
Clerk Colville (Child 42) 240
The Evil Mother (Greek) 240, 241
Fair Annie (Child 62) 240
Hind Horn (Child 17) 240
Lady Isabel and the Elf Knight (Child 4) 240
Lady Maisry (Child 65) 240
Lord Randal (Child 12) 240
Lord Thomas and Fair Annet (Child 73) 240
The Maid Freed from the Gallows (Child 95) 240
The Mother's Malison (Child 216) 240
Ho niópantros sklábos (Greek) 141

Index

Abrahams and Foss 179
actantial model 18-21
Aguiló, M. 120
AIER: Archivo Internacional
    Electrónico del Romancero 8,
    24-25:11
Aitken, R. 65, 71:7
alliteration 206, 209
Anastácio, Vanda 23:3, 25:12, 172
Andalusia: Andalusian ballad
    tradition 23:4, 31, 50:8, 75,
    109-110, 130
Anderson and Higgs 152
Armistead, S.G. 29, 57, 60, 112:4,
    5, 139, 140, 141, 157, 163, 165,
    173:3, 174:15, 235, 243, 244:1,
    245:9,12,14,16,17,19,21,22,
    246:26,29,31
Armistead and Silverman (et
    al.) 23:4, 24:8, 25:12, 139, 141,
    142, 146, 155, 235, 243, 245:5-
    8,10,12,13,15,17–23,25,
    246:26,27,28, 29,32, 268:20
Asociación General de
    Ganaderos 60-65, 72:14
assonance 191
Asturias, Miguel Angel 257,
    268:13
Attias 243, 245:10
audio archives 6, 8, 35, 49:4
Avenary, H. 245:5
Azores: Azorean ballad
    tradition 153, 167-168,

235; islands of: Flores 168,
    173:6; Graciosa 168; São
    Jorge 23:3, 150, 173:6; São
    Miguel 154; Terceira 150

baile del tambor 129
ballads: name for 162, 173:6
Barbeau 244:4
Barry, P. 244:4
Barthes, Roland 255
Bénichou, Paul 83-85, 113-114:16,
    155, 243, 245:11, 246:31,
    268:22
Benmayor, R. 24:8, 243, 245:12,19
Benveniste, G. 246:32
Bernadete Collection 246:29
blind men's ballads 7, 28, 51:16,
    147:3
Braga, Teófilo 120, 150, 157,
    174:14
Bransford and MacCarrell 255
Bráulio do Nascimento 175
Brazil 175-216
Brednick and Sappan 244:3
broadsides 1, 120, 132, 133, 143,
    147:5, 221, 259
Bronson, Bertrand 178

Câmara Fontes, Maria-João 23:3,
    150, 152, 160
Canada: Canadian ballad
    tradition 244:4

321

Webber, R. H. 191, 252
Weich-Shahak, S. 246:32
Wolf and Hofmann 120, 134,
    217:3
women ballad singers 113:10,
    257-258
women in the *romancero* 257-265
Wylie and Margolin 244:2